HUME'S THEOR

To whom...

with love from

Jonathan

HUME'S THEORY OF JUSTICE

JONATHAN HARRISON

CLARENDON PRESS · OXFORD

Oxford University Press, Walton Street, Oxford OX2 6DP

London Glasgow New York Toronto
Delhi Bombay Calcutta Madras Karachi
Kuala Lumpur Singapore Hong Kong Tokyo
Nairobi Dar es Salaam Cape Town
Melbourne Auckland
and associated companies in
Beirut Berlin Ibadan Mexico City Nicosia

Oxford is a trade mark of Oxford University Press

Published in the United States by
Oxford University Press, New York

© Jonathan Harrison 1981

British Library Cataloguing in Publication Data
Harrison, Jonathan
Hume's theory of justice.
1. Hume, David
2. Justice (Philosophy)
179   JC578.H/   80-41600
ISBN 0-19-824619-6
ISBN 0-19-824724-9 Pbk

First published 1981
Reprinted (New as Paperback) 1983

Printed in Hong Kong

To
My Father
and
the Memory of
My Mother

For your mouths lying flat with your faces, you can hardly bite each other to any purpose unless by consent.

Jonathan Swift

PREFACE

Hume's *A Treatise of Human Nature* (subtitled 'An attempt to introduce the experimental method of reasoning into moral subjects') was published between 1739 and 1740. Book I, entitled 'Of the Understanding', contains Hume's epistemology, i.e. his account of the manner in which we acquire knowledge in general, its justification (to the extent that he thought it *could* be justified), and its limits. The theory of knowledge that Hume here espouses is an empiricist one. He thinks that, with the exception of propositions which merely exhibit the relations between one idea and another, all our knowledge is obtained by observation and experience. This means that claims to knowledge which cannot be justified empirically, such as, Hume thought, those made by scholastic metaphysics and by theology, are unfounded, and may not even make sense.

Book II, entitled 'Of the Passions', expounds most of what could be called Hume's philosophy of psychology in general, and his moral psychology (including discussions of the problem of the freedom of the will and the rationality of action) in particular.

Book III, entitled 'Of Morals', is also divided into three parts. Part I, entitled 'Of virtue and vice in general', holds Hume's *moral* epistemology.[1] As we should expect after what he has said about epistemology in general in Book I of the *Treatise*, Hume's account of our knowledge of right and wrong is also an empirical one. Section I of Part I attacks the view that it is reason which reveals to us moral distinctions, and Section II of Part I argues that, on the contrary, we do know of moral distinctions by means of a moral sense. What exactly he means by this is not clear, but the view that comes to be predominant in Parts II and III of the *Treatise* is that

---

[1] For a detailed treatment of this subject, see my *Hume's Moral Epistemology*, OUP, 1976.

moral judgements assert the presence or absence of a sentiment of approbation in mankind. Right actions and virtuous
dispositions arouse this sentiment, and actions which are not
right and characteristics which are not virtuous do not arouse
it, or arouse the contrary sentiment of disapprobation. The
reason, Hume thinks, why some actions and characteristics
arouse approbation is that it is a pleasurable sentiment, which
we feel because we sympathize with the pleasure that these
characteristics or actions give on account of their usefulness
or aggreeableness to their owners or to other people. It
follows from this that, because it is predominantly sympathy
with the pleasure of the consequences of these actions and
characteristics that arouses the sentiment of approval, Hume's
theory is broadly utilitarian, and that because it is an empirical question what actions and characteristics arouse
approval, moral questions, according to Hume, are settled by
observation and experience.

The question, 'What characteristics and actions do in fact
arouse approval in men?' Hume attempts to answer in Parts II
and III of Book III of the *Treatise*. Part II, 'Of justice and
injustice', is the subject of the present volume. In it Hume
attempts to give an empiricist theory of justice. He rejects the
view, approximated to in varying degrees by Cumberland,
Cudworth, Locke, Clarke, Wollaston, and Butler, that justice
is something 'natural', and part of the nature of things, and
that its edicts are eternal and immutable, and discernible by
reason. He maintains, on the contrary, as did Hobbes and
Mandeville, that justice is a matter of observing rules or
conventions which are of human invention, and that, in
consequence, our acquiring knowledge of justice is an empirical
affair of ascertaining what these rules or conventions are.

Because he thinks that justice has been created by man, he
describes it as an artificial virtue. Rules of justice were
invented in order to remedy by contrivance a defect in
human nature, which is that nature has not implanted in man
any motive for a number of different kinds of action, the
performance of which is necessary in order that man may live
in that society without which he cannot survive. Nature,
indeed, has given men no motive for abstaining from the

socially disruptive actions of taking the possessions (not the property, for before rules of justice have been invented there can be no such thing as property) of others; has given men no motive which enables them to co-operate, by guaranteeing that, if one man does something for someone else, this man will not fail to do something for him in return; and has given women no motive for not disrupting the family by not sleeping with men who are not the biological fathers of their children. Hence men must introduce rules prohibiting such actions, and redirect other already existing motives in such a manner as to sanction these rules.

The virtues other than the artificial one of justice, which Hume describes as natural virtues, and which he treats of in Part III of Book III of the *Treatise* (entitled 'Of the other virtues and vices'), are not human inventions. I hope to make Hume's views on the natural virtues and vices the subject of another volume at a later date.

David Hume was a philosopher of the greatest genius. I have sometimes been accused of treating him unsympathetically in my book on Part I of Book III of the *Treatise,* called *Hume's Moral Epistemology.* I do not know whether any of my readers will feel I have made the same mistake again. If so, I am disinclined to apologize for it. Pointing out his merits sounds patronizing, and is in any case superfluous. Hume was a great enough man to be capable of surviving the most rigorous criticism. Indeed I think his stature is more apparent as his work is studied in greater detail and, like a musical instrument which improves the more it is played, the more intensively he is studied, the more rewarding his work becomes. I have learned more about moral philosophy, and indeed about philosophy in general, from Hume than from any other philosopher, and in addition to this, I have acquired the greatest respect both for his literary style and for his personality, two things which cannot quite be dissociated from a writer's thought, however abstract the latter may seem to be. The process of trying to re-create the ideas of a great man from their verbal traces is a highly profitable one, if only because one hopes there is the chance that some of his merits may rub off on to oneself.

In writing this book I have had a great deal of trouble with the summaries of the sections. Originally I wrote full expositions of each section, but to make the book more concise I have taken the advice of the Oxford University Press and replaced these by brief précis (except for Sections III, V, and VI, which are more difficult than the others). It is important to emphasize that these précis are too short to be wholly accurate, and are certainly not complete. Hence it is more than usually necessary that my commentary should be read in conjunction with the work commented upon, Part II of Book III of the *Treatise*. Indeed, I regard it as one of the merits of my book that this must be done, for students are far too apt to read some short, simplified, and palatable account of the work of a great philosopher when they would be very much better off if they spent the extra time and trouble that would be necessary to read and puzzle over what he says themselves, which trouble my book does not save them. I flatter myself that my work is like an old cottage with exposed beams, rougher but more robust and honest than a smoother modern dwelling.

Also in order to cut down the length of this book I have decided to omit my concluding chapter, and hope to include it as the final chapter of my projected commentary on Book III Part III of the *Treatise*.

The reader is advised to use the Oxford University Press edition of *A Treatise of Human Nature*, edited by L. A. Selby-Bigge and revised by P. H. Nidditch, and to make full use of Selby-Bigge's excellent analytical index. All references not preceded by a letter, for example (93), are to the text of this edition. References preceded by the letter 'E', for example (E93), are to the Oxford University Press edition of Hume's *Enquiries*, again edited by L. A. Selby-Bigge and revised by P. H. Nidditch. All references to Hume's essays are to Volume I of *Essays Moral, Political and Literary*, edited by T. H. Green and T. H. Grose, and are preceded by the letters 'Ess.', for example (Ess.93). All references preceded by the letter 'p', for example (p.93), are to the text of my own book. The reader is referred to the excellent bibliography by Roland Hall (*Fifty Years of Hume Scholarship*, published by the

Edinburgh University Press) and to *Hume Studies* (published by the Department of Philosophy, University of Western Ontario).

I am indebted to Mr J. L. Mackie, who read this book for the Oxford University Press, and who must have devoted a good chunk of the winter of 1978–9 to its perusal. He made a great number of stylistic and other suggestions, most of the former and some of the latter of which I have accepted. I am indebted to Professor Peter Nidditch for information on one or two points that baffled me, but did not baffle him. I am indebted to Professor J. C. Smith for a number of professional opinions. I am indebted to my colleague Mr D. A. McQueen for reading part of the typescript. I am indebted to Mr W. R. Chalmers for the Latin translations in the Appendix. I am indebted to Mrs Pauline Davis for the patience and speed with which she typed the manuscript. I am indebted to Mrs Elaine Koss for the care and intelligence with which she has copy-edited my typescript. My thanks are due to the University of Nottingham for the sabbatical leave during which some of the work on this book was done.

J.H.

ANALYTIC TABLE OF CONTENTS

SECTION I

Justice, Whether a Natural or Artificial Virtue?

SECTION II

Of the Origin of Justice and Property

SECTION III

Of the Rules that Determine Property

SUMMARY   77

COMMENTS

SECTION VI

Some Farther Reflexions Concerning Justice and Injustice

SUMMARY

COMMENTS ON I[1]

[1] Section VI is in three parts, headed 'I', 'II' and 'III'.

COMMENTS ON II

COMMENTS ON III

SECTION VII

Of the Origin of Government

SECTION VIII

Of the Source of Allegiance

SUMMARY   190

COMMENTS

SECTION IX

Of the Measures of Allegiance

SUMMARY   203

COMMENTS

SECTION X

Of the Objects of Allegiance

SECTION XI

Of the Laws of Nations

SECTION XII

Of Chastity and Modesty

EPILOGUE

JUSTICE IN THE *ENQUIRY*
SECTION III

Of Justice

¹ This part of Section III, and Appendix III, have not been summarized and
commented upon separately, as have the previous sections, in order to avoid
repetition.

APPENDIX III 288

Some farther considerations with regard to justice

A TREATISE
OF
HUMAN NATURE

BOOK III
OF MORALS

PART II

Of justice and injustice

SECTION I

Justice, Whether a Natural or Artificial Virtue?

JUSTICE an artificial virtue, which produces approbation by a human contrivance (477); external actions are praised only because they are signs of virtuous motives (477); hence no action can be virtuous unless there is *first* in men some motive which produces it *other* than the desire to do it because it is virtuous (478); though an action may be done from a sense of duty alone, there must be some motive which usually prompts men to perform actions of this kind (though it is lacking in this case) or this action would not be a duty (479); where justice is concerned, however, there is no motive preceding the regard for justice itself, which by prompting men to perform just actions makes just actions meritorious (479-80); this motive cannot be self-interest, since this is the normal motive for injustice (480); three reasons why it cannot be regard for the public interest (480-1); it cannot be love of mankind, because there is no such passion (481-2); nor can private benevolence (regard for the interest of the party concerned) be that motive which would make justice a natural virtue, for the justice will remain, even when this motive fails, as when the person awarded an estate will himself receive no benefit from it (482); if private benevolence were the motive which made justice a virtue, one could not explain why one has a more stringent obligation not to take away a man's property than one has to give him something of the same value (482); since men are attached to their possessions because these are their property, it is the fact that it is already unjust to take his property away from someone that explains why it is lacking in benevolence to do this (482-3); and private benevolence is weaker in some people than in others, but our obligation to be just is always equally stringent (483); hence there is no motive prompting men to be just, other than the sense of justice or duty, which shows that our sense of justice is not derived from nature, but is produced by education and convention (483); those motives which make an action naturally virtuous are praised or blamed according as to how nearly they are possessed in their usual strength (483-4); though justice is an artificial virtue, rules of justice are natural in the sense that it is inevitable that men should have invented them, and it is consequently not improper to describe them as Laws of Nature (484).

COMMENTS

(1) When Hume says, 'when we praise any actions, we regard only the motives that produced them' (477) he is most plausibly interpreted as speaking not so much about actions, but as about physical movements. It seems quite reasonable to maintain that praise and blame are not properly applicable to physical movements as such. The very same physical movements which, in a man, are produced deliberately from some motive or other would be morally neutral if performed by a robot or automaton.

Hume is jumping to conclusions, however, when he deduces, from the fact that we do not praise or blame the physical movements, the conclusion that we do praise or blame the motives. There is at least as good a case for saying that we praise or blame the intentions which issue in the movements. The problem is a complex one, and to discuss it in detail would be to digress unduly. (In one place (477) Hume does not say 'motive', but 'certain principles in the mind and temper', but all the examples he gives, e.g. benevolence or paternal affection, are examples of motives.) At first sight it seems as if Hume is expressing the justly criticized view that whether an action is right or wrong depends upon the motive from which it is performed. This, however, is not the case. The view he puts forward here—we shall see that he puts forward a different view in other places—is that whether or not an action is a duty depends not on the motive from which it *is* performed, but upon there being in the nature of man a motive which normally prompts men to perform actions of that kind. Given that there is in the mind of man a motive which normally prompts him to perform actions of a certain kind, it is irrelevant what is the actual motive for any given action of that kind.

(2) Hume's view that a motive is virtuous if it is one that is usual for human beings to have (483) is at first sight most implausible. He also thinks that not only is it virtuous to *have* a motive that men usually have, but that it is virtuous to have this motive *in its usual strength* (483). This view is not open, as might at first sight seem, to the objection that, if he is right, great virtue must be normal, instead of, as it is, exceptional. There is no contradiction in supposing that it is very rare for anyone to possess all the usual motives in their usual strength. But it does imply that courage, to take just one example, would not be a virtue if men were very rarely courageous, that an unusual motive must be reprehensible, and that having more than the usual amount of humanity, as well as having less, are both to be deplored.

However, there is more to be said for Hume's view than might be seen at first sight. Moral assessments of people must bear some relation to what it is reasonable to expect from them, and what it is reasonable to expect from people must bear some relation to what it is common or usual for men to achieve. This latter, since men's achievements must depend to some extent on their motives (one cannot expect men constantly to be performing acts of saintliness or heroism out of all proportion to that degree of courage, chastity, industry, or benevolence that they have by nature been given), is not entirely independent of man's normal emotional endowment, but Hume grossly overstates his case. Though we do not expect or require behaviour from man that is disproportionate to the motivation he has been born with, this does not mean that we condemn it when we get it, or that we would condemn it if we were to get it. Men can, obviously, deviate from the normal in ways which are admirable, as well as in ways which are wrong.

Hume may have had at the back of his mind the idea that vice is a kind of deformity. Just as a swan with a neck that differs in shape from that which swans' necks usually have is a physically deformed swan, so a man whose internal constitution differs from that which men usually have is morally deformed. But though swans with exceptional necks may be ugly—one cannot help but suspect that in choosing the swan, Hume was taking an example especially favourable to his case—men with exceptional motives are not necessarily wicked. They may be, but they may, on the other hand, just be eccentric, or endowed with heroic virtue. Their unusual motivation may, if only because it is more than usually useful to themselves or others, be more than averagely commendable.

Hume might have done better to work with the concept of an ideal man, who is not simply endowed with men's usual motives in their usual strength, but is more a limiting concept from which actual men may deviate in varying degrees. It has been suggested (by Professor C. D. Broad in *Five Types of Ethical Theory*, Kegan Paul, 1930) that Bishop Butler had such a concept of human nature. Such a concept would be analogous to that of a perfect circle, which is not that of a shape that circles usually have, for none of them at all may be perfectly circular, so much as the concept of a shape from which actual circles divagate to different extents. Such a concept, of course, cannot be extracted from observation of actual instances, for no actual circles may be, or, perhaps, even can be, perfectly circular. (There is no reason why this should be any exception to Hume's empiricist principle that all ideas (or concepts) are derived from impressions, for this only applied to simple ideas, and the concept of a perfect circle, or a perfect man, is a complex one, and capable of definition in terms of simple ideas which can be derived from impressions.) It is doubtful, however, whether the concept of a perfect man can provide us with any useful definition of what it is to be virtuous. It is more likely that one defines 'perfect man' in terms of 'man who possesses all the virtues' than that one can define virtue as a quality which would be possessed by a perfect man, or vice as a quality that a perfect man would lack. And it is more plausible—though not *very* plausible—to say that a man who possesses all normal motives in their usual strength is to that extent a perfect specimen of a man than that he is a perfectly good man.

It is odd that Hume should have held that a virtuous motive was one that people usually possessed, in the degree in which they usually possessed it, when it is considered that he usually regarded a virtue as a characteristic which was either *useful* or *agreeable* to its *possessor* or to *others*. It is possible, however, to distinguish between a character-trait, such as industry or honesty, and a motive, such as jealousy or avarice, and it could be that it was Hume's view that it was their usefulness or agreeableness to their possessors or others that made *character-traits* virtuous, and that it was their normality which made *motives* virtuous. It seems plausible to suggest that Hume would have to give a different account of the virtuousness of motives and the virtuousness of character-traits. If character-traits are virtuous according as to whether or not they are useful, motives cannot be virtuous for this reason. Motives are not means to satisfying our wants, i.e. are not useful: they themselves determine what we want, and so determine *what* are the ends which useful things realize. This would suggest that it does not really matter what our motives are, providing that they do not conflict too much amongst themselves or with the motives of others; whatever satisfies them is, by definition, useful, and the usefulness of the character-traits is determined by their ability to provide for us whatever it is that we want.

Very roughly speaking, it could be said that there are two attitudes to morality. According to the first, there is moral law, which is independent of men's wants, needs, and abilities, and it is the duty of men to force their wills to conform to it; they must make themselves ideally rational beings by obeying its dictates, regardless of the difficulty of doing so and the sacrifice it may involve. According to the second, there are men with certain wants and limited abilities, and it is the business of morality to regulate their behaviour in such a way as to enable them to augment their abilities and satisfy their wants. On this latter view it would be pointless for morality to enjoin sacrifices which were out of proportion to the benefits for which it was designed, or to impose demands on human beings which involve the neglect of their human nature. On the first view man is the slave of morality, and is at his best·and most perfect when his will is totally subjugated to its inexorable demands. On the second view morality is the servant of man, and can fulfil its office only by moulding itself to his needs, and taking full account of his limitations. Hume, to his credit, held a view of morality which fell into the second of these two categories, rather than the first.

It is possible, however, that when Hume said that 'when we praise any actions, we regard only the motives that produced them' (477), he was speaking loosely, and that by 'motive' he just meant some internal 'principle' or other. In the very same sentence, as I have said, he uses the expression 'principles in the mind and temper'. If this is what he meant, his claim that external actions are meritorious or the reverse only in so far as they are signs of something 'internal' is almost certainly true. His further claim, however, that this principle is praiseworthy (because it is regarded as praiseworthy) to that extent that it is usual for men to have it, and in its usual strength, becomes no more plausible than it was before.

Hume, who contrived to argue rigorously while at the same time using a rather casual and imprecise vocabulary, draws little or no distinction between the various different moral epithets, and the different things to which these may be applied. It may be that, though he says that actions are praiseworthy only if they issue from virtuous motives, he was simply failing to distinguish between those moral epithets that are properly applicable to *actions*, and those that are properly applicable to *men*. It would be, then, that he thought that an action was evidence of a man's being *praiseworthy* only if it was a sign of his possessing certain motives or 'principles'. This would be very plausible. Hume's view that an action is a *duty*—or at any rate a 'natural duty', a phrase that Hume never uses—if it is the kind of action to which one would normally be prompted by a virtuous motive, however, is less plausible. It might even be argued that he got things precisely the wrong way round, and that a motive is virtuous if it is the kind of motive which normally prompts one to perform actions which are duties or, at any rate, right.

(3) Hume's view, that there is no motive for the performance of just actions except the sense of justice, or the sense that it is our duty to perform acts of justice, is more plausible. It needs, however, to be stated with more care than Hume states it. For, since it is usually in our interest to be just—as he himself points out—on account of the sanctions that are attached to the performance of unjust actions, there is a motive, namely self-interest, which normally prompts us to perform just actions.

Indeed, if there were no motives at all which impelled men to behave justly, no one ever would behave justly—for action without a motive is impossible. Sometimes, however, for whatever reason, men do act justly.

Unfortunately, as I have already suggested, it is not at all clear whether Hume is trying to show that there *is* no motive, independently of a sense of justice, which normally prompts men to perform just actions, or to show that there *would be* no such motives were it not for the 'artificial', man-made human conventions which set up and enforce justice. Sometimes he writes as if he thought the first; sometimes as if he thought the second.

The view that there is, independent of human convention, no motive to justice seems to me to be true. It needs, however, to be fairly carefully stated. Creating rules of justice, as Hume points out, does not create any new motives. These cannot be brought into being by act of Parliament, so to speak. Hence, in a sense, all the motives to justice existed before man-made conventions were established as well as after. In another sense, however, these motives did not exist, for those motives which, after conventions about justice have been established, do impel men not to take the property of others, did not so prompt them before.

There is a related doubt about exactly what Hume's argument, designed to prove that justice is an artificial and not a natural virtue, is. The trouble is that, as he himself states it, his argument proves too much. As he puts it, so far from proving that justice is not a natural virtue, it proves that justice is not a virtue at all. What follows from his first premiss, that actions are not duties unless there is in the mind of man a motive which normally prompts him to perform them, coupled with his second premiss, that there is in the mind of man no motive which normally prompts him to perform just actions, is simply that it cannot be a duty to perform just actions.

There seem to me to be two ways in which we might modify Hume's argument to avoid this embarrassing conclusion, and derive the desired consequence that justice, though a duty, is a duty the performance of which is a manifestation of an artificial, not a natural, virtue.

Firstly, we might modify his *first* premiss and substitute, for the statement that an action is not a duty unless there is a motive for its performance, the statement that an action is not *naturally* a duty unless there is a motive for its performance. The conclusion that justice is not naturally a duty then follows from this premiss, coupled with Hume's second premiss, that there is no motive normally prompting men to act justly.

Secondly, we may allow Hume to retain the premiss that an action can be a duty only if there is a motive which normally prompts men to perform it, and modify his *second* premiss so that it states, not that there *is* no such motive, but that there *would be* no such motive were it not for human conventions. If we accept the first modification, the difference between natural and artificial virtues is that there are motives issuing in the first, but no motives issuing in the second. If we accept the second modification, the difference between a natural and an artificial virtue is that, though there are motives issuing in each, natural virtues have motives which lead us to perform them whether there are human conventions demanding their performance or not, whereas artificial virtues have motives which lead to them only after human conventions have been established.

Since, of course, as Hume himself points out (492), motives cannot be brought into existence by the establishing of a convention, human conventions must affect our motivation by redirecting the motives we already have. Hume himself says that the motive that is thus redirected is self-interest (492). *Before* the establishing of conventions about property, self-interest leads men to take the possessions of others, but *after* conventions have been established assigning to men certain things as their property and imposing penalties upon those who break them, self-interest leads men to respect the possessions of others. Men do this partly from fear of losing the benefits which having such conventions brings, but their main motive is fear of incurring the sanctions by which these conventions are enforced.

It is clear that Hume did think that, antecedently to the establishing of human conventions, there was no motive to justice. Since there would be no such thing as justice or injustice before human conventions establishing justice were set up, there could, *a fortiori*, be no motive to perform acts of justice before there were such conventions (491). (Similarly, there could be no such thing as a desire to revoke before the promulgating of the rules of bridge for, before such rules were formulated, the word 'revoke' would simply have no meaning.)

Unfortunately, however, Hume also tries to prove that there is no motive which leads us to justice, independently of a sense that it is our duty to be just, even *after* human conventions have been set up. The arguments he uses in the section we are considering (480–3) are designed to show that in society *as it is at the moment* there is no motive for justice. He argues here, for example, that in society as it is men do not look to the distant consequences of justice; and that in society as it is justice may demand that an estate be awarded to a man who will do only harm with it; that in society as it is (or in any other society for that matter) there is no such motive as love of mankind as such.

These arguments do not establish that there is *no* motive to justice, whether antecedently to the setting up of human conventions establishing it or not. What they do establish is that there is no motive which *invariably* prompts men to perform just acts. Hence Hume might be thinking, as he argues explicitly later (531-3), that though there are human motives prompting men to be just, they work only intermittently, and so cannot explain why we demand a *rigorous* and *invariable* observance of rules of justice. Incidentally, Hume could have argued, though he does not, that if there is no motive which prompts men to be just, even after rules of justice have been established, there can *a fortiori* be no such motive before they have been established.

My own view of Hume's account of the difference between natural and artificial virtues is this. Some actions are duties because there is a motive in a normal man prompting him to perform them; we may perform such actions from a sense of duty if we are lacking in this motive, and wish to supply the deficiency. Since there is in mankind no motive to prompt men from abstaining from taking the possessions of others, rules have to be established allocating to men what they possess as their property, and the existence of these rules redirects the motives men already have—in particular, self-interest and concern for the welfare of others—to observe these rules. But the motives for obeying these rules are not always adequate, and so they have to be reinforced by the sense of duty, which can in part be inculcated or strengthened by education and the artifice of politicians (500-1). On this account, Hume's claim that an action is a duty only if its performance is a sign of the possession of a motive that most men have in its usual strength must be abandoned as a claim about all virtues; it can be regarded as a claim about the natural virtues only. Similarly, Hume's claim that an action or class of actions can be a duty only if there is in man some motive prompting him to perform it must also be abandoned as a claim about all virtues, and regarded as a claim about only the natural virtues. Hence we get the view that an action is 'naturally' a duty only if there is in man a motive to its performance, lack of which he can remedy by performing from a sense of duty actions that other men perform from the motive in question. The natural virtues, however, and the duties to perform those actions in which the natural virtues normally manifest themselves, are inadequate to cause man to perform all the actions which are socially necessary. They are insufficient to prevent conflict over possessions, for example. Hence rules distributing and safeguarding possessions must be set up and enforced. These rules are set up and obeyed from the normal motives, but men cannot be attracted to them under any designation that they could have apart from human convention (as, of course, we can be attracted to the opposite sex under designations other than those ascribed to them by human convention). We have a duty to obey them not in order to remedy a deficiency in a motive that most men have, for abstaining from taking the possessions of others would not manifest such a deficiency.

I suspect that Hume thinks that our 'artificial' duties are simply assigned to us by the rules of justice which men establish. To say that we have a duty to abstain from taking the property of others is simply tautological, for our property is just that which others have a duty not to take; to say that they have a duty not to take something, and that this thing is our property, is simply to say that there is a social rule assigning this thing to us. There will, of course, be motives, even apart from the sense of duty, to obey such rules; otherwise they will not be obeyed. But such motives cannot be what causes abstaining from taking the possessions of others to be a duty, for the motives presuppose the existence of the rules distributing possessions as property, and so cannot give rise to them. In other words, it is because something is assigned to someone else as his property, which means that it is our duty to abstain from taking it, that we have motives—for example, desire to avoid punishment and desire to avoid wrecking a useful institution—to abstain from taking it. It is not because we have a motive to abstain from taking another's property that it is our duty not to take it. More will have to be said about both the natural and the artificial virtues when we discuss later sections of the *Treatise*.

(4) An answer to the difficulty of making Hume consistent on the question whether there are motives for just actions is, I think, that Hume, though he is not entirely clear about it, is not saying that there is *no* motive to the performance of just actions. Many motives may lead men to behave justly as a means to achieving something else; for example, I may do the just thing because I see that I will be punished or lose my reputation or my job if I do not. What Hume is maintaining is that there is no motive, the *object* of which is the performance of just actions, as the object of hunger is the consumption of food, or the object of parental affection is the welfare of those we suppose to be our children. The object of our desire not to lose our reputations is not justice, even though it may often lead us to act justly. And since there is no such motive, performing just actions can never be a duty, for, unless there were such a motive, omitting just actions would not show a deficiency in a normal motive, and so performing them could not *be* a duty. There would be no motive, the object of which is to perform just actions, either in society as it is, or in a 'community' without justice if such were possible. In society as it is, however, motives which do not

have as their *object* the performance of just actions, have been re-directed by the imposition of penalties for non-performance and various other social pressures in such a manner that they prompt us to perform just actions as a means to their own satisfaction.

What I have just said, however, still does not make Hume's view entirely free from difficulty. It is a minor point worth mentioning that, in society which has justice, not being just often does show a deficiency in a motive that is common to mankind. Injustice, indeed, may well show lack of normal prudence though, of course, it would only do so as a result of human fiat in setting up and enforcing rules of justice. But then, not to send one's children to school may show lack of parental affection (and so be naturally vicious), but only as a result of human fiat in having made a school-leaving certificate a necessary qualification for more than averagely remunerative employment. The main difficulty still remains: if nothing can be a virtue, unless it is something to which there is some motive in the mind of man which prompts him to perform these putatively virtuous actions, antecedently to their being duties, and there is no such motive prompting men to be just, then the conclu-sion is not that justice is an artificial virtue, but that it is not a virtue at all. And even if you make it clear that Hume is talking about motives which have as their *objects* actions of justice, the conclusion that justice is not a virtue still follows, because, whether in society which has or does not have rules of justice, there is no motive in the mind of man which has just actions as its object.

(5) The three paragraphs (482-3) in which Hume gives three special reasons for thinking that private benevolence, or the interest of the party who gains something from the application of a rule of justice, cannot be that motive which causes the performance of just acts to be a duty, are obscure.

In the first of these three paragraphs I take Hume to be saying that abstaining from taking the property of others is not simply a special case of benevolence. If it were, 'a man would not be obliged to leave others in the possession of more than he is obliged to give them' (482). By this I think he must mean that, if justice were just a special case of benevolence, our duty to *abstain from taking* what other people possess would not be more stringent, or not much more stringent, than our duty to *give* to others what they do *not* already possess. He may him-self be suggesting what is commonly asserted by critics of utilitarianism —though Hume, as we shall see, was a utilitarian of sorts—that it would be wrong to take something from one man if you think you can give it to another man who will derive more pleasure from it. The reason why it is wrong is that there is a rule of justice which demands that men do not take the possessions of others, and because this rule of justice will lose its utility if it is not uniformly observed.

In the second paragraph, I think, he is rebutting an objection to this first argument. You cannot explain why it is wrong to deprive someone of something he possesses in order to give it to someone else by arguing that doing so would not in fact bring about more pleasure, since men suffer more from *losing what they have* than from *gaining what they do not have*. This argument will not do, Hume thinks, because the fact that men suffer more from losing what they have *presupposes* that they already regard what they have as their property. As the fact that people lose more from being deprived of what they have than by not acquiring what they do not have presupposes that what they have is their property, it cannot be used to explain why I have an obligation to abstain from taking other people's property.

Hume is partly wrong and partly right about this. That men lose more by being deprived of what they have than by not gaining something they do not have is true only when goods are fairly evenly distributed. When they are evenly distributed, the principle of diminishing utility implies that a man will lose more from having his fifth sheep taken away from him than another man will gain from acquiring a sixth sheep. But doubtless—and this is Hume's main point—the man who has his sixth sheep taken away from him will also be affronted because the sheep he loses is his, quite independently of any loss of utility from losing it. Hume himself makes use of this argument later (503), when he is endorsing the rule that men should be allocated what they already possess. Then, of course, it cannot be argued that they want what they possess because what they possess is their property, before any rules allocating property have been invented.

In the third, the most obscure of these three arguments, Hume seems to use as a premiss the statement that private benevolence is not only in fact weaker in some people than in others, but that it ought to be weaker in some people than in others. If you assume, for the sake of argument, that the people in whom it is weaker are the people in whom it ought to be weaker, it follows that a man whose benevolence is weak will not be as obliged to be as benevolent as a man whose benevolence is strong. All men, however strong or weak their benevolence, have the same obligation to abstain from taking the property of others. (Perhaps Hume's statement that private benevolence ought to be weaker in some persons than in others may be interpreted as meaning that the duty to be benevolent allows of some latitude. There are certain degrees of benevolence where we can confidently say that a man is being more benevolent than he need be, and other degrees of benevolence where we can confidently say that a man is being too little benevolent, but in between these two limits it may not be possible to assign a precise sum which he ought to give. In any case, it seems perfectly fair to argue that people with more money and fewer demands on their time ought to be more benevolent than people with less money and more demands on their time; however much money or time people have, however, they have the same obligation to be just, in particular to abstain from taking the property of others.)

(6) In the final paragraph (484) of the section, Hume says that, though he has been insisting that justice is in a sense an artificial virtue, there is another sense in which it is also natural. It is artificial in that the rules of justice are human inventions or contrivances; hence justice is artificial, as opposed to natural, in the sense in which mountains or rivers are natural phenomena but buildings or computers are not. In another sense, however, justice is natural to man; for man is by nature inventive, and the invention of justice is both obvious and necessary. 'Tho' the rules of justice be *artificial*, they are not *arbitrary*' (484).

Hume says more about this subject in Book III, Part I, Section II of the *Treatise* (473-5). He has just been arguing that it would be absurd to suppose that there are no general principles governing the kind of action we approve of or disapprove of, and that every individual action which arouses in us a sentiment of approval or disapproval does so by 'an *original* quality and *primary* constitution' (473). He then raises the question, 'Whether we ought to search for these principles in *nature*, or whether we must look for them in some other origin?' (473). His answer to this question is that the distinction between virtue and vice is natural, in the sense in which what is natural is opposed to what is miraculous. In the sense of 'natural' in which it is opposed to what is rare or unusual, the sentiments of morality are also natural (474). In the sense of 'natural' in which what is natural is opposed to what is artificial, Hume says that it may in the sequel be discovered that 'our sense of some virtues is artificial, and that of others natural' (475).

In the sense in which what is natural is opposed to what is rare, vice and virtue are equally natural. In the sense in which what is natural is opposed to what is unusual, virtue is perhaps rather more unnatural than vice. 'At least it must be own'd, that heroic virtue, being as unusual, is as little natural as the most brutal barbarity' (475). In the sense in which what is artificial is produced by design, virtue and vice are equally artificial. Hence it is ridiculous to suppose, with some philosophers, that 'virtue is the same with what is natural, and vice with what is unnatural' (475).

To return to the distinction between natural and artificial virtues, it is important to realize that, though Hume sometimes says that our sense of some virtues is natural, and of others artificial, in fact it is not so much his view that it is our *sense* of the artificial virtues that is artificial, as that it is the rules upon which our sense of virtue confers its approbation that are artificial. In the concluding section of the *Treatise*, Hume himself says, 'Tho' justice be artificial, the sense of its morality is natural' (619). Hume thinks that though man makes the rules in which justice consists, man does not himself make his tendency to approve of such rules. This tendency is implanted in him by nature, and is something that he can do little about. (It is not the case that he can do nothing about his tendency to approve of the artificially contrived rules of justice; it can, as has already been mentioned, be strengthened by education and the artifices of politicians.)

Hume, as we shall see, derived the virtuousness of justice from its usefulness; indeed, all virtues, whether artificial or not, are virtues to a large extent because they are useful. (When they are not virtues because they are useful, they are so because they are agreeable.) This rule, that useful character-traits are virtuous, is not a man-made rule, even though the rules that it is useful for men to obey are man-made rules. Furthermore, the rule that useful (and agreeable) characteristics are virtuous applies to all societies and all places and all times; though different societies may have different rules of justice, whenever obeying such rules is useful, our disposition to obey them is a virtue, whatever the rules we are so disposed to obey may be. 'The Rhine flows north, the Rhone south; yet both spring from the *same* mountain, and are also actuated, in their opposite directions, by the *same* principle of gravity' ('A Dialogue', E333).

(7) It seems reasonable to ask whether, if there are no motives which prompt men to perform just acts in a society which has not yet invented any rules about property, etc., there are any such motives after these rules have been established, or is the sense of duty the only motive which prompts men to obey the rules? It seems obvious that there are many such motives, all of which Hume could quite consistently have recognized. Such motives are fear of the consequences, both in the form of legal punishment or social disapproval, for not obeying them; fear of loss of reputation and consequent harm to oneself and one's family; and fear, too, perhaps, of undermining a useful institution with unfortunate repercussions upon oneself. Hence it would be possible for Hume to say that the difference between an artificial and a natural virtue is this. There are motives to natural virtues, even in the absence of human conventions, but if there were no human conventions, there would be no motives which would continue to prompt one to perform

actions which these conventions at the moment enjoin. Hence it would be possible for Hume to say that, where both artificial and natural virtues are concerned, it is our duty to perform that action which is virtuous because not to do so would show a lack of a normal human motive in its usual strength; the difference between the two would be that the motives which normally prompt men to be just could not operate in the absence of human conventions, but the motives which prompt men to be naturally virtuous would operate in their absence. Artificial virtues, then, would be a special case of the rule that no action can be a manifestation of virtue unless it is a sign of the possession of a normal human motive in its normal strength.

I do not think that such a view would be a very plausible one, however, because, as Hume himself may be arguing later (531–5), there would be no human motive, even in a society which had rules of justice, which would prompt men to obey them universally and rigorously. The motives, self-interest, for example, and desire not to do things which harm one's family, which normally prompt men to perform just actions, sometimes prompt them to perform unjust ones. It is, however, man's duty to observe rules of justice inflexibly. This is because, Hume thinks, unless they are observed inflexibly, no advantage will come from having them. Hence these rules must demand an inflexible observance which cannot be explained by the fact that there is a propensity in a normal man to obey them inflexibly, for there is no such motive.

(8) Where natural virtues are concerned, Hume seems to have in mind the idea of the usual man as a standard from which all men who are not usual deviate. His idea of a natural man, however, is not exactly the idea of man as he usually is, but the idea of a man as he would be if his behaviour were not moulded by artificial human conventions. Or rather, since without conventions there would be no words, and without words no communication, and, without either, man would be a totally different creature from, and much inferior to, what he now is, Hume has the idea of a man not moulded by those conventions which regulate property, promising, government, and the relations between the sexes. Such an idea is, of course, an abstraction. There are no men not subject to the pressures that social conventions produce, and Hume perhaps underestimates the difficulty of knowing what men would be like if they were brought up without such conventions. The really puzzling thing about Hume's attitude is why he should regard the usual or normal man, possessing the usual motives in their usual strength, as an ideal from which men who are not usual deviate. Part of the explanation, no doubt, is that he too readily identified deformity with deviation from the usual. Though it is true, however, that a deformed baby

deviates from what babies usually are, it is not necessarily the case that any deviation from this norm is a deformity. In saying that something is a deformity we are both saying that it is unusual and passing a value judgement upon the way in which it is unusual. It is not necessarily the case that what is unusual must be a deformity. And, in any case, when Hume assumed that what was unusual must be a deformity, he was making an assumption which, though it is in fact for the most part true, does not have to be true. Men and other animals have evolved over a long period of time, and during this time characteristics which are deformities have to a large extent been weeded out by the process of natural selection. Hence those characteristics which are usual tend to be those which are advantageous. Hence characteristics which are unusual tend to be characteristics which are disadvantageous, but it is because they are disadvantageous, not because they are unusual, that they are deformities. And, of course, sometimes a characteristic which is unusual may be very highly advantageous, in which case natural selection will tend to favour it at the expense of less advantageous characteristics, and it will become less unusual.

(9) Hence a good way of looking at the distinction between natural and artificial virtues is to regard natural virtues as those characteristics the possession of which is demanded by the economy of one's species. To be lacking in prudence, for example, would be rather like being without a nose, a condition which is both aesthetically displeasing and physiologically inefficient. Here is a better analogy, perhaps: to be lacking in the natural virtue of prudence is like lacking an appetite; it is to be lacking in any natural inclination to perform actions which are in fact good for one (or, in the case of other virtues, humanity, for example, good for others). Hume is then arguing, plausibly, that there is no natural inclination to perform just actions, and hence not having such an inclination is not a natural defect, any more than it is a defect in humans not to have a built-in radar system, useful though such a thing would be. (Lack of parental affection, though a natural vice in men, is no sort of deficiency in reptiles.) But in the case of justice, the fact that there is no natural inclination in man to avoid taking the possessions of others causes so much inconvenience that its absence must be remedied artificially, by the invention and enforcement of rules of justice. (If baby crocodiles did need their mothers' care, crocodiles would have to invent rules forcing mother crocodiles to look after their children.)

A corollary of what Hume says is that the cult of the natural man is misguided. Natural men would be like natural vines, which kill one another because they trespass upon each other's supply of soil, air, sun, and water. Hence vines need to be pruned. Analogous to pruning a vine is the task of compelling men to conform to rules of justice. But though a man, forced to conform to rules of justice, is thereby compelled by man-made pressure to become a person very different from the one he would otherwise be, there is another sense, in which men are behaving naturally when they invent and respond to such pressures. This, indeed, is the way they are made, and a very good thing too.

(10) It is sometimes held that not only are Hume's rules of justice artificial, the sentiments which sanction them and otherwise prompt men to act upon them are also artificial. I, however, have taken the view that it is, according to Hume, only the rules that are artificial; the sentiments which favour obeying the rules spring up of themselves, out of sympathy with the pleasure they produce. This latter view, however, as I have myself pointed out, is only partially true. It would be wholly true if Hume were consistent in thinking that we approve solely of that which is or is believed to be useful (or, where virtues other than justice are concerned, agreeable) for, though we make the rules, we do not make the usefulness of the rules. But Hume also thinks that the sentiment, which to some extent we cannot help having, favouring what is or is believed to be useful, can be strengthened by education and the artifices of politicians; indeed by these artifices, we can even be caused to have a sentiment favourable to rules of justice which are not useful, and which ought to be replaced by other rules. To the extent that this is so, the sentiments which sanction rules of justice, as well as these rules themselves, are artificial. Part of the trouble, as we have seen, is that Hume is not entirely consistent in his view that we approve only of what we believe to be useful and agreeable. If we did do only this, the artifices of politicians could only affect our sentiment of approbation by altering our beliefs about what is useful.

An attempt could be made to save Hume from this inconsistency by arguing that an action is a virtue only if it arouses sentiments of approbation in a man who has correct and complete beliefs about its nature, and is not biased in the ways which Hume allows for in Book III, Part III, Section I. Such an account allows for an irrational and a rational sentiment of approbation, though Hume would not have liked these descriptions of them. The function of politicians, then, is to bias us in favour of obedience to rules of justice, i.e. to cause us to have an irrational and artificial sentiment in favour of acting on them. But since this irrational and artificial approbation, produced by politicians and parents and educators, in fact favours obedience to useful rules, it is an irrational sentiment which favours just what a rational approbation would have favoured if we had had it. There is no difficulty about this. We may have a totally irrational belief that exactly coincides with what we would have believed if we were rational. For example, a man may have an irrational belief that ill will befall him on a Friday, and another man, who has just put a bomb in an envelope addressed to him, a rational belief to exactly the same effect.

Perhaps we can say that it is Hume's view that the sentiment of justice (as opposed to the rules of justice) is sometimes natural and sometimes artificial. It is natural when it results from sympathy with the pleasure these useful rules produce. It is artificial when it is inculcated by politicians, parents, and educators. The latter sentiment is only appropriate, and aroused by something that really is a virtue, when it coincides with the natural sentiment which would be produced by sympathy.

(11) One assumption Hume makes is that, since rules are invented, there can be no natural or innate motive in man the object of which is simply to perform actions which consist in obeying a rule. Hence motives whose object is something else must be made use of in order to enforce obedience. For example, fear of loss of liberty or of pain is an innate motive which can be made use of to compel men to be just, though it does not have as its object the performance of just actions.

Hume's assumptions may be true, but it *is* an assumption, and it could conceivably be false. Presumably man's remote ancestors had no motive which was aimed directly at obeying artificial rules; but many motives, which once did not exist, do so now, and, since a motive the object of which was rule-obedience would be highly useful to man, it might have evolved over a long period of time. Whether or not there is now such a motive is a question I do not feel competent to judge. But, if there is, then Hume would have to say that justice was, after all, a natural virtue. But the rules of justice, which this innate motive gave men some tendency to obey, would be artificial rules all the same.

(12) It is impossible to tell to what extent Hume had Bishop Butler in mind when he argues that justice is not a natural virtue. Butler held that, though it was possible to arrive at one's duty by *a priori* reasoning, it was also possible to regard virtue as that to which one's nature was, as a matter of empirical fact, adapted. Vice consisted in deviating from the economy of our nature, in that it was contrary to the most authoritative part of it, conscience; in that it was contrary to the two superior principles, benevolence and self-love; and in that a proper balance between the particular passions other than the principles already mentioned would prompt us to behave rightly, and to perform actions that were conducive to the happiness of ourselves and others, even if these were not their actual object. Hume's objection to this would be that we are not by nature adapted not to take the possessions of others, and

that justice has to be invented to remedy this defect. Nor are we by nature adapted to justice, but have to have justice imposed on us by sanctions, and our natural tendency to approve of it because of its usefulness has to be strengthened by education.

(13) If Hume were simply claiming that it could not be our duty not to perform certain actions, such as taking the property of others, if we had no motive not to perform them, the claim would not be implausible. For example, it could be argued that we do not have a duty—though it could be an act of supererogation— to give all our goods to the poor, because most men lack adequate motives for doing this. Nor, perhaps, could it be a duty for us to care what is happening to life in remote planets, for this is far beyond the reach of any normal human concern. That this was not Hume's view—indeed, it would be a much more moderate claim than any he makes—is shown by the fact that it was precisely because man had no motive for not taking the property of others that Hume thought he had to be persuaded that it was his duty not to take it.

(14) The claim that the fact that we lack any motive to perform just actions is a defect is more plausible than the claim Hume actually makes, and must be clearly distinguished from it. The claim he makes is that actions are only virtuous in so far as they are signs of virtuous motives, and that a motive is virtuous if it is one that man usually has, possessed in its usual strength. Not only is the claim that something is defective not quite the same as the claim that it is unusual, the claim that something is a defect is also not quite the same as the claim that it is a vice. Nor does the claim that lack of a given motive is a defect suggest that it is a duty to perform those actions to which it would normally prompt us, so much as that it might be wise to perform them, at any rate, if the defect in question is one which harms us. Furthermore, the claim that an action is a manifestation of a defect, as actions perfectly well may be, is quite a different claim from the claim that it is morally wrong, that it ought not to be done, or that to omit it is a duty.

(15) Hume says, 'In general, it may be affirmed that there is no such passion in human minds, as the love of mankind, merely as such' (481). He gives this as his reason for thinking that love of one's fellow men cannot be that motive which, by normally prompting men to perform just acts, makes justice a (natural) virtue. It cannot be that motive, because it simply does not exist.

Hume thinks that though men do love some other men, this is not evidence that there is such a thing as love of mankind. We love some other men because of their personal qualities, from gratitude, or because of their relation to ourselves (because they are our children, for example). He thinks that if there was such a thing as love of mankind as such, this would manifest itself even towards people who had no (useful or agreeable) personal qualities, or to whom we had no reason to feel gratitude, or who stood in no special relation to ourselves. He also thinks that though we are always affected by the happiness or misery of others, this is not a manifestation of love of mankind as such, because (a) they have to be near to us before we can be affected, and their happiness or misery has to be 'represented in lively colours', (b) the fact that we are so affected proceeds 'merely from sympathy', and (c) the sentiment 'extends itself beyond our own species' (i.e. we are affected by the happiness or misery of animals as well as of men).

I find these arguments puzzling. We feel hungrier when we see food (when food is 'near') than when we do not, and hungrier when the pleasures of eating are represented to us in lively colours, but this does not show that there is no such thing as hunger. It does not follow that people do not want to eat meat because they also want to eat things other than meat. And what makes Hume say that the fact that we are affected by the happiness and misery of others proceeds from sympathy, rather than from love of mankind, and why would its proceeding from sympathy show that it did not proceed from love of mankind?

Hume thinks that, if there were in man such a thing as a love of other men, adequate to be that motive absence of which makes us condemn acts of injustice, it would have to be such as to move us to seek the happiness of men remote from us in space and time. There can be little doubt that he is right in thinking that we are not much moved by the happiness or misery of such people. A famine in India or an earthquake in Turkey does not influence us nearly so much as poverty in the family next door, especially if it is the family of a relation, and a relation to whom we owe gratitude. And it is an interesting point, which has puzzled many utilitarians, that men feel a much more stringent obligation to relieve distress which is close to them and suffered by people to whom they stand in a special relationship, than they do to relieve much more intense and extensive suffering in people who live in distant places, and to whom they are in no way connected. If utilitarianism is true, then it is our duty to produce the maximum amount of happiness, which squares ill with the ordinary man's belief that not to relieve distant suffering is not very reprehensible whereas not to relieve near suffering is. It is also interesting that Hume, to the extent that he thinks that an action is (naturally) virtuous if it is a sign of the possession of a normal human motive in its normal strength, cannot be a utilitarian, for on this view not to relieve distant suffering cannot then be vicious if there is no motive in men which prompts men to relieve it. If, then, there is any obligation upon men to help other men, regardless of gratitude, their personal qualities, or the intimacy of their relation to ourselves or the degree of their remoteness, this would have, on Hume's theory, to be an artificial virtue. There would have to be a man-invented rule demanding that any man help any other man, regardless of the above-mentioned facts. There is, however, no such rule, or if there is, it is very far from being stringent.

I argued in *Hume's Moral Epistemology* that Hume had two accounts of sympathy, one in the *Treatise*, and the other in the *Enquiry*. In the *Enquiry* he identified sympathy with benevolence, and sympathetic pleasures and pains were just the pleasures and pains of satisfied or unsatisfied benevolence. This account of sympathy is obviously incompatible with Hume's view that there is no such thing as benevolence, in the sense of love of mankind as such. Hence I shall disregard it. His other account of sympathy is that seeing something which causes pleasure or pain (a man eating or having a cold bath) or is caused by pleasure or pain (a man looking satisfied or agonized) produces in a spectator the thought of pleasure or pain—it is not necessary for the spectator actually to believe that anyone is enjoying pleasure or suffering pain— which thought gets converted into an actual, though sympathetic, pleasure or pain for a variety of reasons which it is not here necessary to go into. This tendency to feel sympathetic pleasure or pain is something which happens 'automatically', regardless of what our attitude to the person in question is, though one would have supposed that people would feel more intense sympathetic pleasures for those they loved than for those to whom they felt indifferent.

For myself, I find it impossible to decide whether Hume was right in thinking that the admitted fact that we do usually feel pain when other people are in pain, and pleasure for their pleasure, is a manifestation of sympathy or love. In either event we may be supposed to have a desire to remove their pain or prolong their pleasure. Perhaps, however, if our pleasure or uneasiness proceeds from sympathy, our reason for wanting this may be to remove our own sympathetic uneasiness or maintain our own sympathetic pleasure. If these proceed from love, on the other hand, our aim is to remove the pain or extend the pleasure for their sakes. Presumably there are empirical tests we can make to find out which of these is the case. Perhaps, if our pain is a sympathetic one, we are content to remove it by keeping away from the vicinity of the people who arouse it, but if it proceeds from love we are not content to remove it in this way. If the fact that we ourselves feel sympathetic pleasures and pains produced in us such a strong desire to remove them as to constitute a motive for performing just acts—though in fact they do not—I do not see that it would matter from Hume's point of view that that motive was not love of mankind as such. So long as it was a motive normally found in man, it might be sufficient to make us say that performing unjust acts showed a want of it. In any case, whether or not there is in a man such a thing as love of his fellow men as such, it is in fact too weak to be that motive which normally prompts men to perform just actions. As Hume quite rightly points out, we are not much concerned by the remote effects of our unjust acts upon people removed from us in space and time, whether what concern we do have proceeds from sympathy or from love.

One final argument of Hume's, designed to show that there is no such thing as love of one's fellow men as such, deserves comment. He thinks that, were there this passion in men, any degree of a good quality would produce a stronger love than the same degree of a bad quality would cause hatred (481). (It is surprising that he did not say that this love for mankind would also produce a weaker hatred of bad qualities than in fact we have, as love between the sexes makes us look both more favourably on the good qualities and less favourably on the bad qualities of those we love.) One point that occurs to me is this. If there were such a thing as love of one's fellow men, and it were universal among men, how would Hume know what degrees of affection would be produced by men's good qualities if it were absent? Since it never would be absent, that question is one which could not be answered empirically.

Hume says, 'But in the main, we may affirm, that man in general, or human nature, is nothing but the object both of love and hatred, and requires some other cause, which by a double relation of impressions and ideas, may excite these passions' (481-2). (By 'other causes' he means 'causes other than the mere fact that someone is a fellow man or woman.) Hume's view is that we love or hate other people only when there is something special about them which arouses love or hatred. For example, we may love someone on account of his amiable personal qualities, or his fine clothes, extensive property, or authoritative position, or hate him for the opposite reasons. We do not love him just because he is a person, but always for some such reason as I have just mentioned. By saying that those things arouse love or hatred by 'a double relation of impressions and ideas' Hume means this. Love is always love of some person (the object of love) on account of our believing that he possesses some quality which arouses pleasure in the spectator (e.g. beauty or physical strength) or on account of our believing that he is related (e.g. by owning) to something that we believe possesses such a property. Hence there is a relation (the first in the double relation) between our idea of the property which produces love and our idea of the person who is the object of our love, mediated by the actual sentiment of love.

The second relation (to make the double relation Hume speaks of) is between the agreeable sensation produced by the quality which is the cause of love, and that other agreeable sensation which is love itself. Hume thinks that it is by these two relations together that love is produced, which is why he thinks that, in their absence, love cannot be felt. This is why he thinks that we do not feel love for our fellow men as such. It does not seem to me that Hume has a viable account of love, but to discuss the account he gives would take me too far away from my present subject. Nor does it seem to me that Hume's remark, 'and perhaps a man wou'd be belov'd as such, were we to meet him in the moon' (482), is consistent with his view that we do not feel love for our fellow men as such.

Hume, too, is in any case wrong in identifying desire for the public interest (which he says, rightly, 'is a motive too remote and too sublime to affect the generality of mankind' (481), which means that it cannot be that motive in which injustice shows one to be deficient) with love. We can be benevolent to people whom we dislike. Hence his remarks about love (481–2) are beside the point.

(16) Hume says, 'A man's property is suppos'd to be fenc'd against every mortal, in every possible case' (483). He himself thinks that there are circumstances in which a man's property ought not to be fenced against every mortal. An overriding public interest may, in time of emergency, mean that rules of property may be set aside, because obeying such rules serves no useful purpose.

(17) Hume thinks that the reason why we condemn lack of paternal affection is that it shows want of a motive usual in man, or, at any rate, lack of this motive in its usual strength. As I have said, it is odd that he should try to derive the meritoriousness of parental affection—Hume mentions only *paternal* affection—from the fact that it is usual, rather than from the fact that it is necessary for the bringing up of offspring. I shall argue, when discussing a later section, that the duty to bring up one's biological children is in fact what Hume called an artificial, rather than a natural, virtue. (Society could have been organized on the principle that the duty of bringing up children is assigned to their uncles, and in some societies it is.)

(18) One further difference between natural and artificial virtues ought to be mentioned. Hume says, 'The only difference betwixt the natural virtues and justice lies in this, that the good, which results from

the former, arises from every single act, and is the object of some natural passion: Whereas a single act of justice, consider'd in itself, may often be contrary to the public good; and 'tis only the concurrence of mankind, in a general scheme or system of action, which is advantageous' (579). Benevolence, for example, is a natural virtue. If I perform an act of benevolence, the person who is the object of my benevolence profits directly from my action. Justice, on the other hand, is an artificial virtue, and consists in following a rule invented by the artifice of man. Any individual just act may benefit nobody at all. It may be just for me not to take the property of someone else, although it is owned by a profligate or a miser, and I and those who have commerce with me would benefit much more from my having use of this man's possessions than does he and those with whom he has commerce. It may, similarly, be a judge's duty to award an estate to a similar miser or profligate, when the consequences of this individual act of justice are equally pernicious. The good which arises from justice arises from a rule's being inflexibly adhered to, even in circumstances when adhering to it does more harm than good. Were it not observed in this rigid way, the benefits from having the rule would be destroyed; if having rules of justice is to be beneficial at all, these rules must be applied even in cases when applying them is not beneficial. More will be said about this at least apparently paradoxical contention of Hume's later.

(19) Hume also says: '*Secondly*, if we suppose, that the loan was secret, and that it is necessary for the interest of the person, that the money be restor'd in the same manner (as when the lender wou'd conceal his riches) in that case the example ceases, and the public is no longer interested in the actions of the borrower; tho' I suppose there is no moralist, who will affirm, that the duty and obligation ceases' (480-1). This is an important passage, because Hume here makes it quite clear that he thinks that we are under an obligation to adhere to a rule of justice, even though no harm would result in the way of our setting a bad example, from our departing from it. This means that he cannot give a very common utilitarian answer to such a question as, 'Why ought I to pay back a loan, when the man to whom I owe the money is rich, profligate and childless, when I could do more good with the money by giving it to charity or even spending it on myself?' This is the answer that I ought to pay back the money because not to pay it back would undermine the confidence of society that loans would be paid back, and so tend to deprive society of the benefits of a useful institution. He must, therefore, give some other explanation of why such loans must be repaid. How he does this will also be discussed later.

SECTION II

Of the Origin of Justice and Property

THE manner by which justice is established is as follows. Man's deficiency in force, ability, and security compared with other animals remedied by society (484-5); society is produced by sexual appetite and concern for offspring (486); and is disrupted by, first, the selfishness and confined generosity of men, together with, secondly, the easy transferability of external goods (484-8); the former, selfishness and confined generosity, since they are usual in men, are not naturally vicious and are in any case without remedy (488-9); but the latter, the transferability of external goods, can be altered by a convention allocating possessions and prohibiting their being taken without the owner's consent (489); this convention not a promise (490); it gives rise to the otherwise unintelligible ideas of justice, property, right, and obligation which are defined in terms of rules of justice (490-1); the object of these conventions is to restrain man's love of possessions, which disrupts society (491-2); these conventions are devices, invented by interest to restrain interest (491-3); without these conventions we would be in the fictional state of nature (492-3); with unlimited benevolence or an abundant supply of external goods man would be in the equally fictional golden age, when justice would be unnecessary (493-5); the fact that justice owes its origin to the selfishness and confined generosity of men shows (1) that the motive which makes justice a virtue is not benevolence (495-6); (2) that the sense of justice is not founded on reason (496); and (3) that justice arises from artifice (496-7); though single acts of justice may be pernicious, it is nevertheless necessary to perform them, since the scheme of which they are part is indispensable to mankind (497-8).

We *approve* of justice because we sympathize with the pleasure of those who benefit from it (498-500); this tendency is augmented by education and the artifice of politicians,[1] although it cannot be *produced* by these (498-501); injustice not so much allowable, as logically impossible, in a state of nature (501).

---

[1] 'Even the clergy, as their duty leads them to inculcate morality, may justly be thought, so far as regards this world, to have no other useful object of their institution' (Ess.114).

COMMENTS

(1) Hume's account of the 'morality' of the natural virtues, given at the beginning and end of Book III, Part II, Section I, goes ill, as I have already said, with what he says about this subject in Book III, Part III, Section I. In Book III, Part II, Section I, he argues that, where natural virtues are concerned, ' 'Tis according to their general force in human nature, that we blame or praise' (483). (He is speaking of motives.) We praise an action only if we regard its performance as a sign of the agent's having a praiseworthy motive, and regard an action as a duty only if it is an instance of a kind of action to which we are prompted by a motive that is usually found in human beings. How can this be consistent with what Hume says in Book III, Part III, Section I, where he claims that natural virtues (like artificial virtues) are approved of because they are qualities useful or agreeable to ourselves or others? If something is praiseworthy if it is usual, how can it be a virtue because it is useful or agreeable?

Something can be done to mitigate this inconsistency, though Hume himself does not do it, or even appear to notice that it is necessary. From the point of view of an evolutionary biologist, it could be argued that a man's motives must usually prompt him in a direction which is useful to himself and others, or man would not otherwise have survived. His motives, like his physical organs, have evolved over an enormously long period of time, and natural selection has weeded out the more harmful of them, leaving us those that normally drive us in directions that are conducive to the survival and prosperity of the human race. Hence a man's motives must impel him in a direction of which a good utilitarian—and Hume, to the extent that he was one—would approve.

This suggestion, however, can bring about only a partial reconciliation between the accounts in Book III, Part II, Section I and in Book III, Part III, Section I of the *Treatise*. Just as natural selection has not yet got rid of the appendix, despite the fact that it is either useless or positively harmful to man, so it has not got rid of many excessively violent primitive impulses, which were useful to man once upon a time, but which are so no longer. Hence many usual impulses are not useful. In any case, to say what is *usual* is also *useful* does not remove the incompatibility between saying that things are virtuous *because* they are usual, and saying that they are virtuous *because* they are useful or agreeable.

Perhaps, however, Hume is giving accounts of the 'morality' of different things, motives on the one hand, and character-traits of men on the other. Perhaps in Book III, Part II, Section I he is explaining what makes a *motive praiseworthy*, and in Book III, Part III, Section I he is explaining what makes a *human characteristic virtuous*. Hence, perhaps, there is no logical reason why giving one account of why a character trait is virtuous (because it is useful or agreeable) should not be quite compatible with giving a totally different account of why a motive is praiseworthy (because it is normal).

The view I have justified may be consistent, but it would be quite extraordinary if it were true. There must be some logical connection between what is praiseworthy and what is a virtue, even if it is only that virtues might not unnaturally be considered to be deserving of praise. (Indeed, we may properly be said to praise someone if we attribute to him some characteristic which we consider, or which is commonly considered to be, a virtue.) Could it really be the case that a motive was praiseworthy because it was normal in man, though, at the same time, it normally prompted one to vice?

Part of the answer to this question is that the word 'vice', as I have used it in the preceding sentence, is not the opposite of 'virtue', as Hume is using the word in the passages we are considering. 'Vice' here means a vicious course of action, not a vicious personal characteristic. The virtues, I think, can be divided into two classes. In the first class fall virtues such as industry and determination, which enable a man to pursue successfully any ends that his predominant motives may set him, whether these ends are good ones or not. In the second class fall virtues like kindness and honesty, which are logically linked to the pursuit of certain ends. One cannot be kind or honest, *whatever* one's ends may happen to be, for to be kind or honest is just to have among one's ends the welfare of others (in the case of kindness), or telling the truth and not cheating or taking what does not belong to one (in the case of honesty).

Where the former class of virtues is concerned, it is quite possible to give an account of why they are virtues, which account is not linked to the praiseworthiness of motives. These virtues serve whatever ends we happen to have. They will remain virtues, even when used in pursuit of an end dictated by a bad motive. Hence it will be perfectly possible for Hume to say, as (sometimes) he does say, that a motive is praiseworthy if it is normal, and a character-trait a virtue if it is useful. But where the second kind of virtue is concerned, this is not possible. For these latter virtues can be exercised only in a way that we are morally in favour of, and if we are morally in favour of them for some reason other than that they can be exercised only in the pursuit of ends to which we are prompted by a motive that is usual in man, Hume must be mistaken. In other words, an account must be given of the praiseworthiness of those virtues that are logically linked to the adoption of a praiseworthy course of action, and if the reason why they are praiseworthy is that they normally prompt one to behaviour which is socially desirable (in Hume's words, useful to ourselves and others), it cannot be that they are praiseworthy because they are logically linked to the pursuit of ends that are set up by motives that are usual.

(2) Hume's account of 'duty' is also inconsistent. Sometimes he says that an action is a duty if it is the kind of action to which we are prompted by a motive that is usual in men (477–8). At other times he suggests that an action is a duty if it is demanded by a rule of justice (490–1).

One might try to argue that there is in fact no inconsistency between these two apparently different accounts, for one is an account of what is naturally a duty, and the other an account of what is a duty as the result of that artifice which establishes rules of justice. This attempt to whitewash Hume, however, will not do. It is scarcely credible that the word 'duty' is being used in a totally different sense when we talk about the natural and when we talk about the artificial virtues. And if it were being used in different senses, and it was our duty, in one sense of 'duty', to perform actions dictated by normal motives, and our duty, in another sense of 'duty', to perform actions which conformed to rules of justice, we would need a *third* sense of 'duty', in order to raise the question, 'Which, in the event of a conflict between "natural duty" and "artificial duty", of these two duties is it our duty to perform?'

One might suggest that it was not Hume's view that actions were duties in two different senses of 'duty', but that actions could be duties for two different reasons. Sometimes actions are duties because they are the kind of actions to which we are led by a normal motive. At other times actions are duties because they are dictated by a rule of justice. This account would square ill with the fact that Hume seems to be *defining* 'duty' in terms of what is demanded by a rule of justice, not simply maintaining that actions that are demanded by rules of justice are thereby made to have the additional feature of being duties (490–1). It would seem to me to be quite extraordinary that two such totally disparate things should both be duties. And in any case, it gives rise to the problem, 'What happens when a rule of justice demands an action to which we are not prompted by a normal motive?' Indeed, as we have seen, Hume sometimes speaks as if there are simply no normal motives which do prompt us to obey rules of justice.

Part of the trouble is that Hume has nowhere given any complete or coherent account of the morality of *actions*, as opposed to the morality of motives and the morality of character-traits. Hence, though he holds that *personal characteristics* are virtues if they are useful or agreeable to their possessor or to others, he never moves on to the natural accompaniment of this view, the view that *actions* are *duties* if it is to the advantage of ourselves and others that they be performed. Had he done so, it would have been quite easy for him to reconcile his account of 'natural duties' and 'artificial duties'. He could simply have said some such thing as that actions are duties if they are advantageous to the agent and others, and then add that some actions are advantageous, whether there are rules of justice or not, but that other actions are advantageous only in a society which has and observes rules of justice. Benevolence, for example, is advantageous whether there are rules of justice or not, but abstention from theft is only advantageous— indeed, it is only possible—in a society which has rules of justice which define and proscribe theft.

Hume could have taken some such line as this, but, if he had, would it have been plausible? The effect would be to divorce the notion of duty, and also the connected notions of 'right', 'wrong', and 'obligatory', from any anchoring they may have to the notion of actually accepted rules, for in a society without what Hume calls justice, there would simply be no such rules.

(3) I use the words 'what Hume calls justice' advisedly. I think that Hume's account of the nature, usefulness, and genesis of these social rules is excellent, but I cannot help thinking that, in describing these rules as justice, he was using the word in too restricted a way.[2] Justice, one is inclined to think, has something to do with the twin virtues of

---

[2] In *An Enquiry Concerning Human Understanding* Hume says. 'But to convince us of this proposition, *that where there is no property, there can be no injustice*, it is only necessary to define the terms, and explain injustice to be a violation of property' (E163). Here, however, he is doing himself an injustice (which injustice does not consist, as it ought if Hume's own definition were correct, in violating his own property). For, even granted that Hume was right in defining injustice as breach of a rule of justice, he did admit of some rules which do not have to do with property, for example, the rules of polite society, and, whether he admitted them or not, there are rules of justice which have nothing to do with property, for example, rules laying down what constitutes an offence against the person.

It is an interesting corollary of the remark I have just quoted, and of other remarks in the same section (E163), that Hume would not have regarded a proposition which was true by definition as one which is shown to be true by demonstration. Hence the fact that there are analytic ethical propositions does not, according to Hume, entail that moral truths can be demonstrated, as can truths about quantity and number. This view, which I think is mistaken, is partly the result of supposing wrongly that truths which result from definitions must be all fairly trivial.

equity and impartiality, but Hume makes scarcely any mention of these, and it is not immediately obvious that these virtues have anything to do with the kind of rule that Hume is talking about. As we shall see, Hume thinks that there are three main kinds of rules about what he calls justice, those that institute property and enforce its stability, those that govern its transference, and those that set up and regulate promises and contracts. Theft, or taking the property of others, is not normally called injustice, nor are any of the various wrongs which private persons can commit in connection with transferring property, nor are promise-breaking or defaulting on a contract. Justice, in the ordinary sense, is certainly *connected* with what Hume calls rules of justice, but not in the straightforward way that any breach of such a rule is a case of injustice. Injustice arises from such rules in two ways. First of all, people may be wrongfully accused and convicted of breaking such rules, or punished for breaking such rules when they have not broken them, or punished more severely for breaking them than they deserve. Secondly, the rules themselves may be unjust in that, to the extent that they allocate possessions to some people rather than others, they allocate these in a manner which is unjust and inequitable. Clearly the terms 'just' and 'unjust', as these are used to assess the rules and the manner in which these rules are applied, cannot be defined, as Hume seems to want them to be, as meaning either conforming or failing to conform to the rules. Impartiality, indeed, to the extent that it consists in simply applying the law without being influenced by considerations which are not, by law, made relevant, logically could not be enjoined by a rule of justice. For it would be logically otiose to have, over and above the rules of law, another rule of law which simply said that these rules of law should be applied. To apply the law impartially is simply to apply it, and, in doing so, not to be guided by any considerations, such as being offered a bribe by one of the litigating parties, that are not to be found in the law that is being applied. A better name for that virtue which Hume calls justice, and for which there is not a word that I can think of in the English language, would be rule-abidingness. (The word 'law-abidingness' would be too narrow, for not all the rules that the rule-abiding man observes have the status of positive *laws*. Many of them are conventions, such as the convention that promises ought to be kept, which do not, or do not always, have any legal force.) The rule-abiding man is not necessarily a just man, for it is not just, though it is rule-abiding, not to steal, to keep one's promises, and to avoid violence. (We do not describe a thief as being unjust, nor do we regard rape as an act of injustice.) Though justice is a virtue which has reference to these rules, it is not a virtue which is manifested simply in obeying the rules, so much as in the framing—if they are framed, and do not just grow up, as they often do—and the applying of them by those who, like judges, lawyers, and policemen, are in an administrative or a judicial position concerned with their improvement. Justice is manifested by legislators in framing laws that are equitable, and by judges, juries, lawyers, and to a lesser extent, policemen, in interpreting, enforcing, and litigating over these laws. For example, a jury may be acting unjustly if it finds guilty a man it believes to be innocent. A judge may be acting unjustly if he passes a sentence which he believes is too severe. A policeman may be acting unjustly if he plants cannabis in the house of a man whose politics he dislikes. A private person may be acting unjustly if he knowingly brings a false action against a neighbour, and a lawyer if he acts for such a person, knowing that his case is groundless.

Though what Hume mistakenly calls justice is an artificial virtue, justice properly so called is not. This follows from the fact that the question whether or not certain rules are equitable (and do not, for example, unfairly favour the rich as against the poor, or whites as against blacks), the question whether certain penalties prescribed by the rules or imposed by judges at their own discretion are or are not excessively severe, and the question whether the rules of justice are being properly applied (that is, applied) cannot be settled by appealing to the rules themselves. There must, therefore, be certain standards or criteria which are not established artificially by convention, by reference to which the rules which are the product of artificial convention may be assessed. Since one—though not necessarily the only one, for their usefulness is also relevant—of these criteria is whether or not the rules are just rules justly applied, justice must, as John Stuart Mill pointed out,[3] be something outside or over and above the rules, and so not, like the rules themselves, artificial. For example, one might, by legislative fiat, change a law imposing the death penalty for attempted suicide, but one could not, by legislative fiat, turn a law which did impose the death penalty for attempted suicide from an unjust law into a just one. One could by legislation make it illegal, instead of legal, to buy guns through the post, but one could not, by a similar act, make it cease to be unjust to try and then sentence a man for buying arms through the post when doing this was not illegal.

Hume himself implicitly allows that there are some criteria by which what he calls the rules of justice may be assessed, for he claims that they are useful, and the habit of observing them is a virtue because it is

---

[3] *Utilitarianism*, Everyman edition, p. 41.

a useful habit. It is obvious that Hume is right, and that the usefulness or otherwise of such rules provides us with one standard by which they can be assessed—though not the only standard, if the rules must also be assessed by their justice. It is also obvious that the usefulness of the rule provides a natural, rather than an artificial, standard by which man-made rules may be assessed. Man may deliberately make or unmake laws, say those prohibiting the sale and consumption of alcohol, but he cannot himself decide whether having such laws is or is not to be useful. However, Hume himself admits of natural controls, unalterable by man, upon the rules. The rules are artificial (and so the habit of obeying them an 'artificial' virtue), but this does not mean that any rules are good rules, or that man can himself decide 'artificially' which rules are to be good rules, and which not.

This gives rise to a problem, which Hume only partly appreciates, namely, what is the consequence for our duty to conform our actions to the rules if the rules are *unfavourably* assessed by their justice and their usefulness? (In Section IX, he considers the related problem: to what extent do we have a duty to obey the civil magistrate when *he* is harmful, and his behaviour unjust?) This problem apparently did not occur to Hume because he was so impressed by the necessity of having almost any, if not quite any, set of rules rather than no rules at all. He does, as we shall see, consider what happens to our duty to be just when it is not useful to have any rules. But of course, the comparison between having the set of rules we do have and no rules at all is not the only comparison that can be made, and it is unrealistic to suppose that it is. There is also the comparison between having any given rule, and not having that rule, or having some modified version of that rule. It would be almost certainly better to have the rules one does have, what-ever they may be, than no rules at all, for without any rules at all life, as Hobbes pointed out, would be nasty, brutish, and short. It is also certainly sometimes better to have rather different rules from the ones one does have, and perhaps, sometimes, to have rules very different from the ones one does have. Furthermore, the act of disobeying one or more harmful rule—say one demanding compulsory military service—is unlikely to bring it about that there are no rules at all.

According to some modern philosophers, who hold one version of a theory which has come to be known as rule utilitarianism, (1) the question whether an action is right or wrong or a duty, which question is settled by asking whether or not it conforms to the rules, and (2) the question whether the rules are useful rules, can be raised quite independently of one another. One never considers whether an action is itself useful when one considers whether or not it is right or a duty, but only whether or not it conforms to the rules. Considerations of usefulness do not, or should not, arise at the level of individual actions, but only at the level at which the rules, to which individual actions conform or fail to conform, are assessed.

Hence there are two questions we must ask ourselves before we decide that any action we are considering is right. First, does it conform to a rule? And second, is the rule to which it conforms a useful rule? It is right if and only if both conditions are satisfied.

This modern view—though not all such views are as extreme as this—seems not implausible, but is in fact quite absurd. The two questions, whether actions are right and whether rules are useful, cannot be kept as separate as the proponents of this view would have us believe. It is obvious that, if the rules are harmful beyond a certain point, it is not our duty to conform our actions to them, and not wrong to break them. In any case, there is no such thing as the utility of a rule *in vacuo*, isolated from the utility of such actions as obeying the rule, condemning people for not obeying the rule, punishing people for not obeying it, encouraging one's children to obey it, and so on. There is no such thing as the utility of a rule, independent of the utility of actions such as these, and to say that a rule is useful is just a shorthand way of saying that actions such as these are useful or—since it is unlikely that all of them will be useful—that actions such as these are useful on the whole. If actions such as these are not useful, then the rule cannot be useful. Hence any suggestion that we divorce the question whether an action is right from the question whether this action itself has good consequences, and consider instead the question whether the rule which enjoined it has good consequences, must return in a circle back to the original question. For to say that a rule is a useful rule is just to say that actions of the kind I have mentioned have or generally have good consequences. One cannot say that the rightness of individual actions depends not on their own consequences, but on the consequences of the rules they conform to, if the consequences of these rules turn out themselves to be the consequences of individual actions.

On the other hand, though, as I have already said, it would be absurd to maintain that it was our duty to obey a rule, however bad the consequences of the rule were; it would be equally absurd to maintain that we do not have some duty to obey rules, even though they have bad consequences or could be replaced by better rules. The logical outcome of such a view would be that we would have to maintain that Britons did not have a duty to drive on the left-hand side of the road, if it were better, because this is the rule adopted almost everywhere else, to have a rule enjoining that they all drive on the right-hand side of the road.

The problem is how to draw a line between those cases when a rule should not be obeyed, because of its bad consequences, and those cases when it should be obeyed, in spite of its bad consequences, because disobedience even to a bad rule is harmful and socially disruptive. Ordinary utilitarianism (now commonly called act utilitarianism) can provide—in theory at any rate, however difficult it may be to apply it in practice—a perfectly simple answer to this question. We should obey a rule, however bad, when the consequences of obeying it are better than the consequences of disobeying it; otherwise we should disobey it.

Hume, however, was not an ordinary utilitarian or, at any rate, not an explicit one. Though he has a utilitarian account of virtues, including a utilitarian account of that virtue which he wrongly called justice, and which we have agreed to call rule-abidingness, he has no articulately formulated general utilitarian theory about what makes an action *right* or what makes it a *duty*, as opposed to what makes a personal character-trait a *virtue*. Sometimes, indeed, as we have seen, he says that an action is a duty if it is the kind of action towards which we are impelled by a motive men usually have, which is not a utilitarian remark at all. At other times he quite specifically states that, though rules of justice are useful, indeed essential, we have a duty to conform to these useful rules even on occasions when our so conforming is pernicious. This statement clearly commits Hume to rejecting any theory according to which we should keep to the rules when and only when the consequences of keeping to them are better than the consequences of departing from them. His view is therefore incompatible with act utilitarianism. To what extent Hume was a rule utilitarian we shall consider later.

(4) Though a man is not denominated just or unjust solely in accordance with whether or not he obeys what Hume calls rules of justice (from which it follows that the virtue of justice does not consist in a disposition to obey such rules), there is a sense of 'justice' in which it refers, not to a virtue in men, but to the institution or system of rules, of adjudication concerning them, and their enforcement. It is in this sense, I think, in which 'justice' is being used in the sentence, 'Let justice be done, though the heavens fall.' In this sense, Hume is using the word 'justice' in a manner which is much more nearly correct (though in this sense it would be logically inappropriate to describe justice as a *virtue*) but rather wider than that in which it is normally used. I say this because Hume uses the word 'justice' to include rules about promising, chastity and modesty, and polite behaviour, whereas these would not normally be so described. (This, I think, is because it is not possible legally to enforce them.) But the difference, between rules

which are clearly rules of justice and rules which are not, is one of degree, and I see no good reason why Hume should not be allowed to use the expression 'justice' in this slightly extended sense.

(5) Hume was prevented from seeing that rules can be criticized because they are unjust by his tendency to define 'just'as 'in accordance with the rules'. To criticize rules because they are unjust, of course, is not at all to criticize them because they are not useful. The words 'just' and 'useful' do not mean the same, nor do their opposites, 'unjust' and 'harmful'. Nevertheless, I am inclined to think that, in the last resort, there can be no conflict between the justice and the usefulness of the rules, and for the following reasons.

It is clearly just that similar people should be treated by the rules (that is to say, by the men who make, enforce, and interpret the rules) in similar ways, whenever this is possible. If people are already being treated unequally by the rules, by some people being given more of a community's resources than others, this introduces a dissimilarity which, prima facie, it would be right and useful to rectify by giving more to the less advantaged than to the advantaged. The reason why it is useful to treat this dissimilarity between people by giving more to the former than to the latter is that, the fewer resources one has, the more one is likely to benefit by receiving further resources. For the extra you give to the rich will probably be spent on luxuries, while the extra you give to the poor is likely to be spent on necessities, and, of course, you do more good with a limited amount of resources if they are spent on necessities than on luxuries.

It may not be possible to treat everyone alike, however, because there may be commodities which not everybody can have, and which cannot be divided, or cannot be divided usefully, and there may be tasks, either pleasant or unpleasant, which not everybody can do, but someone must do, if society is to function, or, at any rate, to function efficiently. To some extent justice could be preserved by casting lots for these emoluments or burdens, or distributing them in rotation, but this is unlikely to be always practicable. There is no reason why, if some people prefer some tasks, and others prefer others, the rules should not allow people the tasks they prefer, or why emoluments should not be given those who want them, rather than those who do not, but it is unlikely that people's preferences should be so conveniently distributed. Even in a world where everyone was similar, then, it might not be possible or desirable that everyone should be treated in similar ways. For the variety of tasks which must be performed in a complex social organization is enormous and heterogeneous, and involves very large differences in interest and power, and so, if all people were similar, very similar people must perforce be given very different functions. Indeed, if all men were born similar, they would have, by education, to be made artificially dissimilar in order satisfactorily to fulfil these varying roles. The dissimilarities introduced by different men's being differently educated to perform different functions, together with the very different stresses and demands made upon them by the very performance of these functions, breeds further dissimilarities. This is not necessarily something to be deplored. Since society is to a large extent like a complex machine, it would be as unreasonable to expect the people who make it up to be similar as it would be to expect all the parts of a machine to be similar. It is perhaps fortunate that to a large extent, though by no means completely, these necessary differences in function can be relegated to that aspect of a man's life which concerns his work. On the golf course he can still be a man, even though professionally he must be an animated cog.

However, men are not all similar, and not all equal. The question therefore arises: 'What differences between one man and another justify the rules, and the people who make and administer the rules, in treating different men differently?' There are the following possibilities.

Merit ought to be rewarded. It is just for the more meritorious to have a larger share of a nation's income than the less meritorious. This remark does not apply so much to moral excellence, as to those excellences which are socially useful. But the fact that it is just that excellence should be suitably awarded in no way conflicts with utility, for it is also, for example, conducive to everybody's advantage that the socially more important roles should attract higher rewards, and that people with the greatest ability should perform them.

It is just that vice should be punished, but it is also obviously useful that this should be done. This is to a large extent because the rules themselves determine what is virtuous and what vicious, or, at any rate, determine what types of conduct incur those penalties which are necessary if the rules are to be enforced. Hence to the extent that the rules are harmful, punishing those who break the rules will encourage harmful actions, but, to the extent that the rules are beneficial, punishing those who are vicious in the sense that they break the rules will encourage beneficial actions. To the extent that there are—*if* there are—moral rules, uncreated by man, and that man-created rules simply codify and enforce these moral rules, then codifying and enforcing these moral rules will be beneficial if these moral rules are utilitarian in nature. It does not follow, however, whatever Mr Justice Devlin may say to the contrary, from the fact that there is a moral rule prescribing or proscribing something and obeying this moral rule is beneficial, that it is useful to have a man-made rule codifying and enforcing this moral rule. If so, it would follow, from the fact that there are useful rules governing the conduct of husbands to their wives and parents to their children, that the actions these moral rules proscribe ought to be legally prohibited, and the prohibition legally enforced. But laws which regulate how much pocket money parents give their children, or which try to enforce courtesy between married people, would obviously be impossible to enforce, and would involve an undesirable interference in domestic matters and an enormous and prohibitively expensive police force, probably consisting of men and women whose marriages had failed and whose children had run away from home. Though to the extent that the rules are useful, punishing those who break them—with the afore-mentioned exceptions—must be beneficial, it is very doubtful whether it is either just or advantageous to punish those who are simply immoral, but whose immorality does not consist in breaking any positive law. This is not to say that the positive laws should not be amended so that these people can be punished, but, again, if the behaviour one wishes legally to prohibit is socially harmful in a way that it is socially benefi-cial to prevent by law, there is no conflict between justice and utility.

In a society which allows some amount of free enterprise, differences in power and wealth are likely to develop. It is very often held that it is unjust that there should be such differences, and it may further be held that one function of a just system of laws is to make people more nearly equal in power and wealth than they will be if left to themselves, even though such inequalities result from the lawful exercise of very unequal abilities for acquiring and retaining wealth and power. Of course, the very same people who maintain that it is unjust that there should be such differences are also likely to maintain that the differ-ences are harmful, as they certainly will be if we consider only the fact that very unequal distributions are likely to result in some people having very much more than they need, while others have barely enough, or not as much as they need. On the other hand, it can be held that redistributing income involves penalizing enterprise, from which everyone, not just the people whose acquired wealth is taken away from them, suffers. It should not be forgotten, of course, that a not inconsiderable amount of redistribution of income is a by-product of the fact that modern governments cannot operate successfully without large amounts of money, which they must take from those who have it, i.e. the rich.

Redistribution of income is often accomplished in the form of giving to the needy, by means of free education, free treatment and nursing for ill health, and maintenance for the old and destitute. It is often maintained that this, too, is a demand of justice. (Personally, I would regard it as a matter of expediency or humanity, rather than justice.) But, if it is a demand of justice, it is also a demand of utility, for people clearly benefit from being given these things, and probably benefit more than the people from whom the money to give these things to them is taken, provided that the former are not pauperized, and the latter not made idle and indifferent in consequence. And if redistributing this money harms both those from whom it is taken and those to whom it is given, I doubt very much whether anyone would want to describe it as just. If it is just, then it is one of those cases in which justice had much better not be done.

If one regards justice as a matter of meeting claims, and a just law as one which meets all the claims that people might have on it, then there must necessarily be some tendency for the justice of laws to coincide with their utility. For the claims different people have must have something to do with their needs, in which case harm will be done if their needs are not met; or with their ability or their services, in which case harm will be done if services are not rewarded or abilities not fostered; or with their legitimate expectations, in which case harm will be done if a state is created in which legitimate expectations are arbitrarily ignored. It is often said that there may be a conflict between what it is just to do and what it is useful to do, but at least to some extent this may be exaggerated because, when we make the comparison, we forget that the utility which we oppose to justice may in fact consist in meeting the claims of people not immediately involved. For example, if we consider it just to spend more money on the education of stupid children than on that of intelligent children, on the grounds that we have a duty of justice to rectify a natural inequality, in spite of the fact that it would be most expedient to spend more money on the education of the more intelligent children (since these are the ones whose skill is most likely to be of use to society), we may be forgetting the claims of the people who would benefit from the services of the more intelligent children, and inadvertently treating these people unjustly.

The claims of justice are in any case so obscure that we would not be departing excessively from its meaning if we simply defined a just law as a law which, so far as possible, treated similar people in similar ways, and, to the extent that it is desirable to treat dissimilar people in dissimilar ways, took account of those differences which it was right to take account of.[4] It may be that the only differences that it is right to

---

[4] For a more detailed account of my views on this question, see my *Our Knowledge of Right and Wrong*, George Allen and Unwin, 1971, pp. 369–75.

take account of are differences that it is useful to take account of. Of course, if it is regarded as unjust that differences that it is right to take account of are not taken account of, this will cause a feeling of just resentment in the people whose interests are thereby ignored, and this will constitute a further utilitarian reason in favour of a just distribution. It is difficult to believe that a family or state which is justly administered will not, other things being equal, be happier than a family or state which is not justly administered. The most obvious, if not the only, cases where there is a conflict between justice and utility will be involved not in the choice of what laws to have, when just laws will be the most useful, but in choosing between prosecuting a law we already have, which might be considered to be the just thing to do, and departing from it for the sake of utility. This, at any rate, is the only type of case that Hume himself recognizes. His view is that justice should take precedence over usefulness, though only because a scheme of things in which justice is the rule rather than the exception, and so usually takes precedence over utility, will be more useful than one where justice is occasionally abandoned for the sake of utility.

There is a point here which cannot be too strongly emphasized. In suggesting that it is just to treat dissimilar people in dissimilar ways only when it is useful to do this, I am giving a utilitarian account of justice. But even if it is not possible to give a utilitarian account of what makes something just, it does not at all follow that one cannot give a utilitarian account of why one ought to be just. This is a point which, I believe, has been overlooked by everybody who has written on the subject. For to say that an action is just is not at all the same thing as to say that it is right to do it, though it will be one reason, among others, why it is right to do it. Utilitarianism, however, is a theory about what it is right to do, not about what is just. Hence, even if we have to give a non-utilitarian account of justice, it may still be the case that it is right to be just only when some good comes of it. If one is not allowed to say that justice is itself a good—and I see no very good reason why a utilitarian should not say this—then at least one can say that, other things being equal, treating people unjustly is not a very good way of producing a harmonious society. Let us suppose (for the sake of argument) what it is by no means clear to me can be sensibly supposed, that one can make one man happier by being unjust to another; one will still be acting in a harmful way if one ignores the former man's just claim. Both men are likely to feel resentful if their interests are ignored, but the first man's just resentment is more likely to be socially harmful than the mere annoyance of the latter, and the first man's resentment, since its justice will make it more likely to attract the support of others than the second man's, is much more likely to be socially disruptive. (Of course, the first man's claim will attract support because it is supposed to be just, rather than because it is just, but the safest way, in the long run, of avoiding the disruption that will be caused by supposed injustice is by performing acts which are just.) It would be no part of this utilitarian view that one ought always to be just. When justice and utility conflict, one ought to perform the useful action rather than the just one, but one thing that makes an action useful is that not to do it would be unjust, and it would be the exception rather than the rule for it to be useful to do what is unjust. This is even more the case when it is considered that, though occasional departures from justice may be useful, harm would result if men made it a rule to perform the useful rather than the just action on all similar occasions.

(6) Though in Hume's view, no human arrangements for the distribution, transference, inheritance, management, or acquisition of property can possibly be unjust—for since 'just' means 'in accordance with the arrangements' the arrangements themselves cannot be unjust —it is possible to criticize these arrangements, though Hume himself does not do so, in other ways. They could be criticized on the grounds that they leave some people to starve, while other people have more than they need; on the grounds that the arrangements do not provide an adequate incentive to people to work, produce, and take necessary risks; on the grounds that they concentrate too much power in the hands of too few people; on the grounds that too few people have too much control over what is produced; or on the grounds that too much equality allows no one any leisure to pursue great enterprises of a kind that governments would not support, and produces on the contrary a dull uniformity of outlook and achievement. All these criticisms are utilitarian in nature, and have to do with the consequences, for good or ill, of these arrangements upon the welfare of the men who have adopted them. They are not necessarily exclusively utilitarian, however. Some people may think, for example, that an equal distribution of property is itself something to aim at, or at any rate, a prima-facie reason for having a certain kind of distribution, quite independently of the goodness or badness of the consequences of such a distribution. Whether this is so or not I shall discuss later.

(7) In defining property in terms of rules, which rules, in a developed community such as ours, will be identical with laws of the land, Hume is clearly right. The precise definition of property in terms of such rules, however, is not easy to give. It looks plausible to suggest that property should be defined in terms of rights, i.e. that something is

someone's property if he has rights over it that other people do not have. These rights in their turn could be defined in terms of duties, so that the right a man has to his property is defined as the duty other men have of not preventing him from treating it in certain ways, and the duty yet other men may have of preventing men from preventing him from treating it in these ways. For example, my owning a house can be defined in terms of my having rights over it that other people do not have, e.g. a right to live in it (but not a right to burn it down). This means that other people have a duty not to prevent my living in it, and some people, e.g. judges and policemen, have a duty to stop other people from preventing me from living in it. This is the account which Hume at least suggests (490-1).

Such an account—or, rather, outline of an account—would be too simple, and for the following reasons.

(i) It is too simple to say that it is the owner who has rights, and other people who have duties. For (a) the owner may have duties, as well as rights, in respect of what he owns, for example, a duty to maintain it in good condition (if it is a car) or a duty to pay compensation for the damage it causes (if it is a dog). And (b) other people may have rights over my property, e.g. a right of way through my land.

(ii) It takes no proper account of the fact that I may temporarily surrender my right over my property without losing possession of it. I may lease my land to someone else, when I cease to have my usual rights over it, but it remains my property because it reverts to me or my heir on the expiry of the lease.

(iii) Hume almost always, though not quite always (520), speaks as if what I own is a material object. But, to take quite a simple case, suppose I own £1,000 in the form of a credit balance in my current account. Then there are no material objects that I own and have rights over. All the material objects concerned are pieces of paper with ink marks on them, and it is my bank, not I, who owns these. My owning £1,000 consists in my having a right to do certain things, e.g. go to my bank and demand £1,000 in notes (the possession of which notes gives me the right, in certain circumstances, to exchange them for goods or services or such things as a seat on Concorde), or to give someone a piece of paper which in effect requests my bank to transfer some rights of mine to him, in exchange for my receiving from him such things as goods or services or whatever. In fact, though I have a right to £1,000, the expression '£1,000' is not a name for a thing belonging to the category of substance, or even 1,000 different things belonging to this category, or even 1,000 unspecified things of this sort (as is 'one thousand and one Dalmatians'), but simply, in this case, a measure of the extent of a person's rights, e.g. a right in certain circumstances to go through certain manoeuvres resulting in his acquiring goods, say, up to the value of £1,000.

The point that, if I have leased or let my property, someone else may have more rights over it than I do, does not strike me as being a very important one, however. All it means is that ownership must not be defined in terms of the rights possessed by someone at a given moment, but that the owner of something must be defined or the person to whom these rights revert at the end of a period during which something is leased, let, lent, or temporarily taken over by the government.

The point that the owner of something is distinguished not only by his rights, but by his duties or responsibilities, may be met by saying that the statement that owners have rights is analytic, but the statement that they have duties is a synthetic one. Owners are distinguished by their rights, and, once so distinguished, may have duties laid upon them, but they could still be owners, even though they had no duties, though they could not be owners if they had no distinguishing rights.

The point that many, if not most, of the things men own do not belong to the category of substance does not in any way show that ownership cannot be defined in terms of rights. If anything, it reinforces the point that to own something is to have rights that other men do not have, for where the property is something 'abstract', all that there is is rights.

It is fair to ask, however, what distinguishes those rights which constitute property from other rights, for example, a right to life or liberty or the pursuit of happiness. It seems to me that the most fundamental notion involved in the definition of property is the idea of having a cluster of rights which are usually of value to more than one person; which may be transferred from one person to another, possibly for a consideration; which may be temporarily transferred, also for a consideration; which revert to the owner after an agreed period; and which may be confiscated in payment of the owner's debts. There is no implication in this definition that what is owned must be a substance. It is unnecessary for all these conditions to be fulfilled for something to be someone's property—for example, if an estate is entailed, the owner will be unable to sell it—but most of them must be, just as a person must have most, but not necessarily all, of a given set of features to be truly said to possess the family face.

It seems to me that it is to some extent a matter of accident that the rights to life and liberty do not give rise to property, and that though people own their houses, they do not own their lives, or own their liberty. The reason for this, I think, has nothing to do with life and liberty not being material things, for a credit balance is not material either, and does not belong to the category of substance. It has, I think, to do with the fact that life and liberty cannot be transferred for a consideration. If they could be, then perhaps we would distinguish between those people who owned their liberty and owned their lives and those who did not.

(8) The reader of the *Treatise* may be forgiven for thinking that Hume puts an entirely excessive emphasis upon property, and the rules which define it, when talking about justice. The psychological and historical causes of this I do not understand. And in any case the appearance that he over-emphasizes property is to some extent illusory. The rules which determine our duty to those who govern us, the laws of nations, and those which regulate the relations between the sexes are also species of those artificial conventions that Hume calls justice, and in the *Enquiry* (E208 f.) he quite properly treats the rules which govern behaviour in polite society as an instance of the same kind of thing. But that he over-emphasizes property is not entirely an illusion. Almost nothing is said about violence which does not arise from conflict over possessions, the need for equal and impartial treatment is barely mentioned, and the need for just distribution and for justice when this concerns punishment and treating people as they deserve to be treated is not discussed at all.

Whatever the psychological and historical explanation of this emphasis may be, one logical mistake behind it is that Hume supposes that serious and prolonged trouble can arise only from competition for goods which are limited in supply, because these are the only things which can be taken by one man from another without losing their usefulness (487). Of the two other species of good things that Hume recognizes, the internal satisfaction of our minds and the external advantages of our bodies, the first, he thinks, cannot be taken away from us at all, and, though the second cannot be taken away from us, they are of no use to the person who takes them (487). I may chop off my enemy's leg, but his leg, unlike his sword, is of no use to me.

Hume is clearly wrong about this. I can take away some of other people's 'internal satisfactions'. It is not at all impossible to take away their intelligence—I can do this by hitting them with a brick—and often quite easy to make other people insecure and unhappy. And though my enemy's leg may be of no use to me, the fact that he does not have a leg may be considerably to my advantage. Of course, one of the advantages of making my enemy stupid or legless will be that it handicaps him in competing with me for possessions, and so, if it is impossible for these to be transferred, a considerable motive for my doing these things will be eliminated. It will not entirely be eliminated, for being stupid or legless will handicap my enemy in even *legitimately* acquiring possessions which are in short supply. Hume discounts envy and revenge as motives for injuring other people because they are directed only against particular persons and operate intermittently. Though he is right about this, it is nevertheless obvious that society must have rules preventing people from injuring other people for whatever reasons, and these rules will not be made unnecessary by the fact that the main reason why some people will want to injure others will be to prevent them from either acquiring possessions they want or taking those they already have, or from anger or malice resulting from competition over possessions.

The reason why Hume says nothing about distributing possessions justly may be that, if he has given an adequate account of justice, it follows that it is logically impossible for goods to be distributed unjustly. For justice is merely a name for those conventions by means of which, among other things, property is defined. A man's property consists precisely of those of his possessions that the rules allocate to him and protect him in using. Hence whatever the rules decree is just, and so the rules cannot legitimize a distribution which is unjust. Similarly, there could be no such thing as an unjust punishment, provided that this punishment was required or permitted by law; no such thing as an unjust power, provided that the power was legally allowable; and no such thing as an unjust man, provided that he did what the law required. Property could not literally be theft, as Proudhon suggested, for theft is taking away someone's property.

Someone who wished to defend Hume could reply that the rules or conventions Hume is talking about are not identical with positive law. They may exist, for example, in a society which might be described as not having a positive law, because the rules enforced in that society are not written down, because there are no second-order rules prescribing what bodies have the power to legislate, and because there are no courts.[5] And Hume counts rules about promising as rules of justice, although these are not always legally enforceable; likewise rules governing the relations between the sexes and how to behave in polite society, although the penalties for disobeying these are social rather than legal. Hence it would be possible for Hume to maintain that there were non-legal rules, which could not be enforced in the courts, prescribing what was a just distribution, or a just price, or a just man, and that, assessed by these rules, a positive law on what it prescribed *could* be unjust. (If

[5] See H. L. A. Hart, *The Concept of Law*, OUP, 1961.

such rules were of great antiquity, they would have a greater effect on men's sentiments than the more recent legal rules (561-2), and so the latter would be likely to be considered unjust when they conflicted with the former, rather than the other way round.) More will be said about this possibility later. For the moment all I need to do is to observe that it seems to be logically possible for any given individual to assess any social convention of any kind as being just or unjust, from which it would follow that justice cannot be defined in terms of either legal rules or social conventions.

(9) Hume thinks that it is a corollary of the fact that justice would be unnecessary if goods were in unlimited supply, or if people were abundantly benevolent, that morality cannot consist in any relations, and, consequently, cannot be discovered by reason (496). I have discussed similar arguments in my *Hume's Moral Epistemology*, but must nevertheless say a few words about this particular argument here. It especially resembles the argument that morality cannot consist in any relations, because all the relations possessed by human and animal incest and human and animal ingratitude are the same, whereas incest and ingratitude in humans are immoral, but incest and ingratitude in animals are not (466-8).

The argument falls into two stages: (i) If reason apprehends moral distinctions, morality must consist of one of the four philosophical relations which give rise to demonstration, viz. resemblance, contiguity, degrees in quality, and proportions in quantity and number. (ii) It cannot consist in any of these four relations, because all the relations possessed by actions performed in a society in which justice does not exist, because it is unnecessary, will be the same as those performed in a society where justice does exist, because it is necessary. The former actions, however, are not immoral while the latter are. This argument can be treated as a variant on the argument about incest and ingratitude, given that it is assumed that the reason for the difference between human and animal incest and ingratitude is that human beings have rules of justice, but animals do not.

It is very odd that Hume should think that all the relations possessed by actions performed in societies which both need and have rules of justice, and those possessed by other instances of similar actions performed in societies which do not need and so do not have rules of justice, should be the same, when there are such enormous differences between the two. For one would have thought that satisfying a human need, arousing sentiments of approval, and being enjoined by human conventions did constitute considerable differences in the relations possessed by the two actions. Part of the trouble, I think, is that Hume, in giving his original classification of the several different kinds of philosophical relations (13-15), has simply omitted any 'moral' relations from his list. (Hume uses the expression 'moral relations' when he says, quite properly, that property is a moral relation, and not a natural one (491). 'Moral' in this sense is used in opposition to 'physical' and is the sense in which Hume described the *Treatise* as 'an attempt to introduce the experimental method of reasoning into moral subjects' (title page).) In these senses, being one's son is a species of natural relation (falling under the genus 'relation of cause and effect'), but being one's heir is a moral relation, and one which would not exist were it not for human convention. Since Hume has not included any moral relations in his original list of relations, it is not surprising that he should think that an action performed in a society which has no rules of justice should not possess any relations different from an action performed in a society which does.

Even if Hume was right in thinking that all the natural relations between the two actions are the same—and it is not obvious that he was —it is evident that their moral relations must be very different. Hume has produced no proof whatsoever that moral relations cannot give rise to demonstration. Since he has omitted them from his original list, he has not even considered the possibility of whether they give rise to demonstration or not. And there is no particular reason why moral relations should not give rise to demonstration, for that if James is Henry's father's brother, James is Henry's uncle, is just as good a demonstrative argument (based upon moral relations) as that if x is the square of the square of y, y is the cube root of x (based upon quantity or number).

However, if Hume is right in thinking that justice is an artificial virtue, in the sense that justice is a matter of observing certain man-made conventions, it will certainly follow that discovering what actions are just will be a matter for inductive reasoning, and that if this is what Hume means when he says that 'the sense of justice is founded not on our ideas but on our impressions', he was certainly right. He may not mean this, however. He may mean that the appeal that justice has for us is a matter of impressions rather than ideas, i.e. that justice's appealing to us consists in our having an impression, which *is* this appeal. Even if he is right about this, however—and one would have thought that to analyse such things in terms of our having indefinable impressions was an over-simplification—I do not see how it would *follow* from the fact that justice's appeal to us is a question of our having a certain kind of impression, that what acts are just is not something which can be demonstrated, even though I agree that what actions are just is *not* something that can be demonstrated. (The fact that our wanting to get the right answer to our question was a matter of our having an impression would not show that it was not reason which enabled us to arrive at the right answer.) Nor would the fact that we established justice from a concern for the public interest show that what actions were just could not be demonstrated.[6] Hume, of course, may be forgetting at this point that he has defined a just action as one that is demanded by a convention, and harking back to his remarks in Book III Part I of the *Treatise*, where he (sometimes) regards a virtuous action as one that appeals to our moral sense. If so, then which actions are virtuous might not have to be discovered by any process of reasoning, whether deductive or inductive. But whether this is so or not, reasoning—i.e. inductive reasoning—is certainly necessary in order to establish what conventions human societies have, and so, if justice is a matter of observing human conventions, necessary in order to determine what actions are just.

Hume seems also to have supposed in this paragraph that justice cannot consist in any relations, and so cannot be a fit subject for demonstrative argument, because it has to be *invented* to satisfy a human need. This argument, too, is not cogent. The most that follows from the fact that justice has been invented is that it consists in moral relations, which, on Hume's view, it does. But many invented things are physical objects and these do possess relations which objects which are not invented possess. Hume presumably thought that it could not be demonstrated what actions were just if justice was a matter of observing invented human conventions because these could be changed by human decision when human needs demanded it. Hence justice could not be eternal and immutable and so could not be demonstrated. (Pythagoras' theorem is both an eternal and immutable truth, and a truth which can be demonstrated.) Here Hume was guilty of a very natural logical error. That an action is contrary to a rule is not something that can be demonstrated *a priori*, because the rules can be changed, and so it is a matter for empirical investigation what the rules are. But this does not in the least show that the hypothetical proposition, that if an action is contrary to a human convention it ought not to be performed, is not an eternal and immutable truth. Similarly, Hume seems to have confused maintaining that, since whether justice is useful or not depends upon certain contingent facts, which may vary from one society to another, it cannot be an eternal *a priori* truth that justice ought to be done (which is true), with the contention that the hypothetical statement,

---

[6] An account of Hume's views about demonstration will be found in my *Hume's Moral Epistemology*, pp. 34–40 and pp. 48–59.

that if justice is useful it ought to be done, cannot be an eternal *a priori* truth (which is false). One might as well argue (as Kant did) that because one cannot know *a priori* what actions have good consequences, one cannot know *a priori* that actions which do have good consequences ought to be performed.[7] Kant comes (wrongly) to the conclusion that the truth of utilitarianism could be only an empirical matter.

(10) In the paragraph we have just been considering, Hume has been concerned with the part played by impressions in our knowledge of justice. In the following paragraph (496–7), he is concerned with the part played by impressions in giving us a concept of justice. What he attempts to prove is *'that those impressions, which give rise to this sense of justice, are not natural to the mind of man, but arise from artifice and human conventions'* (496). And he thinks that this proposition, too, is given additional force by the fact that justice derives its origin from man's competing, from selfishness and 'confined generosity', for a limited quantity of goods.

Unfortunately, it is not clear exactly what Hume is trying to prove, nor why he thinks he has proved it. What he *says* he is trying to prove is that the impressions, which give rise to the sense of justice, are not 'natural', but arise 'from artifice and human conventions' (496). But from the fact that justice is artificial, it does not at all follow that our impressions of justice are artificial. I do not even know what an artificial impression, as opposed to an impression of an artificial thing, would be, so I will assume that what Hume means is that our impressions of justice are impressions of something artificial. Hume thinks that the fact that justice is artificial follows from the fact that it is necessary because men are selfish, or capable only of confined generosity; but Hume specifies more particularly in this paragraph (496–7) how justice so arises. Justice arises, and is artificial, because (a) it would have been unnecessary if man had been born sufficiently benevolent to pursue the public interest 'with a hearty affection', and (b) if he pursued his own interest 'without any precaution'—Hume means 'without troubling to invent rules of justice to restrain it'—he would have run headlong into every kind of injustice and violence. From this it follows not only that rules of justice are artificial, but that they promote men's interest, in the first instance, by restraining it. And he adds that the good that justice was invented to secure could not have been secured by the natural passions of man. (By this he must mean that this end could not have been achieved by these passions in their present strength, for he has said himself that it could have been achieved,

[7] H. J. Paton, *The Moral Law*, Hutchinson, 1948, pp. 92–4.

without any need for man to have invented rules of justice, if a man's benevolence had been stronger than it in fact is.)

The reason why I find this argument so difficult is that Hume clearly intends it to add strength to something he has already said—that justice was invented to prevent strife caused by selfish and avaricious men competing for goods which are limited in supply—but it is difficult to see precisely what this argument adds to what has gone before. The emphasis, perhaps, is on the fact that rules of justice could not have arisen from desire for the public interest—for such a desire would have made them unnecessary—or from self-interest—for this produces injustice, not justice. They are therefore not the natural products of either desire for the public interest, or self-interest, but are an artificial invention, which promotes the self-interest of man in an oblique manner, i.e. by compelling men to perform actions which are not immediately in their interest. But I must confess that I do not think I fully understand Hume's argument.

(11) I said in the preceding section that I did not know what an artificial sentiment would be. It could, however, (I suppose) be a sentiment produced artificially by education and the artifices of politicians. It is not, however, consistently Hume's view that sentiments of approbation, even those directed to rules of justice, are produced artificially in this way. Normally they are supposed to spring up by themselves, by our reflecting on the pleasure that the things we approve of produce.

It is inconsistent both to maintain that sentiments of approbation spring up of themselves to actions we believe to be useful or agreeable, and also to maintain that they are produced artificially by indoctrination. It must not be forgotten, however, that Hume thought that we could approve of what is not useful or not agreeable, if our sentiment was biased in a number of ways which he mentions in Part III of Book III of the *Treatise*, or is based upon false belief. Education and the artifice of politicians may then be held to be two of a number of factors which bias our sentiments; they may, indeed, be the sole reason for our approving of some things, like certain rules of justice.

Hume could then go on to hold that education acts in two ways, either by making us approve of what is not useful and agreeable (in which case our actual sentiments are biased, and for this reason what we approve of is not a virtue), or by making us approve irrationally (though Hume would not have liked the word) of what in fact is a virtue, although we do not in fact approve of it *because* it is useful and agreeable. There is nothing extraordinary about this. A woman may have an irrational belief that her son will do well in his examinations, and his teacher a rational belief to the same effect. Similarly, education might produce artificially a sentiment of approbation which is just that sentiment which would be produced by an unbiased reflection on the utility of something. It must not be forgotten that it is Hume's view that education can only operate by modifying an already-existing tendency to approve of things spontaneously.

(12) Hume has argued that public benevolence cannot be the motive which leads us to obey rules of justice (and that motive, normally present in men, which an act of injustice signifies the lack of) on the grounds that if public benevolence were strong enough to impel men to perform just acts, it would be strong enough to make justice unnecessary (495-6). (It would make justice unnecessary for the same reason that ample affection between married people makes it unnecessary, Hume thinks, for them to have separate property.) I suspect that this remark of Hume's is very largely true, but it is not quite true. There are quite a number of rules that my wife and I need, for example, rules about when to use the bathroom; and the fact that each of us observes the rules out of consideration for the other does not mean that they are unnecessary. Similarly, however much men love one another, rules will be necessary to determine who cultivates which bits of land, or which tasks in a co-operative enterprise are performed by which people. The fact that there will be no need to enforce these rules, if men love one another enough, does not mean that there is no need to have them. However much affection the players in a football team have for one another, rules will still be needed to allocate them different functions, to decide, for example, which of them is to play in goal. Similarly, rules will be necessary to decide who is to farm, who is to make wheels, and who is to be a blacksmith. It could be argued that rules which do not need to be enforced are rules of a degenerate kind, but this may be because rules which do not need sanctions would be useless as human beings are at present constituted. In a society where there was an abundance of affection such rules would be useful, and perform the same functions which enforced rules perform in a society such as ours.

(13) When talking about the natural virtues Hume says that if any man finds himself deficient in a motive normally possessed by other people, he 'may hate himself upon that account, and may perform the action without the motive, from a certain sense of duty, in order to acquire by practice, that virtuous principle, or at least, to disguise to himself, as much as possible, his want of it' (479). Where the artificial virtues are concerned a different account of duty will be necessary. For, in talking about the artificial virtues, he has defined 'duty' as being enjoined by a rule or convention. Given this account of duty, what

account ought Hume to give of the sense of duty? Perhaps he ought to say that, among men's motives, there is a certain irreducible desire to obey rules as such, and that this desire is what the sense of duty consists in. But, whether or not he ought to say this, he certainly does not say it. He does not say it because he thinks that the function of rules or conventions, in terms of which 'duty' is defined, is to redirect motives like self-interest and avarice into channels which, unlike the directions they would naturally take, are not socially harmful. Hence creating new conventions does not involve creating a new motive to obey these conventions. This suggests that the motives to do our duty are self-interest and avarice, and either that there is no such thing as a sense of duty as such, or that the sense of duty is simply avarice and self-interest in so far as these prompt their possessors to obey socially accepted, man-made rules.

If this is what Hume thought—and it seems to me to be unlikely—it would not be a very plausible account of the sense of duty. Self-interest can impel men to do what is enjoined by a social rule only so long as they think their transgression will not pass undetected. Men sometimes do their duty, however, even when doing so is not in their interest. And when they fail to do their duty, because it is not in their interest to do it, they often feel guilt, though guilt is not produced simply by not doing what is to one's advantage. It is, indeed, biologically advantageous to man as a species that individual men should have a tendency to obey social rules when it is not to their advantage to do so, for this fact sometimes makes them perform useful actions, demanded by social rules, even when they can disobey them without being detected. This tendency may, indeed, often be a more effective motive than self-interest, even when it and self-interest do not conflict, for the adverse consequences to ourselves from breaking a social rule may, as Hume himself points out, be too remote to influence our actions.

I shall argue later that, as is really fairly obvious, Hume has yet another account of duty, which is that an action is a duty, not if it is demanded by a rule, and not if not to perform it would be a sign of the lack of motive that men usually have, but if its omission would arouse sentiments of disapproval. Though it is obvious that this is Hume's account of duty, it is not so obvious that it is not Hume's only account of duty.

(14) Hume says, *'Thus self-interest is the original motive to the* establishment *of justice: but a* sympathy *with public interest is the source of the* moral approbation, *which attends that virtue'* (499–500). What Hume is saying here is that self-interest is the motive which prompts men to have rules of justice. This is quite different from saying

that self-interest is the motive which prompts men to obey rules of justice once they have been set up. Self-interest prompts men to *have* rules, although, before the rules have been made, the rules cannot be imposed upon men. Having rules is naturally in men's interest, because there (logically) can be no rules to make people obey rules. But it is not naturally in men's interest to obey the rules, so it must be made artificially in their interest to obey them by their being enforced. Naturally it is in the interest of each man to have rules that other men obey, but not to obey them himself. The result, of course, of each man's following his natural interest would be that the rules never would be obeyed. If, *per impossibile*, everyone but me did obey the rules, I would be unjustly profiting from a practice from which I could benefit only if everybody save me paid his due in the form of those necessary sacrifices that obedience demands. It may be, therefore, that I can, as Kant suggests, decide to disobey the rules myself, but be unable to try to persuade other people to do what I do. For if everybody were to do what I do, the aim I have in disobeying the rules would be defeated.

There is a sense in which there is no inconsistency in this (though Kant thought there was). The consistent policy for an egoistical hedonist is to practice egoistical hedonism himself, but to persuade all other people to be altruists. It is true that if I think it is *right* for me to disobey the rules while others obey them, I ought, since I must think that what is right for me is right for all similar people in similar circumstances, also to think that it would be right for other people to do the same. But this logical demand means only that I must, if I am consistent, *think* that other people would be acting rightly if they were to do what they do. Saying to them out loud that it would be right for them to break the rules is not inconsistent; indeed, it would be inconsistent for an egoistical hedonist to do anything else, for it is in his interests both to disobey the rules himself and to *tell* other people that they would be acting wrongly if they were to disobey them also. Telling someone that it is wrong to disobey the rules is a different action from the action of disobeying the rules, so there is no reason why it should not be right to disobey the rules, and right to tell others that they ought to be obeyed. The consistent egoistical hedonist, however, would be obliged to think that others who also disobeyed the rules while persuading others to obey them were acting rightly; but he would not be obliged to say so.

(15) It has not always been noticed by commentators on Hume that *private benevolence* is not the same thing as *confined generosity*. Confined generosity is concern for the welfare of those to whom we are specially related, and Hume quite rightly points out (487) that it is as much contrary to justice as is self-interest, for the interests of my

family and friends are as likely to conflict with the interests of other people's families and friends as my interests are to conflict with theirs. Private benevolence, however, is a desire for the welfare of the party who benefits from an act of justice, and Hume says that this motive cannot be the one the possession of which the performance of a just act is a sign, because the person who so benefits may be my enemy, or a scoundrel, or a miser, in which case I cannot be supposed to have any such motive (482). There is no reason, of course, why I should be related in any way to the person who benefits from an act of justice, and so no reason why the fact that he benefits should be of any concern to confined generosity.

(16) When Hume talks about our 'uncultivated ideas' of virtue and vice, it might seem as if he means those ideas of virtue and vice which are natural to us, as opposed to those ideas of virtue and vice which are the products of education. This, however, is not so, or, at any rate, if Hume sometimes speaks as if it were so, he is being inconsistent. For he holds that there is a natural tendency in man, which tendency is not the result of human artifice, to approve of what is useful and agreeable. This tendency can be strengthened by education and the artifice of politicians, and to some extent modified by them, but it cannot be entirely produced by such artifices. Even our approbation of the artificial virtues arises from an appreciation of their necessity, not from indoctrination. Though what we feel approval of is artificial—at least, the rules are artificial, even if our disposition to obey them is not—the fact that we do approve of them is a natural fact, which is not brought about by the decisions and choices of human beings, though to a small extent it may be modified by such choices.

Hume, therefore, holds that education and the artifice of politicians cannot be the sole causes of the distinction between virtue and vice. If there were not a natural tendency in man to approve of some actions and disapprove of others in the first place, the words 'honourable' or 'dishonourable', 'praiseworthy' and 'blameworthy' would be without meaning. Education and artifice, however, may assist nature (I think Hume must mean 'intensify the feelings which we would have had anyway') and may sometimes even produce a sentiment of disapprobation for actions which nature herself has not caused us to feel disapproval of. When this happens, the question arises—though Hume himself does not discuss it—whether the sentiment of disapprobation so produced is any less authoritative than the sentiments by nature implanted in us.

It is Hume's view that a sentiment of disapprobation implanted in us by nature must be discounted if it is 'biased', i.e. if it is not the sentiment we would feel were we not affected by such things as self-interest, or by the fact that we are related to the person suffering from the action we disapprove of, or by propinquity in space or time. If a sentiment is produced in us by education or artifice, then presumably it will not have to be so discounted if it is the same as the *unbiased* sentiment which would have been produced in us by nature. If it is not such a sentiment, then it would have to be discounted. It would follow, of course, that nature cannot always be relied upon to produce unbiased sentiments, for if it could, there would be no need of artifice to produce such a sentiment. Again, we might say that a sentiment produced in us by education and artifice is 'sound' if it is a sentiment of disapproval towards a characteristic of men which is harmful or disagreeable, or one of approval towards a characteristic which is useful or agreeable. This, again, implies that we do not always approve of what is useful or agreeable naturally. If we regard Hume as thinking, as sometimes he does think, that an action is right if it in fact arouses a sentiment of approbation (or does not arouse a sentiment of disapprobation) in the majority of men, then it would be difficult for him not to allow that an action was wrong, so long as men in fact disapproved of it, even though their disapproval was produced by education and artifice. He could maintain that an action was not wrong, although generally disapproved of, if the disapproval was biased in one of the ways just mentioned, or based upon mistakes about matters of fact. Otherwise, so long as this sentiment of disapprobation was commonly felt, he would have to accept it as just as good a sentiment for determining what was right or wrong as any sentiment which was produced naturally.

There is in this paragraph an implicit refutation of a certain kind of moral scepticism, viz. the sceptical view that nothing is right or wrong, but that politicians produce in those they govern the delusion that there is, because this makes them easier to rule over. Some such view was held by ancient Greek sophists, and by Bernard Mandeville, writing shortly before Hume.

Hume's reply to this form of scepticism is that, in order for governors to be able to produce, in those over whom they rule, sentiments antagonistic to actions that the rulers do not wish them to perform, words like 'honourable' and 'dishonourable' must already have a meaning, and they would not have a meaning unless nature, as opposed to politicians, had endowed men with a disposition to feel the appropriate sentiments. I think it is also Hume's view that, if politicians tried to alter men's natural sentiments to any considerable extent, nature would be too much for them, and they would not be able to do it.

Is this an adequate refutation of this kind of moral scepticism? I believe he is quite right in thinking that politicians could not give the words 'praiseworthy' and 'blameworthy' a meaning if they did not have one already, and that if they did not have one already, politicians could not use them to produce disapprobation of actions that they wanted people over whom they ruled not to perform. He may well, however, have underestimated, given the resources of modern propaganda, which he could not have known about, the extent to which words like 'praiseworthy' and 'blameworthy' can be used by politicians to mould men's sentiments in the ways these politicians wish. The rulers in Nazi Germany, for example, appear to have been able to persuade some people that it was honourable to inform on their own parents, if their parents were anti-Nazis, and some people have been able to persuade other people that it is wrong to eat meat on Fridays or to eat pork or beans. Hence it is clear that very eccentric or harmful sets of moral codes could become generally accepted, and that, even if the tendency to approve of some things and disapprove of others is an innate one, it could be moulded by education and artifice into forms very different from those it would have without them. The welfare of the people who have these moral codes cannot be ignored beyond a certain point, however, for the fact that these people must be able to survive in competition with other men and other animals imposes a limit upon the forms that moral codes take, just as the same fact imposes a limit on the extent to which convention may cause people to deform their limbs.

This refutation of moral scepticism is, of course, based on the assumption that words like 'right' and 'wrong', 'praiseworthy' and 'blameworthy' would not have a meaning if men did not have the appropriate sentiments. This assumption is discussed in my *Hume's Moral Epistemology* (especially pp. 92 f.), and so I will say no more about it here. It is perhaps worth mentioning, however, that on the view of the meanings of 'obligation' and 'duty' put forward by Hume in *this* section, we could perfectly well know what these words mean without having any sentiments, since they are defined in terms of rules, not of sentiments.

(17) In his final paragraph, Hume makes it clear that it is not his view that in a state of nature it is allowable to take the property of others. His view is, he says, that in such a state there could be no such thing as property; and *consequently* (my italics) there could be no such thing as justice or injustice (501). If Hume is right in thinking that a man's property are those goods that he is (to use a phrase of John Stuart Mill's)[8] 'defended in the possession of' by a human convention,

---

[8] *Utilitarianism*, Everyman edition, p. 50.

then he is certainly right in thinking that there can be no such thing as property in a state of nature, which is by definition that state of society in which there are no conventions. He is wrong, however, in thinking that it follows from the fact that there can be no such thing as property in a state of nature that there can be no such thing as justice in such a state, because, even on his own view, there are rules of justice which have to do with things other than property, for example, rules which regulate the relations between the sexes.

It is, therefore, not the case that it could be allowable, in a state of nature, to violate the property of others. In such a state, there can be no such thing as property. The interesting question still arises, however, whether in such a state it is allowable to take the *possessions* of others. Men can still have possessions in a state of nature, even if they cannot have property. I should make it clear that I am not interested in the material question whether it is in fact allowable, in such a state, to take the possessions of others, but whether, in such a state, it would make sense for men to say that taking the possessions of others was allowable or not allowable. If the word 'allowable' is defined by rules, just as the word 'property', according to Hume, is defined by rules, then it will not only not be allowable to take the property of others in a state of nature, because in such a state there would be no such thing as *property*, but also because in such a state nothing would be allowable or not allowable. (This would be possible, of course, only on the assumption that 'not allowable' was not the contradictory of 'allowable'. If 'allowable' meant 'allowed by a rule' and 'not allowable' meant 'not allowed by a rule',[9] then, in a state where there were no rules, taking the possessions of others would neither be allowable nor not allowable. If, on the other hand, to say something is allowable is to say that it is not the case that there is a rule or convention prohibiting it, then 'not allowable' *is* the contradictory of 'allowable', but it follows from this that in a state of nature everything is allowable, for it can never be the case, in a society which has no rules, that anything is prohibited by a rule.)

Is it then Hume's view that, in a state of nature, nothing is either allowable or not allowable because the word 'allowable', like the words 'property' and 'just', is defined in terms of man-made rules or conventions? Of course, it is clear that it is Hume's view that taking the possessions of others in a state of nature is not a sign of having a vicious disposition, for in such a state there would be no motive impelling men not to take the possessions of others, but this is a view about what is

[9] i.e. it is not the case that there is a rule expressly allowing this.

virtuous or vicious, not a view about what is allowable or not allowable. But if it is neither allowable nor not allowable, in a state of nature, to take the possessions of others, but it is vicious to take the possessions of others, we do get the possibly odd conclusion that, in a state of nature, many things are vicious which are not not allowable. There would, in a state of nature, be virtues and vices, though nothing would be allowable or not allowable. If this view seems a little peculiar it should be remembered that it is perfectly permissible to talk of strength being one of the virtues of the lion (because lions are usually strong) without thereby committing oneself to the view that there are some things that lions are allowed or not allowed to do.

If Hume is suggesting that the word 'allowable' must be defined in terms of man-made conventions, and if he knew what he was doing when he suggested that words like 'duty' and 'obligation' must also be defined in terms of man-made conventions, this is a view that is of great importance. Moral epithets may be divided into two kinds. On the one hand, there are words like 'good' and 'bad', 'virtuous' and 'vicious', which one might describe as value words. On the other hand, there are words like 'right' and 'wrong', 'permissible' and 'impermissible', 'duty', 'ought', and 'obligation'. Such words do not assert anything to be valuable or the reverse, but roughly say that certain actions may be done, must be done, or must be omitted. It could be Hume's view that, though words belonging to the former class have application whether there are man-made conventions or not, words belonging to the latter class have application only when there are man-made conventions.

Hume would be right for the most part about words belonging to the first class. Kindness and industry could perfectly well be virtues, even in a state in which there were no conventions. (They would, in such a state, be qualities useful or agreeable to ourselves or others.) There must, however, be one notable exception. Moral goodness, if Hume is right, could not be a virtue in a state without conventions, because moral goodness is a disposition to do one's duty or to behave rightly, and, if my suggestion about Hume's view is correct, in a state without conventions there would be no duties, and nothing would be right. I see no reason, however, why, as philosophers who follow Kant sometimes suppose, all the virtues and vices should be reduced to moral goodness or the lack of it. Courage, for example, is sometimes considered simply one manifestation of moral goodness, i.e. a disposition to do one's duty even when doing one's duty is frightening. Quite apart from the fact that men can quite easily show courage when they are not doing what they think is their duty, other virtues, such as wisdom, cannot with any show of plausibility be reduced to a disposition to do one's duty.

It is much less likely that Hume is right about words belonging to the second class. Whether all moral words belonging to this class must be defined in terms of human rules or conventions is something that I will discuss later. At the moment I shall content myself with pointing out that, if it is true, it is a truth of very great importance. If Hume held it, then his view is much more daring and far-reaching than it would otherwise be. It ceases to be simply the view that there are certain conventions, necessary to society, which define and regulate property and, as he maintains later in the *Treatise*, government and the relations between the sexes. It becomes the view that all moral rules are a special sort of human convention, and that, in a society which has no conventions—if such a group of men could properly be called a society at all—either nothing would be allowable or not allowable, or, alternatively, everything is allowable. Hume's view would then be widened to such an extent that it becomes not simply the view that rules about justice are artificial, in the sense of being man-made conventions. It becomes the view that morality as a whole, to the extent that it consists of rules enjoining or prohibiting (and permitting, if 'permitted' does not simply mean 'not prohibited') certain acts, as opposed to valuing them, is a human invention.[10] If this is Hume's view, the scope of justice, the only virtue according to him which could not be manifested in a state where there were no conventions, would be widened to include not merely respecting the property of others, but the whole of 'moral goodness', in the sense in which moral goodness consists in a disposition to regulate one's behaviour by the moral rules which enjoin or prohibit certain actions. It would follow that, in talking about justice, he was talking about moral goodness, not merely about rules about property, government, sex, and polite society. Interpreted in this way Hume has a much more important and interesting theory than the one usually attributed to him, though the one usually attributed to him is important and interesting enough. Whether it is right, and whether it is compatible with other things about morality which Hume also says, is another matter.

(18) Hume thinks that men, when they become sensible of the disadvantages resulting from the fact that possessions are transferable, enter into a convention to leave one another in possession of these goods. He says that such a convention is not a promise. (He later (490)

---

[10] A similar view has recently been put forward by J. L. Mackie in *Ethics, Inventing Right and Wrong*, Penguin Books, 1977.

explains that it cannot be a promise because that promises must be kept is itself a convention; hence to derive any obligation we have to abstain from taking the possessions of others from an obligation to keep our promises would be simply to derive one convention from another equally in need of justification.) He likens the conventions by which men abstain from taking one another's possessions to two men rowing a boat, who 'do it by an agreement or convention, tho' they have never given promises to each other' (490). 'I observe, that it will be for my interest to leave another in the possession of his goods, *provided* he will act in the same manner with regard to me. He is sensible of a like interest in the regulation of his conduct. When this common sense of interest is mutually express'd, and is known to both, it produces a suitable resolution and behaviour. And this may properly enough be call'd a convention or agreement betwixt us, tho' without the interposition of a promise; since the actions of each of us have a reference to those of the other, and are perform'd upon the supposition, that something is to be perform'd on the other part' (490).

The analogy between the convention which makes possessions stable and two men rowing a boat is not altogether apt, and, to the extent that it is apt, not altogether in Hume's favour. Though two people may row a boat, or co-operate in performing any fairly simple task, without exchanging any words about it, they may exchange such words. And though they may not then exactly have promised each to perform his share in a common enterprise, certainly one will complain of being let down by the other if either fails to play his part through his own fault. And, if men do discuss out loud how a common problem, which can be solved only by a co-operative effort, is to be dealt with, it is not as obvious as Hume thought, that these men have not made something like a promise. One man, let us suppose, says to another, 'I won't take your goods, if you won't take mine,' and the other replies, 'I agree.' It is difficult to see what they are doing if they are not exchanging promises, or entering into an agreement, even though they do not use (and *ex hypothesi* do not have) the words 'I promise'. Each will treat the other as having been guilty of bad faith if, after having said the words just reported, either of them seizes goods belonging to the other. Hume was reluctant to admit that these men had made a promise because he is later going to attack the social contract theory, which derives our allegiance to a government from the fact that we have promised to obey it. Hume thinks that since our obligation to keep promises is itself a matter of adhering to human conventions, there can be no such thing as an obligation to keep promises in a society which has not yet got any conventions, which he supposes the society he is talking about to be.

He is quite right, of course, in thinking that there can be no such thing as promising in a society which has no conventions. What he does not realize is that the conventions about promising have to grow up somehow, and that, in a society which has neither a convention about property nor a convention about promising, these two conventions could grow up simultaneously. After the dialogue just mentioned, it may be that either of the participants will disapprove of the other for taking the other's goods, and what each will be disapproving of the other for will be taking the goods of the other after this dialogue has been exchanged. In fact, the convention about promising and conventions about other things are likely to grow up together. It is not that first there is a convention about promising, and then a convention about property. There comes to be a convention about promising *and* property, or promising and something else, as a result of one and the same set of actions. And, after all, it is not very likely that a group of men would come together and agree to keep their agreements, and to deliberate about what should constitute an agreement. There came to be such things as agreements when it was appreciated that it was in the public interest that certain things be done, and people said some such thing as, 'Then let's do it.' After this time omitting these things came to be disapproved of partly because it was contrary to private and public interest, and partly because it was seen that collective expressions of intention to do things agreed to be in the public interest would be valueless if, these intentions having been expressed, the things intended were left undone.

Hence Hume was right in thinking that it is not the case that there was first of all the institution of promising, and then subsequently the institution of property, which came into being through people having promised to abstain from taking each other's goods. He is wrong, however, in thinking that our duty to abstain from taking the goods of others is thereby not in any way derived from a promise. Conventions about property and about promising could, and probably did, grow up hand in hand. He is quite right, however, in thinking that our duty to abstain from taking others' goods cannot be derived from our duty to keep our promises. Both are useful institutions, and either obligation can be derived directly from its utility, without reference to the other. The same remarks apply to the institution of government.

(19) It is perhaps surprising that Hume devotes so much space to discussing rules concerning the distribution and transference of property, and hardly mentions the need for laws prohibiting offences against the person. The reason for this may be that he thinks that a man's possessions are the only things of his which can be taken from him and still

be useful to the man who seizes them. Another man's watch may be as useful to me as it is to him, but his leg, though useful to him is totally without value to anyone else. (Kidneys and other organs are perhaps an exception, thought Hume could not have been expected to foresee this.) Hume, however, may be overlooking two points. First, though my enemy's leg is unlikely to be of any use to me, it may be greatly to my advantage that my enemy does not have a leg. Secondly, there are in man violent impulses which may impel him to cut off his enemy's leg, without even reflecting on the fact that it is of no use to him. These impulses may be so strong, indeed, that they are yielded to even when they do the man who acts upon them as much harm as the man who suffers from them.

But I suspect that the main reason why Hume does not discuss violence is that he does not think that here is the proper place to discuss it. I think he thought that abstention from violence was a natural, rather than an artificial, virtue, and perhaps thought that it was one aspect of the natural virtue of humanity.

Up to a point he is right about this. If we accept Hume's theory that moral judgements assert the existence of feelings of approval and disapproval, which are generated by sympathy with the pleasure or pain of those who benefit or are harmed by the action approved of or disapproved of, abstention from violence is a natural virtue. It does harm to the person who is the object of violence, whether artificial rules prohibiting violence exist or not. And violence, unlike theft, can be defined without reference to man-made rules. Theft is taking what a man-made rule allocates to someone else, and so could not occur without such rules. Violence involves harming another person, and people can be harmed whether man-made rules prohibiting harm exist or not. But then, though theft is impossible, without rules allocating possessions, and so determining property, taking the *possessions* of others is possible, whether there are man-made rules or not, and taking a man's possessions does him harm, whether or not these possessions are his property. Again, though my abstaining from taking the possessions of others will not help build a stable society, unless everybody else co-operates with me in likewise abstaining from taking the possessions of others, my abstaining from acts of violence will also not prevent the disruption of society unless other people besides myself abstain from violence. The difference between the two is that, after rules regulating property have been set up, every individual act of violence will do harm, but one act of departing from one of the rules of justice will, all by itself, often do no harm at all. But this, of course, is no reason for not having laws proscribing violence, so violence is something that is both disapproved of because of the harm it does to the man who suffers from it, and further disapproved of because violence is a breach of an artificial rule. This seems to me to show that Hume's distinction between the natural and artificial virtues is to some extent misconceived. For violence is wrong both because it does harm, in almost every case, and because, unlike abstaining from taking the *property* of others, it is both possible and harmful in the absence of any rules at all. However, there is this resemblance between violence and, say, theft. Even cases of beneficial violence, Hume might argue, rare though they are, would have to be punished, even though punishing did no good and no harm. The good of having a rule of justice cannot be secured unless it is applied rigorously even to the cases where applying it, considered apart from the utility of the legal scheme of things of which it is a part, does more harm than good.

(20) Hume thinks that one difference between an act of justice and an act which is a manifestation of a natural virtue is that the good consequences of the latter, unlike those of the former, come about whether or not other people, or myself on other occasions, perform similar acts (579). Is he right about this?

He is right in thinking that there is a distinction between actions which have good consequences, even when other people do not perform similar acts, and actions which have good consequences only when others do the same. If I refrain from walking on the grass, for example, no good will be done unless others also refrain, but if I help a distressed person, some good will be done whether others help him or not. However, Hume is wrong if he thinks that the distinction between acts which do good all by themselves and acts which do good only when performed in conjunction with similar acts peformed by others coincides with the distinction between benevolence (which according to Hume is a natural virtue) and justice. For example, there might be a member of a small and impoverished community who was so needy that no individual person could give him enough money to be of appreciable help to him, but if all members of the community helped, his condition might be substantially alleviated. No good would come of one man giving him as much as this man could afford, though much good would come of them all giving him as much as they could afford. Nevertheless, giving him money would still be a manifestation of benevolence, a natural virtue, rather than of justice, an artificial one.

It is, however, in cases where not much good would be done by one or a few individuals doing something without the co-operation of everyone else that rules are especially likely to be necessary. It is for the very reason that not much good will come of something if it is done by only a few people that rules are likely to be established enforcing such action upon everyone. A system of voluntary payment of income tax would obviously be totally useless. Hence rules are very likely to grow up in just those cases when almost everyone must do something if any good is to come of it, and hence, in such cases, there will be justice in Hume's sense of observing rules. It would be a mistake, however, to suppose that rules cover only cases like this. Many actions which are quite properly prohibited by rules do harm all by themselves. For example, killing people does harm whether it is the general rule or not (though, if killing people were not prohibited by rule, the harm prevented by one person alone abstaining from killing people, in the way of giving people security of their lives, would be negligible).

Hence the distinction between actions which are and those which are not prohibited by rule and the distinction between actions the omission of which does good by itself and actions which do good only when others refrain from doing them do not completely coincide. However, the first distinction may apply at two levels. First, even *before* any actions are prohibited by rule, there will be a distinction between actions which do good by themselves and actions which do good only when most people perform them. Secondly, *after* an action is prohibited by rule, the effects of breaking a rule are likely to be cumulative in that one action of breaking a rule may not do much harm, but if everybody were to break the rule, the harm done is likely to be enormous. Hence the harm done by some actions of rule-breaking is likely to be cumulative on two counts. First, the harm done by that kind of action was cumulative anyway, and secondly, once it has been prohibited by rule, the harm done by breaking the rule is likely to be cumulative. Just as some actions which are not prohibited by rule may do cumulative harm, so some actions which do no cumulative harm may be prohibited by rule. It may even do cumulative harm to perform some actions which would do no harm at all, were they not prohibited by rule.

Another point ought also to be emphasized. Hume mostly thinks in terms of the similarity of actions when he is talking of the necessity for justice. He is thinking of the fact that the harm done by, say, a million repetitions of a similar act will do more than a million times the harm done by a single performance (which single performance, all by itself, may do no harm, and may even do good). However, there are cases where cumulative harm is not done by repetitions of similar acts, but by omissions of dissimilar actions which are collectively necessary to the accomplishment of some useful or necessary purpose. For example, in a complex society, the functions which must be performed by different people in order to achieve an end are no more similar than the functions performed by the different parts of a watch; nevertheless, the performance by one man of his task is as necessary to the good of the whole as is the performance of one of a set of actions which are similar. Each person must play his part in a co-operative enterprise, whether his part in this enterprise is similar to that of other people or not. He ought, perhaps, to play his part, even when playing his part alone is not essential, and even if he could do more good by doing something else, because if everybody else similarly rejected his different tasks, the good secured by the enterprise would be lost.

(21) The problem Hume raises, whether or not I ought to conform to the rules when I can do more good by breaking them than by keeping them, and which he answers by saying that I should nevertheless keep them (we have seen, incidentally, that it is not *always* the case that I should do this, whatever Hume may have thought), is also raised by features of social organizations other than their moral codes. A social system may allocate different tasks, carrying with them different duties to different people. For example, fathers may be allocated the duty of caring for their children, judges the duty of deciding when a rule has been broken, policemen the duty of detecting and apprehending offenders, soldiers the duty of protecting their country; miners the duty of digging coal, and so on. Clearly no people are allocated the over-all duty of *producing good consequences*, and if this, *per impossibile*, were the only duty people were allocated, chaos would result. In general, I suppose, the best consequences are produced by men and women simply carrying out their appointed tasks without looking around them to see if they can do more good by departing from them. But let us suppose that someone does decide that he could do more good by not carrying out his appointed task. (Perhaps, for example, he could produce good by neglecting his own children in order to devote himself to the children of the poor.) Ought he, nevertheless, to carry out the task allocated to him, or ought he to neglect it in order to produce that greater good? One is inclined to say that at least very often he ought not to depart from his appointed task in order to bring about the greater good. Perhaps the reason why he ought not is that other people's appointed tasks and his interlock in order to bring about some desirable, or supposedly desirable, end. He can do good by failing to carry out his, only so long as others go on to carry out theirs. If all the others were to behave as he does, the result would be complete disorganization. This, if I am right, will explain why a father ought to carry out his task of caring for his own children, even though he could do more good by caring for other people's children instead, or why a goalkeeper ought to stay in goal, though he might sometimes help his

team more by temporarily taking over the functions of full back, or why a sentry ought to stay at his post, even though he might be able to save the life of a comrade. It does not follow that there are not occasional exceptions, when a man ought to depart from carrying out his allotted task, because the overbalance of good he can produce in this way is very large. For then, even if everybody did this (i.e. left his role when the balance of good to be obtained by bearing it was considerable), only good would result.

(22) Hume thinks that the question whether I ought to be just (or rule-abiding) in a state of nature would not arise, for a state of nature is, by definition, a state in which there *are* no rules. The question, however, whether in such a state we ought to perform certain acts, such as abstaining from taking the *possessions* (as opposed to the property) of others, which acts would infringe the rules if there were any, does arise. It looks as if the rule I have been advocating, that I ought to perform an act if the consequences of its general performance would be good, would enjoin upon men the duty of abstaining from taking the possessions of others, whether there was a rule demanding such behaviour or not. For abstaining from taking the possessions of others would certainly have good consequences, if everyone were to do it, even in a state of nature. My doing this, without the co-operation of others, however, would do no good at all. (My abstaining from taking the possessions of others will not make life any less brutish unless a very substantial number of people do the same. For this reason Hume says that I would not have, in a state of nature, a duty to abstain from taking the possessions of others. And it does seem rather implausible to maintain that I ought not to take the possessions of others in a society, if one could call it that, where no one else similarly abstains, and so my abstaining from taking their possessions does harm to myself and no good to anyone else.)

I suspect, however, that the fact that we ought to perform actions which would have good consequences if everyone were to perform them does *not* enjoin being just in a state of nature. The solution to this problem may be as follows. I have said previously that I ought to perform a certain action, which itself does no good, if good would result if all people *faced with the choice* between doing and not doing this action were to do it. Clearly the word 'everybody' in the statement 'I ought to perform actions which would have good results, if they were performed by *everybody*' needs some interpretation; left as it stands, this formula would seem to imply that I ought not to walk on the grass, because if everybody, whether they lived in Cincinnati or Timbuktu, were to come and walk on this piece of grass, the grass would be irreparably damaged. Clearly this is absurd, and is not what is intended. Adding the words 'faced with the choice' means that I ought not to walk on the grass only if, everybody actually passing and deliberating upon whether to walk on the grass or not were to walk on it, harm would result. The phrase 'actually passing', indeed, may be omitted, for people cannot contemplate walking on the grass if they are not passing it, or, if they can, and are thinking of getting on a bus to walk on it, then their decision is relevant. If I then make a suitable modification to the rule 'I ought to abstain from taking the possessions of others, if everybody's abstaining from taking them would do good', so that it becomes 'I ought to abstain from taking the possessions of others, if, were everybody considering whether to abstain or not were to abstain, good would result', the rule becomes a good deal more plausible than it was without this modification.

This qualification makes it easier to deal with duties in what Hume called a 'state of nature'. For it entails not that I would have a duty to abstain from doing some such thing as taking the possessions of others, simply because the results of everybody's not taking the possessions of others would be good, but that I ought to abstain from taking the possessions of others if good would result if everybody, *faced with the choice* between taking them and not taking them, were in fact not to take them. The advantage of the modification is that inserting it prevents the rule from entailing that I have a duty to perform acts which would be beneficial if generally performed when there is not the remotest possibility of their being generally performed. The same conclusion can be reached by arguing that I do not have a duty to perform actions which are such that good results would be produced by everybody's performing similar actions, if I *know* that no one else will perform similar actions. This is no exception to the principle for which I have been arguing, as the results of everybody's acting on the rule, 'Do not perform an action, for the reason that good results would be produced by everybody's facing the choice performing similar actions, if you *know* that no one else will perform similar actions', will not be harmful.

The first modification—inserting the words 'everybody faced with the choice'—also has the advantage that it explains why most of the situations to which I have to apply the principle, 'One ought to perform an action, if the results of everybody's performing similar actions would be good', are situations where I have to decide between obeying or not obeying a conventional rule. For only where there is such a rule are there likely to be enough people, faced with the choice between performing the action that is enjoined by the rule or not performing it, for good consequences to be brought about if all these people perform it. Again, only in situations where there is a rule demanding the kind of action which is such that good results would be produced if everybody were to do it, am I likely to know that I will not be the only person to perform actions like this. It follows that, before the principle that I should perform an action, if good consequences would result from its general performance, can be applied, a 'critical situation' must have developed, where enough others besides myself are on the verge of performing actions of the kind in question to mean that good consequences will result if all these people do in fact perform it.

We now have a criterion, which Hume himself does not provide, for telling us when to obey Hume's rules of justice and when not to obey them. This criterion is in no way artificial, though the rules to which it applies are artificial, as Hume quite properly maintains. Altering the rules will not in any way alter the criterion which tells you whether to obey the rules or not; nor can this criterion in any way be altered by any act of volition, though the rules to which it applies can be altered by human acts of volition. Whether or not the principle which provides us with this criterion is fully satisfactory as a formulation of the supreme principle of morality is something which cannot be discussed here.

(23) I next want to turn my attention to some questions, already touched upon, which arise from Hume's contention (497) that not every just (or rule-abiding) action is useful, but that, nevertheless, the rules of justice should be adhered to because having rules is so much better than not having rules. He himself is particularly interested in this because, as we have seen, he thinks it is one of a number of considerations which show that justice is not a natural virtue. According to Hume, if the rules of justice, as they sometimes do, award an estate to a wealthy and childless profligate rather than to one who is deserving, poor, and has a large family, no one benefits from the transaction (482). It is not in the interests of the poor man, though it may be his duty nevertheless, to surrender the estate. Nor has this episode any appeal to anyone's private benevolence or limited generosity. And, in this particular instance, even the public do not benefit, so the transaction can have no appeal to public benevolence, even if there were such a motive. (We have seen that Hume thought that there was not.) Hence there is no motive for the performance of such actions, and justice is not a natural virtue.

However, though Hume is mainly interested in the question of finding a motive for justice other than the sense of duty, his examples raise other issues (which, incidentally, have been much discussed in recent years). Hume says that, in cases like the one I have just mentioned, the public interest is not served by the application of a rule of justice to this individual case. Nevertheless, 'Tho' in one instance the public be a sufferer, this momentary ill is amply compensated by the steady prosecution of the rule, and by the peace and order, which it establishes in society' (497). Though the application of the rule does harm, most other times when it is applied it does good, and the good done by applying the rule greatly outweighs the harm.

This raises the following question. Is Hume saying that the short-term harmful consequences produced by applying a rule of justice to this particular case is compensated by the long-term good consequences that result from the rule's being adhered to? Or is he, alternatively, say-ing that though no long-term good consequences follow from applying a rule of justice in this individual case, the rule ought nevertheless to be applied, because the steady prosecution of the rule would be useful, even if this steady prosecution of the rule in all similar cases is not a *consequence* of the rule's being applied in this case.

The difference between the two possibilities is this. If the steady prosecution of the rule is a consequence of the rule's being applied in this case, this means that the rule's being applied in this case will *cause* the rule to be adhered to in other cases; hence the good from the rule's being applied in these other cases can be listed among the good consequences of the rule's being applied in this case. It follows that an act utilitarian, who holds that actions are justified by the consequences that they each individually have, can easily explain why we ought to apply the rule in such cases. On the other hand, if we simply say that the rule should be applied in the difficult case (because good results from the steady prosecution of the rule, although the rule's being applied in this case does not *cause* the rule to be applied in the other cases), then the good consequences which arise from the rule's being applied in these other cases *cannot* be listed among the good con-sequences of the individual application of the rule to this case. It follows that an ordinary act utilitarian can give no account of our duty to apply the rule in hard cases such as these. This leads to the interesting and allegedly extraordinary conclusion that the rule should be applied in *this* case, because good results from applying the rule in *other* cases, even though the rule would be applied in these other cases, and the good from their application still come about, whether the rule were applied in this case or not.

If Hume is attempting to derive our duty to apply the rule in this case from the fact that applying it in this case *causes* the rule to be applied in the other cases, his conclusions are compatible with act utilitarianism. If, on the other hand, Hume is saying that the rule should be applied in this case, because the steady prosecution of the rule has good consequences, even though this steady prosecution of the rule is not a *consequence* of the rule's being applied in this case, his conclusion is not compatible with act utilitarianism. If, as seems plausible, he is deriving our duty to apply the rule in the hard case from the fact that a steady prosecution of the rule in other cases has good consequences, even if these good consequences are not good consequences of the rule's being applied in the hard case, this would suggest that he was some kind of rule utilitarian, even if he did not, and, at the time at which he was writing, perhaps could not, have explicitly formulated this theory, or been precise about the difference between it and act utilitarianism.

It is my personal opinion, that the view which holds that the reason why rules ought to be observed in the cases when observing them does not do any good, is not that the rule's general application *results* from its application in this difficult case, is the more plausible of these two possible views. I also believe that it is more plausible to maintain that this view was Hume's. It is more plausible to maintain that my duty to apply the rule in the difficult case does not derive from the fact that the rule's being applied in other cases are *consequences* of its being applied in this case, because it is really very implausible to maintain that a failure to apply the rule in this one case *will* result in the rule's not being applied in other cases. (This is especially true when the failure to apply the rule is not generally known. Breaking a promise made in secret will have no tendency to cause other people to break their promises, and so since we think that even promises made in secret ought to be kept, there must be at least one failure to apply a rule the immorality of which failure cannot be explained by its having the bad consequence of *causing* others to fail to apply the rule.) And it is more plausible to maintain that this view is Hume's, for otherwise it would be difficult to explain the emphasis he repeatedly puts on the fact that public benevolence is not a motive for being just in those difficult cases we are considering. If applying the rule of justice in a difficult case were to cause the rule to be applied in other cases, public benevolence—if there were such a thing—*would* be a motive to being just in the difficult cases. Furthermore, it is Hume's view that even a promise which has been made in secret ought to be kept (480-1). Breaking a promise made in secret can set no bad example, nor can it tend to undermine the general confidence that promises will almost always be kept. Hence breaking of the rule (of justice) that promises be kept will not in this case cause this rule not to be applied in other cases, and so will not destroy the utility of having the rule.

I cannot over-emphasize, however, how extraordinary the view I have attributed to Hume is. According to it, I ought to obey a rule of justice (even though my obeying it does no good, and even though it does positive harm) on the ground that it is a good thing that we have the rule, even though it is still a good thing that we have the rule, whether I obey it or not. Since it looks as if having the rule can be a good thing only if some acts of obeying it have good consequences, even if mine does not, it seems to follow that I ought to obey a rule of justice because other people's obeying it has good consequences, and that I ought to do this even if my obeying it has no tendency to make them obey it likewise.

The situation may, indeed, be even more extraordinary than this. It could be that it is useful to have a rule, even though *every* individual act of obeying it does more harm than good. It might, for example, be that *everybody* who stole could and would do more good with the money he stole than the person from whom he stole it, and, in spite of this, it could still be the case both that we ought not to steal, and that the rule prohibiting stealing was a good and useful rule to have.

The reason for this is as follows. The situation we are envisaging is one in which everybody who obeys the rule could do more good by breaking it, *so long as others do not do likewise.* If everybody who could do more good by breaking the rule than by keeping it were to break it, the result would be disastrous, and civilized society would dissolve.

To take a homely analogy, a factory might employ one hundred hands, though only ninety-five were necessary to maintain its full output. In such a case, it is obvious that every individual factory hand could do more good by staying at home to cook for his or her children than by going to work; the output of the factory would be unaffected. But if all—or even, perhaps, more than five—of the hands who could do more good by staying at home than by going to work were to stay at home, the output of the factory would cease altogether.

It is fairly obvious that the situation is the same with rules of justice. It is essential, for example, that if promising is to be a useful institution, people must have confidence that promises will be kept. Otherwise, as Hume points out (520-1), no one would help me gather my harvest today in return for a promise to help him with his harvest tomorrow, and we should *both* lose our crops. The breaking of any one promise, or even a few promises, however, will do nothing to undermine this confidence that promises will be kept. But if all the promises which, if broken severally, do nothing to undermine this confidence, are broken collectively, then people's confidence in promise-keeping will be totally undermined. It is simply the case that a number of repetitions of an act which does no harm and which even does some good, may collectively prove calamitous. More generally, the good or harm done by a number of acts performed together is not necessarily equal to the sum of the good or harm each of them does when performed in isolation.

Hume, in *An Enquiry Concerning the Principles of Morals*, likens justice to a vault, 'where each individual stone would, of itself, fall to the ground; nor is the whole fabric supported but by the mutual assistance and combination of its corresponding parts' (E305). Since the removal of any one individual stone would cause the whole vault to tumble, a better analogy, and one more in keeping with Hume's view, would be that of a bridge being supported by a large number of pontoons. Not only are none of the pontoons individually capable of supporting the bridge, though collectively they are, each individual pontoon, by itself, can be removed without in the least affecting the stability of the bridge. The engineer who built the bridge left a wide safety margin. However, if more than a certain number of pontoons are removed, the bridge will fall to the ground. (*A fortiori*, it will fall down if they are all removed.) This analogy is better than that of the vault, because it is not Hume's view—and, if it were, it would be an implausible one—that a rule of justice must be kept on absolutely every occasion, if the good resulting from having this rule is not to be lost. If it were, he could not maintain, as he does, that public benevolence cannot be a motive to every single act of justice. The utility of having any 'rule of justice' would be lost by the performance of any given departure from it, which in precisely what Hume is denying. For example, awarding an estate to a wealthy profligate rather than to a deserving poor man with a large family would have the good consequence of maintaining the whole of the utility of the rule demanding it.

It follows from all this that, if one has a duty to obey a rule of justice in one of the difficult cases we are considering, this duty cannot be derived from the duty of acting in such a way as to perform actions which have good consequences. Perhaps, then, we simply do not have a duty to obey a rule of justice in a case like this. One good reason for thinking that we do have this duty, however, is that, if something is right for me, then the same kind of thing must be right for any similar person in similar circumstances. Hence, if it is right for me to disobey a rule of justice because the consequences of breaking it are better than the consequences of keeping it, then it must be right for everybody faced with a similar choice to break such a rule. However, if everybody faced with the choice between breaking and keeping a rule of justice in these circumstances were to break it, bad, and possibly even disastrous, consequences would result.

It does not follow from this that there ought to be *no* exception to keeping rules of justice. If the heavens were to fall as a result of keeping a rule of justice then, doubtless, one ought to break it. But, in this case, if everybody were to keep the rule in similarly dire circumstances, the consequences would, like the consequences of just one person's keeping it, also be disastrous. Perhaps a rule of justice should be kept if and only if the consequences of everybody's keeping it are better than the consequences of everybody's breaking it—which, as we have seen, may be the case even if the consequences of my alone keeping it are *worse* than the consequences of my alone breaking it.

This principle might be made general enough to provide a statement of the supreme principle of morality. (The view that this is a correct statement I have elsewhere christened cumulative-effect utilitarianism.) It might be maintained that, in every situation with which we are faced, we ought to act not in such a way as to produce the best consequences, but in a way which would produce the best consequences if everybody faced with a similar choice acted in the way we are considering acting. Choosing between breaking and keeping rules of justice would be only one special example of the application of this principle. An example which does not concern the choice whether to break or keep a conventional rule might be my duty to vote—supposing, for the sake of argument, that there is no social convention prescribing voting—when it could be argued that I have a duty to vote, even when I could do more good by not voting, because if *everybody* similarly placed who was faced with the same choice were not to vote, harm would result. And it must not be forgotten that the rule that we are considering as a possible candidate for the position of being the supreme principle of morality might enjoin upon us the duty, not of keeping a rule of justice, but of breaking it, when the consequence of everybody's always breaking it in circumstances like this would be better than the consequences of everybody's always keeping it in these circumstances.

There are, however, other ways of explaining why we have a duty to obey a rule of justice, even when breaking it would do more good than keeping it, than by saying that we have a duty to perform actions which would have good consequences, if generally performed, rather than a duty to perform actions which are such that they themselves have good consequences. One is to explain these duties as a way of not risking the possibility that enough others besides myself might break the rule to cause its utility seriously to be impaired. My breaking a rule will do no harm, but if enough other people also break it, harm will be done. Hence I ought to keep it, as a way of insuring against the possibility that I might not be the only person to break it, and that, if so, my breaking it in conjunction with others also breaking it would do harm. This theory can quite easily explain why I have a duty to adhere to rules of justice, even when my breaking them can pass undetected. There is still a risk that other people may unilaterally break a rule of justice, even though their breaking it is not a consequence of my bad example (which it cannot be if my breach of the rule is secret). And it can also explain why I do not have a duty to keep to a rule of justice if I can do *much* more good by breaking it than by keeping it, though I may have such a duty if I can only do a little more good by breaking it than by keeping it. For a little good to be obtained by breaking the rule may not justify the risk of destroying the good from having the rule, while a large amount of good may justify such a risk.

This theory, however, is circular, and begs a question it ought not to beg. Agreed that there *is* a risk that enough other people besides myself may break the rule of justice to deprive this rule of much, or even all, of its utility, the assumption that, if they do, things will be made any better by my alone keeping it while others break it is exactly the same kind of assumption as that things would originally have been made worse by my breaking it while they keep it. For as the utility of the rule is not affected by one breach of it, though it is seriously damaged by a number of similar breaches, so the harm done by a number of breaches of the rule is not affected by my keeping it while others break it. In such cases it is simply a myth or prejudice to suppose that there is anything analogous to the last straw which allegedly breaks the camel's back. No individual straw ever does the camel any harm, though collectively straws do harm camels. No individual breach of a rule of justice is *ever* the breach which causes a number of breaches to change from doing no harm to doing harm. Since whatever the situation, my breaking or keeping a rule of justice will *never* make any difference to what good or harm is done, there is nothing to insure against. What I am supposed to be insuring against is just the possibility that mine might be the breach which makes all the difference; i.e. that breach which, in conjunction with all the other acts of breaking the rule (which are going to occur whether I break or keep the rule or not), substantially damages the utility of the rule. If I am right, there is no possibility of there being such a breach and so no possibility to insure against.

Since this may be a difficult point, I should like to illustrate it by another example. Sometimes my duty to vote is derived from the risk, admittedly very small, that my not voting might make all the difference, because the candidate I would have voted for got either the same number of votes or one vote less than the candidate who got most votes. This supposes that the number of voters is small enough for every individual vote to be counted, and in many elections this is not so. In many elections the system of counting will not be sufficiently precise for one vote ever to make any difference. It might be that even if votes are counted in fives, my vote might just make the difference between a vote of five being recorded and not being recorded. But suppose votes are counted like coins by being weighed in a machine which is not sensitive enough ever to record the weight of a single ballot paper. Will not this be a case when my individual vote will never make a difference, although numbers of votes collectively will? No, it may be replied, for some ballot paper must tilt the scales, and, even if it was not my ballot paper that did this, perhaps, if my ballot paper had not been on the scales, the ballot paper that did tilt the scales would not have done so.

Let us therefore take another example. A highly sophisticated reaper-binder might in the future be constructed—if wheat were to become more valuable than it is now—so that it decides, before harvesting, into just how many sheaves it is going to bind the wheat in order that it should not be left with some wheat which is not enough to bind into a sheaf. In this case, no individual ear of wheat is every going to make a difference to how many sheaves the harvester binds the corn into, and so it will make no difference to the amount of money the farmer gets for his crop. It would be wrong, however, to conclude that there is no point in the farmer's sowing corn because the sowing of no individual corn seed will ever make a difference to the amount of money he gets. In a case like this, therefore, there is no risk at all that sowing or not sowing any individual seed will make the difference between the farmer's getting one sum and another smaller sum for his crop. I think it is a case like this that my duty to keep a rule of justice most resembles. If my breaking the rule does harm all by itself, then I have some duty to prevent this harm. If, as in some exceptional cases there may be, there is some risk that my breaking the rule might be that breach which totally deprives the rule of its usefulness, then I do have some duty to insure against this remote possibility. But even when my breaking the rule does no harm (or even when it does some good) and even when there is no risk of mine being the crucial breach which destroys the utility of the rule, because there can be no such breach, I still have a duty to apply the rule if everybody's breaking the rule would do harm. There is no contradiction whatsoever in supposing that a large number of repetitions of an action which does no harm, do harm; in fact, it happens. And even my duty not to take the risk of my breach of a rule of justice being that breach which destroys the utility of the rule is augmented by the fact that if everybody were to take a risk like the one I contemplate, the utility of the rule would be destroyed.

(24) Discussing this alternative explanation of our duty to obey a rule of justice, even when to do so does more harm than good, leads me to consider an objection to the first explanation (viz. that I ought to obey the rule, because if everybody faced with a similar choice were to disobey it, harm would result). This objection is that, when all the circumstances of the action are taken into account, the view that I should act on a rule which would produce good consequences, if it were acted upon by everybody, prescribes nothing in any way different from what is prescribed by the rule that I should perform actions which themselves have good consequences. Hence it cannot explain why I ought to obey a rule of justice, even when my obeying it has bad consequences, for it will lead to the conclusion, which was just the one we wanted to avoid, that we ought to *disobey* the rule of justice when disobeying it has better consequences than keeping it.

The reason for thinking that, when the action which breaks a rule of justice is described fully enough, the consequences of its general performance *are* no different from the consequences of its individual performance, is this. It is alleged that, if I go into sufficient detail, it is possible to assess precisely the contribution made to the general good secured by the rule which would be made by my own act of keeping or breaking it. Just what this contribution will be, will depend upon just how many other people keep or break the rule. But given that it is fixed just how many other people are going to keep it, and how many other people are going to break it, then the contribution made by my act of breaking it must be quite determinate, though it may be much greater than all the other acts of breaking it because my act of breaking it is the last straw that breaks the camel's back. But, if tracing out in detail the consequences of my proposed act, taking into consideration the number of other people who will keep or break the rule of justice, makes it in principle possible to determine exactly the contribution made to the general good made by any act, then, if everybody performs acts precisely similar to mine, in circumstances where just that number of people also keep or break the rule of justice, the consequences of this general performance must be just the same as the consequences of the individual performance. Hence this theory cannot explain why it is my duty to keep a rule of justice rather than break it, by saying that the consequences of everybody's breaking the rule in similar circumstances will be bad, even though the consequences of my breaking it are good. For the consequences of everybody's breaking rules of justice in cases *precisely* like mine, where the same number of people break it or keep it, and where exactly the same contribution is made to the good of the rule by my keeping it, will be just the same as the consequences of my breaking it.

This is a better objection than another rather similar one, which I shall now consider, and it is important not to confuse the two. It is this. If only we specify the action I am contemplating performing in enough detail, I get a class of which this action is the only member. In this case, the consequences of the performance of every action of the class will be just the same as the consequences of performing *it*, because to perform it *is* to perform every action in this class. There are no others. For example, if I specify my action as the breaking of a promise by a man with a scar 5.7 centimetres long on his cheek, five foot nine and a half inches tall, two hundred and thirty-three pounds in weight, with so many hairs on his head, five minutes after breakfast on the thirteenth day of a month, then the consequences of the breaking of all such promises are just the same as the consequences of the breaking of this promise, for it is the only one of its kind.

This latter objection may be dismissed. Every action has some specification—perhaps even an infinite number of such specifications—such as this, which makes it unique. If everyone were to find such a specification—as everyone easily could—for any breach of a rule that he was contemplating performing, then all the breaches of these rules which themselves had good consequences would be admitted and performed, and bad consequences result.

The former objection cannot be dismissed for this reason. It rests on the assumption, which I have already questioned, that it is possible to isolate the part played, in contributing to the good consequences of having a rule, by any individual case of obeying it, or to isolate the harm done by the individual case of disobeying it. We saw that, in the case of the reaper-binder, no individual wheat stalk could make any difference to the number of sheaves bound; nevertheless, obviously, taken altogether wheat stalks do make such a difference. I believe that the situation is the same where the contribution of every single act of obeying a rule to the usefulness of the rule is concerned. There is simply no such thing as the difference made to the usefulness of the rule by any one act of obeying it, and hence no such thing as the *detraction* from its usefulness by any one single act of disobeying it. Consequently, in however much detail we trace out the effects which the act of disobedience I am contemplating performing will have, the answer is still that it makes no difference. Nevertheless, a number of similar acts of disobedience may make a difference. In any case, *in practice* it would be impossible to trace out and determine the effects of disobeying the rule on the usefulness of having the rule, and hence we would still have to refrain from acts of obedience which apparently had no harmful effects, or even had good effects, on the grounds that repetitions of such acts would certainly have harmful effects.[11]

---

[11] Classical philosophers who have written on this topic include not only Hume, but Richard Price, William Paley, Alexander Smith, John Austin, and John Stuart Mill. Among contemporary writers, the reader is referred in particular to David Lyons (*Forms and Limits of Utilitarianism*, OUP, 1965) and M. G. Singer (*Generalisation in Ethics*, Eyre and Spottiswoode, 1963). My own views may also be found in 'Utilitarianism, Universalisation and our Duty to be Just', (*Proceedings of the Aristotelian Society*, 1952–3) and in 'Rule Utilitarianism and Cumulative-Effect Utilitarianism' (in the *Canadian Journal of Philosophy*'s special volume on John Stuart Mill and Utilitarianism).

SECTION III

Of the Rules that[1] Determine Property

SINCE this section is difficult, a more detailed exposition of it may be helpful. In the preceding section, Hume has shown the necessity for having rules in order to prevent society from being disrupted by quarrels over possessions. In this section he proceeds to determine what these rules must be. A rule which simply declared that possessions must be stable, but did not lay down which things were to be possessed by which people, would obviously be useless.

He starts by rejecting one possible answer to this question, namely that 'particular' goods be allocated to those particular persons to whom they are most 'suitable', for example, those who would derive most benefit from them. He rejects this idea for the following reasons. Some goods will be equally suitable to more than one person, and so will not tell us to which of these persons these goods must be allocated. Such a rule would be 'loose and uncertain', i.e. it would be very much a matter of opinion to whom certain goods *were* most suitable. The looseness of this rule, combined with the fact that men are 'passionate and partial', would give rise to controversy over possessions which would be incompatible with the peace of society. Hence utility demands that we not be guided by the 'particular' utilities of certain ways of allocating goods; a 'more extensive' view demands that we ignore particular utility in distributing goods in framing rules of justice. 'Whether a man be generous, or a miser, he is equally well receiv'd by her [justice], and obtains with the same facility a decision in his favour, even for what is entirely useless to him. It follows, therefore, that the general rule, *that possession must be stable*, is not apply'd by particular judgments, but by other general rules, which must extend to the whole society, and be inflexible either by spite or favour' (502). He means that the rules must be such as can be applied in particular cases without consideration of the benefits or losses to be derived from such applications.

Hume supposes a group of men in a savage and solitary condition, wishing to form a society; they are sensible both of its advantages, and of the fact that it would be impossible without rules making possessions

---

[1] The word 'that' occurs in the Table of Contents; in the heading to the section itself Hume uses 'which'.

stable. A group of people, accidentally detached from their own societies, would be in such a position, but, in setting up such a society, they would only be doing in a short space of time what in fact has been done by men over a long period of time. Hume thinks that the principle for distribution of goods which would commend itself would be '*that every one continue to enjoy what he is at present possess'd of*' (503-4). The reason why such a division would attract them would be that custom makes them prefer what they are used to, to what they have never had, and so will not miss, even though the latter be greater.

However, though goods may be allocated initially to their present possessors, it would be pernicious to allow no other rules; it would be necessary, for example, to have a rule demanding that goods sometimes be taken away from their *present* possessors and restored to their *former* possessors: otherwise 'restitution wou'd be excluded, and every injustice wou'd be authoriz'd and rewarded' (505). Hence circumstances other than present possession must be allowed to make something someone's property, and Hume thinks the most important of these circumstances are 'Occupation, Prescription, Accession, and Succession' (505).

'Occupation', or 'first possession', is an odd word for such things as seeing something first, being the first person to catch something, or the first person to occupy a piece of land which does not belong to anyone else. It would be highly undesirable not to have some such rule, for otherwise some goods would be unallocated, and so give rise to violence and disorder. Furthermore, 'first possession always *engages the attention* [my italics] most; and did we neglect it, there wou'd be no colour of reason for assigning property to any succeeding possession' (505).

Hume next raises the question—not, one would have thought, too soon—What is meant by "possession", as opposed to "property"?' (There must be a difference; of course, because I may possess something that is not my own.) Possession he thinks is to be defined in terms of causation: to possess something is to have power over it. The fact that having power over something admits of degrees—Hume seems to think that this is because the *probability* with which we may successfully exert power over a thing admits of degrees—means that there is no 'certain standard, by which we can decide such controversies' (506). We might (my example) have much more power over a mole hill we possess than over a mountain. Not only will there be disputes about whether a man possesses a thing at all—Hume says 'property *and* [my italics] possession'—there will also be disputes as to the *extent* of a man's possessions. Hume says, 'A person who lands on the shore of a small island, that is desart and uncultivated, is deem'd its possessor. . . .

The same person landing on a desart island, as large as *Great Britain,* extends his property no farther than his immediate possession' (507).

It seems to me that disputes about the extent of what a man possesses can be reduced to disputes about whether he possesses a thing *at all*. To say that the man's possession does not extend to the whole of the island the size of Great Britain is to say that he does not possess those regions of the island which are *far* removed from him.

However, after a long passage of time, it may be impossible to determine who was the *first* possessor of certain goods. In this case, we allocate goods not to their first possessor, but by *prescription*, to some-one who has possessed these goods for a long period of time, however he may first have come by them. This is not simply because it may be impossible to determine who the first possessor of these goods was; even when it is possible to determine this, and their first possessor is known, the mere fact that it was a long time ago that he acquired these goods, which have in fact been possessed for many years by someone else, will affect us in such a way as to make us regard their actual possessor as having a greater right to them than their first possessor. Hume says, 'And this may be receiv'd as a convincing argument for our preceding doctrine with regard to property and justice. Possession during a long tract of time conveys a title to any object. But as 'tis certain, that, however every thing be produc'd in time, there is nothing real, that is produc'd by time; it follows, that property being produc'd by time, is not any thing real in the objects, but is the offspring of the sentiments, on which alone time is found to have any influence' (508-9).

We acquire goods by *accession* when they are connected 'in an inti-mate manner' with other goods which are already our property. 'Thus the fruits of our garden, the offspring of our cattle, and the work of our slaves, are all of them esteem'd our property, even before possession' (509). By 'even before possession', I think Hume means that these things are considered our property by accession, even when we have no power (possession he thinks has to be defined in terms of power) over them, as we do not if our cow calves on a neighbouring ranch. This is because accession connects something which is our property with something else, and hence we also connect them with the relation of property. (Hume says 'connected in the imagination', but he does not mean that we imagine that our sheep is the mother of a certain lamb. And it may be worth noting that, though it is the sheep which is connected to the lamb by a relation, which, according to Hume, makes us want to connect them still further by supplying another relation, the lamb is our property, not the sheep's.) Though it is not essential, it helps us to acquire goods by accession if they are smaller than the goods we already possess; for example, lambs are smaller than sheep. I shall postpone any consideration of the second footnote (509 n.), a long and difficult one devoted to the topic of accession, until I come to comment on this section.

The last of the relations which give rise to property is *succession*, for example, inheriting an estate from one's father. (What gives rise to accession is a relation between something that is already one's property and other goods; what gives rise to succession is a relation between the owner of property and other people.) Hume says, 'The right of *succession* is a very natural one, from the presum'd consent of the parent or near relation, and from the general interest of mankind, which requires that men's possessions should pass to those, who are dearest to them, in order to render them more industrious and frugal' (510–11). But succession also depends upon the imagination, although Hume does not specifically say so, in that, for example, a father is already related to his son; hence our mind passes easily from the idea of the father to the idea of the son; hence it will disturb us if we do not connect them by further relations when we have the power to do so; hence we have a propensity to make the son heir to the father's property. (The son, of course, no more belongs to his father than the lamb does to the sheep; Hume does not notice that at least three *different* relations are supplied by us to connect by further relations things which are already related. We make one of these things the property of the other, as when we make what someone *possesses* his property; or we unite them by the relation of being the properties of the same owner, as when we make crops the property of the owner of the land they grow in; or by the relation of owning the same property at different times, as when we make a son heir to his father's house. The first of these is what is involved in present possession, occupation, and prescription; the last two are what is involved in accession and succession, respectively.)

In an important footnote (504 n.) Hume states that, though it is very likely in the public interest to have the rules about property we do, it is not solely from an appreciation of their advantages that we adopt them. He suspects 'that these rules are principally fix'd by the imagination, or the more frivolous properties of our thought and conception'. He says it is very difficult when two or more causes co-operate to produce an effect—as in this case the imagination and a perception of their advantages co-operate to bring it about that we have certain rules about property—to say which of these causes is the 'principal and predominant' one. He leaves it to his readers to make up their own minds whether utility or imagination is more important in determining

rules about property, but it is fairly clear that he personally thinks that
the imagination is.

Hume thinks that the imagination operates in producing the rule,
that what people presently possess should be their property, in the
following way. He says that he has already observed (235-8) that when
two objects are related in certain ways, the mind has a propensity to
ascribe to them additional relations in order to complete their union.
The example he has already mentioned (237) is particularly striking; the
relish of a fig and a *fig* are already related by the relations of causation
and temporal contiguity (i.e. simultaneity). As a result of this, we
suppose that they are also related by the relation of spatial contiguity
(i.e. that they are in the same place), although our doing so in this case
results in the absurdity of our supposing that certain impressions of
taste have a spatial location, when in fact they are nowhere, and when
spatial predicates cannot even meaningfully be ascribed to them.

In the case of the figs, however, the fact that two things are related
in certain ways causes us to *believe*, mistakenly, that they are related in
a further way. In other cases, the fact that things are related in certain
ways makes us *cause* them to be related in another way, as when we
put objects which are related by being similar in size next to one
another. Hume thinks that, when we cause something which someone
already *possesses* to become his *property*, we are causing two things
which are already related in one way (by the relation of present possession) to be related in a further way (by the relation of property) in
exactly the same way as we do when (my example) we sort eggs into
large eggs and small eggs, or cabbages into red ones and green ones.
Only in this former case he thinks that this natural propensity of the
mind is helped by the fact that the relation of possession *resembles*
the relation of property, in that one's possessions are what one has
physical power over, and property is what the 'laws of society' give us a
conventional and constant power over. Hence 'the same love of order
and uniformity, which arranges the books in a library, and the chairs in
a parlour, contributes to the formation of society, and to the well-being
of mankind, by modifying the general rule concerning the stability of
possession' 504 n.).

In another footnote (505 n.) Hume criticizes an alternative account
of why occupation gives rise to property. (He must chiefly be thinking
of John Locke.) According to this account, everyone possesses his own
labour, and so possesses whatever his labour is joined with. Hume
makes three objections to this account. Firstly, sometimes we occupy
something without joining our labour to it, as when we graze our cattle
in a meadow. Secondly, Locke's account reduces occupation to a

species of accession, which Hume thinks is a 'needless circuit'. (In other words, what is 'joined' to my labour, which labour I already own, becomes mine by accession in the same kind of way as the lamb belonging to a sheep I already own. Hume presumably regards it as a needless circuit, because he thinks he has explained directly how occupation gives rise to property, without deriving it from some other principle. He does not notice, however, that reducing occupation to accession would have the advantage of reducing by one the number of principles about property.) Thirdly, Hume thinks (rightly) that we can join our labour to anything only in a figurative sense (though he does not notice that we also own our labour in only a figurative sense); what, literally, we do is alter it by our labour. Hume thinks that this alteration forms a relation between us and the object altered, which relation gives rise to property, according to the principles he has already mentioned. (Presumably he means we add the relation of property to complete the union between us and that which we have altered by working at it.) Hume does not say so, but one would have thought that altering something by means of our labour (providing it is not already owned by someone else) and occupying something would be two distinct reasons for assigning something to somebody as his property.

The difference between clearly possessing something, and clearly *not* possessing it, is one of degree. How are the disputes to which this fact gives rise to be settled? Hume argues (506 n.), as he has done already, that reason and the public interest will not enable us to decide them. The imagination, which Hume has already said has a great deal to do with what makes us say that something is someone's property, will also provide no precise standard by which such disputes can be decided, for the qualities (Hume usually says relations) which operate upon the imagination, like the 'quality' of having power over something, also vary in degree. To modify an example of Hume's, it is because of the imagination that we say that the man who owns opposite banks of a small stream owns the stream, but does not own a large river in the same circumstances, but the difference between a small stream and a large river is one of degree. It is because of the imagination that we say that a person who lands on a small desert island owns the whole of it, but does not own the whole of a large one, but the difference between a small desert island and a large one is again a matter of degree. I shall say more about the imagination when I come to comment on this section.

The most important and interesting part of this section, which, presumably because of its difficulty, Hume relegates almost entirely to footnotes, is his account of the manner in which man's imagination disposes him to allocate property according to certain principles. That certain principles appeal to our imaginations is intended to be only a partial explanation of how we come to have the rules allocating property we do; we also partly have these rules because, sometimes, of a perception of their utility. For example, in the case of succession, we realize that passing property from father to son will increase industry and frugality. Sometimes we come to have these rules because having them *suits* everybody. For example, in the case of present possession, everyone would prefer to be left in possession of what he has, rather than have a larger quantity of goods that he does not have at the moment. But the major reason why we have the rules allocating property we do is that they appeal to man's imagination. It is, for example, solely because it appeals to the imagination that we would give the bottle of French wine to the Frenchman, the bottle of German wine to the German, and the bottle of Spanish wine to the Spaniard. In doing so, we are following our tendency to relate by a further relation (in this case, that of property) those things which are already related by other relations (that of having the same country of origin).

Though Hume thinks that it is useful, indeed necessary, for mankind to have rules allocating goods, he does not think that perception of their usefulness has much to do with our acceptance of the rules we have. We have these partly because we perceive them to be useful, and partly because they appeal to our imaginations. He mentions only one unequivocally utilitarian argument for any of his five rules for allocating property. He says that it is natural that men should be moved by the fact that it is in the general interest of mankind that men should be allowed to pass on their property to those who are dearest to them (because this makes them more industrious and frugal) as *one* reason why men should favour having a rule allocating a man's property to his children on his death. He mentions the advantages of having *some* rules for allocating as yet unallocated goods, but not the advantages of having the rule of allocating such goods to their *first possessor*. His general attitude is that, though it is extremely important and necessary that men should have rules allocating goods, it is a matter of minor importance *which* rules men actually adopt. Hence at least no harm is done by man's propensity to adopt rules to which he is favourably disposed by 'the imagination, or the more frivolous properties of our thought and conception' (504 n.). Indeed, in so far as the imagination does cause men to have some rules, and enable them to come to some decision when the possession of goods is in dispute, to that extent the fact that men are guided by the imagination is wholly beneficial.

COMMENTS

(1) Is Hume in this section trying to justify our using the rules for allocating possessions which he mentions, or is he simply trying to explain how it comes about that we use them? (In discussing this question we should bear in mind the possibility that the difference between these two apparently distinct tasks may not be as great as one might imagine.)

Hume's predominant view is that virtues are those characteristics of men that as a matter of fact arouse in people the sentiment of approbation. We can also say, with a little filling in, that it was sometimes his view that an action is a duty if, as a matter of fact, people would feel disapprobation of its omission. We must remember, of course, that it is not its arousing *any* sentiment of approval that makes a characteristic a virtue or an action a duty. The sentiment must be based on adequate information on matters of fact, and not be biased by such things as that we are related to the person who performs the action we are morally assessing, or that our personal interests are affected. But, given that we make these allowances, what is right and virtuous is determined by the brute fact that people feel approval of certain things. It is just a fact that people feel about actions and characteristics in the way they do, and the question whether they are justified or not justified in feeling in this way cannot arise. People's feelings are the criterion by which the morality of actions and character-traits are assessed, and there can be no other more ultimate court of appeal to which the deliverances of these feelings can be taken. We can justify particular actions by showing that they fall under a rule, the rule being determined by what *kind* of action people feel approval of. We cannot, however, justify the rule, but simply have to accept it. It can be argued that Hume's theory is no worse off in this respect than any other theory about the epistemology of morals. On any theory, one might say, he can show that some actions are right by showing that they are actions of a kind which are right, but at some point we simply have to accept the fact that actions of certain very generic kinds *are* right. The distinctive feature of Hume's theory is not that the fact that this very generic kind of action is right cannot itself be further justified, but that this fact is an empirical one and not, say, something we recognize by rational intuition.

This suggests that the question, 'Why do we feel approval of such-and-such?' on Hume's theory, is not a different question from the question, 'Are we justified in feeling approval of such-and-such?' For example, if we approve of a rule of justice because it is useful, then the fact that it is useful both explains why we approve of it, and, though it does not justify our approving of it—for this is an ultimate fact which cannot be justified—it does provide us with a criterion by which other actions of the kind of which we approve can be shown to be right. If we approve of qualities which are useful, their being useful is both the reason why we approve of them, and the fact which justifies us in approving of any given useful quality. This suggestion, however, would be an over-simplification.

There must be some difference between a causal explanation of how it comes about that people have a disposition or tendency to feel approval of certain characteristics, and an explanation of why these actions are right. Though it may be that the fact that people approve of industry because it is useful is the same fact as that industry is a virtue because it is useful, the fact that people approve of industry because they have been brought up to do so is certainly not the same fact as that industry is a virtue because people have been brought up to approve of it. Nor is the fact that I would not approve of industry if my thyroid gland had been seriously injured in early youth the same kind of fact as that I would not approve of industry if I did not believe it to be useful.

Hence not just any kind of causal explanation of how it comes about that men approve of something is the same thing as a justification of our approving it. It is only so when it gives the characteristics of that thing which arouses our approval. Although *arousing* approval is a way of *causing* approval, for all arousing is causing, not every kind of causing approval is a way of arousing it, for not all causing is arousing. Nor must it be forgotten that there is a distinction between the question, 'Why do we approve of such-and-such?' and the question, 'Why do we have a disposition to approve of those characteristics we do approve of?', that is, on Hume's view, 'Why do we (have a disposition to) approve of utility?' Hume's answer to this last question is that we approve of utility because we sympathize with the pleasure of those to whom the useful characteristic in question gives pleasure. It is, presumably, a brute fact about human beings that they are disposed to feel sympathetic pleasures and pains, a brute fact, that is, that utility pleases: if it were otherwise, as it could have been, then characteristics other than useful ones would be virtues, and characteristics other than harmful ones would be vices.

One reason why I raised the question whether Hume was trying to justify our having the rules of justice we do have, or trying to explain why (i.e. show how it comes about that) we have them, is this. It is clearly his view that in part we have these rules because we perceive them to be useful, but that, to a much greater extent, we have them because certain relations, for example, the relation of parent to child, or that of stream to the land which encloses it, appeal to the imagination, and make us feel impelled, perhaps irrationally impelled, to be guided by them in assigning property to one person rather than another. In such passages it seems to me that he is not attempting to justify our having the rules we do have, but simply trying to explain how it comes about that we have them. And the reason why we have these particular rules is often, if not usually, nothing to do with their usefulness as compared with possible alternative rules. But though the reason why we have the rules is usually nothing to do with their usefulness, the reason why we approve of justice is that justice is a useful characteristic. There is no inconsistency in Hume's saying that we approve of justice because it is useful, but do not have the rules about property we do because of an appreciation of their usefulness (but because certain, possibly frivolous, characteristics of things appeal to our imagination). It may well be that a tendency to be moved by features other than their usefulness may be a useful tendency, just as a tendency to want to eat certain foods on account of their flavour, not their nutritional value, may in fact lead us to eat foods that are of nutritional value. This tendency to want to eat what, on the whole, is good for us, has, of course, evolved by a process of natural selection over a very long period of time. Hume does not suggest, nor at that time could he have suggested, that the usefulness of our tendency to be impressed by features other than usefulness is useful because it has evolved by a process of evolutionary selection. He could not have realized that over a long period of time, any tendency to be impressed, for whatever reason, by features which are harmful has been eliminated by a process of natural selection.

(2) What are the implications of Hume's account of the reasons why we have the rules about property that we do for the *rationality* of these rules? It follows, I think, that we do not always, or even usually, select these rules from an appreciation of the advantages of having them. To this extent, if it is rational to have rules from an appreciation of their advantage (as I think it is), we are not behaving, or not always or even often behaving, in a rational way in adopting them. On the other hand, it is essential, and therefore rational, to have some rules, and so the imagination, in that it causes us to have rules, does make us behave in a way which is in fact rational, even though we do not behave in this way from a *realization* that it is rational. Very often, I think, it is Hume's view that there is *no* good reason for allocating property in one way rather than another. However, it is essential that property be allocated in some way or other, and hence the imagination, in causing us to

plump for one way rather than another, causes us to behave rationally. When there is no good reason for adopting one course of action rather than another, but it is essential to adopt one or other of these courses of action, it *is* rational to do something like decide which course of action to adopt by tossing a coin. Being guided by the imagination, however, where property is concerned, is unlike tossing a coin. For in the case of property the imagination causes us to behave in this rational way, by something like a blind instinct, without our realizing that it is the rational thing to do.

Does Hume think that men believe property *ought* to be allocated according to the rules by which he thinks it is allocated, and, if so, what bearing has his view, that our acceptance of these rules is largely due to the fact that they have a 'frivolous' appeal to the imagination, upon the rationality of our belief that property ought to be allocated in this way? And does Hume *himself* think that property ought to be allocated according to these rules? If he does think that, what bearing has his account of how it comes about that we have these rules upon the rationality of his *own* belief? Finally, what bearing has his belief that our acceptance of these rules is determined largely by the fact that the imagination is (irrationally) impressed by relations such as present possession, occupation, and so on, on his own, prima-facie inconsistent view that, if I may at first speak very imprecisely, morality is determined solely by *utility*?

Hume himself could not consistently have thought that property always ought to be distributed according to these rules, because he thought that, though some rules are necessary, it very often does not matter which rules we have. ('And as to the public interest, it seems not to be in the least concern'd on the one side or the other' (513 n.).) It follows that, in the cases when it does not matter which rules we have, it cannot be the case that we ought to have the rules we do have, rather than an alternative set of rules which would do just as well (i.e. we ought to have some member or other of a set of rules, though it is not the case that we ought to have any particular member of the set). Hume almost certainly thought, however, that once we have acquired a set of rules, we ought to adhere to them, because the consequences of our not doing so would be socially disruptive. I believe he thought this not only in the case when there was nothing to choose between the rules we have and their alternatives, but even when the alternatives were better than the rules we have.

Hume, incidentally, was not a full-blown utilitarian. He never expressed the view that we ought to act in such a way as to *maximize* happiness; his view was that virtues were characteristics which were useful or agreeable to ourselves or others. His view, in other words, was not a view—as utilitarianism is—about what makes actions right, but a view about what makes character-traits virtues. Justice is a virtue for this reason (because it is useful to ourselves and others), but it does not follow from this that we ought to have the rules of justice that we do have. (There is no inconsistency between saying that we ought to obey the rules we do have but at the same time maintaining that we ought to try to improve them.) It does not even follow that we ought *always* to obey the rules we have. (For the same reason, it does not follow from the fact that *generosity* is a virtue that we ought always to be generous.) Indeed, it may be regarded as a criticism of Hume's moral philosophy that he does not provide us with any standard by which it can be determined what we ought to do; the statements that valour is a virtue, and that discretion is a virtue, though they may tell you that you ought for most part to be valorous and also for the most part to be discreet, do not tell you anything at all about in what circumstances you ought to be valorous when you cannot also be discreet, or discreet when you cannot also be valorous.

If Hume thinks that rules of justice ought to be obeyed, does he think that other men also think this, and, if so, does he think that their opinion that rules of justice ought to be obeyed is a rational one? (It may be, of course, that he thought that he himself had a rational view that rules of justice ought to be obeyed, but that other men had an irrational, but true, opinion, which was the result of the operation of the imagination already mentioned, that they ought to be obeyed.) It is difficult to see how he could think that the generality of men had a rational opinion to the effect that rules of justice ought to be obeyed, when, according to him, the imagination had such a predominant effect in causing such men to adopt rules of justice. If it is the imagination which causes men to think that the owner of a sheep has a right to the lambs to which it gives birth, does it not follow that man's opinion that there is such a right must be an irrational one? This, however, does not quite follow. On Hume's view, to say that men have a right to the lambs produced by their own sheep is to say that as a matter of fact there is a rule of justice allocating to them these lambs, and, of course, men have a rational opinion that there is such a rule (and there *is* one). The situation is, then, that men have a rational opinion, for example, a right to the lambs to which their sheep give birth—for the rules allocate to them these sheep—but adopt the rules which determine these rights irrationally, because of their imaginations. Hence, if the reason why men think we ought to have these rules is that their imagination disposes them to be in favour of these rules, then men's opinion that they ought to have them is irrational. Hume's own opinion that we ought to have them, however, since it is determined by their utility, and the usefulness of men's being guided by their imaginations, is a rational opinion. (In other words, Hume himself sees through the operation of the imagination, which causes other people to adopt certain rules of justice.)

There may seem to be some tension between, on the one hand, Hume's view that justice is a virtue approved of by men because of its utility, and, on the other hand, his view that men by and large do *not* adopt the rules of justice they do because they appreciate their utility, but because they are seduced into having them by the imagination. If justice is useful, then the rules of justice which the just man obeys must by and large be useful, and, if justice is approved of because it is believed to be useful, then the rules of justice, obedience to which justice consists in, must be believed to be useful, at least to the extent that it is seen to be better to have them than not to have any rules at all. The only way I can see to resolve this tension is to say that justice is useful, and is seen to be useful, because it is necessary, and it is seen to be necessary to have *some rules or other* even though it is not always more useful, and is not seen to be more useful, to have the rules of justice we do have rather than an alternative set.

It is also necessary, and may be seen to be necessary, to obey rules of justice once they are established because these are the ones we have, and departing from them would be harmful.

(3) Implicit in what Hume says about the imagination is a criticism of that philosophical theory known as intuitionism. (The word was not current in his day, though a very modern version of it was put forward by Richard Price in *A Review of the Principal Questions in Morals*, published in 1758. Price, writing after Hume, was very much concerned to defend his view against Hume's criticisms, though he does not say anything about what Hume says about the imagination.) According to intuitionism, it is not the case that we ought to act in such a way as to maximize happiness or good. Instead, we have a rational insight into a number of moral truths, such as that debts ought to be paid and promises kept, and our duty to obey these rules cannot be derived from the fact that these are useful rules for society to have.

Intuitionists do usually recognize that the moral principles that we accept because of our rational insight into their validity are in fact useful. They think that the utility of these principles cannot justify them, however, because they think we ought to go on acting on them even when doing so does no good, or even does harm. Some of them admit a duty to perform actions which produce good consequences as one of a set of rules the validity of which we intuit. Usually this rule reinforces the others, but sometimes it and they conflict. When they do conflict, there is no rule which determines when we should, say, keep our promise but not do good, or alternatively, do good and break our promise. It seems to me, however, that it is inconceivable that it is just coincidence that the rules that intuitionists think we intuit are useful. It is one advantage of the type of utilitarianism that I defended in the previous chapter that it explains why I have a duty to do things such as keep my promises, and why I do not always have a duty to keep my promises, but may break them if the advantages to be gained are considerable. It also explains in what circumstances I should break a promise in order to do good, rather than keep it although keeping it does harm.

If anyone were to maintain that we have a rational insight into the moral truth that we ought not ourselves to appropriate lambs to which other people's sheep give birth, Hume would have said that there was no such rational insight. Indeed, there could not, given his epistemological views, be any such insight, for the propositions that we are alleged to intuit are synthetic ones.

They do not involve one of the four philosophical relations which make demonstration possible, and of course, they can be denied without self-contradiction. It was Hume's view that all synthetic propositions could be established only by observation and experience. The reason why we think that there is rational insight into this truth is simply that our imagination disposes us to allocate the lambs to someone to whom the sheep are already related, rather than to someone to whom they are not. In other words, we think we can apprehend a truth, when in fact the idea of arranging things in a certain way has something like an aesthetic appeal (504 n.). It is an interesting question to what extent Hume's criticisms of the rules for allocating property can be widened to apply to other allegedly intuited moral tenets, the truth of which also can be established neither by demonstration, nor by observation and experience. Consider taxation, for example–as John Stuart Mill does in Chapter V of *Utilitarianism*. Some people may think that they have rational insight into the truth of the proposition that men ought to be taxed equally, others that they have such insight into the truth of the proposition that men ought to be taxed in proportion to what they earn, others that they have rational insight into the truth of the proposition that men ought to be taxed more than in proportion to what they earn. Can they be sure that, in thinking this, they are not simply being influenced by the imaginative and the quasi-aesthetic appeal of making the amount of payments proportionate to the number of people, or making it proportionate to their incomes? Is the appeal of the principle of an eye for an eye and a tooth for a tooth any more rational, or is it that the symmetry of treating someone in exactly the same way that he has treated someone else appeals to people? In this case, of course, feelings of vindictiveness are also satisfied, but would they not be still more satisfied if the punishment was more severe than the crime? Is there not some similar aesthetic appeal in the idea that punishment should be proportional to the crime or, in Marx's slogan, 'From each according to his abilities, to each according to his needs"?[2]

(4) What Hume says about the imagination, predominantly in the footnotes in this section, may be regarded as a criticism of legal reasoning as well as a criticism of moral reasoning. Consider, for example, the story he tells of the two messengers (507 n.–508 n.), each delegated to search for a new abode for their respective peoples. When they come across an empty town, the slower of the two runners, seeing that his rival will enter the town first, throws his spear, and with it pierces the gates. The problem is, does this cause the city to become (by first occupation) the property of the people whom the slower messenger represents, or does it become the property of the compatriots of the faster messenger, who actually entered the gates first? Hume himself quite reasonably hints that the problem is insoluble. But, if the case were put before a judge, if this were possible, he would have to come to a decision about the ownership of the disputed town, and then, if Hume is right, there is *no* rational decision he could come to. If he decided in favour of the messenger who pierced the gates with his spear, this could only be because his fancy was more affected by the relation, between him and the uninhabited city, constituted by the fact that this messenger was first to pierce the gates with his spear. If he decided in favour of the messenger who entered the city first, this could only be because his fancy was more impressed by the relations between the messenger and the city, constituted by the fact that he had entered the gates first. But the force with which these two relations impress the imagination is not a rational process, and not a matter which admits of argument. Hence cases such as that concerning the ownership of the city, which must frequently have to be made or pleaded for by judges and lawyers, are entirely irrational. The same is true of the other

[2] A view which would, if applied, encourage people to have very small abilities and very large needs. I am myself not convinced that the rules of justice advocated by Professor Rawls (in *A Theory of Justice*, OUP, 1972), because, as he repeatedly says, they seem reasonable to him, do not simply owe their attractiveness because of some such appeal of certain relations to which Hume draws our attention.

examples that Hume gives. There are no rational procedures for deciding whether a letter belongs to the person who wrote it, or to the person who owned the paper on which it was written; or for deciding whether a picture belongs to the person who painted it, or to the person who owned the canvas on which it is painted. We have to make a decision, and we are determined to decide in the way we do by the fact that certain things impress the imagination more than others. We may think we are deciding whom the letter or the pictures in fact belong to, but really they belong to nobody, antecedently to our deciding that they do. To take another example, we may decide that a cup belongs to the owner of the metal from which it is made rather than to the person who has made it, but on the other hand decide that a ship belongs to the ship builder rather than to the owner of the wood he used to construct it. We decide this because the metal can be returned to its original shape, whereas the wood cannot. But, whatever we may think, in doing this we are not deciding to whom the cup or the ship belongs. Antecedently to our so deciding, there is no one to whom it does belong. We are deciding to whom it *shall* belong. It is the fact that the 'stronger' the relation between the person and the goods, the more the imagination is determined to make these goods his property, that causes us to decide in different ways in the two different cases.

(5) So far, though I have said much about the implications of Hume's account of the part played by the imagination in causing us to assign possessions, I have said nothing about whether this account is correct. I shall now proceed to do this.

It seems to me that Hume rather impishly underrates the extent to which our decisions about what goods shall belong to what people are determined by their usefulness. For example, in speaking of accession, he says, 'This source of property can never be explain'd but from the imagination; and one may affirm, that the causes are here unmix'd' (509 n.). By saying 'the causes are here unmix'd', I believe, as is suggested by 504 n., he means that accession is explained solely by the imagination, and not, as in other cases, partly by the imagination and partly by a perception of the utility of having one rule rather than another (504 n.). But Hume is quite wrong not to assign any part to utility in our decision to allow property to be acquired by accession. It would obviously be very inconvenient not to allow lambs to be the property of the owners of the sheep, or not to allow cabbages to be the property of the owners of the seed from which they grew and the land on which they were planted.

The organizational difficulties involved in handing over to Jones the cabbages which grew from seed planted by Smith, and to Smith the cabbages which grew from seed planted by Jones, would be immense. It is possible that both Smith and Jones would buy inferior seed and neglect the seedlings if they knew that the cabbages grown from their seed on their soil would not accede to them. Nor is it just because of the imagination that we allow small streams but not large rivers to be the property of the owners of the land through which they flow; it would be undesirable to give the landowner a control over navigable rivers, control which he might use to hamper the traffic. For similar reasons, it would be contrary to the interests of everyone who used the sea if it were partitioned out among different nations. Hume is quite right in thinking that our acceptance of our rules about property are not *solely* determined by our perception of their utility. Whether he is right in thinking that, to the extent that they are *not* determined by our believing them to be useful, they *are* determined by the imagination, is another matter.

According to Hume, our tendency to be guided, in allocating property, by such things as present possession, first possession, prescription, accession, and succession, is just an instance of a general tendency possessed by man to dispose of any relations he may have in his gift, so to speak, to objects which are already related, in preference to objects which are not related. In Hume's words, 'if there be any relations, which depend on the mind, 'twill readily conjoin them to any preceding relation, and unite, by a new bond, such objects as have already an union in the fancy' (504 n.). An example of this tendency would be arranging things in order of size; the ones which are *already* related by the relation of being closely similar in size, we *put* in the relation of being spatially contiguous to one another. Hume says, 'Thus for instance, we never fail, in our arrangement of bodies, to place those which are *resembling* in *contiguity* to each other, or at least in *correspondent* points of view; because we feel a satisfaction in joining the relation of contiguity to that of resemblance, or the resemblance of situation to that of qualities' (504 n.). (I do not know what Hume means by 'correspondent points of view'. I feel that putting two similar vases at either end of a chimneypiece, arranging books with the large ones at the ends of a row and the small ones in the middle, would be an example of arranging things in correspondent points of view—i.e. symmetrically— but do not know how to justify this feeling.)

Hume regards this tendency in the human mind, to cause objects to be related which are already related, to be a special case of a law that he has already remarked upon (10-13). An idea or impression tends to cause us to have other ideas which resemble it, or which are ideas of objects which have been found to be contiguous in space or time with it, or ideas of objects which have been found to be causally connected with it. I think that this is what he means when he says that 'they are already united in the mind' (504 n.). It is difficult to see, however, that our tendency to *arrange* things in such a manner as to *cause* objects, which already resemble each other in certain respects, to resemble each other in still further respects—for example, to put all objects which are already similar in colour in the same place—is an instance of this law. Let us take, for example, our tendency to assign land to its present possessor. This cannot be an example of association resulting from causation, because before property was assigned to its present possessor there was no such thing as property to stand in causal relation to anything. Nor can it be an example of association resulting from contiguity in space or time, for the same reason. The best Hume could say would be that observing the fact that people have possessions calls to mind the idea of property, because, as he thinks, having something as one's property resembles being possessed of it (504 n.–505 n.). But this, of course, will apply only in the special case when we not only cause things which are already related to be related by a further relation, but cause them to be related by a further relation which resembles the relation by which they are already related. Hume says (504 n.–505 n.) that this resemblance strengthens the tendency to arrange things already related in such a way that they become related in yet further ways, but he nowhere suggests that it is the foundation of this tendency. It is in any case thoroughly implausible to hold that we cause people to have as their property those things to which they are related because the relation of property resembles the relation or relations by which they are already related. Hume may be right, however, in thinking that this happens sometimes. It may sometimes be because we confuse being possessed of something with having it as one's property that we come, by insensible degrees, to regard those things that men are already possessed of as their property. It is worth pointing out that though causing things related by one relation to become related by another can hardly be an instance of associating ideas with impressions, or with other ideas, it could be because we associate property with certain already-existing relations that we feel disposed to cause the things to which people are related by these relations to be related by the further relation of property. The view, however, that property and the antecedently existing relations are *associated* in the mind—Hume says 'united in the mind'— suggesting as it does that it is because of past experience that they are so associated, is implausible. In any case, questions about the psychological causes which influence us in arranging things in certain ways rather than in others are empirical. Hume can hardly be acquitted of the charge of pronouncing on them on totally insufficient evidence.

Hume also greatly underestimates the difficulty with which we would be faced in trying to arrange things in such a manner that those things which are already related become still further related. For objects are not normally related to one another in just one way, but in several different ways. In Hume's example (509 n.–510 n.), where we award the Spanish wine to the Spaniard, the French wine to the Frenchman, and the German wine to the German, the bottles might not only be from different places, but be of different sizes, or contain wines of different colours, to mention just two out of a large number of possibilities. Books are not only related by being of similar size, but by being bound in similar ways, by having similar colours, by being written by the same author, by being about the same subject, by being written by authors whose names begin with the same letter. Nowadays, indeed, Hume's way of arranging his books would be regarded as eccentric. Hume has no explanation of why some of the relations strike the imagination, while others do not. And indeed, in arranging things in such a way that those already related become still further related, we are not normally guided by certain relations rather than others because these are the ones which appeal to the imagination most. If we are grading apples, we arrange all the ones that are similar, in that they come from the same type of tree, together, rather than those which are similar in size or colour, because the tree from which they come affects their flavour more than does their colour, and because people buy apples for their flavour. In arranging books, we put all the ones by the same author, or on the same subject, together, rather than those of the same size, and usually arrange our books alphabetically. We do not do this because these features appeal to the imagination more than their size, but because if we do this it is much easier to find them. If we are arranging furniture, we do not necessarily put all chairs of the same size together, or even in 'corresponding points of view'; they have to be arranged in such a way that people can walk about the room, so that the chairs are at tables and in other places where people want to sit, and so that armchairs are facing the fireplace, rather than having their backs to it. In Hume's example of the wine (509 n.–510 n.), giving the Spanish wine to the Spaniard, and so on, might impress everyone by its justice, but giving the cheap bottle to the poor man and the expensive bottle to the rich man might not achieve such universal acclaim. Hume's views about what determines us to allocate property work best in those cases where it does not matter very much how a distribution of property is made, but where it is essential that we be guided by something.

Indeed, in allocating property, it is impossible *not* to allocate goods to people to whom they are not already related. For, so long as we allocate property on some principle or other, and not in a purely random fashion, we *must* have some way of correlating individuals to items of goods. However bizarre the principle we opt for, we must be bestowing goods of certain kinds to men of certain kinds; consequently, the men must already be related in some way or other to the goods. For example, if we are distributing cows, we might allocate large cows to large men, or fat cows to fat men, or black cows to black-haired men, or to the man nearest them or farthest from them, or to the man whose name was drawn from a hat at the same time as the cow's name was drawn from another hat. In all these cases, there would be some antecedently existing relation, however trivial, which determined us, by allocating property on its basis, to unite the man to the goods by the further relation of ownership. Hence Hume's claim, to the extent that it simply consists in the contention that property is distributed on the basis of antecedently existing relations, is unfalsifiable so long as property is distributed in accordance with a principle, however trivial. It is not until he makes the claim that certain relations impress us more than others—present possession rather than similarity of colour, for example—that it comes to have any significant content. In such cases, Hume underrates the part played by considerations of utility and convenience in our selection of certain features on which to base one distribution rather than others. His psychological explanation of how it comes about that certain things rather than others move us to be guided by them in allocating property is implausible. However, his contention that there is a large irrational element, not based on utility, in our choice of the principles according to which we distribute goods is not unconvincing. (It is this fact which gives some strength, I suspect irrationally, to intuitionism. It must not be forgotten, of course, that Hume thinks it is a good thing that we are not guided wholly by utility in settling such matters.)

Hume's views about the imagination in general are very complicated, and his remarks on the subject are scattered throughout the whole of the *Treatise*. According to him, it has the following functions. *One* function of the imagination is simply to have mental images, something which Hume does not clearly distinguish from having concepts, holding beliefs, and envisaging possibilities. A *second* function of the imagination is to rearrange mental images that are copies of impressions in such a way that they form mental images that are not copies of any impression, which is what happens when, for example, we fabricate a mental image of a centaur. (Again, Hume does not clearly distinguish producing a mental image of a centaur from having a concept of a centaur, or from having beliefs or entertaining possibilities about centaurs.) A *third* function of the imagination is to pass from one idea (or mental image) to another, or from an impression to an idea, as when having an impression of thunder causes us to frame an idea of lightning. The *fourth* function of the imagination is supplementative. We have a tendency, when perceiving things, to fill in the gaps in our impressions, caused by blinking, turning our heads, or going away and returning to the same place, with ideas resembling the impressions we would have had if our perceptions had not been thus interrupted. For example, we fill in the gap in our impressions caused by our leaving the room when the fire is blazing, and returning to dying embers, with ideas just like the impressions we would have had if we had not left the room, but remained watching the fire. *Fifthly*, Hume also says that the imagination has the reverse function of turning an *idea* into an *impression* when we sympathize with someone else's feelings or beliefs, for example, of turning our idea of someone else's pain conjured up because we see him writhing and hear his screams, into an actual impression of pain. It is, *sixthly*, a great extension of the original concept to call by the word 'imagination' our tendency—if Hume is right in thinking that there is one—to believe falsely that things which are related in certain ways are also related in other ways, for example, to believe that the taste of a cherry, which is caused by the cherry and is contiguous in time with the cherry, is also (impossibly) contiguous in place with the cherry. And it is, *seventhly*, a still greater extension to regard it as a function of the imagination to cause us to arrange things in such a way that objects already related by some relations become, by our act, also related by others.

It is this seventh function of the imagination, which he nowhere distinguishes from the others, that Hume has in mind when he talks about the allocation of property. I am not saying we do not do what Hume says we do. In arranging anything in accordance with a principle, say books alphabetically, we must be doing just this (i.e. causing the position of the books on our shelves to be correlated with places in the alphabet). But Hume seems to think that he has *explained* why certain relations attract or impel us in such a manner as to cause us to want to make them related by still further relations.

This I do not think he has done. One difficulty with what Hume says is that the principles by which he says the imagination operates do not appear to be always the same. He starts off (10) by saying that the imagination is guided by resemblance, contiguity, and causal connection in passing from one idea to another, or from an impression to an idea.

Later much greater emphasis—sometimes exclusive emphasis—is placed on causal connection, especially in explaining why we pass from an impression to an idea (because similar impressions have been found to be constantly conjoined with similar ideas in the past). And later still the imagination appears not to be guided by the three relations of contiguity, resemblance, and causal connection, but by any relations whatsoever, in such a manner as to cause us to believe that things related in some ways are also related in others, or to cause us to make things that are related in some ways become related in others. (A good many of the relations which Hume thinks impress the imagination in such a way as to incline us to add to them the relation of property are causal relations. Possession is, he says, a causal relation, and so when we make what people are presently possessed of their property we are adding property to a causal relationship. But length of time is not a causal relationship, nor are contiguity or resemblance, so when we make something someone's property because he has possessed it for a long time, the imagination is being worked on by a relation other than the three Hume originally mentions (10).)

(6) Is there any inconsistency involved in Hume's assertion that it is a very good thing that rules of justice are not always selected by men because they perceive them to be useful? Hume in fact makes a number of different contentions of this kind, which can easily be confused with one another. The first is that it is useful to adhere to rules of justice which *already exist* even in circumstances where more good can be done by departing from them than by keeping to them. The second is that any attempt to *bring into existence* rules which apportion goods to those individual people who would derive most benefit from them would in fact be harmful (502). The third is the contention that it is often a good thing that even those rules about property which do not allocate goods to those who would derive most benefit from them are not selected because of their utility.

The first of these three contentions has already been discussed at some length. The second suggests that if we aim at producing utility we will not succeed, and that we may better produce utility if we do not aim at doing so. It may be argued there is nothing contradictory about this, any more than there was anything contradictory about Alice's discovery that the way to get to the house was to walk away from it rather than towards it, or in the claim that in order to be happy it is necessary not to try to be happy. Nevertheless, it would be a little peculiar if nature were so arranged that we could not produce utility except by not aiming at it. Indeed, though there is nothing contradictory about producing utility though not aiming at it, to be aiming at producing utility by not aiming at it would be to be in a contradictory frame of mind. On the other hand, there would be no contradiction involved in aiming at producing utility by not aiming at producing it *directly*. In any case, we could not produce utility *simply* by not aiming at it; there would have to be *special* ways of not aiming at it which, unlike the other ways, did produce utility, and we would have to know which these special ways of not producing utility were in order to adopt them. (Alice, of course, was aiming at reaching the house even after she realized that the only way of doing so was to walk away from it.) The resolution of this apparent paradox is to be found by distinguishing that utility which is the consequence of adopting a rule, from those utilities which are specified in the rule adopted. What Hume is saying is that a rule which mentions or takes cognizance of utilities in specifying how goods are to be distributed will not have utility as its consequence. Furthermore, if we wish to produce utility, we must do so by aiming at it indirectly, i.e. by having rules which do not take utility into consideration in deciding how goods are to be apportioned. About this there is nothing contradictory, or even particularly paradoxical. In fact, I believe it is true.

The third contention amounts to saying that the consequences of our *not selecting* rules, which do *not specify* that distribution should take place in accordance with utility, on account of their utility, are in fact good. Hume is not here, I think, advising us not to adopt rules because of their utility. He is simply saying that we often do not in fact do this, and the consequences are nevertheless good, perhaps better, though not necessarily so, than they would have been if we always selected our rules because of their utility. There is nothing any more paradoxical about this than there is about saying that it is healthier to eat when we are hungry than it is to eat from a conscious desire to assimilate the right amount of nourishment.

(7) I shall end by commenting on some tricky passages, which I omitted from my summary, because to have included them would have made it difficult for the reader to see the wood for the trees. Hume presumably relegated them to footnotes for the same reason.

In a footnote (506 n.–507 n.) to a passage where Hume points out that it is sometimes impossible to determine where possession begins and ends, because possession admits of degrees, he gives the following example. 'A person, who has hunted a hare to the last degree of weariness, wou'd look upon it as an injustice for another to rush in before him, and seize his prey. But the same person, advancing to pluck an apple, that hangs within his reach, has no reason to complain, if another, more alert, passes him, and takes possession.' Hume argues that since it takes a great deal of work to reduce the hare to that state of immobility which is natural to an apple, this forms a stronger relation between the person and the hare than the relation between the person and the apple. Hence the imagination is inclined to unite the hare to the person by the further (moral) relation of property but not to unite the apple to him, though he has the same power over the apple as he has over the hare.

This shows that power over an object (in terms of which Hume has defined possession) is not always sufficient to cause us to want to assign something to a man as his property. (In the example just given, the man must also have altered it by his labour.)

He makes the converse point when, later in the same footnote (507 n.), he argues that we sometimes gain something as a possession simply by seeing it, without having any power over it at all. This does not usually happen. It would be odd indeed if just seeing our neighbour's field made it our property. Something becomes our property in this way only when it does not already belong to anyone else, and when becoming able to see it is the result of considerable labour and difficulty, as when a continent is discovered and becomes the property of those who first saw it.

Even where discovery and possession occur, these are not sufficient to make something someone's property if this discovery or possession does not have the *intention* of making what he discovers or what he possesses his property. Hume thinks this is because it strengthens the relation (the connection is not so great, but it must be helped by such an intention), but I suspect that the reason is not that, but that where no one has any intention of acquiring something as his property, the question whether it shall be allocated to him as his property does not usually arise.

Hume is inclined to draw three morals from the examples I have just mentioned, together with the examples of the two messengers, which he discusses later in the same footnote (and I duscuss on page 91). (i) Neither possession nor modifying something with our labour is a necessary or sufficient condition of something becoming our property. (ii) Because of all the quirks which determine us to assign something as someone's property, such assignment is the work of the imagination rather than reason. (iii) Many disputes about property are simply insoluble. For example, such a dispute will be insoluble if a 'weak' relation, which appeals but little to the imagination, inclines us to assign something to one man as his property, and a similar relation makes us want to assign the same thing to another man.

In the second footnote to page 509 Hume discusses the following miscellaneous points. The fact that accession gives rise to a right to property depends *wholly* upon the imagination, and 'one may affirm, that the causes are here unmix'd'. By this he means that (though he has said previously (504 n.) that concern for public interest *and* the imagination are the reasons why we assign property, it is difficult to determine the weight of the parts played by each), the fact that accession makes us assign things to people as their property is solely due to the imagination. As I have said (pp. 92–3), Hume must be wrong about this. It is by accession that the eggs laid by our chickens become our property, but it is clearly in the public interest that this shall be so, for if they did not, men would have little incentive to keep and take care of chickens.

In the second paragraph to this footnote (509 n. 2), Hume argues that the relation to a man which gives rise to a tendency to make something his property admits of what he calls degrees. The imagination may have a tendency to assign something to someone as his property when it is related to something which is already his property, and a third thing to him when it is related to the second thing, and so on. Hume thinks that this relation weakens at each remove, but clearly it does not always weaken. One is as strongly inclined to assign the eggs from the chickens of the eggs from my chickens to me as my property as one was to assign to me the original eggs themselves.

The next paragraph to 509 n. 2 contains an example, already mentioned, which is intended to be a minor illustration of the same principles of the imagination which ascribe property by occupation, prescription, and accession. The arbitrator awards each bottle of wine to the person who belongs to the nation which produced it. The example could be made more complicated. Let us suppose that a large bottle of Spanish *rosé* wine, a medium-sized bottle of German hock, and a small bottle of Burgundy have to be allocated to a small white Spaniard, a medium-sized French Arab, and a large German Negro. The imagination would then have to choose between Hume's principle and the equally attractive principle of giving the white wine to the white Spaniard, the *rosé* to the French Arab, and the red wine to the German Negro, or giving the large bottle to the large man, the medium-sized bottle to the medium-sized man, and the small bottle to the small man. The imagination, doubtless, would boggle at the task. This, however, is no objection to what Hume says. He himself gives examples where the imagination is torn between the opposing claims of various frivolous relations, each of which appeal to it, and where no rational decision can be taken.

In the next two paragraphs (510 n.–511 n.) Hume is concerned to resolve what he thinks is an apparent inconsistency between his present view and what he has said elsewhere. Here he thinks that it is easier where succession is concerned for the imagination to allocate a new object to the owner of another object if the new object is smaller than the one already owned. For example, he will be readier to say that Great Britain has dominion over the Orkneys than to say the Orkneys have dominion over Great Britain. But, says Hume, 'I have already observ'd, that the imagination passes with greater facility from little to great, than from great to little, and that the transition of ideas is always easier and smoother in the former case than in the latter' (510 n.). Hume reconciles this inconsistency in the following way. The imagination does not pass from the idea of the owner to the idea of the large object, and *then* to the idea of the small one. There is not in fact this easy passage from large object to small one, which it would be inconsistent for Hume to recognize. There is simply one passage of the imagination from the idea of the owner to the idea of the complex whole of the large object combined with the small one, and this one passage of the imagination does not take us with much force unless we are related to the greater part of the whole. This solution of Hume's difficulty does not strike me as being satisfactory, for he is left with the problem of explaining why we assimilate small objects to large objects, but not large ones to small ones. Since we would expect him to say that this assimilation has something to do with the imagination, passage from large objects to small ones as compared with small objects to large ones leaves us with precisely the same problem which Hume thinks he has solved.

In the next three paragraphs (511 n.) there are three more examples of the effect of the imagination upon accession, the first two of which have to do with the assimilation of large to small. He thinks that it is because of the aforesaid principles which govern the imagination that no nation is supposed to have property in the sea, but 'friths and bays naturally belong as an accession to the proprietors of the surrounding continent'. (The continents are larger than the friths and bays, but smaller than the ocean.) And the same thing explains why, as we have already seen, the owners of the banks of a small stream own the stream, but men do not own large rivers flowing through their property. Again, it seems obvious that utilitarian considerations are not as irrelevant as Hume thinks. It would be very inconvenient if the owners of the banks were allowed to own and control shipping on a navigable river, and very inconvenient if nations were to own and control navigation of large parts, containing important trade routes, of the high seas.

Hume's third example of accession concerns *alluvion*. The owner of the bank of a river acquires land by alluvion when the banks are imperceptibly enlarged by this process. If, on the other hand, a large piece of land gets deposited on his banks all at once, he is not deemed to own it until it is joined to his land by the growth of vegetation. Hume thinks that the decision that the land is his is thus shown not to be a rational one, but one that is due to the fact that the imagination can pass easily from the idea of the banks to the idea of the extra land if the land is added imperceptibly, or is joined by vegetation, but not when there is a sudden addition not so joined. One suspects that too many irreducible principles governing the imagination are being introduced. On the other hand, one cannot help agreeing with Hume that there is no rational principle which would dictate that new land joined to land which some-one already owns becomes his when conjoined to it by vegetation, but not if it is not.

Hume lastly discusses a number of examples of something which *resembles* accession, though it is not, strictly speaking, a case of it, and for which Hume has no name. The problem concerns who owns a property which is composed of the properties of different persons, but so conjoined as not to admit of separation. Some of these cases admit of division, though not of separation; others admit of neither separation nor division. The cases where division is possible have, Hume points out, been distinguished into two types of cases by Roman Law. First there is *confusion,* as when the corn in my bag gets inextricably mixed with the corn in yours. Second there is *'commixtion'*, as when my wine gets into vats already containing wine of which you are the owner. Hume says that Roman Law in principle regards each separate grain as belonging to its original owner, but cannot do the same with the wine. It cannot, however, do this with either in practice, so in each case the compound has to be divided properly between the two owners in that proportion which the original parts bore to one another. An atomic physicist, presumably, would see no difference of principle between the two cases. Presumably Hume's point, though he does not say so, is that the imagination makes a difference between the two cases because we can retain distinct ideas of the different grains of corn, but not of the different units of wine. There does not seem to be anything irrational about the decision that the property, resulting from 'commixtion' or confusion, should be divided between the owners of the original parts in the proportion which held between the parts.

Another case when two properties are so united as to admit of neither separation nor division arises when one person owns a house and another the land on which it is built. Hume thinks that our imagina-tions will dispose us to ascribe the whole property to the owner of the most considerable part if it is possible to pronounce what it is. (In this example, the two properties are inseparable only in practice, for in principle the house can be moved to another site.) He says, 'One part of a compound object may become more considerable than the other, either because it is more constant and durable; because it is of greater value; because it is more obvious and remarkable; because it is of greater extent; or ·because its existence is more separate and independent' (512 n.). These principles may vary in degree and may conflict. Hence there will be cases 'where the reasons on both sides are so equally ballanc'd that 'tis impossible for us to give any satisfactory decision. Here then is the proper business of municipal laws, to fix what the principles of human nature have left undetermin'd' (513 n.). It follows from these remarks of Hume's that there are three cases to be considered: (i) where there is a reason for adopting one principle rather than another; (ii) where there is no such reason, and our decision is determined by the attractiveness to the imagination of certain features of the case; and (iii) when even the imagination leaves the matter undetermined, and a rule has arbitrarily to be adopted by human decision. It would have been better, and more in accord with Hume's usual view, if he had said that *all* these cases were determined by man-made civil law, but that sometimes there were good reasons for the law, sometimes certain other laws were attractive to the imagination, and at other times, when even the imagination was no guide, a decision had to be taken in a manner which was wholly arbitrary. It is not that the features which attract us cause something to *be* a law, so much as that, because of the features which attract us, we *make* something a law. It seems to be Hume's view that since the imaginations of all men are similar, there will be a wide amount of agreement among civil laws everywhere.

Hume next illustrates his contention, that many problems concerning separation are insoluble, with a number of cases which have to do, not with separating two (or more) *objects* from one another, but which might be described as having to do with separating the *form* of an object from its *matter* (513 n.). He first points out that there are no consistent principles in civil law, for though the superficies yield to the soil and the writing to the paper, the canvas yields to the picture. Hume is particularly concerned with the problem: 'Who is the owner of a cup made from the metal of another, or of a ship made from the wood of another?' Sabinus thought that the owner of the matter (the metal or wood) should own the whole on the ground that the matter is the 'foundation' of all its qualities, because it is more constant and durable. Proculus thought that the man who made the cup or the ship was its owner, as the form was the most obvious and remarkable part. Hume mentions with some approval the solution of Trebonian, which was that the cup belongs to the owner of the metal because it can be restored to its original form, but the ship belongs to the man who made it, because it cannot. Hume comments that this solution depends partly upon the fancy, which is irrationally (or non-rationally) more attracted, for the reason Trebonian has given, by the relation between the man who made the ship and the ship, than between the man who made the cup and the cup.

What strikes me about the controversies Hume discusses is that what they appear to be arguing about is who *is* the owner of the composite property, as if either were the owner before a judge had come to a decision on the question. In other words, Hume and the 'civilians'— Hume means writers on civil law—he mentions talk as if it were a fact, which it was someone's business to discover, whether the man who made the ship or the owner of the wood from which it was made owns the ship—which is what you would expect from a natural law theorist, but not from Hume—whereas it is more a question of a judge's deciding that, say, the man who made the ship is to be the owner.

There is, indeed, some parallel between a judge's decision that the shipwright is the owner and an umpire's decision that Grace is out. If the umpire decides that Grace is out, then Grace *is* out, and Grace is not out until the umpire decides that he is. The umpire might have been mistaken, in that he judged that Grace had been caught, when in fact Grace had not touched the ball with his bat or glove, but this does not mean that Grace is not out, even though the laws of cricket say that a man shall not be (caught) out unless he has hit the ball with his bat, or touched it with his glove. Conversely, Grace is not out, even though a ball he hits has been caught by a fieldsman, if the umpire does not judge him to be out. He should have judged him to be out, but did not, so he is not out. The laws of cricket, accurately interpreted, should say, 'the umpire shall pronounce a batsman to be out if he is caught, and when this pronouncement has been made he is out'.

Similarly, the law can demand that a judge award a picture to the man who painted it, even if he did not own the canvas he used, but, if the judge fails so to award it, then it is not the painter's property, but the property of the owner of the canvas. There are in fact two stages at which the allocation of property is a conventional matter. First of all, it may be that the law, which is itself a convention, should declare that pictures are the property of the man who paints them; but, if it does not do that, then such pictures are not the property of the painter in these cases. Secondly, even if there is such a law, but a judge misinterprets it and pronounces a picture to be the property of the owner of the canvas, it becomes the property of the owner of the canvas (unless the judge's decision is set aside by a higher court). Whether a picture belongs to the painter or the owner of the canvas is a matter—as Hume usually recognizes—entirely settled by human convention. Hence Hume should not speak of the greater attractiveness of certain relations making something someone's property, but of the attractiveness of certain relations causing men to decide that something shall be someone's property. In more complicated cases, this is still more obvious. A case may not be neatly covered by a rule of law, but may resemble cases that are so covered in some respects, while differing from them in others. It is then a matter for human decision whether the new case sufficiently resembles the old to be decided in the way the old cases were decided. It does not follow from this that there is no right or wrong about such decisions. It may be that a new case resembles a case which was decided in one way but resembles more a different case which was decided in the opposite way, and is wrongly decided in the way in which the first case was settled. If so, a judge has made a wrong decision, but, nevertheless, the property is owned by the man he decides it is. This is a straightforward corollary of property's being a conventional matter. Hence the natural law way of thinking of property, according to which something is someone's property antecedently to the existence of human conventions deciding that matter, and according to which the function of legislators is simply to see that each man gets what naturally is his property, and the function of judges to award to someone what is, independently of human decision, his property, is just wrong.

(8) Hume says, 'And this may be receiv'd as a convincing argument for our preceding doctrine with regard to property and justice. Possession during a long tract of time conveys a title to any object. But as 'tis certain, that, however every thing be produc'd *in* [my italics] time, there is nothing real, that is produc'd *by* [my italics] time; it follows, that property being produc'd by time, is not any thing real in the objects, but is the offspring of the sentiments, on which alone time is found to have any influence' (508-9). In other words, since property is affected by time, this shows that property is not a natural (Hume should not have said 'real') phenomenon, for natural phenomena are not affected by time. (Hume's arguments to show that property is not only not *natural*, but that being someone's property is not a *physical* feature of a thing, are to be found on pages 515, 516, and 527 of the *Treatise*.) Time can have an effect only on our sentiments, and this just shows that being someone's property is determined by the sentiments of disapprobation we feel when someone other than the owner treats this thing in various ways, such as trying to sell it, and do

not feel when the owner treats it in these very same ways. (I am assuming here that by 'sentiments' Hume means 'feelings' and not 'opinions', but clearly time does also have an effect upon our opinions, if only in producing the opinion that someone has been in possession of something for a long period of time.) These opinions may then have a further effect on our sentiments if the opinion that someone has been in possession of something for a long time causes us not to feel disapproval of his treating it as if it belonged to him.

Is Hume right in thinking that time can have an effect only on our sentiments? Time is usually regarded as the universal destroyer, in which case it must have an effect on things other than men's sentiments. But perhaps to say that time destroys is only a manner of speaking, and what really destroys are moth and rust, which take time to corrupt. Is the case then any different with people's sentiments? Is there any difference between the fact that, if a house is occupied over a period of time, the wind and the rain and woodworm and dry rot may, during that time, cause its condition to deteriorate, and the fact that, as this time gets more advanced, we will progressively be less ready to disapprove of its occupiers for treating it as their own? Personally, I cannot see that there is any difference. Neither the alteration to the house nor to men's attitudes to the occupiers is, strictly speaking, caused by *time*; the one is caused by the elements and insects, the other by men's belief that the house has been occupied for a long time. This belief, if it is rational, is caused by the *fact* that the house has been occupied for a long time. Hume may be confused between the true proposition that position in time can have no effects (and of course, on a relational theory of time, there could be no such thing as position in time, as opposed to position in relation to other *events* occurring in time) and the false proposition that the length of the time interval between an occurrence and some other occurrence can have no effects.

What is true is that the fact that, after a long period of time, a house becomes the property of the occupier, is not just a natural effect of agencies operating on the house during this period, but that this change happens because human beings have decided that, after a long period of time, a house shall become the property of the occupier. But a decision by a judge, or in a more rudimentary society by people in general, that a house belongs to the occupier, is an event (or series of events) in time, just like any other, and has causes, just as do any other events. It is true that these decisions are caused by the beliefs that a given interval of time has elapsed (coupled, perhaps with another belief that, after such a time has elapsed, the rules demand that the house becomes the property of the owner) rather than by the *fact* that such a time interval has elapsed. But, as I have said, the beliefs about the time interval may result from the time interval, and hence the lapse of time does indirectly produce the decisions. It is not the mere passage of time which produces the decisions; it is the fact that, during this time, the passage of the days and the seasons has had such an effect in the mind of man as to cause him to have beliefs about the length of the time interval. Hence the alteration which takes place when something becomes someone's property because of long possession is no different from any other alteration which takes place in it.

Hume says that property 'is not any thing real in the objects' (509). The question whether property is 'real' is an elusive one. People really do own things, and it really is the case that there is a difference between something's being owned by one person and its being owned by another, albeit this difference is not a physical one. If you take the question, 'Is property real?' in an obstructively simple-minded way, the answer is that it depends on the nature of the property, for I may own real silk, or imitation pearls, with equal ease. The most natural supposition is that Hume uses the word 'real' in opposition to 'imaginary', but in this case, again, houses I own are real, though houses I fantasize about owning are imaginary, in which case there are no such houses. I may also, of course, imagine I own something which is not at all imaginary, but belongs to someone else. In this case, again, the house I imagine I own is real, though it is not (really) the case (is really not the case) that I own it. In more complicated situations, when I own money in a deposit account, or futures in tea, there will not exist any physical objects which I own, though in the latter case such objects may exist at some time in the future. What in fact I have in all cases of ownership is a right, the right to treat a material object in ways in which people who are not its owner do not have a right to treat it, a right to go to a bank and be given notes on request, a right to sell any tea that is produced at a given date for whatever price it will fetch at that time. Even in the case where I have a deposit account at the bank, which does not involve me in owning any material object at all, it is wrong to say that what I own is not something real. For I really do have the right to draw money from the bank up to this amount. When I have a thousand pounds 'at the bank', though there are no notes which are mine, it is not a case of my owning something which is not real, or even a case of my owning something not being a real feature of what I own. It is rather that there are no objects involved in my ownership at all, though perhaps some very unsophisticated people believe that there are.

(9) Hume's main target in this section is presumably Locke. Locke

held that there were certain principles about property—for example, the principle that men have a right to those things to which they have joined their labour—the truth of which were discerned by reason.

Hume's criticisms of this view are as follows: (i) Reason cannot discern any such truths, for reason can only discern necessary connections between ideas if one of the four relations which he says (Book I, Part III, Section I) give rise to demonstrative knowledge (resemblance, contrariety, degrees in quality, and proportions in quantity and number) is involved. Hume thinks that none of these relations *is* involved. He sometimes seems to go further than this, and implies that no relations are involved in property at all, for property is nothing real in the object. Normally, however, he does appear to think that when I say that something is my property, I am making a verifiable statement about it. Though being someone's property is not a physical feature of the thing that someone owns, as it depends upon the sentiments which his treating it in certain ways arouse in mankind, there is no reason why only statements ascribing physical properties to things should be empirically verifiable. If the owner treats a thing in certain ways, e.g. selling it, no disapproval is aroused, but, if other people treat this thing in the same way, disapproval or some other hostile attitude is aroused. It somehow seems to escape Hume that there could be demonstrative truths about feelings of approval or disapproval, just as much as there can be demonstrative propositions about proportions in quantity and number. The proposition, that if someone disapproves of something, it cannot be the case that everybody approves of it, is such a truth. I argued on page 48 in *Hume's Moral Epistemology* that Hume was led into thinking that there could be only four relations which gave rise to demonstration by his erroneous identification of a proposition with an idea (or mental image). This led him to think that the only relations which gave rise to demonstrative knowledge were those which must hold between two ideas so long as these remain the same, and which cannot be altered without altering the ideas. There is no reason at all why he should regard 'property' as a meaningless word, on his own view, for it is determined by impressions of approval or disapproval, or other hostile sentiments, and we can have ideas of these impressions, as we can of all impressions of reflection. It is usually held that Hume's view is that reason can tell us the truth only of analytical propositions, which cannot be denied without contradiction, whereas statements such as that we have a right to that to which we have joined our labour are synthetic. (Hence, according to Hume, they can be known to be true only by observation, in this case either by observation of men's sentiments of approval, or by observation of what rules they have adopted to govern the distribution of property.)

(ii) Reason cannot discern the truth of statements, such as that men have a right to that to which they have joined labour, because this is not a natural fact, existing independently of the conventions which, partly because of their usefulness, men have adopted to govern the distribution of property. It is something which is only the case because men have deliberately decided to make it the case. Hence men have a right to that to which they have joined their labour only if they have decided to have a rule which allocates goods to the person who has joined his labour to it. Whether they do have such a rule is an entirely empirical matter, which only observation of the practices of mankind can decide.

(iii) It is not a fact, independent of empirically ascertainable human conventions, that men have a right to that to which they have joined their labour. The fact that a man has joined his labour to something gives rise in men to a tendency to add to this relation that further relation of property. It is not found that having joined one's labour to something makes it one's property, so much as that this fact tends to make men want to make something the property of the person who has joined his labour to it. Whether men yield to this tendency or not is again a matter for empirical observation, not for reason.

(iv) Hume has a psychological explanation of how it comes about that people like Locke mistakenly think that reason apprehends such truths as that a man has a right to that to which he has joined his labour. This is similar to that by which Hume explains how it comes about that men mistakenly think that there is a necessary connection between a cause and its effect. In this case we mistake a propensity of the imagination to pass from an impression or idea of one event (e.g. smoke) to an idea of another (e.g. fire) when similar impressions have always been found to be constantly conjoined in the past, with a necessary connection between the objects of these impressions. We think we can apprehend as an *a priori* necessary truth the fact that fire causes smoke, when all that is really true is that, because an idea of fire has become associated with an idea of smoke as a result of past experience, we find that it does some violence to ourselves to suppose that one of these impressions might occur without the other. With the allegedly *a priori* and necessary principles about property, discernible by reason, the case is similar, though not quite the same. In this case there has been no constant conjunction between something's being joined to someone's labour and his having a right to it. A fact about something which causes us to want to make that thing someone's property is confused with the statement that, antecedently to its having been made someone's property, it is necessarily his property, whether man makes it so or not. Locke, in fact, confused synthetic, necessary, *a priori* truth about how things are, independently of human convention, with synthetic, contingent, empirical facts about men's tendencies to be attracted by certain features of things in allocating property. There is no question whether something is someone's property naturally and independently of convention if he has joined his labour to it. The question before man is whether or not *to make* something someone's property, for the reason that he has joined his labour to it. After such a decision has been made a question arises about what decision has actually been taken, but this question is an empirical one, and totally opaque to *a priori* reasoning.

SECTION IV

Of the Transference of Property by Consent

SINCE the rules for the allocation of property cannot give property to the man who has most need of it, it is necessary that men be allowed to exchange what they do not need for what they do, which exchange also makes possible what Adam Smith describes as the division of labour (514); since property is nothing real, delivery (or a symbolic delivery where this is impossible) is necessary in order to help the imagination conceive the mysterious transition of property, by producing an impression related to the transition (515); symbolic delivery resembles the superstitious practices of the Roman Catholics, which have a similar function (515-16).

COMMENTS

(1) The first of only two paragraphs in this short section, in which Hume points out the advantages of allowing property to be transferred with the consent of the owners, is extremely straightforward, and can scarcely be quarrelled with. It is, however, worth emphasizing the fact that one of the benefits that Hume rightly sees in allowing property to be transferred is that this practice makes possible the division of labour. Hume, in pointing out the advantage of such a division, was to a slight extent anticipating his friend Adam Smith's celebrated treatment of this subject in *An Inquiry into the Nature and Causes of the Wealth of Nations*, first published in 1776, more than thirty years after the *Treatise*.

It is a little peculiar that Hume should speak as if there were a law of nature (in his sense) permitting the transference of property. It would have been less peculiar if he had simply said that there was no law of nature prohibiting it. The 'law of nature' guaranteeing the stability of possessions, in other words, prohibits only the transference of property *without* the owner's consent, for obvious utilitarian reasons. There are, however, laws facilitating the transference of property, and protecting the new owner after it has been transferred.

(2) The second paragraph is much more difficult to understand; indeed, it is extremely obscure. The crux of its difficulty is this. Why does Hume regard property, and so *a fortiori* both the stability and

transference of property, to be 'a quality perfectly insensible, and even inconceivable'? After all, he devotes a substantial part of the *Treatise* to writing about it. Should he consistently have done this if he was making use of and clarifying a notion that he himself says we are incapable of conceiving, and so presumably do not have?

The answer to these questions are to be found in Section VI (527). He thinks that the transference of property is inconceivable because he believes (rightly) that there is no physical or perceptible mark which distinguishes the property of one person from that of another, no physical or perceptible change which takes place when it ceases to be the property of one person and becomes the property of another (527). Clearly Hume is right about *this*. There is no physical difference between a sovereign which is mine and one which is yours, and so when I give you my sovereign, its physical properties are in no way altered, and it looks and behaves precisely as it did before. Changes *may* happen to it; for example, it may change its spatial position from my pocket to yours, but it cannot be this that constitutes its becoming your property, for it could become yours even though it remained in my pocket. Hume, of course, is committed to the view that all ideas are copies of impressions, and that any words which cannot conjure up ideas which are copies of impressions are meaningless (Book I, Part I). Hence if there are no physical and sensible marks of something's being some-one's property, remaining his property, or being given or sold to some-one else, it could be argued that there ought, according to Hume's own view, to be no such thing as an idea of property, or of its stability or transference, for there are then no impressions from which these ideas may be derived. It is then the *absence* of these ideas which is the defect which delivery, whether real or symbolic, is supposed to remedy.

Strictly speaking, however, Hume does not actually say that property is a quality perfectly insensible and inconceivable. He says that property is inconceivable only 'when taken for something real, without any reference to morality, or the sentiments of the mind' (515). In other words, the notion of property will seem incomprehensible if we look for a physical or sensible feature of those things which are property, but not if we look to a difference in the sentiments people have about them. Though no physical or sensible change takes place in anything when it ceases to be mine and becomes yours, people feel quite differently about your treating it as you please after it becomes yours from the way they felt about your treating it in this way before.

Hume's remarks about the incomprehensibility of the notion of property are all the more extraordinary when it is considered that he himself has gone a long way to providing a perfectly adequate account of the notion of property in Book III, Part II, Section II of the *Treatise*. There he suggests that the notion of property is a conventional one; something is someone's property if there is a convention in his society which allocates to him the right to use it. It would be quite wrong to suppose that there are *no* impressions corresponding to the idea of property defined in this manner. Though we do not come by the necessary impressions simply by observing the objects which are someone's property, we do acquire them by observing the manner in which people behave with respect to them. We observe that when an object is treated in certain ways by one man (its owner) people do nothing to prevent him, but that they do prevent others from treating it in exactly similar ways. The impressions from which we derive our idea of property, then, are impressions of the manner in which people behave.

Though Hume, in the paragraph we are discussing, suggests that the difference between what is one's property and what is not is to be defined in terms of morality (i.e. in terms of the difference in the moral sentiments aroused in us by an object's being treated in a given way by its owner and by someone else), in this he must be mistaken. It is true that we do disapprove of people treating what is not theirs in a manner which would arouse no disapproval if it were theirs. There must, however, as Hume himself would have agreed, be some further difference between these two types of behaviour, which explains why we approve in the one case but not in the other. The difference consists in the fact that in the first case we are breaking a social or legal convention, whereas in the second case we are not. In any case, since taking what is not one's own, or otherwise treating what is not one's own as if it were, does not always and necessarily arouse sentiments of moral disapproval, the idea of property, and the idea of what arouses moral disapproval when it is treated in certain ways, must be distinct.

If we have *no* idea at all of property and its transference, as will be Hume's view if we regard him as maintaining that the idea of property is *incomprehensible*, because no perceptible physical changes happen to something when it acquires a different owner, it is very difficult to see how our idea of property can be enlivened by the present impression produced by the act of real or symbolic delivery. An idea which does not exist at all can scarcely be enlivened by anything. Nor is it at all easy to see how there can be a relation of resemblance between the *impression* of the delivery—the key of a granary changing hands, for example—and the *idea* of the transference of property if the idea of transference of property is non-existent. An idea which does not exist cannot resemble, or fail to resemble, any impression. And even the idea of delivery is not simply the idea of a key passing from a spatial position in one person's hand to a spatial position in another's. The change of the key's spatial position must be regarded as involving a change in its ownership, and so is no less obscure than the idea of the change of ownership of the granary which it is supposed to enliven.

There is, however, a more charitable interpretation of Hume, according to which he is perfectly well aware, though he sometimes impishly disguises the fact, that the idea of property is a social and conventional one, and that we should not even expect it to be derived from any visual inspection of objects which are someone's property. On this interpretation, the conventional idea of property is more difficult to apprehend than perceptual ideas. For example, the idea of something changing *ownership* is more difficult to grasp than the idea of its changing *place*. The function of delivery, on this view of Hume, is then to enliven the idea of the transference of property not because this idea is non-existent, which would be absurd, but because it is somewhat more obscure and recondite than the idea of a *perceptual* change. It is fairly easy to see, if Hume's view is correct, that there is the necessary resemblance between the idea of property being transferred from me to you, and the idea of an object physically passing from my hands to yours. One of the reasons why the idea of property changing hands is less easy to grasp than the idea of something changing its spatial position, or changing physically in some other respect, is that the change in position to the object is categorical, whereas its changing its owner is hypothetical. Change of ownership is a *dispositional* change. A piece of goods changing its ownership on a certain date consists roughly in a large number of hypothetical facts to the effect that, if a certain man (the new owner) were to treat this object in certain ways before this date, various sanctions, such as being sent to prison, would be applied to him which would not be applied if he were to treat this object in the same ways after this date. It is worth pointing out that Hume is bound to have some difficulty in giving an adequate account of the meaning of words for dispositional properties, for though you can have an idea or image of chalk's being white, it is impossible to have an idea or image of its being soluble in (as opposed to dissolving in) sulphuric acid, especially when it does not actually dissolve. It is partly for this reason that Hume, in Part III of Book I of the *Treatise*, has difficulty in finding an impression from which our idea of causation can be derived, and why, in Part I of Book III, he has difficulty in finding an impression from which our idea of immorality can be derived.

It is, however, difficult to believe that even on the second, more charitable, interpretation of Hume, his view for the need for delivery is correct. There is a much easier and more plausible way of explaining why a real or symbolic delivery is required if property is to be transferred. Though the idea of property is an idea of something conventional, it would be utterly impossible for a physical object to change its owner without some non-conventional changes taking place to it, or in connection with it. It is inconceivable that the change which takes place to a thing when its owner changes should be a conventional one only. If one thing is one person's property, and another thing another's, this must be because a convention lays it down that the first person may treat the first thing more or less—it is, of course, quite untrue that we can do exactly what we like with our own—as he pleases, but not the second, whereas the second person may treat the second thing more or less as he pleases, but not the first. If, however, there were no non-conventional difference between the two things, it would be impossible for a convention to lay down which thing belonged to which man. If they were utterly indistinguishable, no rule could specify that the one which was such-and-such was the first man's and the one which was so-and-so was the second man's, for it would then be impossible to replace the expressions 'such-and-such' and 'so-and-so' with different descriptions identifying different objects. (Differences in the situation of the two things are perfectly good distinguishing features for this purpose; indeed, they are very frequently made use of, and, where things so resembling as coins are concerned, very little else can be made use of.) It is not that, if the two things were indistinguishable, there would be no way of *telling* which was one man's and which was the other's—though this, too, would be true. If the rule could not specify which thing was which man's, one thing could not be one man's and the other thing the other's.

What I have said about ownership *a fortiori* applies equally to change of ownership. If no non-conventional change occurs to something when it changes its owner, it cannot change its owner, for there is no way in which a conventional rule can specify that something has changed hands unless it lays down that before something happens to it it is one man's, but after this thing has happened to it it is another's. Just as one thing cannot be one man's and another thing another's, unless there is some difference between them in addition to, and presupposed by, this *difference* in their ownership, so the same thing cannot belong to one person at one time, and another person at another time, unless there is some further change to the two things in addition to this *change* in their ownership. Obviously, we cannot normally expect such a change conveniently to *happen* to a thing just at the time we wish to buy it or sell it or give it away, so we have to produce it artificially. We can do this by changing its position, e.g. by handing it from me to you, or by means of some such symbolic delivery as Hume mentions, but the most convenient way of effecting the change is to use words, spoken or preferably written, for these are the changes we can easily produce, and the ones which are usually the most *precise* and *discriminating*. Before Smith says to Jones, 'You can have this' and Jones says, 'Thank you', this was Smith's; after these words have been spoken it is Jones's. This is because there is a special convention laying down that if Smith says these words, and Jones makes the appropriate formula of accept-ance, the object they are referring to ceases to be Smith's and becomes Jones's. (We say that Smith has *given* it to Jones, rather than sold it, because Jones transfers no money or property to Smith in return.)

It is very often convenient to use the same words which describe the transaction to *perform* the transaction. Hence someone may accomplish that operation described as 'giving' by using the words 'I give . . .', or the operation described as bequeathing by using the words 'I bequeath . . .'. Such operations could not be performed in the absence of human conventions; saying certain words cannot change the physical constitu-tion of that which is given or bequeathed. They have the effect they do, of causing something to cease to be one person's property and become another's, only because this is the function that they have by conven-tion been given, and because the effect they have is a conventional effect (i.e. an effect on conventions). Men have decided that, after these words have been said, the things referred to shall be treated as the property of a different person from the one they belonged to before. Without the use of words it would be difficult, if not impossible, to deliver property actually or only symbolically, for words—or at any rate gestures—are necessary in order to make it clear that, when an object is passed from the hands of one person to those of another, it is being sold or bartered, rather than lent, offered for inspection, or given to someone to hold.

The saying of certain words is enough to make that non-conventional difference which, I have argued, it is necessary there should be, between a thing at an earlier and a later date, in order that before this date it should be one man's, but after this date another's. It is not enough, however, to provide any adequate safeguard against fraud; for example, if Smith says the words, 'I give you, Jones . . .' when only he and Jones can hear, there is no proof that these words have been spoken. There is no way of settling a dispute between Smith and Jones, if Smith were to say that no gift had been made, when it had, or if Jones were to say that a gift had been made, when it had not. Actually delivering the gift, when this is feasible, helps to some extent, for that Jones actually possesses what he alleges he has been given is some evidence, though not conclusive evidence, that he has been given it. It is better if the presentation of the gift be witnessed, but witnesses' memories fail, and they may have motives for lying. Written documents indelibly marked and, better still, indelibly witnessed, provide the best possible evidence that a gift or sale has been made. Indeed it is sometimes so necessary that there be a proof of gift or sale that the conventions regulating these transactions disallow the possibility of unproven gifts or sales by making unwitnessed or undocumented or unsigned gifts or sales not valid, or of no effect. Where two or three—witnesses and witnessed—are gathered together, it is 'natural' that there should be some ceremony, but it is not just love of ceremony that leads to delivery. My friend can derive no benefit from my giving him my money if I keep it in my own pocket, nor my buyer from my granary if I do not give him the keys. The imagination, in some sense or other, not necessarily Hume's, determines the exact form the ceremony takes, and this, perhaps, explains why many such ceremonies are more dramatic than they need be. But it is not this appeal to the imagination or to man's love of ceremonial that is the essential thing about those events which are, so to speak, the vehicles by which property changes hands. The essential thing is that some non-conventional event should take place, which provides a foundation for a rule to the effect that before this event has taken place a thing is one man's, and after it another's. It is less necessary, though still very highly desirable, that this non-conventional event shall, if possible, leave a permanent, easily recognized, and non-imitable trace as a reliable sign that it has occurred. As an added insurance it should be witnessed, if possible in a way which also leaves such a trace.

It is perhaps a little surprising that Hume, in this section, speaks as if the translation of property were always barter, and says nothing about the function of money in enabling us to exchange goods and services. *Buying*, in fact, is just that species of exchanging in which money (instead of goods) is exchanged for goods, and *selling* that species of exchanging in which goods are exchanged for money (instead of goods). What distinguishes money from goods (or from other goods, if you prefer to use the term 'goods' widely enough to include money) is that people acquire money not merely because it is useful or desirable in itself, but because it can be exchanged for a wide variety of other goods. Money, in fact, to the extent that it consists of coins or notes, can be regarded as a set of tokens, entitling their possessors to a certain quantity of goods, without it being specified what goods. Since these tokens are only entitlements to buy, I do not need actually to possess them. A record of how much I am entitled to buy may be kept in the form of a bank account. If I buy a Rolls Royce and pay for it by cheque, this operation is performed without any tokens changing hands at all. I may have a million pounds in the bank, but this does not mean that the bank keeps a million pound notes for me, or a hundred thousand ten pound notes, or twenty thousand fifty pound notes. (The bank, indeed, will own notes to only a fraction of the sum total of all the notes the customers are entitled to draw.) When I buy a Rolls Royce and pay for it with a cheque, my bank reduces my account by the same amount, and the seller's account is correspondingly increased, but no notes, or anything else, change hands. I have a right to draw £10,000 less in notes than I could before, and the seller £10,000 more, but it is very unlikely that either of us will ever exercise this right.

What must be said about Hume's remarks about delivery, in the light of the fact that most goods are paid for by cheque? I suppose that handing over the cheque may be counted as a kind of symbolic delivery, made necessary not by the size or immobility of the goods, but because in this case no physical object is ever handed over from one person to another. (Even the handing over of a cheque is inessential, since directions may be posted directly to one's own bank, as is the case with a banker's order.)

There are also other examples where property is exchanged, and where the reason why an actual delivery cannot take place is not the size or immobility of the goods sold. If I sell a share in a company, nothing can be delivered for, though I own part of the company, I do not own any particular part of it that might be delivered. (Hume himself makes a similar point about promising (520).) If I sell someone all the oil, if any, in my back garden, it may be that this cannot be delivered, not only because it is difficult to move, but because there is not any. If I buy or sell futures in coffee beans, the goods that 'change hands' may not yet exist, and it is possible that they never will. All that can change hands, in such cases, is a piece of paper entitling me to dispose of such things should there ever be any.

(3) In the *Enquiry* Hume quite correctly points out that it is impossible to transfer property by an act of will alone, and that some overt sign is necessary to accomplish the transition. (If all I did were to think hard to myself, 'That watch is now Smith's', everything would go on precisely as before.) It follows that it would be just plain *impossible* to transfer property without some overt act, and that the reasons for delivery cannot be to *make comprehensible* some transition which might well have occurred, though less obviously, without delivery. 'It is evident, that the will or consent alone never transfers property . . . but

the will must be expressed by words or signs, in order to impose a tie upon any man' (E199 n.).

Even when goods are physically handed over, words or signs would be needed to make it clear that this act was one of transferring property as opposed, say, to giving someone something to hold.

(4) It is perhaps surprising that Hume did not think that what he regarded as a difficulty with promising (517), that promising alters our obligations, which means altering people's sentiments (his view), or the relations possessed by actions (his opponents' view), which things could not be altered, did not apply to the transference of property. For transferring property from one man to another also alters these obligations. Men will *lose* obligations not to interfere with the way in which the former owner treated what is no longer his property, and will *acquire* obligations not to interfere with the way in which the new owner now treats it. Hume's difficulty, however, as I shall later argue, is the result of confusion.

(5) It follows from what I have said that Hume's comparison between the mysterious transition of property and the Roman Catholic 'superstition' in religion is not apt. Hume says, 'the *Roman catholics* represent the inconceivable mysteries of the *Christian* religion, and render them more present to the mind, by a taper, or habit, or grimace' (515–16). There is, however, whatever may be thought of the Christian religion, nothing incomprehensible about the idea of the transference of property, and the function of delivery, real or symbolic, is more practical than the one of making the idea of its 'transition' more lively and comprehensible.

It is an interesting point that Hume's remarks here suggest that the doctrines which the taper, the habit, and the grimace were supposed to make more present to the mind were incomprehensible rather than false. In this he anticipated the views of the modern logical positivists.

It may be a little naughty of Hume to aim, as was his wont, his criticism at the Roman Catholics, when he must have been perfectly well aware that all branches of the Christian religion were to some extent open to the same criticism.

SECTION V

Of the Obligation of Promises

A more detailed exposition of this section is also necessary. Hume thinks that (the habit of) promise-keeping is another of the artificial virtues. The rule which enjoins promise-keeping is an artificial rule. For (1) there could *be* no such things as promises, in the absence of human conventions, and (2) if there were, there could without these conventions be no obligation to keep promises (516). (It follows from what Hume says, incidentally, that it would be possible for there to *be* promises which men were not under an obligation to keep, and that he would have disagreed with those philosophers who thought that the proposition that promises ought to be kept was an analytic proposition, not a synthetic one.) Promises cannot occur (Hume says 'be intelligible') without human conventions, and a man 'unacquainted with society, could never enter into any engagements with another, even tho' they could *perceive each other's thoughts*' (my italics) (516). If promises could occur without such conventions there would have to be 'some act of the mind attending these words, *I promise*; and on this act of the mind must the obligation depend' (516). There is, however, no act of the mind in which promising could consist. For (1) this act cannot be the act of *resolving* to do something, for I am not obliged to do what I simply resolve to do. (2) It cannot be *wanting* to perform the action I promise to perform, for I am obliged to perform it, whether I want to or not. (3) Nor can it be the act of willing the action I promise to perform, for, since the action I promise is future, this willing would have to take place in the future (if, Hume might have added, it takes place at all), not at the time I make the promise. The only alternative that remains is that the act 'attending' the words 'I promise' is the act of willing oneself under an obligation (516). This would have the advantage of explaining why we are bound only by our own consent (though Hume does not notice that this fact would also be explained if promising were resolving or willing, but not if it were wanting) (517). Willing onself under an obligation, however, is impossible, since our obligations can be altered—on Hume's view—only by altering people's sentiments of approbation or disapprobation, and sentiments cannot be altered at will (517). 'A promise, there-fore, is *naturally* something altogether unintelligible [i.e. would be unintelligible were it not for human conventions], nor is there any act of the mind belonging to it' (517).

Hume's reason for thinking that to will oneself under an obligation is impossible, on his *own* view (which is, very roughly, that we are under an obligation to do something if it is an empirical fact that its omission would be generally disapproved of), is that human sentiments cannot be altered at will except by an omnipotent being. His reasons for thinking that it is impossible, on the view of his *opponents*, who held that morality was discovered by reason, are discussed in a footnote (517 n.). He claims that he has shown in Book III, Part I, Section I that, if moral distinctions are discovered by means of reason, morality must consist in a relation. Hence, if willing oneself under an obligation is to be possible, it must *change* the relations of something. But it is impossible simply to change the moral relations of objects without first changing these objects in other respects, i.e. in Hume's language it is not possible 'immediately' to change those relations in which morality consists. (Hume is right here, for this would follow from the modern doctrine, which is obviously true, that the moral properties of things are resultant attributes which are wholly dependent upon their other properties.) But, since an 'immediate' change is just what the change in our obligations which we are supposed to will when we make a promise must consist in—i.e. this change is supposed to be a 'pure effect of the will', which involves our changing our obligations without first changing anything else in the universe—promises have no natural obligation. (It is not clear to me why he simply does not conclude that promising is just impossible, if it consists in willing oneself under an obligation, and this is impossible. One would expect his argument to be: if promising is a non-conventional phenomenon, it must consist in willing oneself under an obligation, and, since this is not possible if morality consists in relations apprehended by reason, it cannot in that case be a non-conventional phenomenon. But that his argument really is that promising is impossible, because it must consist in *immediately* willing oneself under an obligation—i.e. altering one's obligations without first altering anything else—is suggested by the fact that later in this section he seems to regard promising as an impossibility which we have to put up with on account of its usefulness! I shall argue in my comments that, though promising *changes* one's obligation, there is no reason why it should immediately change one's obligations.) Hume next considers the possibility, that the change in the universe (i.e. the new object) which alters those relations in which our obligations are supposed to consist, is the occurrence of the act of willing a change in our obligations itself. His reply is that this view is a 'sophism'; if the change we must produce in order to bring about a consequential change in our obligations were simply the occurrence of that volition which is the act of willing such a change, a volition would have to be its own 'object', i.e. a volition would have to consist in the act of willing that obligation itself, which is impossible. Alternatively, this view may be considered as leading to a vicious infinite regress of a volition, the object of which is another volition, the object of which is another volition, and so on *ad infinitum*, which regress is never terminated, as it ought to be terminated, in a volition which has as its object something other than a volition. (For example, one could choose a cream bun, or make up one's mind to choose a cream bun, or decide to make up one's mind to choose a cream bun, but this series must obviously at some point terminate in the act of making up one's mind to do something other than make up one's mind—in this case, in the act of choosing *a cream bun*.)

Hume now turns his attention to his second objective, to show that even if, *per impossibile*, there could *be* such things as promises without human conventions, they could not do what promising must do to be successful, i.e. alter our obligations. The same reason, Hume thinks (that one cannot alter people's moral sentiments by an act of will), which makes it impossible for there to be such a thing as willing oneself under an obligation, would also make it impossible for willing onself under an obligation actually to change one's obligations (518).

Hume next uses the same argument, which he earlier used to try to show that justice in general was not a natural virtue, to try to show that promise-keeping is not a natural virtue. Before an action can be a manifestation of a natural virtue (or before it can naturally be a duty to perform an action) there must be some motive usually found in normal men which prompts them to perform it. There is, however, no feature of keeping promises which could attract us, and provide us with any motive for performing them, other than the fact that they are a duty (518-19). In this respect, keeping promises is unlike helping others in distress, to which there is a motive in normal men independent of its being a duty, which causes helping others in distress to be a duty.

In the next paragraph (519), Hume makes it clear that he thinks that, if promise-keeping is a natural virtue, three conditions must be fulfilled. (a) There must be *'a peculiar act of the mind* annext to promises'. (b) There must be *'an inclination to perform, distinct from a sense of duty* '. (c) The inclination to perform must arise 'consequent to this act of the mind'. I think that by 'consequent to this act of the mind' Hume must mean that the object of that motive which would make promise-keeping a natural virtue must be some feature of that act of the mind which would have to accompany our saying the words 'I promise', if promising were to be a natural phenomenon. This third follows from the first two. For if promising must be both attractive to a normal man, and a natural phenomenon, in order to be a natural virtue, it follows that it must be some feature of this natural phenomenon which is the object of the motive in mankind whose existence would make promise-keeping naturally virtuous. Hume might have added that this feature of promise-keeping which attracts normal men must not be a feature of the promising alone—for this could explain only why we are motivated to make promises, whereas *making* promises is not a virtue—but something about the complex fact, performing an action after you have promised to do it.

Rules about promising are invented by men to remedy a defect in their natures, which, if left to themselves, would not supply men with any motive for co-operating in acts which would be of benefit to the co-operating parties. 'Your corn is ripe to-day; mine will be so to-morrow. 'Tis profitable for us both, that I shou'd labour with you to-day, and that you shou'd aid me to-morrow' (520). There is in man, however, no motive which would, if there were no human conventions about promising, *cause* me to labour with you today. Generosity is commonly not strong enough (519). And self-interest will be inoperative, because I can not foresee any reason for thinking that you will help me tomorrow, even if I do help you today, especially as you are not likely to be particularly grateful to me for a service which you know is rendered only out of egotism (519). Hence if things are just left to nature, 'I leave you to labour alone: You treat me in the same manner. The seasons change; and both of us lose our harvests for want of mutual confidence and security' (521). The same argument applies to the exchange of goods as well as of services, when these goods cannot actually be delivered. This will be the case when the goods in question are either not present, like a 'house, twenty leagues distant', or not 'individual' (520). Property appears to be not 'individual' when it consists of *any* one or more things of a certain kind (e.g. '[any] ten bushels of corn, or [any] five hogsheads of wine'), without its being determined *which* things of this kind are someone's property (520). For example, I may own a share in a company making slippers, without there being any answer to the question, 'Which part of the company do I own?', though for I own part of it, I own no particular part of it. In this case, I could not hand over ('deliver') the part I own, even were this physically possible, for there is no distinguishable part, owned by me, to be handed over.

Just as with a similar defect in our nature (namely, that there is no natural incentive to abstain from taking the possessions of others), that defect in our nature which prevents us from exchanging services, and property which is large, absent, or not 'individual', must be remedied, not by altering human motivation, which is impossible 'unless aided by omnipotence', but by redirecting the motives we already have (521). This is done by inventing a sign, the words 'I promise', which subject a man to the penalty of not being trusted if he uses them and then does not perform what he says he promises (522). The use of the words 'I promise' has also the function, the importance of which Hume exaggerates, of distinguishing between what I do out of generosity and what I do as part of a bargain, as they are not used in the former case (521–2). (I do something for somebody, or give him something, without extracting a promise from him in return.) The institution of promising therefore redirects self-interest, or causes it to seek its end in 'an oblique and artificial manner' (521). If I help you gather your crops today, in exchange for a promise that you will help me with mine tomorrow, I perform my part of the bargain from the self-interested motive of getting later help from you, and you help me from the self-interested motive of not incurring the penalties attached by convention to promise-breaking. These motives would not lead to the desired effect in the absence of the convention of promising and the penalties imposed by this convention on promise-breaking. Hume at first quite rightly says the 'form of words *constitutes* [my italics] what we call a *promise*' (522), but later, in a passage that I shall discuss, he says, 'A resolution is the natural act of the mind, which promises express: But were there no more than a resolution in the case, promises wou'd only declare our former motives, and wou'd not create any new motive or obligation' (522). Hume thinks that the invention of promises is an obvious one, not at all beyond the capacity of human nature (522).

Hume describes self-interest as being the first (natural) obligation to the performance of promises (523). Since promise-keeping is in the public interest, we will (by sympathy, presumably, though Hume does not say so, with those who are hurt by our undermining this useful institution) feel disapprobation when promises are broken. This disapprobation will be strengthened (though it cannot be created) by education and the artifices of politicians (523), as is the case with our approval of justice generally.

Hume seems to think that, because it is not made obligatory, to do something merely because we have expressed a resolution to do it, we must '*feign* a new act of the mind', that of willing oneself under an obligation (523). He believes that he has demonstrated that such an act of the mind is impossible, but suggests, very oddly, that we have no alternative but to put up with this impossibility because of the usefulness of promising. He appears to think that the impossibility of willing one-self under an obligation does not hinder promising from being an artificial virtue, as it *does* prevent it from being a natural virtue (523).

Hume asserts that the fact that our obligation to keep our promises is not a natural one is confirmed by the following considerations. An act of the will (at this stage Hume must be assuming that, if promise-keeping were a natural obligation, it would have to consist in an *act of the will*, presumably the act of willing oneself under an obligation) without being expressed can confer no obligation (523). (A promise, obviously, would have to be made known to the promisee before it could be either obligatory or useful. Hume has earlier (516) contended that men would not be able to bind themselves in the absence of human conventions, even if they could 'perceive each other's thoughts by intuition'. His idea may be that, if one *could* will oneself under an obli-gation, one ought to be able to do this without having to say the words 'I promise' out loud.) 'The expression [saying 'I promise'] being once brought in as *subservient to the will*, soon *becomes* the *principal part* [Hume earlier said 'constitutes'] of the promise [all italics mine] ' (523), which is equally binding whether the promiser intends to do what he promises or not. Some intention, over and above simply saying the words 'I promise', is necessary, for 'tho' the expression makes *on most occasions* the whole of the promise [my italics] ' (523), a man will not be bound if he utters the words 'I promise' without intending to bind himself, perhaps because he does not understand what the words mean. Hume seems to think that it is *contradictory* that, though a man *is* bound, although he does not intend to do what he promised, he is *not* bound if he uses the words 'I promise' without any intention of binding himself, either because he does not know what the word 'promise' means, or because he is 'in jest only' (523-4). He appears to think that these contradictions can be accounted for on the theory that promise-keeping is an artificial, but not on the theory that it is a natural, obliga-tion (524). (There is, however, no 'contradiction' to be accounted for, for the intention which is necessary, if we are to be put under an obliga-tion by our saying the words 'I promise', is an intention *to become bound*, whereas the intention, the absence of which does not mean that we are not bound, is an *intention to keep the promise*. He is right, however, in thinking that it is because of human convention that a man who says 'I promise', without intending to bind himself, is not bound, whereas a man who says 'I promise', without intending to do what he promises, is bound.)

Hume thinks that creating a new obligation, which he has shown to be impossible, is so 'mysterious and incomprehensible' that it may be compared to *'transubstantiation,* or *holy orders'*. Here the use of certain words, coupled with an intention on the part of the priest, is supposed to change the nature of an external object, e.g. turn wine into the blood of Christ, in the case of transubstantiation. The effects of taking orders (524), in so far as these are supposed to produce some (natural) effect on the person ordained, other than the conventional effect of changing his legal status (524 n.), also resemble the effects of promising. Promises have to serve a useful human purpose and may be made as contradictory as this purpose requires (524). The fact that we are less worried about what happens to us in the next world than about what happens to us in this, however, enables us to be consistent about the monstrous doctrine that a priest may render a ceremony ineffica- cious by withholding his intention. Where the awful consequences of being consistent affect us only in the next world, which concerns us less than this one, we do not take the trouble to avoid them. Since it seems obvious that the mere use of certain words can have no effect in, say, changing the fate in the next world of a baby, it has been assumed that an *intention* on the part of the priest to change its fate must be neces- sary. This doctrine *has* been consistently maintained, even though it has the 'terrible' (and, I think Hume thinks, immoral) consequence that a priest can publicly baptize a baby, but render the ceremony inefficacious by privately and deceitfully withholding his intention. It is equally inconsistent to allow a promise the agent does not intend to keep to have the same effect in binding the promiser as promises the agent does intend to keep, but this inconsistency has to be allowed because of the inconvenient social consequences of not regarding promises that the promiser intends to break as binding (525). I think he has it at the back of his mind that it is an inconvenient consequence of the view that promising consists in a mental act (which is distinct from the saying of the words 'I promise') of willing oneself under an obligation that, if one were to say 'I promise', but secretly decide not to will oneself under an obligation, one would not have promised, and so not be bound.[1]

Hume thinks that the fact that promises extracted by means of force

---

[1] 'If the secret direction of the intention, said every man of sense, could in- validate a contract; where is our security? And yet a metaphysical schoolman might think, that, where an intention was supposed to be requisite, if that inten- tion really had not place, no consequence ought to follow, and no obligation be imposed. The casuistical subtilties may not be greater than the subtilties of lawyers, hinted at above; but as the former are *pernicious*, and the latter *innocent* and even *necessary*, this is the reason of the very different reception they meet with from the world' (E200 n.).

are not binding is another reason for thinking that promise-keeping is not a natural virtue. I think the idea Hume has in mind is that if promising had some 'natural' effect, it would have this effect from whatever motive it was done. (The consequences of pulling a trigger are the same, from whatever motive the trigger is pulled.) You would expect, in this case, that promising would have the same effect, whether the motive was fear of being killed by a brigand, if one does not promise him a ransom, and fear of not being treated by a surgeon, if one does not promise him a fee. It is, I think Hume is saying, just a decision, made for the convenience of society, that people are to be bound by the latter, but not by the former promise (525). This proves that the effect of promising is artificial (i.e. that it is the result of human artifice) rather than natural. What Hume means is that it is a human decision to enforce by means of sanctions the promise to the surgeon, but not to enforce the promise to the brigand. To impose sanctions is something human beings can decide, whereas they cannot decide to make or not make something morally obligatory.

COMMENTS

(1) Perhaps it would be best to start by clearing up a confusion, which vitiates Hume's argument to some considerable extent. He seems to think that to put, or will, ourselves under an obligation involves altering the moral properties of something, which on his view would involve altering people's sentiments. 'Immediately' altering moral properties of something, i.e. altering its moral properties without first altering it in some other respect, he rightly thinks is impossible (517 n.). But, of course, altering something is not impossible, and, as a result of our altering it, we may alter its moral properties; we may even alter it in order to alter its moral properties. For example, by marrying a woman you may cause it to become morally permissible to sleep with her, but this does not mean that you simply will an alteration in the moral properties of a projected act, e.g. change it from being morally wrong to being morally permissible to sleep with a given woman. You alter your relationship with the woman in some non-moral respect, by marrying her, and so cause the act of sleeping with her to change from being an act of sleeping with a woman to whom you are not married, which is immoral whether you will it to be immoral or not, to being an act of sleeping with a woman to whom you are married, which is morally permissible whether you will it to be permissible or not. In other words, whether a certain *kind* of action is immoral or not has nothing to do with what anyone wills, but whether a projected action

is a certain kind of action or not can be something to do with what one wills.

What I have just said applies to promising. By uttering the words 'I promise to marry you' you cause a projected action, marrying someone, to change from being an action you have not promised to do to being an action you have promised to do. In this way you may cause it to be obligatory, when it was not obligatory before. But, of course, you have in no way altered the moral fact, that keeping one's promises is obligatory, by deliberately altering a future action from being one you have not to one you have promised to do. You have changed the action, not the rule, nor do you in any way alter people's moral sentiments about promise-keeping or promise-breaking when you make a promise. You have, of course, altered their sentiments towards an action you perform if, before performing it, you promise not to, but this is only because you cause this action to be one of a kind towards which they had hostile sentiments already.

(2) Hume, I think, is entirely right in regarding promising as something which could not occur without—he says 'would be unintelligible without'—human conventions. Promising is conventional in two ways. First of all, it is just a human decision that there is some word which, uttered before an act is performed, causes the omission of this act to incur social sanctions of various kinds. Secondly, it is just a matter of convention that the English words 'I promise', or equivalent words in other languages, have this function.

It seems obvious to me that all that is necessary to bind ourselves to perform a certain action is to say the words 'I promise' before we perform it, provided, as Hume himself says (523–4), we understand what the words mean, bind ourselves intentionally, are not in jest, and provided also we do not do such things as promise something to a tree, mistaking it for a man. Hume's arguments to show that there is no act of the mind 'attending' the words 'I promise', the occurrence of which puts us under an obligation, seem to me to be admirable. He is right in thinking that if promising consisted in such an act of the mind, promises would not have to be expressed (516). Promises have to be expressed, even if we could know one another's thoughts by intuition. Obviously I cannot make a promise without saying something to the person I am promising, or using some gesture (e.g. shaking hands) which conventionally fulfils the same purpose. Hume comes close to saying, though he does not actually say, that saying 'I promise' cannot be stating that some act of the mind was taking place for, if it did, promising could occur without my saying 'I promise', or some such words, which it cannot: 'promises wou'd only declare our former motives, and wou'd not create any new motive or obligation' (522). He is right, too, in thinking that the act of the mind 'attending' the words 'I promise' cannot be the act of resolving to do the thing I promise, for resolving to do something does not oblige me to do it, and I am obliged to do what I promise whether I resolve or intend to do what I promise or not (516, 524). He is also right in thinking that there can be no such thing as willing myself under an obligation, if this consists in simply altering the obligatoriness of a proposed act and altering nothing else (516-17, 517 n.). He does not, however, consider carefully enough the possibility, which we have seen to be the truth, that one can alter one's obligations by simply altering the features which an act would have, if performed, without in any way altering the fact that certain acts are right and others wrong, if performed. Why, then, does he think that an act of willing oneself under an obligation must be 'feigned' (523)?

Perhaps, however, he does not think that such an act must be feigned, and it is possible that another interpretation may be put on the words which suggest that he does think this. His actual words are as follows: 'The difficulties, that occur to us, in supposing a moral obligation to attend promises, we either surmount or elude. For instance; the expression of a resolution is not commonly suppos'd to be obligatory; and we cannot readily conceive how the making use of a certain form of words shou'd be able to cause any material difference. Here, therefore, we *feign* a new act of the mind, which we call the *willing* an obligation; and on this we suppose the morality to depend. But we have prov'd already, that there is no such act of mind, and consequently that promises impose no natural obligation' (523).

It would be nice to think that he was not saying that the invention of promising involved the feigning of an impossible act of the mind, but that philosophers have unnecessarily invented a new act of the mind, in order to explain why keeping promises is obligatory. 'We' in this case would refer to philosophers, instead of mankind. Perhaps, however, the most likely interpretation of this passage is simply that people have to invent this act of the mind, in the sense that people have to pretend that there is an act of the mind in order to convince themselves that their obligations can be altered by making a promise, for they cannot see how their obligations can be altered simply by saying certain words. It would then be nice to suppose, too, that Hume thinks they are just mistaken about this, and that our obligations *can* be altered, just by our saying certain words. And he does say, 'the expression makes on most occasions the whole of the promise' (523). And the reason why he thinks it does not make the whole of the promise *always*, is not that some mental act having to do with the promised act is also sometimes necessary, but that the words 'I promise' have to be said intentionally, by someone who knows what they mean. However, I do feel that he is attracted by the idea of usefulness being so important that even what is impossible and contradictory must be pressed into its service. For he says, 'since every new promise imposes a new obligation of morality on the person who promises, and since this new obligation arises from his will; 'tis one of the most mysterious and incomprehensible operations that can possibly be imagin'd' (524). And he does delight in the contradictions which he thinks are involved in promising (524), and may suppose these to be of the same order as feigning an impossible act of will.

So I really must conclude that Hume does think that we have to suppose that there is an impossible act of the mind, willing oneself under an obligation, in order that promising should be effective, and that he thinks this because he cannot see how the saying of certain words can alter our obligations. Why this should help, when he thinks he has shown that willing ourselves under an obligation cannot alter our obligations, any more than the saying of certain words can, he does not explain. Since, of course, there cannot be an impossible act of the mind, Hume cannot mean that we must invent, in the sense in which the spinning-jenny was invented, such an act, but must mean that we must invent, in the sense that people invent false stories, the fact that there is such an act. Quite how our supposing wrongly that there is such an act of the mind can make promising obligatory, he does not say. An extra premiss seems to be needed. Given that, supposing there is an impossible act of the mind that enables us to believe that promise-keeping is obligatory, we need the premiss that everybody's supposing promise-keeping to be obligatory is as good as promise-keeping's actually being obligatory. If all that people did was to suppose that promise-keeping was obligatory, this *would* be as good as promise-keeping's actually being obligatory, but it is clear that Hume thinks that promise-keeping is obligatory, and not just supposed to be, and he is surely right.

It is difficult to see why Hume gets himself in such a muddle, when he has himself given a perfectly correct account of promising, which is that the promising consists in the saying of the words, 'I promise to do so-and so', the saying of which words has, by convention, been assigned to it by society the function of making us liable to certain penalties if we do not do so-and-so. There is no earthly reason why society should not impose penalties on the omission of an action, if it is omitted after certain words have been said, but not impose any penalties for the omission, if these words have not been said. Since this is a socially useful institution, weakening it by breaking our promises comes to cause moral disapprobation.

It is natural to proceed from the topic of the impossible acts introduced in promising to consider the other contradictions which Hume thinks are involved in promising (524). He should not, and I think does not, mean that promising is contradictory in the sense that its specification is contradictory; if this were so, promising could not occur (although, of course, it also cannot occur if it involves the impossible act of willing oneself under an obligation, for what involves the impossible must itself be impossible). He must mean that it is contradictory in the sense that beliefs or attitudes or policies or behaviour can be contradictory. Contradictory beliefs, etc., do occur, and there is no impossibility of willing the impossible. He then must mean that our treatment of promises is contradictory (or perhaps better, inconsistent) in the sense that sometimes we regard an intention as necessary to put us under an obligation, at other times we do not. There is no contradiction or inconsistency, for the intention that is necessary is an intention to put ourselves under an obligation, whereas the intention that is not necessary is an intention to perform the action which is promised. It is not absolutely obvious to me why Hume supposes that the contradictions which he thinks are involved in promising show that promising is an artificial, rather than a natural, virtue. He would be right if by 'natural' in this context were meant that part of human nature which is exclusive of human beings, i.e. nature as opposed to man, for contradictory beliefs, attitudes, and policies are a human phenomenon. But, of course, human contradictions are not necessarily artificial or invented. People do not deliberately produce in themselves contradictory beliefs; they just occur. However, Hume is not far from being right on this point. The distinction made between an intention to bind oneself, which is necessary if one is to be under an obligation, and an intention to do what one promises, the absence of which does not absolve one from the obligation to do what one has promised, though not, as Hume supposed, contradictory or inconsistent, does mean that human beings have deliberately decided to treat the latter as binding, but the former as not binding. They do this on the grounds that it would not harm the usefulness of the institution of promising not to compel the keeping of unintentional promises, but would totally defeat the purpose of having this institution if promises made without the intention of being kept were not enforced. This entails that there are rules governing promising, which rules must be human inventions, though it does not actually entail that promises are human inventions (though they are). Nor should it be forgotten that, though man makes the rules, he does not make the usefulness of the rules, and the fact that it is useful to enforce promises that the promiser has no intention of *keeping*, but not promises he has no intention of making, is not in any way the result of human decision or artifice.

Hume's other argument to show that promises are human contrivances, viz. that the fact that we do not regard promises made under the threat of force as binding (525), is similar. It amounts to saying that it is a man-made rule, decided upon on account of its usefulness, that such promises shall not be binding. His conclusion here, however, is not that the obligation to keep our promises is man-made, but that promising is a human contrivance. It does not follow (though again, it is true) from the fact that there are man-made rules about promising that promising is a human contrivance, though the rules about it will be man-made. Hume does not clearly enough emphasize the fact that, though man deliberately invented promising, and deliberately enforces promise-keeping, he does not deliberately make it the case that promise-keeping is obligatory, and a virtue. If an artificial virtue were, as the phrase suggests, a disposition caused to be a virtue by a human decision that it should be a virtue (as opposed to being caused to be a virtue by some *other* human decision), then, as Hume ought to have realized, he has himself proved, by what he says about willing obligations, that there can be no such thing as an artificial virtue. What is artificial is that which is a virtue, not its being a virtue. Since the fact that promise-keeping is a virtue depends on its usefulness, and since what is useful is not something that men bring about, that certain promises ought to be kept and others broken is not the result of human fiat, though which promises are enforced and which are not is the result of human fiat. In other words, men decided to invent and enforce promise-keeping, and decided which kinds of promises to enforce and which kinds of promises not to enforce. However, the rules saying whether we ought to keep the man-made rules are not themselves man-made; nor are our approval of rule-keeping in general, and keeping the rules about promising in particular, man-made. Hume ought to have remembered a remark of his own about justice, which I have already quoted. 'Tho' justice be artificial, the sense of its morality is natural.' Though promise-keeping be artificial the sense of its morality is natural.

(3) Why does Hume think that, if promises are to be 'intelligible naturally', or a non-conventional phenomenon, it follows that 'there must be some act of the mind attending these words, *I promise*' (516)? He himself does not say why, but I think the reason must be this. Words themselves are conventional phenomena; it is always an arbitrary human decision that a word has the meaning or function it does have,

and not some other meaning or function, or no meaning at all. Hence, if promising consisted only in saying the words 'I promise', promising would be conventional, or an artificial human contrivance. Of course, all words, not just the words 'I promise', are conventional, but where strings of words forming declarative sentences like 'The cat is on the mat' are concerned, there is an extra-conventional element, namely, the phenomena these words describe. Though the meaning of these words is fixed by convention, whether there is a cat on the mat or not is something we cannot decide by deciding what these words are to mean. It would not follow from the fact that a sentence describes something 'outside itself' that what it describes is something natural; conventional phenomena can also be described by sentences, which are themselves conventional phenomena. However, if there was nothing that a sentence described, the uttering of a sentence would be a wholly conventional matter. If by 'act of the mind *attending* [my italics] these words *I promise*' Hume means 'described or asserted to occur by the words *I promise*', it follows that what he was looking for, and what he thought would have to be found if promising were to be a natural phenomenon, was something natural, which, when I say 'I promise to do so-and-so', I am describing or asserting to be occurring. At least one way, though not the only way, in which an act of the mind could attend the saying of the words 'I promise to do so-and-so' would be that these words are used to assert that this act of the mind is occurring.

If promising is just saying the words 'I promise', and not doing something distinct from saying these words, which I then use these words to report, it follows that promising is a human contrivance, for that some words should have this function, and that it should be the words 'I promise' that have this function, is entirely a matter of human decision. Though many philosophers have questioned it, it does seem to me—and I think it pretty obvious, really—that to promise *is* just to say the words 'I promise' in suitable circumstances (not when acting a part in a play, for example). Promising is not an occurrence which saying 'I promise' reports—i.e. not an act of the mind attending the words 'I promise'— because saying 'I promise' does not report anything; these words, indeed, are not used to make any sort of statement at all. If, *per impossibile*, these words did report the occurrence of something, they could not be used to report the occurrence of a promise for two reasons. If they did, the promise could occur without my saying the words 'I promise', or using any equivalent words or gestures, which would simply report this act, which might occur without being reported. Secondly, I could say the words in appropriate circumstances and, because I said that I was making a promise when I was not, *not* make a promise. In fact, if I say the words 'I promise' in the right circumstances, I must be making a promise. The whole purpose of promising would be defeated if one were allowed to say 'I promise' in normal circumstances and *not* make a promise.[2]

I suspect that it was partly because Hume took it for granted that there must be something, the actual promising, distinct from the saying of the words 'I promise', which saying these words required or described or stated to occur, that he supposed that there must be an act of the mind 'attending' the saying of these words. Since to suppose that there must be *anything* occurring over and above the saying of the words 'I promise' is just a mistake, it is not surprising that Hume could not find it. However, promising binds one, and one cannot get oneself bound without uttering the words 'I promise', or something equivalent. One could not allow, as Hume insists, something covert, which saying 'I promise' simply reported, to be the promise, for this would allow people deceitfully to pretend to promise by saying 'I promise' without actually promising. It would obviously be highly inconvenient to allow business men to say 'I promise' to their customers and not have bound themselves.

A rather botched attempt has been made by some philosophers to escape these two difficulties by maintaining that when I say 'I promise' I *am* reporting an occurrence, not an occurrence which is distinct from my saying the words, but my saying the words 'I promise' themselves. (They should add that I am also claiming that the circumstances are right; that the person saying 'I promise' knows what the words mean and is not joking, for example.) On this view the sentence 'I promise to do such-and-such' enables the person using it to make a statement which is about itself. In this case, if I say the words, my statement that I am saying the words is true, and if my statement that I am saying the words is true, I must be saying the words. Since saying 'I promise to do such-and-such' is not reporting anything outside itself, this view avoids the difficulties we have been considering, that it is impossible for the promise to occur without the words, or the words without the promise.

This view must be rejected, however. To say 'I promise' is, as I have

[2] 'It is evident, that the will or consent alone never transfers property, nor causes the obligation of a promise (for the same reasoning extends to both) but the will must be expressed by words or signs, in order to impose a tie upon any man. The expression being once brought in as subservient to the will, soon becomes the principal part of the promise; nor will a man be less bound by his word, though he secretly give a different direction to his intention, and withhold the assent of his mind' (E199 n.–200 n.).

already said, not to make a statement of any sort, and so, *a fortiori*, not to report the occurrence of anything at all. For it would be just plain ridiculous to respond to anyone who said 'I promise to do such-and-such' in ways in which it would be quite appropriate to respond to a statement, for example, by saying 'I agree', by saying 'That's true' or 'That's not true', by saying 'I believe you, or 'I don't believe you', by saying 'You are lying' or 'You are mistaken'. And this inappropriateness is not the kind of inappropriateness involved in saying something in odd circumstances, e.g. saying 'It's a fine day' to someone who is crying out for help. There are circumstances in which it is quite appropriate for me to say 'It's a fine day', but none in which it is appropriate to say 'That's true' to someone who has just said 'I promise to do such-and-such'.

The view that when I say 'I promise' I am making a statement, may gain some spurious plausibility from the times when I say some such thing as 'I'll take you to the match tomorrow. And that's a promise.' The words 'And that's a promise' do seem both to cause my remark to be a promise, so enabling me to promise, and at the same time to be a statement. However, though the words 'And that's a promise', in conjunction with my previous words, do turn the whole string of words 'I will. . . . And that's a promise' *into* a promise, they do *not* make a statement. There is no possibility of my saying 'And that's a promise', and at the same time not promising, in this kind of situation; nor is there any possibility of my saying 'But that's not a promise' when it is a promise. 'And that's a promise' is not like 'And that's a widgeon', which informs someone, rightly or wrongly, that something is a widgeon. It is more like 'And you're goalkeeper', said by the team captain, which does not report the pre-existing fact that the person addressed is a goalkeeper, but turns him into one by assigning him this function or office.

The words 'And that's a promise' *could* have the function of making a statement. For example, if I were trying to explain to someone what a promise was, I could say 'I promise to increase your pocket money. That's (an example of) a promise', which would be true if I really did intend to make a promise. I could say, deceitfully, 'Shut the door. That's a promise', which would be false. But in the cases discussed in the previous paragraph, my saying 'That's a promise' turns what I am saying into a promise. The words 'And that's a promise' only, cannot function by themselves to make a promise because without the preceding words, what I was promising would not be specified. That 'And that's a promise' is furthermore shown not to make a statement by the fact that one cannot say 'I agree' or 'That's true' to someone who has just said 'And that's a promise', when he says this to make a promise.

It is a great pity that Hume does not fully realize that all promising is is saying the words 'I promise' in suitable circumstances. (He does, as we have seen, realize this sometimes (523).) He would not then have been tempted to talk about our having to feign the impossible act of willing ourselves under an obligation (523), or talk of 'one of the most mysterious and incomprehensible operations that can possibly be imagin'd' (524). It is at this point that he compares promising to '*transubstantiation*, or *holy orders*' (524-5). He thinks that there is as much difficulty in seeing how saying 'I promise' can affect our obligations as there is in seeing how the priest's words can affect the nature of a material object (by turning it from bread into flesh) or a man (by making him holy). Because we cannot see how saying the words can be efficacious in either case, we have to have a real intention, in the case of transubstantiation or holy orders (or marriage or baptism), and feign one in the case of promising. For myself, of course, I cannot see that it is any easier to explain how an *intention* can change bread into flesh than a *word* can—both are impossible—nor can I see that there is any difficulty at all in seeing how saying 'I promise' can change my obligations. Hume himself gets the answer right when he says 'I mean so far, as holy orders are suppos'd to produce the *indelible character*. In other respects they are only a legal qualification' (524 n.). By this he means that he has no difficulty in seeing how the ordination ceremony —which, like promising, consists simply in the saying of certain words —can turn a man into a priest, in so far as it merely affects his legal status, for a priest simply is a man who has endured the ordination ceremony, being properly qualified, the ceremony performed in the stipulated manner by a duly appointed person, and so on. It is clear that it is the fact that such ceremonies make changes in other respects that Hume does not understand. Similarly, there is no difficulty in seeing how deceased men and women can be turned into saints, if to be a saint is simply to be a person in respect of whom the canonization ritual has been properly performed. A man can be made a BA, or an OBE, or given 'out' in precisely the same way. What Hume fails to realize fully is that saying 'I promise' changes our obligations in just the way in which the marriage ceremony changes the legal status of the men and women who undergo it. Saying 'I promise to do such-and-such' brings the action that I promise to perform under the conventional rule that attaches penalties to the non-performance of this action if these words have been said, which it will not incur if they have not been said. And we *ought* to obey this rule because it is a useful one, and disobeying it might tend to disrupt it, or would disrupt it, if everybody else also disobeyed it.

Hume is quite right to distinguish the two questions, whether promising could exist without human conventions, and whether it derives its obligatoriness from human conventions (516). There could have been rules about promising, which rules we ought to keep, even if promising were a natural phenomenon, and did not owe its very existence to rules. There are rules about the use of the countryside, for example, even though the countryside, or parts of it, is a natural, as opposed to a man-made, phenomenon. The point he is making is that the promise is brought into existence by the rules about promising, as the operation of castling is brought into existence by the rules of chess, or the crime of revoking by the rules of contract bridge. His best view, though he is, as we shall see, not consistent about it, is that the words 'I promise' are like a pawn in chess. A pawn is, by definition, anything which can move according to the rules laid down for a pawn in chess, and a promise is any symbol which carries out certain functions given to it by men. What this function is we shall see later.

Hume's argument to show that if, *per impossibile*, there could be such a thing as promising, if there were no human conventions, it could not, without these conventions, be obligatory, need not detain us long. His main premiss, that an action cannot be a duty unless there is in a normal man some motive prompting him to perform it, is simply false. His other premiss, that without human conventions enforcing promise-keeping, there would be in men no motive for keeping their promises, needs a little clarification. There is no such class of actions as the actions which would be promised if there were such an institution as promise-keeping. Any action at all can be promised, and there is no need for these actions to have anything in common. Hence there will be a motive for performing some of these actions, which could be promised, but not others. There can, however, be no such thing as a motive the distinctive features of which is to perform the actions which would be promised, if there were such a thing as promising, for these actions can have no common feature which could be that feature of them which attracted us, and so gave us a motive for performing them. There is, however, a class of actions which could exist in the absence of human conventions, which class might be described as actions which it would be very useful if they could be made capable of being promised. Examples of this class of actions would be helping someone else with his harvest tomorrow. It would be useful if such things could be promised, for then I could, by promising something in return, offer others an inducement to help me with my harvest today. Hume is quite right in thinking that neither benevolence, self-interest, gratitude, nor any other motive in normal men would, except very occasionally, prompt them to do such things as help other people with their harvests in the absence of their being able to receive a promise of help in return.

(4) Perhaps one reason why Hume raised the possibility that there was an act of the mind, which consisted in willing oneself under an obligation, is this. It is, Hume thought, a common view, the view of ordinary men, that promising consists in willing oneself under an obligation. It also seems natural for philosophers to suppose that when I say 'I promise to do such-and-such' I am stating something—the discovery that not all sentences make statements is a fairly recent one in the history of philosophy—and, if so, still more natural to suppose that what I am stating is that promising is occurring. Then, if promising consists in willing oneself under an obligation, it follows that what we are stating to be occurring when we say 'I promise . . .' is an act of willing oneself under an obligation. Hume's arguments to show that there can be no such thing as an act, which is the act of willing oneself under an obligation *and nothing else*, are conclusive. It seems to me to be just possible that the reason why he thought an act of willing oneself under an obligation had to be feigned was that, if promising is to occur, statements expressed in the words 'I promise . . .' would have to be true, and so in order for us to suppose that promising did occur, we would have to feign an act of promising, or willing oneself under an obligation, the existence of which would make them true. This might well be a correct account of how some philosophers have wrongly supposed that there must be some act of willing oneself under an obligation, distinct from the saying of the words 'I promise . . .'. It does not seem plausible, however, to suggest that ordinary people must feign such an act. But what I have said is little more than speculation about Hume's possible mental processes, and not an account of anything he actually says.

(5) Hume, as we have seen, thinks that if promises are a nonconventional phenomenon, there must be some act of the mind attending the words 'I promise'. This act of the mind cannot be that of willing oneself under an obligation, for this is impossible. Hume's argument to show that willing oneself under an obligation is impossible, if, as he himself supposes, the morality of something consists in its being generally approved or disapproved of (517), is straightforward. So, really, is his argument to show that willing oneself under an obligation is impossible on the view of his opponents, that the morality of actions is apprehended by reason (517 n.), which view is discussed in Book II, Part I of the *Treatise*. I can, however, think of no reason why Hume should think

that it is 'still more evident' that willing oneself under an obligation is impossible on the views of his opponents than it is on his own view, unless this reason is that it is to some extent possible to alter people's sentiments, given enough time, but is quite impossible to alter the moral 'relations' of actions without first altering them in some other respect.

It should be noticed, however, that Hume's argument is designed to show that it is impossible to change the moral properties of things 'immediately', as the 'pure effect of the will' (517 n.). By changing the moral properties of things immediately, he means changing these properties without first changing in some other way the things which possess these properties. He is quite right in thinking that it is impossible to do this. We can change a man's obligations by warning him or marrying him, but we cannot alter his obligations without first altering him in some other way. Hume is, however, perhaps not as clear as he ought to be that the obligation resulting from a promise is not the effect of an 'immediate' change in the moral properties of things. Hume is quite right in thinking that we can only change the moral properties of things by first changing their other properties, but, of course, saying 'I promise to do such-and-such' before doing such-and-such does change the non-moral properties of such-and-such; it causes such-and-such to be an action the performance or omission of which has been preceded by the saying of the words 'I promise to do such-and-such'. Hence if these words have been said in the appropriate kind of context, my saying them causes a future action to be one of keeping or breaking a promise, which it would not have been otherwise. Hence saying 'I promise' does change our obligations, not immediately, but by first altering in some other way the action I promise to perform.

(6) Hume remarks, 'When a man says *he promises any thing*, he in effect expresses a *resolution* of performing it; and along with that, by making use of this *form of words*, subjects himself to the penalty of never being trusted again in case of failure' (522). This remark is a little puzzling, in view of his contention that a promise has still been made and is still binding even if the person making it has no intention of keeping it (516), and in view of his claim, 'the expression makes on most occasions the whole of the promise' (523). Hume, of course, could not possibly have been expected to be familiar with the modern distinction between expressing something and making a statement about it, drawn by Professor Ayer in *Language, Truth and Logic. Expressing* pain by saying 'ouch', and sadness by saying 'alas' is not the same thing as saying 'I am in pain' or 'I am sad'. It could not be Hume's view, or, at any rate, ought not to be his view, that when I say 'I promise . . .' I

am making a statement about my resolution to perform the action I promise, for then it would follow that I had not promised, if I did not have the resolution, whereas Hume rightly thinks I have promised. And it may well be that expressing a resolution does not entail having the resolution expressed. One can certainly express regret without feeling any regret. (Though the statement 'He expressed the resolution [intention] of doing-such-and-such' does not entail 'He was resolved [intended] to do such-and-such'; 'He expressed *his* resolution [intention] to do such-and-such' does entail 'He was resolved [intended] to do such-and-such'.) Nevertheless, I think that if one has expressed a resolution or intention, one has not promised; this follows from the fact that promises are commonly contrasted with mere expressions of intention. Promising 'contextually' implies that one intends to do what one promises, in the sense that if one promises, one knowingly leads others to expect that one will do what one has promised, but if their expectations are disappointed, this does not mean that one has not promised. Similarly, if one says 'It is raining', one knowingly leads others to expect that one believes that it is raining, but if one does not believe that it is raining, it does not follow that one has said what is false.

(7) When Hume is speaking of the need for promising to facilitate commercial transactions (520), he speaks of goods which, because not 'individual', e.g. 'ten bushels of corn or five hogsheads of wine', cannot be transferred by 'mere expression and consent'. What does he mean by 'mere expression and consent'? Earlier he has said, 'One cannot transfer the property of a particular house, twenty leagues distant; because the consent cannot be attended with delivery, which is a requisite circumstance.' *Delivery,* or rather, mutual delivery (*A* hands something over to *B* at the same time that *B* hands something over to *A*), is necessary, because where there is not immediate mutual delivery, trust that a later delivery will be made must be assumed, which Hume thinks is impossible where there can be no promising. Some form of *expression* (which need not be in words) is necessary, over and above delivery, in order to indicate that material objects are being handed over as part of a bargain, and not for some other reason. They are needed, for example, to distinguish giving someone my hedge clippers from bartering them, trying to get someone to repair them, or just to inspect and admire or carry them for me. But where there are no promises, goods cannot be transferred by *mere* expression and consent, by *A* saying to *B* some such thing as 'I'll swop you twenty cigarette cards for ten marbles' (expression) and *B* saying 'You're on' (consent)—for simultaneous mutual delivery is necessary if there is to be no reliance at all on promising and trust.

I should perhaps make it clear that, whatever Hume may have said to the contrary, it is possible to promise without using the words 'I promise', and not only for the reason that one can promise in French or Greek as well as in English. When one says that one will do something, one can, if the context in which these words are said is suitable, be described as having promised to do that thing. Indeed, it is much commoner for promises to be made without than with the words 'I promise', and I suspect that using these words rather adds to the solemnity of the promise than creates a promise. When one says to someone who has no interest in the matter that one is going to do something, then one has not promised; but if one says to someone 'I'll meet you at four o'clock', then one probably has promised, or, if the arrangement was too casual for one to be described as having promised, one is still under some obligation to do what one has said one is going to do.

I have also spoken as if promising puts one under an obligation to do what one promised, as Hume did. Promising, however, does not always make it obligatory to do what one has promised, even when there is no element such as misunderstanding, or threat of force. For one's obligation to keep a promise can always be overridden by greater obligations which one might not have foreseen. For this reason it might be better to speak of making a promise as giving rise to a prima-facie obligation (or prima-facie duty) to do what one has promised, or as putting one under *some* obligation to do what one has promised.

If someone who says 'I promise . . .' is making a statement about the very words he is using when he promises, then, presumably, he must be making the *same* statement about these words that someone else who says, in the third person or past tense or both, that he is promising . . ., or that he promised. . . . Quite apart from the fact that someone saying 'I promise' is not making a statement at all, but performing the activity reported by corresponding statements in the second or third person, or in the past tense (just as someone swearing is not making a statement, let alone the same statement as anyone else reporting the fact that he is swearing) there is the following conclusive argument against this. It is quite possible to say some such thing as 'I am now talking in English', which both makes the same statement as does 'He is now talking in English', said of the speaker by someone else, and is about the words he himself is using to make this statement. But in this case someone just reports that he is talking in English, but does not say what it is that he is (in English) saying. For him to say what it is that he is saying is impossible, for if anyone were to try, what he would be saying would be something like 'I am saying in English "The cat is on the mat"', and in that case he is not saying in English, 'The cat is on the mat'; he is saying in English 'I am saying in English "The cat is on the mat"'. Hence if someone (Robinson, let us say) were to try to say what he is promising, and at the same time to make a promise, he would find it impossible. What he would have to say would be some such thing as 'I am uttering the words "I promise to have tea with you, Smith"', from which it would follow that he had not uttered the words 'I promise to have tea with you, Smith', but the different words 'I am uttering the words "I promise to have tea with you, Smith"'. Furthermore, anyone who utters the words 'I am uttering the words "I promise to have tea with you, Smith"' is precisely not making a promise, because he has not *used* the words 'I promise to have tea with you, Smith' (which are in quotation marks) but only mentioned them. The only way in which one could use the words 'I am uttering the words "I promise to have tea with you, Smith"' to make a true statement would be to have two voices, and to say with one voice 'I promise to have tea with you, Smith' and with the other 'I am uttering the words "I promise to have tea with you, Smith"'. In this case, he would be using the first sentence to make a promise, but not to make a statement, and the second sentence to report the occurrence of the words 'I promise . . .', but not to make a promise.

It follows from this that if Jones reports that Robinson is making a promise, by saying 'Robinson is promising Smith to have tea with him', he could not possibly be making the same statement that Robinson is making when he says 'I promise to have tea with you, Smith', assuming, for the sake of argument, that Robinson is making a statement at all, which he is not. For Jones must be, roughly, saying 'Robinson is uttering the words "I promise to have tea with you, Smith"', or some words which perform the same function, and he knows what these words mean, and the circumstances are appropriate. (For example, Smith must not be deaf.) But if Robinson were to make this statement, what he would be saying would be, 'I am uttering the words "I promise to have tea with you, Smith", or some such words which perform the same function, and I know what these words mean, and the circumstances are appropriate.' But anyone saying this has not made a promise, for the reason that has been given, namely, that he has not *used* the words 'I promise to have tea with you, Smith', which occur only within quotation marks in the sentence that he has used.

In any case, where statements are concerned there are two questions which can be asked about them. Firstly, one can ask the question whether the appropriate conditions have been fulfilled for someone correctly to be described as having made a statement at all, and, secondly, if he has made a statement, we can raise the question whether he has made a true statement. But where promising is concerned, there are not these two questions. We can ask whether the appropriate conditions have been fulfilled for someone to be described as having made a promise, but we cannot then go on to ask whether or not he has made a true promise (as opposed to truly having made a promise, which *ex hypothesi*, he has). The latter question simply does not make sense.

(8) It looks obvious that Hume's argument to show that promise-keeping is an artificial virtue (he himself never quite puts his conclusion in this way, but it is the way of putting it that makes it properly analogous to his view that justice is an artificial virtue) should be this. In the absence of human conventions, promising could not occur, and could not alter our obligations. But with human conventions promising could occur, and could alter our obligations. And he does say that his arguments—and he himself is uncomfortable about them—prove more than that promises cannot *naturally* occur and *naturally* alter our obligations, but that they cannot occur or alter our obligations *at all*. For example, if we can only alter our obligations by altering our sentiments, and cannot alter our sentiments (517), and promises must, if they occur at all, alter our obligations, it follows that they cannot occur at all. Similarly, it follows from the same two premises that they cannot alter our obligations. Again, if willing oneself under an obligation is impossible, it is impossible to create an obligation to keep promises by creating a convention that they ought to be kept, for creating a convention boils down to a large number of acts of will on the part of a large number of individual people, and it is difficult to see how, if one act of will cannot alter our obligations, a large number of acts of will can alter our obligations. Hume's view, however, if he were consistent, ought not to be that we by convention cause promise-keeping to be obligatory, but that by convention we cause promise-breaking to be penalized, and promise-breaking is wrong, whether human beings will or conventionally decide that it shall be wrong or not, simply because it is useful that promises generally be kept. Promise-keeping is a convention, but it cannot be a convention that conventions ought to be kept.

SECTION VI

Some Farther Reflexions[1] Concerning Justice and Injustice

THIS is the last of the sections that I shall summarize in full. In the opening paragraph, Hume repeats that it is upon the observance of three 'fundamental laws of nature, *that of the stability of possession, of its transference by consent*, and *of the performance of promises*' that the 'peace and security of human society entirely depend' (526). He states that though these rules impose restraint upon men's passions, they are nevertheless the offspring of the passions they restrain, and are simply 'more refined ways' of satisfying these passions (526). (He elsewhere (489) says that self-interest, which in the absence of justice would lead men to take the possessions of others, itself imposes, by creating these rules, this restraint upon itself.) Thus there are no 'peculiar original principles' prompting us to perform just actions; our ordinary motives suffice. Hume seems to think that it *follows* from this that justice is an artifical virtue—that it is a human invention, to which man is impelled by normal motives, other than a desire to be just as such. To be a natural virtue it would have to be the object of a distinct and irreducible passion (like our desire for food or drink). The rest of this section is taken up by three arguments in support of the view that justice is not a natural virtue. I shall summarize them one by one.

I. Hume argues that the 'vulgar' definition of justice, as 'a constant and perpetual will of giving everyone his due', *presupposes* that there are already such things as rights and property (man's due) existing antecedently to and independently of justice. He says he has already briefly pointed out the fallacy of this opinion (490-1), and proceeds to do so in more detail. He thinks that justice cannot be defined as giving every man his due, for, on the contrary, man's due must be defined in terms of justice, i.e. a man's due is whatever (an artificial rule of) justice assigns to him (526-7). It would follow from this that the function of creating rules of justice cannot be to enforce rights which men already have. Making rules of justice actually creates these rights, which do not exist until after they have been made.

If, *per impossibile*, justice were giving every man his due, rights and

---

[1] The table of contents says 'reflections'.

property would have to be something existing in nature, something already there to be respected, whereas Hume thinks that rights and property are assigned to people by artificial, man-made rules of justice. If rights and property existed antecedently to and independently of rules of justice, they would have to consist (1) of some sensible quality, or (2) some relation between one inanimate object and another, or (3) of an external relation between an object (the property) and persons (their owners), or (4) some 'internal' relation. (1) It cannot consist of any sensible quality, for a thing's sensible qualities do not change when the property changes hands. (A thing does not change its colour, for example, when it is sold by one person to another.) (2) Nor can it consist of any relation between the property and other inanimate objects, for the same reason. (A mill, for example, can change hands without changing its situation.) (3) It cannot consist of any 'external and corporeal' relation to intelligent beings (the owners of the property) for it can stand in all these relations to 'brute beasts' *without* becoming their property. (For example, an animal can occupy a territory, just as much as a man can, but this does not make this territory the animal's property.) Hence neither occupation, for example, nor any other external corporeal relation is what property consists of, though it may be because of these relations that we assign something to someone as his property. Since corporeal relations between things and human beings do not constitute property, but give rise to it, they must create property by altering what Hume calls (4) 'internal' relations, (perhaps it would have been better if he had said 'intentional' relations) between goods and the minds of people. They alter these internal relations by causing people to have 'a sense of duty in abstaining from that object, and in restoring it to the first possessor'. Hence property is whatever we have a duty to abstain from taking; it is not so much the case that we have a duty to abstain from taking a thing because it is antecedently and independently someone's property; property is *defined* as whatever we have a 'sense' that it is our duty not to take (which implies, I believe Hume thinks, that it is whatever we have a *duty* not to take) (527).

Hume thinks it *follows* from what he has said that justice is an artificial virtue. This can be denied only if, contrary to what he thinks he has just proved, nature has endowed such things as not taking that to which we are not externally related by, say, the relation of occupation, with a moral beauty or deformity (527-8). (His argument consists in maintaining that there are two sets of facts about property, natural facts, such as that a given man actually occupies a certain piece of land, and conventional or artificial facts, such as that there is a rule preventing other people from, say, damaging this piece of land.) Hume thinks that, if justice were a natural virtue, interfering with the land someone occupies would of itself produce disapproval, as being in a hot room makes us feel hot, or as being in the presence of the opposite sex makes us feel sexual desire. His view then is that these natural facts do not by themselves affect our sentiments; we do not disapprove of damaging land someone occupies, unless this is proscribed by a rule allocating to men the land they occupy.

Hume next gives two reasons for thinking that nature has *not* attached the pleasurable sentiment of approval simply to abstaining from taking goods to which certain other men (the owners of these goods) are related by the aforementioned 'external' and 'corporeal'—and so 'natural' and non-conventional—relations, e.g. occupation (528). Firstly, if nature had annexed approval to conduct with respect to material objects which stood in certain external, corporeal relations to people (e.g. occupation) this would be obvious, which it is not. If the sentiment of approval had been aroused by such behaviour, there would have been no need for us to try to convince ourselves that property existed antecedently to rules of justice by means of a circular definition, i.e. by defining justice in terms of property and then defining property in terms of justice (528).

Secondly, rules of justice have all the marks of being artificial, none of being natural. Hume mentions three such marks. (1) 'They are too numerous to have proceeded from nature' (528). (Hume is thinking of such facts as that the emotional and physical structure (which is natural) of men from different places is very similar, whereas their customs (which are artificial) are very different.) (2) 'They [rules of justice] are changeable by human laws' (528). (You cannot successfully introduce legislation abolishing the natural appetite between the sexes, for example.) (3) They 'have all of them a direct and evident tendency to public good, and the support of civil society' (528). (Hume here forgets that many natural phenomena have this tendency.)

Hume ends this first part of Section VI by making two comments on the last of these three marks of being artificial. Firstly, he draws a distinction between those things which are designed to produce the public good, and those things which have this tendency, although they are not designed to have it. (Hospitals, for example, are designed to produce the public good, but a drug factory may produce the public good though designed to promote the interest of a limited liability company.) Hume thinks that rules of justice tend to produce the public good, although they have not been consciously designed to produce it (529). (His usual view (504 n.), which is less extreme, is that rules of justice *partly* owe the fact that they bring about the public good to deliberate intention on the part of man, *partly* because the effect the imagination has in causing us to choose them is beneficial, though not designedly so.) He argues, correctly, that, even if rules of justice had been intentionally chosen by men in order to bring about their general welfare, these rules would still have been artificial. Hume's second comment on the third of these three arguments is to suggest that rules of justice cannot owe their origin to the fact that they have been deliberately invented in order to produce the public good, because, if men had had enough benevolence to make them do this, they would have had enough benevolence to make these rules unnecessary in the first place. The motive for their invention is in fact not desire for the public good but self-love, which induces men 'to adjust themselves after such a manner as to concur in some system of conduct and behaviour' (529). Since this system is in the interest of each individual man (and adopted by him for this reason) it follows that it is in the public interest.

II Hume's second argument can very roughly and crudely be summarized: all virtues other than justice—the natural virtues—admit, like all natural qualities, of variations of degree; justice and injustice do not admit of such variations; therefore justice is not a natural virtue (529–30).

Hume makes no attempt to prove the first of his two premisses, that other virtues and vices admit of degrees, though I agree with him that it is true. He thinks the second premiss, that justice and injustice do not admit of degrees, follows from the fact that 'rights, obligations, and property' do not admit of degrees. Something is either one's property, or it is not; it cannot be more or less one's property. One either has a right to something, or one has not. One either has an obligation, or one does not have it. Though one may not have many rights or have them only for a short period, the rights one does have, for the time one has them, are 'absolute and entire'. One may have the right to make use of a hired horse only for a day, for example, but, for the period that one does have the right, one has as much right to it as its owner does on every other day.

Hume thinks that it *follows* from the fact that right, obligations, and property do not admit of variations of degree that we acquire or lose these things instantly, 'without any of that insensible gradation, which is remarkable in other qualities and relations' (530).

In a final, and very peculiar, paragraph in this second part of Section VI, Hume contends that 'in our common and negligent way of thinking' we find it difficult to accept *'that property, and right, and obligation admit not of degrees'* (530). This is because property and rights depend partly on public utility, and partly on 'the propensities of the imagination', both of which admit of degrees (531). They may incline us, for example, to the belief both that *A* does have a right to *A*, and that he does not. Hence *referees* often divide an estate between parties who have equal claims to the whole of it. *Civil laws*, however, are unable to do this, and so 'are necessitated to proceed on the most frivolous reasons in the world. Half rights and obligations, which seem so natural in common life, are perfect absurdities in their tribunal; for which reason they are often oblig'd to take half arguments for whole ones, in order to terminate the affair one way or the other' (531).

III. Hume's argument in II for the artificiality of justice relied upon the (alleged) fact that justice does not admit of degrees; his argument in III, an extremely difficult one, rests upon the inflexibility of justice (531–3). It is only by supposing that the laws of justice are artificial or man-made that we can explain how it is that they must be obeyed in all the cases to which they apply (are inflexible), do not admit of exceptions, and are not rules about what must be done usually or for the most part (531). In the absence of artificial conventions, men are not restricted by inflexible rules, but adapt themselves to the particular situation in which they find themselves. Men have certain motives, and act in such a way as to achieve the goals at which these motives are directed; the way in which they can achieve these goals depends upon the circumstances in which they find themselves, upon 'our immediate situation within ourselves, and with respect to the rest of the universe' (531). Men may 'form something like *general rules*' (531) for their conduct, but these are only rules to the effect that behaving in such-and-such a way usually achieves certain results; there is no reason why men should not depart from these rules, when acting in this way does not achieve these results, or when they have no longer any desire for the results. Rules of justice, however, do not admit of exceptions, for the very reason that they are invented to prevent the chaos which would result if people followed their inclinations; since there is no natural motive in man the function of which is to prevent him from taking other people's possessions, chaos would result if everyone simply acted upon the rules of thumb which enable them to achieve what they want.

I have disentangled the above argument from a slightly different argument, which Hume has already used (479 f.), and which he repeats in this section, without himself clearly distinguishing it from the earlier one. It is that there is in nature no motive which impels men to abstain from taking the property of others and, since what is naturally virtuous is determined by what motives men normally or naturally have, justice cannot be a natural virtue. The argument that is peculiar to this section may be regarded as an extension of this one, for it can be looked upon as putting forward another reason why justice cannot be founded, as are the natural virtues, upon normal human motivation. The first is that there *are* no motives to found it on; the second is that, if there were any such motives, they could not account for the inflexibility of justice (for what satisfies a motive will depend upon the circumstances, whereas justice must be done in all circumstances). For example, respecting the possessions of others will sometimes satisfy a natural motive, at other times not, but possessions *must* be respected in either event.

In a final paragraph, Hume re-emphasizes another point that he has already made (498), namely, that justice has two 'foundations', firstly interest, secondly morality (533). Justice is founded on interest in that each individual man perceives the necessity of creating rules of justice, that it is to his interest to have these rules, and to his interest that they should be enforced. It is founded upon morality in that obeying and enforcing rules of justice is seen to be useful to men collectively, and so, by sympathy with the pleasures of the people who benefit from its usefulness, arouses the pleasurable sentiment of approbation. 'After that interest is once establish'd and acknowledg'd, the sense of morality in the observance of these rules follows *naturally*, and of itself' (533). By this Hume means, though he does not here say so, that obeying and enforcing rules of justice is seen to be useful, and therefore (by sympathy with the pleasure of the people to whom it is useful) arouses the pleasurable sentiment of approbation. Though the rules are artificial, that the rules arouse this sentiment is a natural phenomenon, over which man has no control. Men invent and enforce the rules of justice, in other words, but it is not within their power to decide that inventing and enforcing such rules should arouse in them approval. Though the existence of this feeling of approval is natural, it can to some extent be augmented artificially by 'the public instructions of politicians, and the private education of parents' (533–4).

COMMENTS ON I

(1) By describing the rules enforcing the stability of property, allowing its transference, and constituting and enforcing promise-keeping as 'laws of nature', Hume does not intend, inconsistently, to suggest that there is a law existing independently of human convention, to be discovered. He simply means that the necessity of having such laws is obvious, and that it is therefore natural for man to invent them. Their existence is as much a natural phenomenon as is the existence of cities

and railways and factories, although these too are artificial, for man and
his creations are as much part of nature as anything else.

(2) One of Hume's main contentions in these three sections is that
the motives for our abstaining from taking the possessions of others
can, unlike our desire for food, be reduced to other motives. Other
motives, like self-interest, will explain why we set up rules of justice
and act on them. There is no need to postulate an irreducible desire in
the mind of man, the object of which desire is the performance of just
acts as such. There cannot be such a motive because, if there were,
there would have to be something about the physical features of other
people's possessions which moves us not to take them, just as hunger,
which is a natural motive, is something which is aroused by the physical
features of certain material objects, e.g. their smell. But Hume shows,
to my mind conclusively, that there are no physical features which
could constitute property (527). There are no sensible qualities of the
property, or relations of it to other objects, or relations of it to animate
beings (its owners) which necessarily change when ownership of the
property is transferred. Hence, Hume thinks, being someone's property
must consist in the sentiments of approval or disapproval that behaviour
concerning this thing (e.g. taking it) arouses in human beings; this fact,
Hume thinks, entails that property is a conventional notion. I suspect
that he thinks it *follows* from the fact that property is a *conventional
notion* that there cannot be any *original motives* inclining us to respect
it, not derivable from the other motives we possess, for he argues (quite
correctly) that we cannot produce a new motive by introducing a new
convention. The convention can only change our behaviour by appealing to motives that we possessed before the convention was introduced.

Unfortunately, at this point (527) Hume makes a mistake which in
other places (e.g. 619) he does not make. He says that what makes
something someone's property is its arousing in people a sense that it is
their duty not to take it. But, of course, the non-conventional physical
properties of possessions cannot arouse a sense that it is our duty not
to take them. And in any case, as Hume himself points out, no one can
introduce a convention to the effect that certain behaviour must appeal
to the sense of duty. What kind of things we feel morally impelled to
do or not to do is not something that human beings can decide upon;
they have no choice. Hume should have said that that internal relation
between the possessions and the minds of people, which is property,
does not consist in certain behaviour concerned with these possessions
(e.g. taking them) directly arousing moral sentiments of disapproval. It
must first of all have been decided that this kind of behaviour should be
prohibited. Then, because the system of behaviour which constitutes

there being rules is approved of (because of its usefulness), we have a sense that it is our duty to obey the rules and enforce them. It is the *rules* which are conventional, and which can be changed in the manner in which conventions can be changed; our duty to obey the rules is not conventional at all, and it is not normally Hume's view that it is (619). Put more simply, property is a conventional notion, but not a moral one. It must be defined, not in terms of people's moral sentiments, but in terms of that complex behaviour on the part of its members which makes us say that society has a rule prohibiting taking others' goods.

(3) Is Hume right in saying that the definition of justice as *'a constant and perpetual will of giving every one his due'* (526) is circular? (He gives a more detailed argument for this on pp. 490-1). This definition is circular because all it means is that it is in accordance with the conventions to give each man what the conventions demand that he be given. That it is just to respect the property of others simply means that it is in accordance with man-made conventions not to interfere in another man's use of goods when the conventions demand that we do not so interfere. For this definition of justice to be useful 'due' would have to be defined independently of human convention; but, Hume thinks, it cannot be.

It is not difficult to produce examples where behaviour in accordance with the man-made conventions which Hume wrongly thought consti-tuted and determined justice is unjust. For example, if one of a father's two children is left the whole of his estate without good reason, it might well be deemed unjust for him not to give the other a share, and so rectify an act of injustice committed by his father. Hume's definition of 'due' is also too narrow. For the law may sometimes allow a judge some latitude concerning how severely a certain offence is punished, and then, if he gives a severe, though perfectly legal, penalty which is more than the man deserves, he is acting unjustly, and giving the man more than his due, even though he is not contravening any man-made convention. If the law demands that men do not leave their estates to Jews, then it may be demanding behaviour which is unjust, for it might be that a Jew has the best claim to someone's estate. Furthermore, the law itself may be described as just or unjust. For example, it could be thought unjust for it to be legally compulsory for the poor to pay as much tax as the rich. The law itself, however, cannot conform or fail to conform to law.

One might help Hume a bit by distinguishing between what might be called legal and moral justice, and between what is legally and what is morally due. Then one might say that legal justice consists in behav-ing in accordance with the law, and something is legally a man's due if a law demands that he be given or left in possession of it. An action is morally just if it conforms to the moral law, and is morally a man's due if the moral law demands that he be given it or left in possession of it. The propositions that legal justice consists in giving a man what is legally his due, and that moral justice consists in giving a man what is morally his due, are both analytic propositions. The proposition that it is always morally just to give a man what is legally his due is a synthetic one, and false at that.

Just as we can define implication in terms of disjunction, or disjunction in terms of implication, but not both, there would be no harm in defining 'just' in terms of 'giving a man his due' or defining 'due' in terms of what it is just to give him, so long as we do not do both. If either definition is correct, then the proposition that it is just to give every man his due is an analytic one, but it is not for that reason necessarily unimportant. For an analytic proposition may explain how two concepts—in this case, the concepts of 'due' and 'just'—are necessarily related to one another, and it may not be unimportant to know this.

Hume, incidentally, needs two distinct concepts, one of what is demanded by convention, and another of what is morally right, in order to do full justice to his own theory, however inconsistent this may be with what he himself sometimes says. For there is, on his view, first of all the fact that certain classes of action are enjoined by artificial rules, and secondly the fact that we feel moral approbation of behaviour in accordance with the rules on account of its usefulness. Hume has not adequately considered what would happen if the artificial conventions were harmful, as they perfectly well might be, but it seems that what he ought to say is that in this case conforming to the rules is wrong because conforming to the rules evokes the painful sentiments of moral disapprobation from sympathy with the pain experienced by those who are hurt by it. It would then follow, if Hume does not allow himself a distinction between moral and legal justice, that behaviour which was just, because it consisted in giving a man what the law demanded, was wrong, because the law in question was a very harmful one.

Hume does not have to define 'just' as meaning any kind of behaviour which the law demands, though it looks as if he does in fact want to do this (490-1). The law demands both that we abstain from rape and that we pay men and women equally for equal work. To rape a woman is not to behave unjustly[2]—which is not at all to say that it is not

---

[2] Though the law that prohibits rape is one item in that collection of laws, and practices connected with them, which is collectively called justice. 'Justice' in this sense is not a word for a virtue, incidentally.

morally wrong—but to pay some of one's employees more than others without good reason is unjust—and, incidentally, would be unjust whether it was prohibited by law or not. Hence it is necessary to say that behaving unjustly does not consist in disobeying any kind of law, but in disobeying only laws of certain sorts.

(4) Hume argues, quite correctly, that property cannot consist in any of the sensible qualities of a thing; its ownership may change, while its sensible qualities all remain the same. Change of ownership must, however, show up somewhere by making a difference to what sensible properties we are aware of. Otherwise we would never know whether a property had changed hands or not, and the whole object of allocating different things to different men would be rendered impossible to achieve. The way in which change of ownership makes such a difference is that we have sensations of men behaving differently towards a man's using a piece of goods when it is his property, from the way they behave if it is not. If the owner of a house enters through a ground floor window, we will have no sensations of men in blue uniforms coming to take him away, but if a burglar does the same, we may have such sensations. Property shows up in our sensations of policemen and lawyers and judges and documents. Without them it would be a meaningless word.

(5) Hume is quite right in thinking that ownership is not a sensible and physical property of a piece of goods, and in thinking that, *a fortiori*, change of ownership is not a change in a thing's sensible and physical properties. There must, however, be some sensible physical change which takes place to a piece of goods when it changes hands. Though a thing may not change any of its intrinsic properties, its relational properties must change in some way or other. For if they did not, there would be no way of telling that it had changed hands, and so the whole idea of apportioning different objects to different people would be entirely useless. One thing could not be yours and another mine if there was no difference between them. These physical and sensible marks of a change of ownership are, of course, not *just* sensible and physical marks. They are sensible and physical marks to which a certain conventional significance has been attached by man. Otherwise there would be no way of distinguishing between a mere change in the relational properties of a thing, and a change which meant that the ownership had changed. If I say the words, 'I bequeath to my wife my second-best bed', then this bed later becomes hers because of the meaning these words have, not because of the bed's physical properties, and because of the conventional legal system which confers upon these words the power of transferring the ownership of the bed to the wife of

the deceased. But something physical, usually the saying or writing of words, must occur if property is to change hands. Without such an occurrence, everything would go on just as it had before. There must also be some difference in the physical properties of the words used, say, for giving and exchanging, or there would be no way of giving as opposed to exchanging. Every different facet of ownership must have its appropriate, albeit conventional, physical mark.

The relation between the words and the thing which, say, changes ownership, must be an intentional rather than a physical one. Otherwise altering the position of the document transferring some object would alter its legal status. The intentional relation in question is the relation between a description (e.g. 'my second-best bed') and the thing described (my second-best bed). This presupposes that there must be some other difference, over and above the saying of words such as 'I bequeath to my wife my second-best bed', between my second-best bed and other things. Otherwise there would be no way of picking out what it was I was bequeathing, and my bequest would be ineffective.

(6) Hume says, 'If nature had given us a pleasure of this kind [a pleasure arising from the sensible and physical features of property, and having nothing to do with conventional rules], it wou'd have been as evident and discernible as on every other occasion; nor shou'd we have found any difficulty to perceive, that the consideration of such actions, in such a situation, gives a certain pleasure and sentiment of approbation' (528). One doubts whether it is as easy as Hume supposed to decide whether our attitude to something is a response to its physical or conventional features.

Let us take an example that Hume would have approved of. Some buildings are sacred, and they are sacred, perhaps, because a ceremony of consecration has been performed over them, i.e. they have been consecrated. Now it seems to me that a sacred building is simply one which has been consecrated and that this is the only difference between a building which is sacred and one which is not. Performing such a ceremony, unlike treating it for dry rot, can make no difference to a building, except in so far as it alters the way that people behave in it when they know or believe that this ceremony has been performed. People, many people, at any rate, who have an especially reverent attitude to a building which has been consecrated suppose that there is some difference between a consecrated and an unconsecrated building, over and above the fact that a ceremony of consecration has been performed in the one case, but not in the other. They must be mistaken, of course. Any tests we can perform will show that there is no physical difference between the two buildings. If 'sacred' means anything different from 'consecrated', being sacred will be in principle an undetectable property, and 'sacred', in consequence, like the 'imaginary qualities of the peripatetic philosophy', a meaningless term. But that people are capable of believing that some buildings are sacred in any way other than that they have been subjected to a ceremony of consecration shows that it is not as easy to decide as Hume supposed whether the sentiments we feel towards things—sacred buildings, for example—are aroused by physical (or natural) properties, or conventional ones.

(7) Hume says, '*Secondly*, because, if men had been endow'd with such a strong regard for public good, they wou'd never have restrain'd themselves by these rules [the artificial rules of justice]; so that the laws of justice arise from natural principles in a manner still more oblique and artificial. 'Tis self-love which is their real origin; and as the self-love of one person is naturally contrary to that of another, these several interested passions are oblig'd to adjust themselves after such a manner as to concur in some system of conduct and behaviour. This system, therefore, comprehending the interest of each individual, is of course advantageous to the public; tho' it be not intended for that purpose by the inventors' (529).

I suspect that by 'they wou'd never have restrained themselves by these rules' Hume means 'they never would *need* to have such rules to restrain themselves'. This is just a very much shortened version of an argument he uses in the *Enquiry* (E184-6), and I shall discuss it in another place (pp. 266-7). His point is that, if men had had a degree of benevolence strong enough to lead them to set up rules of justice, this very degree of benevolence would have made such rules unnecessary. Hume thinks that the motive for adopting rules of justice is self-love. What I think he means is that we adopt rules of justice, although doing so limits our own freedom to encroach upon the possessions of others, because we foresee that we will gain more than we will lose, by the fact that these rules will also restrict the freedom of others to encroach upon our own possessions.

Though what Hume says is true, I doubt that this is entirely a matter of artificial convention. Let us suppose that there is something that two people both want. They could then concur in allowing each to have half of it. The result is a compromise between what, for each of them, is the best thing, having it all, and the worst thing, not having any of it. Each is forgoing a chance of getting it all, and avoiding a risk of getting none of it. They both gain, for, because of the principle of diminishing utility, the extra half they gain if they get it all is of less value to them than the half they lose if they get none of it. Furthermore, each will gain the benefit of getting his half of the thing without violence and

disruption. Hence each will agree to leave the other in undisputed possession of one-half of it, because he sees that it is in his interests to do
this. If they agree upon a rule to the effect that all disputed possessions
are to be divided equally between them, then an equal distribution
becomes just in the sense that it is demanded by a rule which they have
adopted. But, one suspects, an equal distribution would be the just one,
even if, from greed and stupidity, they could not agree upon a rule, and
one reason for the rule they adopt is that it accords with what would be
the just distribution antecedently to their adopting it. If we use the
word 'fair' instead of the word 'just' to describe this equal distribution,
then it is more obvious that fairness does not depend upon human convention. 'Fair', unlike 'just', does not have the connotation of being in
accordance with law.

(8) Hume states, 'I shall begin with observing, that this quality,
which we call *property*, is like many of the imaginary qualities of the
peripatetic philosophy, and vanishes upon a more accurate inspection
into the subject, *when consider'd a-part from our moral sentiments* [last
italics mine]' (527). Hume's criticism of the peripatetic philosophy is
contained in Book I, Part IV, Section III of the *Treatise*. There he
suggests that a number of words—in particular the words 'substance',
'accident', 'faculty', 'occult quality', and *'sympathies, antipathies, and
horrors of a vacuum'*—are without meaning. There are no impressions
of such things from which our ideas of them could be copies, and so
such words, standing for no ideas at all, are devoid of significance. It is
not Hume's view that the word 'property' is without meaning, so much
as that it would be without meaning if it stood for an idea which pur-
ported to be a copy of an impression of sensation, instead of one which
was a copy of an impression of reflection, i.e. the impressions of the
sentiments of approval which the different ways of behaving towards
possessions arouses in men.

(9) It would appear to be Hume's view that an action can be a
manifestation of a natural virtue only if it is the sign of a passion which
is such that it is aroused by the physical features of something. Thus
hunger and sexual appetite are aroused by the physical features of a
thing—the smell and texture of certain physical objects, food, or the
shape and appearance of a woman, for example. If there are any mental
features of things—intelligence, perhaps—which cannot be reduced to
physical features—and these, as some of them must be, are natural—I
see no reason why Hume should not be allowed to say that an action is
a natural virtue if it is the product of a desire which is aroused by the
physical or mental features of things, though this is a correction which
he has himself omitted to make. But, even so, the number of desires

which are of the right kind to count as the kind of desire which makes a man's actions naturally virtuous is much more limited than Hume supposed. Desire to care for one's children would be a natural passion if it is a desire to care for human beings to whom one is related by the physical relation 'biological father of', but the desire to care for human beings for whom society has allocated to us the task of caring is an artificial one, in that it has as its object something which we can only do if there are certain rules, in this case, rules demanding that we care for our biological offspring. A desire to maintain one's position in society is not a natural passion, because our position in society is determined by conventions. Desire for money is not a natural desire, for we do not desire money on account of its physical features, but for its purchasing power, and money has purchasing power only because of a convention which determines that printed bits of paper, produced by a man who is authorized by conventions to do so, can be exchanged for goods or services. Desire to become chairman of a board of directors or to become a vice-chancellor are obviously conventional desires in that sense; even the desire to own a car is conventional, for owning, as Hume rightly insists, is a conventional relation, and a man may not just want a physical object answering to a certain physical description; he may want a physical object, answering to this description, but want it partly because it is the kind of object—say a vintage Rolls Royce—often possessed by people with a social status to which he aspires. I suspect that our 'natural' passions are so inextricably mixed up with conventional ones, and our aims and outlook on life by our position in society, that the number of purely natural passions is very few.

COMMENTS ON II

(1) Hume is guilty of a cross division when he says that justice does not admit of degrees, but that the other virtues (the natural virtues) do admit of degrees. 'Justice' is ambiguous. It may be a name for that quality of character which manifests itself in performing just acts, or it may be a name for the class of actions demanded by rules of justice. Clearly justice, in the first of these two senses, *does* admit of degrees. A man may perform just acts seldom, or frequently, or almost all the time, or fail to perform them from small or great temptations, and be designated more or less just accordingly. A man can be more or less just in precisely the same way as a man can be more or less benevolent.

Hume, of course, is not talking about justice in the sense in which it is a name for that disposition in the just man which leads him to perform just acts. He is using it as a name for the rules of justice, and the acts which conform to them. In this sense it is much more likely that he is right in thinking that justice does not admit of degrees. A judge's decision, it can be argued, is either just or unjust, it cannot be more or less just; and a man either conforms to a rule of justice or fails to conform to it. He cannot conform to it more or less. But if, as it is, it is justice in this sense that Hume is talking about, it could be argued that the same is true of the natural virtues. For though a man may be more or less benevolent, his benevolent acts cannot be more or less right, and though he may be more or less courageous there can be no question of the rectitude of an action which shows courage admitting of degrees. Though an action, as well as a man, may be more or less *courageous*, it cannot be more or less *right*. There are no such words as 'righter' and 'rightest', and no such phrases as 'more right' and 'most right'.

(2) Hume says, 'For whatever may be the case, with regard to all kinds of vice and virtue, 'tis certain, that rights, and obligations, and property, admit of no such insensible gradation, but that a man either has a full and perfect property, or none at all; and is either entirely oblig'd to perform any action, or lies under no manner of obligation' (529). In this context, where Hume is contrasting artificial and natural virtues, this suggests that he thought that not only property, but all rights and obligations, were artificial. Probably what he had intended was that a *right* is something which someone is protected in doing by a man-made rule, or to which he has a claim which man-made rules demand he be conceded. An obligation, on this view, would be an action which was enjoined upon a man by a man-made rule. Though it seems to me that Hume is entirely right about property, and that the rules instituting and regulating property are man-made, it is much less obvious that he is right about rights and obligations generally. Legal rights and legal obligations are clearly man-made and artificial. But most people do not suppose that any moral issue concerning what they ought to do is entirely settled by the positive law of the country in which they live. For example, the fact that a speaker has a legal right to hold a meeting is not commonly supposed by those of a left-wing persuasion to give him the moral right to speak, and, whether they are right or wrong about this, the fact that it is possible for them to believe it shows that the notions of a legal right and a moral right are distinct. The same is true of obligations. Everyone thinks that they have some moral obligations—for example, a moral obligation to support their children at a university—which are not legal obligations, and so the fact that legal rights and obligations are artificial does not show that all rights and obligations are.

This point does not entirely settle the matter, however. A disciple of Hume's could defend the Humean position by distinguishing between two sorts of conventions, legal conventions and some more fundamental conventions (i.e. moral ones) which cover areas of life on which the law makes no pronouncement, which sometimes conflict with the former, and sometimes override them when they do. (Strictly speaking, one would have to say that the former always override the latter but point out that the moral conventions are such as to take account of the legal conventions, and to make pronouncements about what one ought to do in the event of a conflict between what the legal conventions enjoin, and what the moral conventions *would* enjoin, in the absence of the legal ones.) Even when property is concerned, this Humean philosopher would have to say, there are legal as well as moral conventions, and the fact that property is a wholly legal notion does not mean that there are not moral as well as legal conventions governing its use. For example, the rule demanding that one morally ought to respect other people's property (i.e. that one morally ought to respect possessions which one is under a legal obligation to respect, which is a synthetic proposition, not an analytic one) is a moral rule which dictates how one ought to behave with respect to other people's property, and doubtless it admits of exceptions. Even Hume himself has to allow, and does allow, that there are unusual circumstances in which the legal rules about property have no moral force, since, in these exceptional circumstances, the public interest demands that they be overridden. A general, for example, may have the right to defend a town which is being attacked by the enemy by burning the suburbs ('Of Passive Obedience', Ess.284). And Hume says very sensibly, 'The maxim, fiat justitia et ruant coeli, let justice be performed, though the universe be destroyed, is apparently [Hume means evidently] false, and by sacrificing the end to the means, shows a preposterous idea of the subordination of ethics' (ibid.). The question whether there are such things as moral conventions which are distinct from legal ones, but which are nevertheless artificial, is one which I shall have to discuss later. Unless there are such things, Hume must be wrong in thinking that all rights and obligations are artificial, and wrong, therefore, in thinking that the fact that they do not admit of degrees shows that they are artificial.

(3) Is Hume right in thinking that the notions of right and obligation do not admit of degrees? It is true that we have such expressions as 'Riff has more of a right to beat his wife (since she also beats him) than Raff has to beat his' and 'Man is under more of an obligation to his daughters than he is to his sons (since his daughters cook for him, though his sons do not)'. But despite appearances, I do not think that this

shows that rights and objections do admit of degrees. Riff's having more of a right to beat his wife than Raff has to beat his is compatible with neither Riff nor Raff's having a right to beat his wife. The degrees which the expression 'more of' indicates are not degrees of rights, which is meaningless, but degrees of the strength of a claim to have a right, or degrees of the unequivocability with which a right may be laid claim to, or the degrees to which the claim to having a right may be justified. And the fact that a man may be under more of an obligation to his daughters than to his sons means that his daughters have done more of those things which tend to put their father under an obligation to do things for them in return than his sons have. Each individual act which the father may be under an obligation to perform in return is absolutely and completely obligatory, and not obligatory in some degree or other. There may be fewer acts which he is under an obliga-tion to perform for the benefit of his sons, and the services which he is under an obligation to perform for his sons may be of less moment, but each individual act which he is under an obligation to perform for them is simply obligatory, and not obligatory in some degree. And, as with rights, the factors which tend to make an act obligatory may vary in the force with which they have this tendency, and obligations may be more or less equivocal, but obligations themselves do not admit of degrees. Furthermore though both rights and obligations may vary in the ease with which they may be overridden, this does not mean that, when they are not overridden, they admit of degrees. Travellers may be near or far from their destinations, and may be more or less easily diverted from their course, but when a traveller is at his destination, he is at it, and his being there does not admit of degrees.

(4) Whether rights and obligations do admit of degrees or not, why does Hume think that their not admitting of degrees would show that they were artificial notions, having reference to and having to be defined in terms of man-made conventions? There are, of course, an enormous number of natural qualities which do admit of degrees. Colour, weight, size, velocity, and innumerable others all do. Shape, however, does not always seem to admit of degrees. Though we may speak of an object's being more or less square or more or less round, we are really talking of the degrees to which an object may approximate to being square or round; there are no degrees of being quite round or exactly square. One could argue, I think, that concepts like round or square are intentional ones, instances of which are not to be found in nature, and their measuring up to them is like, if I may misuse an example of Professor Ryle's, winning a race or hitting a bull's eye. These are artificial phenomena, for what counts as either of these is

determined by the rules of racing or of darts. I must confess however, that I am not entirely convinced by my own argument. And mathematical concepts often do not admit of degrees. That there is one owl in an oak does not seem to be an artificial phenomenon, but being one is something which does not admit of degrees. And the fact that there was one owl in an oak or that the courses of the planets are elliptical are facts that are quite independent of anything man may decide.

Let us assume, then, that some natural things, which have nothing to do with human convention and artifice, do not admit of degrees. It must follow again that Hume is wrong in thinking that rights and obligations not admitting of degrees would show that they are not natural phenomena. But why should Hume suppose that the fact that rights and obligations do not admit of degrees shows that facts about rights and obligations are facts about human conventions, or that rights and obligations are conventional phenomena, tied by the meaning of the words 'right' and 'obligation' to the existence of humanly created rules? What I am about to say is little more than guesswork, but I think that the thought at the back of his mind may be this. Since everything in nature is a matter of degree, and hot and cold, fast and slow, large and small, heavy and light merge insensibly into one another, the idea of something which does not admit of degrees, which is not in a state of perpetual flux (and, in II, the idea of instantaneous change) is a human fiction. Just as, although nature does not contain a disjunction, and everything either happens or does not happen, the law, which contains intentional concepts, may prescribe that a man repays a debt either in money or in kind, or is punished by a fine or imprisonment, so that the law may prescribe that someone loses a right to something at an instant, though nothing in nature can happen instantaneously. The idea that something must be done at some time or other during the year is again a 'fictional' notion, for everything in nature happens at some particular time. Hence anything which contains a mention of something's happening instantly or being done at some time or other, or something's being done or something else's being done, must involve human concepts, and human concepts are the artificial construction of man. Not everything which contains such concepts is a *law*. Propositions, beliefs, and intentions involve the same kind of notion. But all the things which do contain such 'ideas' are artificial in the sense that propositions are things which human beings create for various purposes, and intentions are things which human beings arrive at or formulate.

The idea of artificiality is not quite the idea Hume wants, however, if my suggestion about what he is driving at is correct. For medicines and houses are artificial phenomena, but there can no more be a disjunctive or indefinite medicine than there can be a disjunctive or indefinite cabbage. And intentions are not exactly *created* by man. If they were, they would have to be preceded by yet further intentions, and so to suppose that all intentions are artificial would lead to an infinite vicious regress. The fact to which Hume wrongly indicates by saying that rights and obligations are artificial might be better described by saying that rights and obligations are intentional. They are the intentional objects of mental acts, which acts may have a kind of object—for example, either to do one thing or to do another—which cannot, as instantaneous happenings and disjunctive actions cannot, be found in nature. But in this case, it does not follow that rights and obligations are artificial, in the sense that rules are artificial, for rules are only one kind of intentional phenomenon. If rights and obligations had no reference to man-made rules, but facts about them remained facts whatever men decided upon or did, they could still contain notions not to be found in nature. For just as a man may intend either to beg, borrow, or steal some money—there is no such act, of course, as begging, borrowing, or stealing—so a man may have a duty to educate any one of his children, without having a duty to educate any particular one. Since laws, which are both artificial and intentional phenomena, are not the only intentional phenomena there are, Hume's argument, interpreted in the way I have suggested, would not show that rights and obligations are artificial, but would perhaps show that they are intentional. If so, they are intentional in the way in which human thoughts and plans are intentional, rather than artificial in the way in which the *products* of human thinking and planning are artificial.

(5) Hume, however, does not argue only that justice must be an artificial virtue because rights and obligations do not admit of degrees. He also argues that justice must be an artificial virtue because the *change* from having a right to something and not having it takes place *instantly*: 'this right both arises and perishes in an instant; and that a man entirely acquires the property of any object by occupation, or the consent of the proprietor; and loses it by his own consent; without any of that insensible gradation, which is remarkable in other qualities and relations' (530). It presumably *follows* from the fact that rights and obligations do not admit of degrees that the change from having to not having a right or an obligation does not take time; nevertheless the two points ought to be distinguished from one another.

One can, of course, gradually lose one's rights, but this, Hume must think, consists in *instantly* losing one right after another over a fairly long period of time. Losing them rapidly must consist in losing them instantly one by one over a comparatively short period of time. Again it may take a long time to acquire a right to something (and a long time to lose it), but Hume could say, this simply means that losing a right may be the termination of a long or short process, but at the end of either process, the right is lost instantly. One may have to occupy a property for a long time before one acquires a right to it, but nevertheless, after this process has been gone through, one acquires it instantly. One might argue, in a parallel way, that though it may take a long or short time to reach one's destination, *arriving* at one's destination is instantaneous, or that though it took the horses a long time to get to the end of the course, winning did not take any time at all. To say that it took a long time to win or that it took a long time to beat Smith at chess, means that the race or the game was a long one, and that it took a long time to reach the end result, but the conventional change from not being the winner to being the winner is instantaneous. Again, litigation may take a long time, but if, as a result of litigation, one is awarded rights which one did not previously have, the change from not having these rights to having them is again instantaneous. The acquiring of the rights can be dated, but not timed. Furthermore, it does not just so happen that one loses rights instantly; one cannot meaningfully ask the question, 'How long did the expiry of your right to use a hired horse take?'

It might be considered a difficulty with Hume's view that in some cases the length of time needed to acquire a right may be indeterminate. For example, it may sometimes be quite clear that five years is not long enough to acquire a prescriptive right to a property which one has possessed for this period, and that ten years is long enough to acquire such a right. There may be intermediate periods, however, such that it is impossible to say whether a person who has occupied a property for these times has or has not acquired a prescriptive right to it. But this does not mean that the change from not having a right to having a right is not instantaneous. It simply means that the law has not fixed a definite instant when this change takes place.

The fact that the period over which one has to occupy property in order to acquire a prescriptive right to it is indeterminate (and taking an indeterminate time is not the same thing as taking a long time) can be turned into another argument for the artificiality of the rules of justice. For, one may say, this kind of indeterminacy is a feature of artificiality. Nothing in nature can take place, but not take place at some time or other. One cannot have visited one's bank manager on some day last week but not on a Monday or a Tuesday or a Wednesday, and so on. But one can *intend* to visit one's bank manager some day next week, without intending to visit him on Monday or intending to visit him on

Tuesday, or intending to visit him on Wednesday, and so on. A man cannot be at Bath or Bristol, without being at either, but he can intend to go to Bath or Bristol, without intending to go to Bath, and without intending to go to Bristol. If justice is artificial, then it can be, unlike natural things, indeterminate, for men may not have specified, and not made up their minds about, what shall be done in a number of eventualities. For example, it may not have been decided whether a man who has occupied a property for seven years, three months, five days, and seven and a half hours shall or shall not have acquired a prescriptive right to it.

Hence this argument of Hume's for the artificiality of justice seems to me to be substantially correct. But Hume, as we have seen, fails to make an explicit distinction between the conventional rules regulating such things as property, and so on, and moral rules. It may be, for example, that a man has a legal right to be protected in the use of something without having a moral right to be so protected. Do moral rights similarly arise and perish in an instant? If so, it seems unlikely that the fact that rights do this shows that they are conventional phenomena unless moral rules, as well as legal conventions, are decided upon by man. And it seems very unlikely that they *are* decided upon by man for, as I have argued elsewhere,[3] it is impossible to change our rights and obligations except by altering our circumstances. By getting married, for example, we can acquire both legal and moral rights and duties, which we did not have before, without changing either the positive law or the moral law, but there are procedures for changing the positive law when there are none for changing the moral law. If I do not like it that it is immoral to sleep with my neighbour's wife, there is in principle nothing I can do to make it not immoral, though there would be in principle things I can do to make it not illegal, if it were illegal, and there are in principle things I can do to make it not *considered* immoral, difficult though this may be to achieve in practice. Hence, so it seems, moral rights and obligations are not conventional, and so the fact that legal rights do not admit of degrees, and arise and perish in an instant, does not show that all rights and obligations are conventional and artificial. If in the eighteenth century a man wanted to enclose his land, he could acquire the legal right to do so by getting a private Act of Parliament passed, which act gave him legal rights which he did not have before. But, though this change in his legal rights would or could alter his moral rights, there could be no such process as getting himself a moral right which he did not have before.

(6) Hume ends II by oddly asserting that, though it is a maxim of

---

[3] *Our Knowledge of Right and Wrong.*

philosophy and of law that rights and obligations do not admit of degrees, in our common way of thinking we maintain the opinion that they do admit of degrees. I doubt whether he is right about this, and his arguments are not conclusive. He thinks that the fact that rights and obligations admit of degrees is indicated by the fact that utilities and the propensities of the imagination, which give rise to rights and obligations, admit of degrees. But, to the extent that rights and obligations depend upon utilities, I think that all that follows is that claims to having a right, or the reasons which tend to cause one to be under an obligation, admit of degrees. If these are equal in the strength they give to opposing claims, then a judge will have to make a decision one way or the other, but in making such a decion he is allocating to one man rather than another a (legal) right which does not admit of degrees. Hume thinks that the fact that referees sometimes divide a property between two claimants shows that each claimant has a right in some degree to the whole of the property. This is not so. The referee does not decide that they each have half a right to the whole property but that they each have a whole right to half the property. It is true that we sometimes say such things as that they each have some right to the property, or that they have an equal right to the property, but that does not show that rights admit of degrees. For having *some right* to a property is compatible with not having a *right* to it, and one man's having *as much right* to a property as another is compatible with neither's having a *right* to it. Despite appearances, what we are talking about is not the rights, but the strength of their claims to having a right. And a man may certainly have some claim to a right to a property, or have an equal right to a property as someone else, without having a right to the property, and so without his *right* to the property admitting of degrees. Two men's having equal rights to something sometimes means that what the one man has a right *to* is equal to what the other man has a right to. For example, that a divorced man and woman have equal rights to see their children just means that each has a right to see as much of their children as the other. (The statement that each has as much of a duty to support them may be interpreted as meaning that they each have a duty to contribute as much to the support of their children as the other.) Hume's remark, 'Half rights and obligations . . . are perfect absurdities in their tribunal; for which reason they are often oblig'd to take half arguments for whole ones, in order to terminate the affair one way or the other' (531) is perfectly just, but there is nothing wrong, so far as I can see, with giving the whole of a property to two people, each of whom has an equal claim to it, if it is incapable of being divided, and the matter cannot equitably be settled in any other way. It seems to me that those remarks of Hume's which I have just discussed are inconsistent with his own contention (529–30), made when he is arguing that the notion of imperfect dominion does not make sense, that 'A man that hires a horse, tho' but for a day, has as full a right to make use of it for that time, as he whom we call its proprietor has to make use of it any other day; and 'tis evident, that however the use may be bounded in time or degree, the right itself is not susceptible of any such gradation, but is absolute and entire, so far as it extends' (529–30).

COMMENTS ON III

(1) Crudely and formalistically interpreted, Hume's third argument has two premisses and a conclusion. The first premiss is that in the ordinary course of nature the mind does not restrain itself by universal rules. The second premiss is that the rules of justice are universal and inflexible. His conclusion is that justice is not a natural virtue, i.e. the rules of justice are artificial.

Part of the difficulty of understanding this very difficult argument is that though one would expect it to be of the form, 'natural virtues are not inflexible; justice is inflexible; therefore justice is not a natural virtue', it does not, without emendation, fit into this form. This is partly because, as it stands, it commits the fallacy of four terms. The conclusion states that rules of justice are artificial, but what should be the major term, and contain the predicate of the conclusion, is not about artificial things, but about the ordinary course of nature, a term which does not appear in the conclusion.

This difficulty can perhaps be partly overcome by assuming that Hume thinks, as he probably did think, that in the ordinary course of nature there is no question of obeying or failing to obey rules of justice. If we add the extra premiss that all natural virtues are something that manifest themselves in the ordinary course of nature—though one suspects that this assumption is (a) not strictly speaking true and (b) begs the question that justice is not natural—one can then form Hume's argument into a valid sorites: all natural virtues are things that manifest themselves in the ordinary course of nature; whatever manifests itself in the ordinary course of nature is not inflexible; justice is inflexible; therefore justice is not a natural virtue. But even allowing Hume all these points, there is the following difficulty. It is clear what he means by saying that justice is universal and inflexible. By saying that justice is universal he means that the rules of justice demand a certain course of action in *all* of a class of cases, e.g. that the deceased's property should always be passed on to the eldest son. By saying that justice is inflexible he means that these universal rules should not be departed from. But what does he mean by saying that the same universality (and presumably, though he does not say so, inflexibility) is not to be found in the ordinary course of human actions, where observing or failing to observe a rule of justice is not in question?

At first (531) he appears to be talking about actions designed to serve some end which the agent has. He seems to be saying that when we are acting in order to obtain things which result from our actions, there is no particular reason why we should perform an action' when it does not have the results in question. He says, 'As each action is a particular individual event, it must proceed from particular principles '[he means motives], and from our immediate [particular] situation within ourselves, and with respect to the rest of the universe' (531). Freely interpreted, this means that each action—where no rule of justice is relevant—is the result of some particular motive, and that the possessor of this motive has to take into consideration facts about that particular action, and its relation to the agent and the rest of the world, in order to determine whether that motive would be satisfied by performing it. There is no need to consider whether that particular motive would have been satisfied by other different actions, performed in other and different circumstances. Though man may sometimes be guided by general rules (honesty is the best policy, for example), these rules always admit of exceptions, and, when a case is exceptional, the rule may simply be departed from.

It does not seem obvious to me that these rules always admit exceptions. It seems very unlikely that the rule that successful athletes should not drink excessively admits of any. But I think that Hume's more important point concerns not the *universality* of these rules, but their *inflexibility*. Some may be universal, in that they do not admit of degrees, but none is inflexible; if a certain case is an exceptional one, there is no reason to adhere to the rule. If one of our maxims, to use a word of Kant's, does not secure for us the end it is a rule for obtaining, there is no reason why we should not simply depart from it. Justice is different, in that its rules may *not* be departed from in exceptional cases. When a rule of justice, which for the most part produces a good result, and was instituted for the sake of the good result it produces, does not produce this result, it must still be adhered to, whereas, as we have seen, a maxim for securing some advantage may be departed from as soon as this advantage is not secured.

On the next page, however, Hume says, 'No action can be either morally good or evil [should he not have said 'morally good or evil *naturally*'?), unless there be some natural passion or motive to impel us to it, or deter us from it; and 'tis evident, that the morality must be susceptible of all the same variations, which are natural to the passion' (532). Here, perhaps, he is arguing that justice cannot be (naturally) morally good or evil because justice is still a duty, even in cases where there is no motive for performing it (and in any case, those just actions which it is our duty to perform do not admit of degrees or gradations of goodness). We have to add the qualification 'naturally morally good or evil' for Hume, otherwise he would get the conclusion that justice is not morally good or evil at all. We would also have to amend his argument so that he does not assert that there is no motive at all leading to the performance of just actions, for otherwise all that follows is that just actions will not be performed at all. We must say instead (a) that there is no motive the *object* of which is the performance of just actions and (b) that the other motives which do lead us to perform just actions, even though their performance is not the object of these motives, would not lead us to perform just actions except in a society which had set up rules and enforced justice (for in such a society there would be no just actions, and we could never be faced with a choice between performing one and omitting one).

These two arguments do not seem to me to be quite the same. (1) The first makes no mention of there being *no* motive for the performance of just actions, and to the extent that it is valid at all, it would be equally valid whether there was such a motive or not. (2) The second argument means that, if the morality of justice depended, as with all (natural) virtues, upon there being a motive for the performance of justice (as there is a motive for the performance of benevolence) then justice would admit of gradations, which Hume thinks it does not. Hume appears to be arguing from the fact that justice does not admit of *exceptions* on page 529, and from the fact that it does not admit of degrees or *gradations* on page 531, and makes things even more confused by adding, without distinguishing it from the others, an argument that he has already used (477 f.), to the effect that justice cannot be a natural virtue, for it is still a duty, even when there are no motives for performing it. Perhaps we can say that it is Hume's view that justice is not a natural virtue (a) because there is no motive the *object* of which is the performance of just actions, and the motives which do lead us to perform just actions, although this is not their object, do so only because they are so moulded by human conventions; (b) because if the rectitude of a just action depended upon such a motive, the justice of a just action would admit of gradations, which it does not; and (c) because if the reason why justice is a virtue is that there is in man a motive leading him to perform just actions, it would not be a duty to be just in cases when a rule of justice did not promote that end which it was invented to produce.

There is one interesting and important point to be found in Hume's remarks. The reason why we may depart from the maxims we adopt in order to secure whatever end we happen to have—we may depart from our norm 'Go early to bed in order to work hard on the following day' if, for some reason, going early to bed will not enable us to work hard on the following day—but may not depart from a rule of justice in order to secure the end the rule was instituted to secure, is that rules of justice have to do with enforcing behaviour concerning a number of different people who have to co-operate in order to secure a desired end. *I* might secure more good by departing from rather than adhering to a rule of justice, but, in order that the rule secures the advantage that such rules were intended to secure, I have to co-operate with other people, and if everyone like me unilaterally departs from a rule of justice for the sake of some good, chaos will result. Since maxims are intended to secure only my own ends, I may depart from them in exceptional circumstances without risking this chaos. This is why maxims may be flexible, but rules of justice may not be. There is nothing naturally vicious about the fact that maxims are not inflexible, for to depart from a maxim when acting on it does not bring about the end for the sake of which it was adopted is just the natural human thing to do. It is because, when the natural human thing to do is done by everybody, chaos results, that inflexible rules of justice have to be instituted to regulate and improve upon this natural unregulated way of behaving.

There is a parallel here between Hume and Kant for, if we interpret the latter with some latitude, we may regard him as saying that the categorical imperative is necessary simply because maxims designed to secure an end will not fit into a system of universal legislation. Hence we have to control them by the categorical imperative, and ask ourselves how it would stand if our maxim were to be a universal law, and acted upon by everybody. Kant could then be regarded as saying that, if everybody were to be flexible about a rule of justice (and, say, award an estate to the poor man rather than to the miser) chaos would result. Hence we cannot will that rules of justice should be anything other than inflexible. Hume's account of the difference between the flexible rules designed for securing our ends and the inflexible rules of justice is very similar to Kant's account of the differences between hypothetical and categorical imperatives. Though the content of Kant's categorical imperative, or what it enjoins, is very different from the content of

Hume's rules of justice, and Kant's account of the manner in which we know that we have a duty to obey the categorical imperative is very different from Hume's account of how we know that we have a duty to conform our actions to rules of justice, Hume and Kant both agree that hypothetical imperatives are flexible and categorical imperatives are not. Both think that one does not have to act on a maxim if one has no desire for the end one obtains by acting on it, and both think that one may depart from a maxim when one no longer wants this end, whereas neither thinks the same is true of rules of justice, in the case of Hume, or of the categorical imperative, in the case of Kant.

Hume's arguments in this chapter are strong, but not absolutely conclusive. Being someone's property is not a physical feature of the thing in question, and is in fact a conventional fact about it, which has to do with the rules by which society allocates it and to whom it is allocated. But it does not *follow* from the fact that property is not a physical feature that it is a conventional feature. Being one's best move in chess is not a physical feature of a physical event, but neither is it a conventional one, for if a given move is not one's best move, there is nothing anyone can do about it. Hence, though property is conventional, and many rights and duties are conventional, there is no reason why moral rights and duties, which must in any case be distinguished from legal ones, should not be non-conventional phenomena. Though rights and duties do arise and perish in an instant, and though their doing so can be explained by their being conventional, moral rights and duties also arise and perish in an instant, although there are reasons for thinking that these are not conventional. Hume, indeed, may be confusing artificiality with intentionality. Though maxims are flexible, and rules of justice are not, it does not follow from the fact that they are inflexible that they are conventional. For the rule, that a rule of justice may not be departed from in an exceptional case, is a moral rule about a conventional rule, and, to the extent, which Hume exaggerates, that it is true at all, it would mean that there are two inflexible things, the conventional rule to which the moral rule demands inflexible adherence, and the moral rule itself, which is also inflexible, for moral rules, also, may not be departed from. (Moral rules may admit of exceptions in that they do not demand certain behaviour in such-and-such cases, but they logically cannot admit of exceptions in that, whenever they do demand certain behaviour, then what they demand is what we ought to do.)

SECTION VII

Of the Origin of Government[1]

THE interest everyone has in observing rules of justice is so great that it
is difficult to see how these rules would ever be broken (534); they are
broken because ideas of what is near affect our passions more than do
ideas of what is distant (534-5); and the advantages gained from
observing justice are remote as compared with those of departing from
it (535); this will produce a tendency in people to break rules of justice
which will be reinforced by the fact that each person will know that
others will have the same tendency (535); it would seem that the very
fact that men have this tendency would prevent them from adopting a
remedy (535-6); but in fact it is its own remedy since, from a distance
in time, the difference between future near pleasures and future distant
pleasures is inconsiderable (536); we are, until the time comes when we
have to make a choice between these pleasures, capable of forming a
just assessment of their relative amounts (536-7); hence *before* the time
for a choice comes, we can adopt a remedy, which is to appoint civil
magistrates whose interest it will be, by enforcing justice, to prevent us
from indulging our preference for near over distant pleasure (537); the
magistrates will have the subsidiary function of judging disputes between
parties who are not impartial (537-8); the magistrates will also have the
function of compelling individuals to play their part in necessary large-
scale enterprises (538-9).

COMMENTS

(1) Many writers, for example Hobbes and Locke, have suggested
that men surrendered power to the magistrates in order to gain the
protection of these magistrates against other men. According to Hume,
man's main reason for surrendering power to the magistrates is in order
that they shall protect him against *himself*. It is because of his own
short-sighted tendency, which he is unable to alter, to prefer near to
distant advantages, that he does not act on rules of justice, and so

---

[1] 'Given a world of Knaves, to produce an honesty from their united efforts'.
Carlyle. Quoted by J. B. Schneewind in *Sidgwick's Ethics and Victorian Moral
Philosophy*, OUP, 1978.

harms himself by depriving these rules of any utility. For the same reason he needs magistrates to enforce the rules, and to decide impartially when they have been broken. The fact that man also needs magistrates because he foresees that other men will also break the rules is, according to Hume, only secondary. Indeed, Hume speaks as if the only reason why other men's transgressions were harmful was that these would make it psychologically impossible for me not to transgress myself (535). Obviously Hume is wrong about this. I do need the law to be enforced in order that I may be protected from other people taking my property, and harming me in other ways, though I may also need it to prevent me from taking the property of others, which also harms me, though indirectly. Other people's transgressions against me are contrary to my interest in two ways. They both harm me immediately, and tend to deprive me of the benefit of having rules of justice, by undermining these rules. My transgressions against other people are contrary to my interest only in the second of these two ways.

Perhaps, then, all men need rules of justice to be enforced, both for the short-term reason that they shall be protected against other people, and for the long-term reason that these rules must be obeyed by everyone if they are to be of advantage to anyone. It is not, however, in a man's interest to have them imposed upon *himself*. Though Hume is right in saying that it is in *man's* (collective) long-term interest to have rulers who impose justice on *man* (collectively), it is not in any *given* man's interest to have rules of justice enforced upon *him*. What is in the interest of each individual man is to have rules of justice imposed upon others, but not on himself. If he ever did meet together with other men to decide whether to have rulers, it would be in his interest to agree that the rules of justice should be imposed upon everybody, excluding himself, if this were possible. Obviously, however, if all men were in favour of having a ruler who imposed the law only upon others, no one would be in favour of having a ruler at all. The proposal, 'Let us all have a ruler who imposes rules of justice upon other men, but never upon ourselves', would be contradictory. Since men see that it is in their interest to have a ruler, they must accept one who will impose rules of justice upon everybody without exception. But though it is in their interest to accept, or even demand, such a ruler, and to agree, if necessary, that he should impose these rules upon all and each of them, it does not follow from this that it is in their interest to obey the rules, once the ruler has been established, in circumstances in which they can disobey the rules without being detected. Though Hume is right to maintain that it is in everybody's interest to *have* rulers who enforce rules of justice, he is wrong in holding that it is in everybody's interest to act on these rules. What is in every man's interest is that other people should act on the rules, while he himself does not. There is, however, very little chance of his succeeding in this enterprise, for each man will realize that it is in the interest of other men to disobey rules of justice, if they can, while it is in his own interest that other men should keep them. Rules of justice are therefore enforced not because, as Hume supposes, each man sees that it is in his long-term interest to be compelled to act upon them, but because each man sees that it is in his interest that all other men should be compelled to act upon them. It is other men, not I myself, who adopt magistrates to impose rules of justice on me. Though Hume is right in thinking that it is in man's interest that man *collectively* selects rulers who impose rules of justice on him which he is too weak and short-sighted to impose upon himself, it is in each individual man's interest to select rulers who impose rules of justice on everybody but himself. Since this is impossible, he must try to engineer a situation in which everybody acts on rules of justice but himself. Since men, for the most part, will succeed only to the extent of imposing rules of justice on other men, the result is the same, but less edifying. And it means that Hobbes was nearer the truth than Hume in saying that men adopt magistrates to impose rules on others, rather than on themselves.

It is worth pointing out that, though it is in each man's interest to have rules of justice which are imposed only upon others, if each man were, *per impossibile*, to succeed in doing what it would be in his interest to do, so long as other men did not behave in a similar fashion, the result would be that all men broke rules of justice, which would be *contrary* to each man's interest. To the extent that men attempt to be the only exceptions to obeying rules of justice, they are acting in a manner which would defeat its object, if everyone were to act in the same manner. They are also aiming at producing a situation which is unfair, in that it is unfair that I should benefit from other people's acting on rules of justice, without making my own contribution to their usefulness by acting on them myself.

It is also worth pointing out that the very thing that makes it necessary, according to Hume, to have rulers who enforce rules of justice (the fact that men prefer their short-term to their long-term interest) reduces the effectiveness of the means that are adopted to enforce them. For they are partly enforced by punishing those who break them, and, from the nature of the case, the punishment must occur after the crime. Consequently, man's tendency to prefer short-term to long-term advantages will frequently lead him to break rules for advantages which, though not usually adequate to compensate him for what he loses if he is punished, have less psychological effect on his will, as they are less remote in time. Since each man is in favour of having rules of justice because they impose good behaviour on other men, Hume is wrong in thinking that each man is in favour of having these rulers in order that he himself may be compelled to conform to rules of justice. Hence Hume's explanation of how man can limit his own tendency to prefer the short-term advantage of breaking rules of justice to the long-term advantage of keeping them—viz. that by appointing a government, he adopts a means of preventing himself from yielding to the temptation of breaking rules of justice before this temptation actually occurs—is unnecessary. For each man adopts rules to limit *other* men's tendency to be moved by the short-term advantages of breaking these rules, and has to surrender his own liberty to break them as the price he has to pay for conformity from other people. The statement that man (collectively) adopts rulers in order to overcome his tendency to prefer near to distant pleasure, however, is perhaps compatible with each individual man's wanting rulers to overcome other men's tendency to prefer near to distant pleasure.

(2) Plato, in *The Republic*, raised the question whether it is better to *be* just, without seeming it, or to *seem* just, without *being* it. In reply to Glaucon, who suggested that being and seeming just was a compromise between the worst thing, which was to be just, without seeming it, and the best thing, which was to seem just, without being it, Plato represents Socrates as maintaining that it is best to be just even if, as a result of being just, we incur all the punishments set apart for the unjust. Since I have, in the foregoing pages, represented the just man as acting on rules of justice because he realized that it was impossible for him to secure the advantages of justice being generally observed without incurring the inconvenience of reluctantly observing it himself, I need to offer some defence of my view against Plato's.

Plato, however, when he talked of justice, was not talking about the same thing as Hume. Plato used 'justice' as a word for virtue in general, whereas Hume was using it for one particular virtue. Hume, in fact, was using it as rather an odd word for the virtue of observing the conventions that society must have if it is not to collapse into total disorder. In asking whether it was better to be virtuous or to seem virtuous, about virtue in general, however, Plato was conflating a large number of questions. There is no such thing as virtue. There just is a large number of different virtues, and the question whether it is better to be or merely to seem virtuous may have a different answer in the case of each one of them, and the answer to the question may depend upon the circumstances. If you are a self-employed farmer, for example, it may be better to be industrious without seeming so, than to seem industrious without being so; if you are a factory hand, exactly the opposite is likely to be true. Both the farmer and the factory hand, however, will probably be better off if they seem honest without being so, than if they are honest without seeming so. In general, perhaps, it is better to have rather than seem to have those qualities which are virtues because they are useful or agreeable to ourselves, but to seem to have rather than have those qualities which are virtues because they are useful or agreeable to others. Justice, in Hume's sense, which he regards as a characteristic which is useful to others, is something which it is better to seem to possess than to possess. The best thing for any individual person is to gain the benefits of living in a society which is stable, because justice is the rule rather than the exception, but to obtain the advantage of other people's being just without himself paying the price of having to be just. Fortunately, it is comparatively rare for anyone to be able to do this; by and large honesty is the safest policy, though it may be possible for some people to make dishonesty pay for short periods of time, and some especially clever or lucky people to make dishonesty pay for fairly long periods of time.

It must not be forgotten, of course, that, though it is better for any individual to seem just without being it, than to be just without seeming it, it is better for society that people are just than that they seem so, and better for me that other people are just than that they seem so. Hence Thrasymachus was acting contrary to his own principles in recommending injustice to others. A more consistent man would have contented himself with practising injustice, but advocating justice. In recommending injustice to others, Thrasymachus was defeating his own end, which was to secure the advantages of other people's keeping the rules, while not losing anything by keeping them himself. The maxim on which he was acting, incidentally, could also not be 'universalized', in the sense, which may or may not have anything to do with Kant, that if everyone were to adopt the maxim, 'Practise justice, while justice is the rule rather than the exception', justice would cease to be the rule, and become the exception.

Mr. D. G. C. Macnabb, in *David Hume* (Hutchinson, 1951), defends Plato by arguing that it is in the interest of men to obey rules of justice, whether these rules are enforced or not, and whether they can escape detection or not. According to Macnabb, the pleasures of conversation and society are much greater than any material advantage one can gain from breaking rules of justice, and, if I am dishonest, evasive, and bullying, I will lose these. What Macnabb says is true, but his argument nevertheless begs the question. For my dishonesty, evasiveness, and arrogance will only cause me to lose the pleasures of social intercourse with others so long as I also seem to them to be dishonest, evasive, and arrogant, which supposes that not only have I broken rules of justice, but that I have broken them and been found out. This is contrary to the hypothesis.

(3) The question then arises: 'Is it in the short-term interest of rulers, as it is with all other men, to play their part in society, merely because doing so is enforced?' (Hume thinks it is clearly in the long-term interest of all men, rulers and ruled alike, to play their part in society.) Or are the rulers in an exceptional position, in that though the ruled obey the rules because they are compelled to do so, it is *naturally*, so to speak, in the short-term interest of the rulers to be rulers? By saying that it is *naturally* in the short-term interest of someone to do something, I mean that it is in his interest to do this thing, whether or not he incurs the conventionally laid-down penalties for not doing it.

I think it is Hume's view that though the ruled have, because of their short-sightedness, to be compelled to act on the rules of justice, although it is in their long-term interest to act on them, the rulers have a short-term interest in justice which does not depend upon compulsion (537). He may indeed have thought it an obvious truth that though the ruled can be made to play their part in society by being forced to obey the rules by the rulers, there are no super-rulers to see that rulers play their part in society by enforcing, and even obeying, the rules themselves.

There are two questions, which Hume only partially distinguishes. Firstly, there is the question, 'Why is it naturally in the interests of rulers to *rule*?' Secondly, there is the question, 'Why is it naturally in the interests of rulers—if it is in their interests—to obey the rules themselves?' These two questions are clearly logically independent. However, the questions are connected, in that one answer to the first question may be that it is naturally in the interest of the rulers to rule because rulers are in a better position than anyone else to *break* the rules.

One notorious answer to these questions, held by some ancient Greek sophists, and also discussed by Plato in *The Republic*, is that it is 'naturally' in the interest of rulers to rule because, by doing so, they are able to exploit the ruled for their own advantage. In its extreme form, this view holds that the rules themselves are in fact invented by the rulers for their own advantage, and that the rulers are clever enough to hoodwink the ruled into thinking that it is their duty to obey the rules. The rulers themselves, however, will be wise or clever enough to see through this deception, and will ignore the moral and social constraints which impose conformity upon other men. Hence the rulers will be guided by 'nature', and do what is 'naturally' to their advantage, whereas the ruled will be artificially constrained by the rules to do what is to the rulers' advantage. The Marxist theory that rules are made in the interest of the dominant social class bears obvious similarities to this view.

Hume, however, thinks that rulers and ruled alike will have an *obligation* to obey the rules, and that it is in the interest of rulers and ruled alike to obey the rules. This is because it is in everybody's interest to have rules. However, he thinks that it is 'naturally' in the interest of the rulers both to govern and to obey, whereas it is in the interest of the ruled to obey only because obedience is imposed upon them by the rulers. Presumably he thinks that there must be someone who has a 'natural' interest in enforcing justice, i.e. an interest which does not depend upon the sanctions of punishment, or such rules never would be enforced.

Hume's answer to the question, 'Why do the rulers have a (natural) short-term interest in ruling?' is this. The rulers have a natural short-term interest in ruling for two reasons. Firstly, 'being indifferent persons to the greatest part of the state' they have 'no interest, or but a remote one, in any act of injustice'. Secondly, 'being satisfied with their present condition, and with their part in society, [they] have an immediate interest in every execution of justice, which is so necessary to the upholding of society' (537). The first reason will explain only why the rulers do not disobey the rules themselves. The second reason is necessary to explain why they actually enforce rules of justice. Since the rulers, as Hume points out in the following paragraph, will also judge disputes, the first reason will explain why, *if* they judge disputes at all, they will judge them impartially. The second reason is necessary to explain why they *will* judge disputes.

One suspects that Hume exaggerates the indifference of the rulers to the gains they may acquire by breaking rules of justice. The rulers' indifference to the greater part of the state will at most explain why they judge impartially disputes between other members of the state. It will not explain why they judge impartially disputes between *themselves* and other members of the state, instead of adopting the doctrine that the king can do no wrong, nor will it explain why they obey the rules themselves—and, of course not all rulers do obey the rules themselves.

The second reason, a reason why rulers *enforce* rules of justice, needs more elaboration than Hume gives it. He is trying to say that while the rulers have an immediate interest in the prosperity of the state, the ruled have only a remote one. For this reason the rulers enforce justice, judge disputes impartially, and compel the ruled to engage in enterprises which are of long-term benefit to everyone, but which benefits the ruled will ignore because of their preference for short-term over long-term interest. Though Hume does not enlarge upon why the short-term interest of the ruler is more intimately bound up with the welfare of the state than is the interest of the ruled, it seems possible that he might have agreed to the following. (1) The ruler is more concerned with the welfare of the state because it is the state over which he rules, just as I may be more concerned than another about the state of a house because it is my house. (2) The ruler's income will be in part derived from taxation, which will depend upon the prosperity of the country over which he rules. (3) If justice is not enforced to some extent, he will not have a state to rule over. (4) His prestige will depend upon the power of the state, which will depend upon its prosperity, which will depend upon rules of justice being enforced. However, it is very questionable whether, with the exception of (1), these interests on the part of the rulers in the enforcement of justice are any more short-term interests than are those of the ruled. And (1) is not exactly a short-term *interest*, so much as an immediate concern in the welfare of the state. A man who cares for the welfare of his children, even though he does so because they are his children, does not thereby have a short-term interest in the welfare of his children. And just as people other than he can care about the welfare of his children, so people other than rulers can care about the welfare of the state.

My conclusion is that it is not much more in the interest of the rulers to enforce justice than it is in the interest of those over whom they rule to do this. I suspect that the answer to Hume's problem is very often, though perhaps not always, that rule-observance is as much or nearly as much imposed on the rulers as it is on the ruled. The idea of a ruler who is above the law, and imposes laws on other people because it is in his 'natural' interest to do so, is more often than not a myth. In a country which approximates to democracy rulers cannot with impunity disobey the law, and must enforce it, because if they did not enforce it they would lose their jobs. And they become rulers not so much from love of natural gain, but from love of power and prestige. A so-called absolute monarch would differ from this in degree only. There would be many things he could do with impunity which a ruler who was not absolute could not do. But still, he is surrounded by other powerful men, and without the ring of Gyges cannot cheat them beyond a certain degree without losing that support without which he cannot rule. It is, indeed, because of rules that he has the power that he has—rules which assign him power because he is the son of his father, and which decree that men shall obey him. The same rules dictate that he shall hold levees, receive ambassadors, and appoint generals. Like everybody else, he must do what is expected of him, just as his power derives from other people doing what is expected of them.[2] It is because it is expected of them that his troops obey him, and if they obey him partly because they will be shot if they do not, those who shoot them do so because that is what is expected of them. Not only is the ruler's power derived from the rules, the rules which give him power also prescribe his duties and circumscribe his behaviour.

(4) Hume speaks as if the device of government, which involves having men whose short-term interest it is to see that rules of justice are enforced, consists in certain men being *put* in the position of being rulers. Again, he is over-simplifying. For one thing, men are often not put in the position of being rulers. They seize this position without being asked. For another thing, at some time or other men will not only have to put other men into the pre-existing office of being a ruler. The very office of being a ruler will have to be invented by them. It is, of course, a very speculative question how rulers first came about, but it seems very likely that in wartime some men, as Hume suggests (Ess.114–16), saw a need, and partly from love of power, and partly from concern for the success or survival of that community, took it upon themselves to fulfil it. (It is fashionable to be disparaging about the love of power as a motive, but, if some men did not love power, it is likely that there would be no one to perform certain functions which are useful to society, from which it follows that love of power is, as one might expect, a motive which has a survival value.) Hence, though government is necessary to mankind, it seems possible that governors were not, as Hume here supposes, deliberately invented by men as a conscious device to remedy a situation brought about by a deficiency in their natures (preference for short-term interest), so much as something which, like Topsy, just grew, as the result of certain impulses

---

[2] 'Nothing appears more surprising to those who consider human affairs with a philosophical eye, than the easiness with which the many are governed by the few; and the implicit submission, with which men resign their own sentiments and passions to those of their rulers. When we enquire by what means this wonder is effected, we shall find, that, as Force is always on the side of the governed, the governors have nothing to support them but opinion. It is, therefore, on opinion only that government is founded; and this maxim extends to the most despotic and most military governments, as well as to the most free and most popular. The soldan of Egypt, or the emperor of Rome, might drive his harmless subjects, like brute beasts, against their sentiments and inclination: but he must, at least, have led his *mamelukes*, or *praetorian bands*, like men, by their opinion' ('Of the First Principles of Government', Ess.109–10).

which make some men enjoy ruling and other men enjoy obeying. That these impulses have the desirable result of producing a government, which is necessary to mankind, is a manifestation of the tendency in man to have impulses which, like hunger, prompt him to perform actions which are to his advantage, though man's advantage is not in fact their object. It seems likely that this tendency, which moralists like Bishop Butler ascribed to the unseen hand of Divine Providence, is one which has been biologically selected because it is of advantage to mankind.

(5) It is not clear whether Hume is saying that rulers are *put* into power by the people over whom they are to rule, *after* which time it becomes their short-term interest to enforce justice, or whether he is saying that they choose to become rulers because they see that it is in their short-term interest to enforce justice. His view that government is a device adopted by man suggests the former, which is also suggested by the words, 'But this being impracticable with respect to all mankind, it can only take place with respect to a few, *whom we thus immediately interest* [my italics] in the execution of justice' (537). The latter view is suggested by his words in the very next sentence: '. . . *have no interest*, or but a remote one, in any act of injustice; . . . *have an immediate interest* [all italics mine] in every execution of justice . . .' (537).

The first view, that rulers are put into power by men, from an appreciation of the advantages of having rulers, invites the question: 'How do men make it in the short-term interest of their rulers to govern?' By offering them a salary, perhaps, and paying them in proportion to their success, or, since many men enjoy ruling for its own sake, simply allowing some men to rule, and removing them from power if they are unjust. It is, in this case, in the short-term interest of the rulers to enforce the rules of justice only because the ruled retain some control over them, which implies that the 'ruled' are in some way more powerful than the 'rulers' or, what is more likely, that rulers are observing some set of conventions which demand that they remain in office only so long as they enforce the rules of justice to the satisfaction of those over whom they rule. Even this latter implies that some power remains with the ruled, as a set of conventions which are not in any way enforced by the ruled will not be obeyed by the rulers for very long. That Hume is talking, implausibly, about some past historical act is suggested by the fact that he must have known that some contemporary rulers are not subject to the judgement of the ruled upon the manner in which they enforce rules of justice, except to the extent that government which is bad beyond a certain point is likely to produce insurrection.

The second view, that rulers become rulers because they see that it is to their short-term interest to enforce rules of justice, has the advantage that it does not suggest, improbably, that men get together to select leaders from a rational appreciation of the disadvantages of not having them. It is at least compatible with, if it does not entail, the view that certain men become rulers not because they are chosen by the multitude, but because they want to rule, and so impose themselves on the ruled, partly from an appreciation of the advantages of being rulers, partly because they enjoy ruling. Once they are in the position of being rulers, they enforce justice, decide disputes, make new legislation, and organize co-operative enterprises, for such reasons as Hume has given. An enlightened ruler—though perhaps Hume forgets, at this point, that not all rulers are enlightened—sees that his power and affluence depend on the state over which he rules being undivided and prosperous. Hence, though it is necessary to have rulers, it is neither the case that the ruled select rulers, nor that the rulers become and continue to be rulers, from either an interested or a disinterested appreciation of the advantages of this institution. It is just another example of that harmony between the wants of different people which causes human desires to lead their possessors to bring into existence goods which their possessors were not aiming at bringing about, as a side effect of their aiming at other things.

We have seen that Hume was wrong in thinking that it is, apart from avoiding the punishment for breaking them, in the interest of individual men that they observe rules of justice; what is in the interest of individual men is that other men observe them. Having rulers who enforce rules of justice does not, strictly speaking, make it in the interest of all men to observe rules of justice. What it does do is to make it in the interest of all men to observe these rules so long as they cannot break them without being detected. Hume has said explicitly that it is in the interest—short-term interest—of rulers to *enforce* rules of justice. Is it in the interest of rulers to obey the rules themselves, or is it, as it is with all men, in the rulers' interest that all other men but them observe rules of justice, so long as rules of justice are not imposed on them? Could the rulers be in a better position than other men to escape having these rules of justice imposed on them, either because they are more easily able to escape detection, or because they can *make* rules which favour themselves? I think that the answer to this question is that it is bound to be easier for rulers than for others to put themselves, in one way or the other, in a privileged position. I am conservative enough to feel that, to some extent, they are entitled to do so, and cynical enough to believe that this very fact is one of the main reasons why some men want to be rulers. It is better to be ruled by men who become rulers because they can then break the rules we have with more impunity than other men, and because they are able to make special exceptions of, or even make rules in favour of, themselves when they do not positively break the rules, than not to have any rulers at all.

I would not like to end my discussion of this point by giving the impression that I think that self-interest is the only motive from which some men rule, and other men obey. I have already suggested that some men enjoy ruling, and perhaps other men also enjoy both ruling and obeying. I do not at all wish to deny—any more than did Hume—that some men rule, and other men obey, from a sense of duty, from love of admiration or esteem, or from concern about the welfare of those who would be harmed by their failure to rule, or of their failure to obey. On the other hand, I cannot disguise from myself the fact that unless it were predominantly in the interest of the rulers to rule, and the ruled to obey, no one would rule, and no one would obey, and ordered society would perish. However, there is no reason why the term 'interested'—Bishop Butler said something similar—should be construed so narrowly as to suggest that someone satisfying his desire for, say, money or power, is acting in an interested way, but someone satisfying his conscience, his desire for the approval of others, or his desire to see his community flourish, is not acting in an interested way. It has been held that the term 'interested' is used in such a manner that organizing the maximum satisfaction of one's wants, whether the wants in question be for wealth and power, or a satisfied conscience and the prosperity of one's compatriots, is behaviour which is interested and, if this is not the way in which the word actually is used, it would produce less confusion if it were. In this more accurate sense, it can be in men's interests to rule even if they gain little materially from ruling, or even if they lose by doing so.

(6) Though Hume, in this section, speaks as if government were necessary to enforce justice in any society, it appears in the next section (VIII) that he thinks that magistrates are not necessary in *poor* societies in times of *peace*. They are not necessary in poor societies because the differences in men's worldly goods will not be great enough to offer much temptation to transgress rules of justice. Even in poor societies, however, government is necessary in wartime. 'An *Indian* is but little tempted to dispossess another of his hut, or to steal his bow, as being already provided of the same advantages; and as to any superior fortune, which may attend one above another in hunting and fishing, 'tis only casual and temporary, and will have but small tendency to disturb society' (539). Civil war is much more feared than any other

kind of war, because in civil war men cannot face their enemies together, but have to face them single, and in civil war their enemies will be men whose 'commerce is advantageous to them' (540). Foreign war in a society without government necessarily produces civil war. 'Throw any considerable goods among men, they instantly fall a quarrelling, while each strives to get possession of what pleases him, without regard to the consequences. In a foreign war the most considerable of all goods, life and limbs, are at stake; and as every one shuns dangerous posts, seizes the best arms, seeks excuse for the slightest wounds, the rules of society, which may be well enough observ'd, while men were calm, can now no longer take place, when they are in such commotion' (540). It is perhaps worth notice that this is the first place that Hume explicitly acknowledges that society may be disrupted by anything other than quarrels over goods. Weapons are goods, but posts are not, and what men fear to lose is not so much their property, which is transferable, as their life and limbs, which are not.

(7) Hume says, 'It has been observ'd, in treating of the passions, that men are mightily govern'd by the imagination, and proportion their affections more to the light, under which any object appears to them, than to its real and intrinsic value. What strikes upon them with a strong and lively idea commonly prevails above what lies in a more obscure light; and it must be a great superiority of value, that is able to compensate this advantage. Now as every thing, that is contiguous to us, either in space or time, strikes upon us with such an idea, it has a proportional effect on the will and passions, and commonly operates with more force than any object, that lies in a more distant and obscure light. Tho' we may be fully convinc'd, that the latter object excels the former, we are not able to regulate our actions by this judgment; but yield to the sollicitations of our passions, which always plead in favour of whatever is near and contiguous' (534-5). These remarks, which are intended as an explanation of *why* we prefer near to distant pleasure, are a summing up of what Hume says in Book II, Part III, Section VII of the *Treatise*, entitled 'Of contiguity, and distance in space and time'.

(8) Hume says, 'Whoever chuses the means, chuses also the end' (536). This remark is highly reminiscent of a similar one by Kant, who says: 'Who wills the end, wills [so far as reason has decisive influence on his action] also the means which are indispensably necessary and in his power.'[3] Hume's saying and Kant's are, of course, converses of one another. It is possible that they are both right, and that since choosing a

---

[3] H. J. Paton, *The Moral Law*, pp. 84-5.

means implies choosing an end, and choosing an end implies choosing a means, choosing a means is equivalent to choosing an end.

I think that, perhaps interpreted with some small amount of latitude, both statements are true. What they amount to is that all that choosing some distant end consists in, is choosing to perform some action which is a means to that end. He who chooses to smoke chooses lung cancer, and he who chooses lung cancer chooses (if smoking is the only way of getting cancer) to smoke. Hume should have said, 'Whoever chooses the means, chooses also the ends which he *believes*, rightly or wrongly, result from these means.' Kant's *proviso*, that 'who wills the end, wills the means', is true only so long as reason has decisive influence on his action, and is presumably intended to exclude weakness of will. Someone may will not to have lung cancer, and yet not will the means (giving up smoking) because of this weakness of will. Personally, I think that this is a qualification which Kant did not need to make. Someone may *want* to avoid getting lung cancer, and still smoke, or may resolve to avoid getting lung cancer, and still smoke, but the only form in which his choosing not to get, at some future time, lung cancer can manifest itself at *this* time is in his actually choosing actions which he believes will result in his not getting lung cancer.

It would be irrelevant to consider what use Kant makes of his remark. But what use does Hume make of it? This becomes clear if we take the contrapositive of what Hume says, which is that whoever does (or can) not choose the end, does (or can) not choose the means to that end. This is why anyone who does not prefer large distant pleasures (the end) is unable to choose the means to the greater pleasure, if this entails losing the nearer small one. The impossibility of his choosing the end—large distant pleasure—is psychological. The impossibility of his choosing the means, given that it is impossible for him to prefer the end, is logical.

Kant, incidentally, thinks his statement would be true, were it not for weakness of will, or is true, except when there is weakness of will. Hume thinks his statement is true, even when there is weakness of will, for it is precisely a case of weakness that he has in mind. In this, as we have seen, Hume was right and Kant was wrong.

(9) Hume says, 'This gives rise to what in an improper sense we call *reason*, which is a principle, that is often contradictory to those propensities that display themselves upon the approach of the object' (536). When *both* the object which gives me great pleasure and the object which gives me small pleasure are remote in time, I prefer the one which gives me great pleasure, even though I know that, upon their nearer approach, I will again choose the less pleasurable, but also less

distant, of the two objects. Hume describes this as 'what in an *improper* [my italics] sense we call reason' because preferring one thing to another, or desiring one thing more than another, is not a process of reasoning. It does not consist in inferring one proposition from another, nor does it consist in believing anything, nor in deliberating upon what to do. I am, when I view the two objects from a distance, in a reasonable frame of mind, though my not being in such a frame of mind does not consist in my having false beliefs. I believe correctly that one thing is more pleasurable than another, even when I prefer that which is least preferable. In Book II, Part III, Section III of the *Treatise*, Hume says that reason cannot influence the will, but that we wrongly suppose it can because 'certain instincts originally implanted in our natures, such as benevolence and resentment, the love of life, and kindness to children; or the general appetite to good, and aversion to evil, consider'd merely as such' (417) are so calm that they are readily confused with 'the determinations of reason'. Hence we wrongly suppose that an action, proceeding from one or other of these principles, proceeds from reason, because neither makes any disorder in the soul. A preference for a greater to a lesser good is presumably one manifestation of 'the general appetite to good and aversion to evil, considered merely as such'. Though perhaps Hume even here thinks that it is mistakenly called reason because of its calmness, it would seem that there is more to be said for calling a preference of greater goods to smaller ones 'reasonable' than that we do this because we mistake reason for something quite different.

(10) Hume speaks as if rulers and ruled were different people or groups of people. Are his remarks applicable to a democracy, where the people who are ruled are alleged to be the very same people as the people who rule?

Whatever may be true of some ideal democracy, Hume's remarks do apply to the countries today which are called democratic. (I do not intend the phrase 'which are called democratic' to be disparaging. I see no reason to regard democracy as an ideal from which all existing institutions fall short, even if democracy were practicable.) The statement that in an ideal democracy rulers and ruled would be the same, for the people rule, and the people are ruled, would be only a subterfuge to hide the fact that, in any actual democracy, the minority must inevitably impose its will to a greater or lesser extent on the majority. In an elective oligarchy like our own, the rulers are selected periodically by people who have little hand in choosing that small group of people from whom the selection must be made; who have little control over what their rulers do between the times when they select them; whose rulers do not necessarily do the things they said they would do when they needed to persuade people to vote for them; and who cannot decide on individual items of policy, but only on large packages of items, so that they must vote for some policies they do not want in order to secure others they do want. Hence the rulers cannot do what all the ruled want, and may not be doing what any of the ruled want. The rulers, in fact, are clearly different from the ruled, but simply have to get some rough, ill-informed, over-all approval from the ruled, at periodic intervals, for what they do.

(11) All actual governments may be regarded as falling between two extremes. One extreme is where rulers and ruled are identical, and rules of justice are imposed by everybody upon everybody. The other extreme is where a person or group of persons, who is himself not subject to rules of justice, imposes rules upon everybody else. In the first case, which is obviously impracticable except perhaps in very small communities, everyone is subject to the same rules, and plays an equal part in deciding what they shall be and in enforcing them. In the second case, the rulers decide what the rules shall be, and impose them upon the ruled. In the first case, the rules adopted are likely to be in the interest or supposed interest of the majority of people, who may be wise enough not to impose rules which are against the interest of the minority to a divisive extent. In the second case, it might seem as if the rulers would make rules which were simply in their interest. Even if these rulers had unlimited power, however, it would not be in their interest to ignore the needs of the ruled completely. For their wealth and power will be largely dependent upon the wealth and power of those over whom they rule, and it is consequently to their advantage to make rules which enable their subjects to prosper. Hence they will themselves be bound, from interest if not from necessity, to obey the rules that they impose on others. For if they totally ignore the interest of those over whom they rule, the latter will become so impoverished and discontented that their own power and prosperity will be undermined. Even a farmer must consult the interest of his sheep to the extent that he would not prosper unless his sheep were healthy and well fed, and, for these reasons, men might have much the same rules imposed upon them as they would have adopted themselves had they the power to settle this matter. Actual rulers, of course, fall somewhere between these two artificial extremes. No ruler is quite above the law, and no ruler is quite as much subject to it as the men over whom he rules.

(12) Hume does not suppose that men are in favour of having a government only from self-interest and that they obey it once it has been set up only from interest and duty. In his essay 'Of the First

Principles of Government' he says that 'affection to wisdom and virtue in a sovereign' has great influence in prompting men to obey him. He thinks, however, that such a motive is merely derivative, since it presupposes, before it comes into operation, that a government has already been set up from some other motives. For the sovereign, before he becomes the object of affection, 'must antecedently be supposed invested with a public character, otherwise the public esteem will serve him in no stead, nor will his virtue have any influence beyond a narrow sphere' (Ess.112).

(13) I do not suppose that Hume thought that men ever met together to decide whether or not to have a ruler to enforce rules of justice, and who he should be. If this were ever to happen, however, there would, from the point of view of each individual voter, be four abstract possibilities. He could vote for a ruler who would impose rules of justice on (1) everyone, or (2) no one, or (3) everyone but him, and on (4) him but not on anyone else. Each man's first preference, in such a situation, would be (3), to have a ruler who imposed rules on everybody but himself. Each would realize, of course, that he stood no chance of getting his first preference adopted. No man would run any risk of having his last preference (4) adopted, for having rules imposed upon one man only would be of no advantage to anyone. The alternative (2), of having no rules, is similar to the one which men are meeting together in order to avoid, and they are already sufficiently familiar with its disadvantages. Hence the only possibility left (1) is for them to vote for a ruler who will impose rules of justice upon everybody. Though each man will have no hope of getting his first preference agreed upon, however, he may hope to obtain it surreptitiously, by voting to have a ruler who imposes rules of justice on everybody, but deciding to break these rules when he can. Since everyone will realize that this is what the others will also aim to do, each will be in favour of rules of justice being sufficiently well enforced to prevent the others from breaking them, and, as a result, each will be in favour of having rules of justice which have the undesired consequence that he himself cannot easily depart from them. The selfishness of each man, therefore, will curb the selfishness of all the others.

This, as I have said, is an artificial and impossible account of how and why rulers come to be chosen. Man has biologically selected impulses to conform to what society wishes and to obey rules, even when it is not in his interest to do those things, just as bees have an impulse to sting those who approach their hive even though they lose their lives by doing so.[4] And some men will have similarly biologically

---

[4] See my *Our Knowledge of Right and Wrong* and Richard Dawkins, *The Selfish Gene*, OUP, 1976.

selected impulses to rule.[5] Hence a system of rulers imposing rules of justice which might have been adopted because of a rational appreciation by those ruled of the advantages of having rulers, will in fact be adopted as much from a natural desire to dominate, on the part of some men, and innate docility, on the part of others, as from rational egotism.

---

[5] 'The love of dominion is so strong in the breasts of man, that many not only submit to, but court all the dangers, and fatigues, and cares of government; and men, once raised to that station, though often led astray by private passions, find, in ordinary cases, a visible interest in the impartial administration of justice. The persons, who first attain this distinction by the consent, tacit or express, of the people, must be endowed with superior personal qualities of valour, force, integrity, or prudence, which command respect and confidence: and, after government is established, a regard to birth, rank, and station has a mighty influence over men, and enforces the decrees of the magistrate' ('Of the Origin of Government', Ess.115).

SECTION VIII

Of the Source of Allegiance

MEN capable, especially when poor, of living without government, which is produced by foreign war, and the civil war which this leads to (539-40); this fact explains why government was at first monarchical (541); since a society which had no government preceded a society with government, it was natural for men to try to found our duty of allegiance upon obligations which were recognized before government came into existence (541); this explains why it has been thought that men ought to obey the government only because they have promised or contracted to do this (541-2); those who maintained that justice is natural must derive our duty of civil obedience from a promise, for government is plainly artificial, but promising, the origin of which is lost in antiquity, may be supposed (though wrongly) to be natural (542); our duty of obedience to the government, however, cannot be derived from our duty to keep our promises, because civil obedience and promising were both invented and are both morally obligatory on account of the inconveniences they remedy (542-3); and because government was invented from the need to preserve order in society, which is a different need from that from which promises were invented (543); and because promise-keeping is the effect of government, rather than its cause (543); and because civil obedience is no more closely connected with promising than it is with the other 'laws of nature' (544); and because men may bind themselves by a promise to do what is already in their interest (543-4); and because if this interest is as general and avowed as that of promising (as it is) it will have an obligation independent of that of promising (544-5); and because, since promising and civil government alike depend directly on an obvious interest, there is no need to derive either from the other (545); and because the moral obligation to obey the government is independent of our moral obligation to keep our promises, since both institutions are advantageous in their own right (545); and because the advantages of promising (facilitating commerce) are different from the advantages of government (enforcing law and order) (545); and because civil government would have been necessary, had promising never been thought of, and promising is more dependent on government than government on promising (546); appeal to authority, which is legitimate in morals (as men must know what gives them the pleasure and pains which constitute moral good and evil), shows that the moral obligation of allegiance does not arise from a promise (546-7); for (1) magistrates conceal the fact that they derive their authority from a promise; (2) if government depended on promises, these would be made explicitly; (3) even a tacit promise cannot be made unintentionally, but subjects are not aware of having made such a promise; (4) men imagine themselves bound to rulers whom they would not have promised to obey, because they are the successors of rulers of great antiquity (too great for men to have promised them obedience); (5) dwelling within the dominions of a government cannot be regarded as a tacit promise, for most people do not have any choice; (6) a man who made it clear from infancy that he did *not* consent to being governed would not be regarded as absolved from the duty of allegiance; (7) a man is bound to obey an absolute ruler, whom he has neither promised nor consented to obey; (8) we believe a promise reinforces an already-existing obligation to obedience (547-9).

COMMENTS

(1) I find all the arguments which Hume uses to show that our duty to obey the government is not a special case of an antecedently existing duty to keep our promises, and that, in consequence, we have a duty to obey the government whether we consent to do this or not, absolutely conclusive, and can only wonder that the contrary view has survived until the present day, in spite of his arguments.

Hume's attitude to our duty to keep our promises and our duty of allegiance to the government is utilitarian. Both duties, he thinks, arise from the fact that they (government and promising) are useful human institutions, which can exist and retain their usefulness only if promises are usually kept and the government usually obeyed. Hence even if people had promised to obey the government, which they seldom have, it would be a needless circumlocution to attempt to derive our obligation of allegiance from our obligation to keep our promises; our obligation, as well as our interest, both to keep our promises and obey the government, follow directly from their usefulness. But Hume's argument in this section is so lucid, so forceful, and so wittily expressed that I have no inclination to elaborate upon it.

(2) It is not always clear whether by 'the source of allegiance', in the heading to this section, Hume means 'the psychological causes of our coming to feel that we have a duty of allegiance' or 'the reasons which cause us to have, and to be justified in thinking that we have, a

duty of allegiance'. When he makes remarks such as, 'Our civil duties, therefore, must soon detach themselves from our promises, and acquire a separate force and influence' (544) he seems to be speaking about the former, i.e. about what causes us to feel that we owe allegiance. When he elaborates upon the usefulness, or indeed, the absolute necessity of government, to any community of more than a certain degree of size and affluence, he appears to be trying to justify our feeling that we have a duty of allegiance to the government, by pointing out how dire would be the consequences of our not having a government. But the two questions, 'How does it come about that we feel that we owe allegiance?' and 'What justifies us in feeling that we owe allegiance?' are not as distinct in Hume's philosophy as they might seem to be to us. This is because he regards morality as an empirical science, the problems of which, roughly speaking, are settled by finding out what sentiments of approbation men actually have, and what arouses them. What in fact arouses our sentiments of approbation is the usefulness and agreeableness of certain characteristics (from sympathy with those to whom they are useful or agreeable); hence to say that our approbation is aroused by the usefulness of something is both to assign its cause, and to give it a justification. For the same reason, to say that our approbation of allegiance is caused by our perception of its usefulness *is* to justify it; at least, our approbation of allegiance, which is *explained* by governments being believed to be useful, is *justified* if they are shown really to be useful. This last observation explains why, though governments are useful from their first inception, they are not at once approved, according to Hume, independently of our having promised to obey them. It takes time for us fully to appreciate their usefulness, and so to approve of allegiance, not because it is a special case of promise-keeping, but for its own sake. Hence we would have an obligation to obey the government, because it is in fact useful, before we felt approval of obedience, because of the time it would take for our appreciation of the usefulness of government to arouse in us a special feeling of approval of obedience to it. (It follows from this, it might be supposed, that '*Education,* and *the artifice of politicians*' (546) might cause our sentiments of approbation to deviate from their natural tendency to be aroused by what is useful, but Hume usually seems to think not so much that this alters the direction of our sentiments, as that it intensifies the sentiments favouring what is useful which we already have.)

(3) If commentators on Kant's *Fundamental Principles of the Metaphysics of Morals* may point out that jewels, to which Kant likened the good will, do not shine by their own light, perhaps I may be forgiven for remarking that plants which are grafted on other plants—as, Hume

thinks, the duty of allegiance is at first grafted on our duty to keep our promises—*never* take root of themselves (542).[1]

(4) '*All men*, say they, *are born free and equal*' (542). What does this sentence mean, and what is Hume's attitude to it? Men, of course, are not all free and are not all equal. They are not all free, in that there are many things, including legal restraints, which often prevent them from doing what they want. They are not all equal, in that they are often very dissimilar, and dissimilar in respect of the degrees in which they possess desirable characteristics like strength, intelligence, beauty, and so on. Nor, of course, are they *literally* any more free or equal when they are first born than at any other time. (Perhaps, at this time, they are more equal, but less free.) The statement, then, is conveying something by means of a figure of speech, presumably, that all men are similar in some very fundamental way which entails that they all have equal rights, or if they do not all have the same rights, that there are certain ways in which they all ought to be treated alike, even if there are other ways in which they may be treated differently. It is, however, very difficult to see in what ways men are all similar, over and above their all being men, and what rights they all have, or in what ways they all ought to be treated alike, over and above the formal claim that similar men ought to have similar rights and be treated in similar ways. And the claim that all men have a right to equal consideration is but very little better. For all it amounts to is that we should treat men equally in giving them whatever rights they do have, and, since this claim is compatible with the rights we are supposed to consider being very different, it adds up to very little. There is a sense in which men are certainly equal; for there is a sense in which moral rules apply to all men alike. All men must keep their promises, for example. But this just means that all men must keep their promises *if* they have made any, just as all men, whether fathers or not, should care for their children *if* they have any, and all men, whether murderers or not, should be hanged *if* they have committed murder, and all men, whether serfs or slaves or not, have the same duty to their overlord or owner *if* they have one. Hence the assertion that men have this kind of equality or rights is of very little value, for it is compatible with their actual rights and duties being very different. Again, we may be all equal before the law, in the sense that the law applies to everybody, but in this sense our being equal before the law is compatible with the law's assigning to different people very different rights and duties. In this sense, a law

---

[1] Mr Mackie tells me that some jewels do shine by their own light, and some grafts do root by themselves.

which hangs coloured men for raping white women, but does not hang white men for raping coloured women applies equally to all men; that they are *all* hanged *if* they are coloured, treats all men alike in just the same way as does the rule that they are hanged *if* they are murderers. Again, if there is a God, it seems reasonable to suppose that there is a sense in which all men are equal in his eyes, but, since it is improbable that he looks upon all men the same, it may just mean that he looks upon all men the same unless there are reasons for looking upon them differently. And, of course, God may look upon all men the same in that he will look upon *any* man who is a saint differently from the way he looks on *any* man who is a sinner, while he looks upon men differently in that he looks upon saints differently from sinners. Hence the statement that men are all equal in the eyes of God is profoundly uninformative, unless it is coupled with a view about *what* things cause God to look upon men differently.

The clear implication of the statement 'Men are born free and equal' is that inequalities of power and freedom are all artificial. To the extent that 'free' means 'free from the coercion of conventional rules', as opposed to the limitations on our actions imposed by lack of physical strength and competence or mental ability, then all differences in freedom are artificial, for the conventions which restrain men's freedom are artificial. And to the extent that 'power' refers to the power conferred on people by their position in society, which is a position allocated to them by a system of rules rather than by superior ability, then all differences in their power will be artificial. However, freedom from the coercion of rules, and the power conferred upon someone by his position in society, are not the only kind of freedom and the only kind of power. For example, differences in power founded upon strength, intelligence, and personality are not artificial; and differences in freedom from restraint other than the restraints imposed upon men by human conventions are not artificial. To this extent, then, the statement that men are born free and equal is simply not true. It could be true if all differences between one man and another were the result of environment and not inherited—Descartes appears to have thought something of the kind, and many modern socialists appear to want to believe it— but this is quite certainly untrue.

Not only is the statement that no inequalities between men are innate, but that they are all the result of artificial human convention, quite certainly untrue, the statement that conventional differences do not justify us in treating men differently is also untrue. Having more property than most is a fact about some men which could not exist apart from human conventions, as Hume has shown, and having more money (as opposed, say, to having more land) than most men is doubly conventional, for property depends upon conventions, and the purchasing power of money also depends upon conventions. But having more money or property does justify us in treating men differently, if only in that we might be justified in asking a rich man for money, when we would not be justified in asking a poor man for money, or in that we might have a duty to give money to a poor man, where we would not have a duty to give money to a man who was rich. There is no reason why we should not ask a rich man to pay more tax than a poor man (because he can afford more) or do jury service in preference to a poor man (because he can afford the time). Indeed, conventional differences are enormously important in assessing how people ought to be treated. The organization of society involves the existence of an enormously complicated hierarchy of rank, authority, power, social position, and so on, the existence of which depends on a highly intricate set of conventions determining what powers and rights people have, and what they have to do, and what is due to them. It is because of conventions that the Queen signs bills and opens Parliament, the Speaker presides in the House of Commons, the Archbishop of York supports the monarch at the coronation, that the vice-chancellor's secretary does what the vice-chancellor says (if the vice-chancellor does what the vice-chancellor's secretary says, this results from nature rather than convention), that presidents preside and soldiers fight and ministers conduct services and centre-forwards score goals and conductors conduct. To say that, because all men are born equal, none of these conventional differences should be taken account of in determining how men and women are to treat one another would be utterly and completely absurd. There may be some deep sense in which all men are brothers, but if, because I think this, I treat the managing director like the tea boy, I am likely to please neither of them. It is not permissible for a soldier to treat his commanding officer just like any other man, on the grounds that the difference between them is purely conventional, nor a priest his bishop, nor a tenant his landlord, nor a Member of Parliament his whip. Nor can one's obligation to take account of these conventional differences depend upon one's consent. The soldier may have volunteered, but he may not have done so, and, once he is in the army, he is bound to obey orders to which he does not consent.

One might argue that, though there are conventional differences between one man and another, and though these, as well as natural differences, determine how men ought to be treated, natural differences are always prior to conventional differences, in that the latter ought always to be founded upon the former. Differences of rank should be founded upon differences of ability, for example. There are obviously some good utilitarian reasons for wishing that this were so, but it would, equally obviously, be going much too far to argue that we should take account of conventional differences only to the extent that these are founded upon natural differences. It would be disastrous, for example, if I did not obey my commandng officer in an emergency, on the grounds that he had bought rather than merited his commission. Nor should we disrupt the fabric of existing society on the grounds that we should ignore conventional differences that are not founded upon natural differences, say, differences of merit. One might think, however, that one ought to try to bring about a society in which all conventional differences were so founded, but personally I have grave doubts about whether even as much as this is true. (I shall assume without argument that it is simply impossible to have a society in which there are *no* conventional differences between one man and another.) One consequence of such a doctrine would be that conventional differences, even when appropriately founded upon natural ones, should not be allowed to pass on to later generations, on the grounds, for example, that a son may not have the ability which enabled his father to acquire money or a crown or a seat in Parliament; but there are strong utilitarian arguments against not allowing parents to pass on some of the advantages in wealth, education, and social position to their children, even were it practicable totally to prevent them. (It is obviously impracticable to prevent educated parents from educating their children, for example.) One of these utilitarian arguments is used by Hume (510–11); if parents are not allowed to pass on their wealth to their children, this deprives them of a strong incentive to acquire wealth, and everybody loses as a result.

Conventional advantages may be distributed proportionately to natural ones, or they may be distributed equally, undesirable and impracticable though this latter would be. Conceivably they could be distributed inversely in proportion to natural advantages; indeed some case, on the grounds of equality, can be made for doing this. If people are unequal in respect of natural endowments, the way to make all men as equal as possible over all is to give advantages of rank and money and social position and prestige to those who are *poorly* endowed by nature. Indeed, if we consider that we ought to bring about a state in which everybody is as equal as possible, then this would be the way to do it. The utilitarian arguments against this, however, would be overwhelming. It would mean rewarding the useless more than those endowed with valuable qualities (which must inevitably discourage people from acquiring the latter) and putting the weak and the stupid in positions of authority. And the idea of holding back on egalitarian principles those with the greater potentiality of development would be the height of folly. A gardener who put his best plants in the worst soil rather than the other way round, on the grounds that plants were by nature equal, would get but poor results, and plants, unlike men, do not need leaders and doctors and teachers and scientists. Of course, in many societies, probably in most, the question of how conventional advantages are to be apportioned only arises to a limited extent, and in Hume's day it arose less than in ours. It is to be hoped that men, actuated mostly by self-interest and limited benevolence, will be led by the fact (sometimes attributed to providence) that men's interests for the most part coincide, into courses of action which benefit the community as well as themselves. This higgledy-piggledy arrangement has some appeal to those whose faith in human wisdom is small, and who have a preference for liberty rather than order. To sum up, men are not naturally equal, nor should any attempt be made to make them so by means of artifice and convention. Inequalities that are due to convention, i.e. the fact that men occupy different positions in an enormously complex hierarchy, carrying with them different duties, rights, responsibilities, powers, authority, and functions determined by an equally complex system of man-made rules, are useful, desirable, and often absolutely necessary. It is desirable that men should occupy those positions which they are fit to occupy, but impracticable, and often undesirable, to allow their natural fitness for such positions to be the only factor which determines what these positions shall be, partly because the positions they or their parents actually have must be given some weight, partly because the idea of a committee which apportions all positions—some may be so apportioned—according to merit is odious, unfeasible, and would leave too little freedom for individual initiative. I do not know quite what is left of the claim that men should be treated equally when these facts are recognized. There is, of course, the rather empty claim that all similar men should be treated similarly, which does not tell one what differences between one man and another justify one in treating them differently. And it may well be that very large differences in wealth mean that human resources are being used uneconomically— for some will be deprived of necessities so that others may live in luxury—and that very large differences in power, to the limited extent that these are avoidable, may leave many open to exploitation. On the other hand, too equal a distribution will leave little incentive to those with greater than average ability, allow no more leisure to those capable of benefiting themselves and others from having it, and make the necessary use of power the subject of interminable and fruitless discussion.

Men, therefore, are not equal, are not born equal, and ought to be treated unequally, whether they consent to this unequal treatment or not. They ought, however, always to be treated humanely, regardless of any difference of colour, rank, or natural ability between one man and another.

It looks as if everything that I have said about equality applies automatically to freedom. For if not everybody can or ought to be equal in authority, it follows, or so it can be argued, that not everybody can or ought to be equal in freedom. For those people who are superior to others by reason of the position allocated to them by a set of man-made rules must be precisely those people to whom these rules allocate more freedom. The ones ruled over must have less freedom, because they are ruled, and the ones who rule must have more freedom, because, since they rule, they have powers which the ruled do not have. The argument, however, is erroneous. The freedom of those who rule can be as much, if not more, circumscribed than those over whom they rule. The rules of the system may impose upon the ruled a duty to obey, but also impose on the rulers a duty to rule, and the latter may be more, not less, onerous than the former. One must, furthermore, distinguish between two different ways in which rules may restrict the freedom of the people governed by those rules. One's freedom may be restricted by the rules or commands of one's superiors, or it may, so to speak, be restricted by the rules themselves, i.e. by rules which have grown up without any person or group of persons making them. The freedom of the ruled may be restricted in the former way, whereas the freedom of the rulers is restricted only in the latter, but the freedom of the rulers may be more restricted in the latter way than the freedom of the ruled is in the former. The freedom of the men at the very top of the hierarchy may be very substantially restricted by the rules, even though their freedom cannot be restricted by the commands of their superiors, for, *ex hypothesi*, they have no superiors. For the same reason, one may be more restricted in a community where one has some say in what rules there are, than in a community—one governed by an absolute monarch, for example—where one has no such say at all. For the rules made by a democratic community may be numerous and restrictive, especially if they are made by a frightened and repressive majority, while those autocratically laid down by an absolute monarch may, though arbitrary, be fairly undemanding, especially if he feels his position is invulnerable. I have personally little doubt that I would rather live in a community in which there were few rules in which I had no voice than one in which there were numerous and restrictive rules, but where I occasionally had the rather dubious privilege of voting against the majority that brought them into existence. Perhaps I ought to end by pointing out that when I oppose being restricted by rules to being restricted by people, I do not suppose that there can be disembodied rules which impose themselves on people. The distinction is rather one between rules which are explicitly promulgated by rulers, and enforced by special machinery constituted for the purpose, and a less obvious but nevertheless real set of conventions which have grown up over the course of time, and the breach of which carries sanctions of more subtle sorts.[2]

(5) If it is Hume's view, as I suspect it was, that the words 'free' and 'equal' (as opposed to 'similar') are words which take their meaning from their reference to a system of conventions established by men, then it follows, in the absence of any such conventions, not that all men are free and equal, but that in the absence of such conventions, though they may all be free, they are neither equal nor not equal. For if 'free' means 'not constrained by conventions which prohibit certain actions', then, if there are no such conventions, all men are certainly free. But if 'equal' means 'having the same status in a system of rules', then, if there is no such system, men are neither equal nor unequal. It seems absolutely impossible to me that there should be a viable system of rules which does not establish inequalities, for, to be effective, such a system must put some people but not others in positions of power and authority. In this sense there is nothing wrong with inequality. There is, in the same sense, nothing much right with freedom. A world in which all men were free would be a world in which men were not governed by any human conventions, and in such a world man's life would, as Hobbes pointed out, be nasty, brutish, and short.

There is, however, another sense of 'free' in which it means 'able to do what one wants'. In this sense, men may be more free in a world in which there are rules limiting their freedom than in a world in which there are no such rules. For the main way in which man's freedom is limited is by the unregulated actions of other men, by his being prevented from doing what he wants by other men doing what they want, or by their failing to co-operate with him in enterprises which would get him what he wants, but which are such that other men will not co-operate unless such co-operation is made legally compulsory. Man's freedom can be increased by the existence of rules restricting his freedom because, though the existence of such rules does prevent him from doing things that he wants to do, it also prevents other men from doing

[2] 'One thinks himself the master of others, and still remains a greater slave than they.' Rousseau, *The Social Contract*, Everyman edition, p. 3.

things that they want to do, and his freedom may be more restricted by
other men doing what they want to do than it is by the rules preventing
him from doing what he wants to do. It is obvious that the world is not
divided into countries which are free and countries which are not free.
Freedom from the restrictions of man-made conventions is a matter of
degree, and, beyond a certain point, quite undesirable.

(6) Hume's philosophical views about the reasons why we owe a
duty of allegiance to the government are mixed up with a certain
amount of anthropological speculation about how government in fact
first arose. He supposes that very poor primitive societies (like the
American Indians of his day) neither needed nor had a government
except in time of war; that government was first established by people
meeting, selecting a ruler, and promising obedience to him; and that
governments were originally monarchical because they were modelled
upon single military leaders made necessary by war, and not upon
families ruled by a single head. Fortunately, Hume's utilitarian view
that we are under an obligation to obey the government because it
is a useful institution does not in any way depend for its correctness
upon speculation about how governments actually arose. If governments are useful we have an obligation not to undermine them, however they come about in actual fact. (It seems reasonable to suppose
that different governments came about in different ways.) The social
contract theory that Hume is criticizing, however, *is* vulnerable to
speculation about how governments arose. The obligation of our forefathers to obey the government could not have arisen from a promise if
our forefathers never actually made a promise, whether explicit or
implicit, and any view about what their duties were must depend
entirely upon determining exactly what it was they promised, and
what was promised to them by their chosen rulers in return. One
would have supposed that it was now quite impossible to do this. Our
own obligation to obey our own contemporary governments must turn
upon the exact nature of whatever explicit promises we have made
in the comparatively rare cases when any such promises *are* made, and
upon what exactly we have implicitly committed ourselves to by doing
such things as choosing to live in a country—supposing emigrating to be
possible—or accepting social security, free medical treatment or education, or the protection of the police and the armed services. I suspect
that whatever obligations we acquire as a result of accepting such things
are duties of gratitude rather than of promise-keeping. I also suspect
that what have been described by philosophers as explicit promises of
allegiance are oaths of allegiance rather than promises, which makes
implausible the suggestion that the government promises anything in

return. It seems fairly obvious that, though some part of our obligation to obey the government arises from gratitude, and some from honouring commitments, there is some residual obligation, which I personally think is more considerable than either of the first two, which arises simply from the fact that government is an institution necessary to the wealth and happiness of mankind. The point should be made that there is no reason why a utilitarian should not admit that some of our obligation of allegiance arises from gratitude and from honouring commitments, provided that he offers a utilitarian account of these last two duties. Plausible utilitarian accounts of them have been put forward, one of them by Hume. It is not my present business to inquire into their adequacy.

(7) If I am right in thinking that both the justification of having a government and the reason why we have a duty to obey it are utilitarian, it follows that any dispute about what kind of government one should have, and whether it should be democratic, autocratic, monarchical, oligarchical, communist, or fascist, should be settled by appeal to the advantages or disadvantages of the different possibilities. To a very large extent, one's opinion about what kind of government is best will then turn upon matters of fact, which are usually difficult to ascertain with any degree of certainty, and are not such as to make a philosophical training a very good excuse for having the temerity to pronounce upon them. I suspect that the following very general observations may have some weight. (1) There is some presumption against altering whatever kind of government one happens to find oneself with, especially if the alterations are considerable, and even more so if they have to be accomplished by means of force. There is, I think, some tendency for governments, like clothes and houses, to grow up not entirely ill adapted to the circumstances obtaining in the country that has them, and to the kind of people that live there, and the actual government, which may have evolved and adapted itself to human needs over a long period of time, may have advantages over some idealistic blueprint, which has not been tried, or not tried in circumstances just like those prevailing in the country upon which reformers may wish to impose it. (2) Since people, and, still more, circumstances, vary considerably from one part of the world to another, and the actual institutions on which a reformed government has to be built may be very different from one another, it would be wrong to suppose that the government which is best for one place and time will be best for a different place and a different time. Hence a democrat who supposes that all governments should be democratic, or a communist who supposes that all governments should be communist, is making the mistake of taking it for granted that institutions,

which may work quite well in his own country—though doubtless not as well as he thinks they do—will work equally satisfactorily in very different conditions, and in countries with very different traditions. (3) People apparently vary enormously in their natural endowments, especially in ability. Any decision taken on utilitarian grounds concerning the relative merits of a democratic, as opposed to some more oligarchical type of government, must depend very largely upon one's assessment of the extent of this variation, and of the extent to which it is inborn, rather than the result of environmental factors. Clearly the greater are such variations in ability, the weaker will be the case for democracy, and in a world in which such variations in ability were enormous the case against democracy would be enormous. Though similar men should be treated in a similar way, if men are very different, such differences may well justify very unequal treatment, perhaps even to the extent of making desirable a world which is ruled over by a hereditary oligarchy which might be in the interest of rulers and ruled alike. (It is my personal opinion that differences in the suitability of men to rule are very great, great enough by themselves to justify such an oligarchy; what probably makes hereditary oligarchy impracticable is the rather unpredictable way in which it is handed down from one generation to another.)

SECTION IX

Of the Measures of Allegiance

THOSE who think that we are obliged to obey the government because we have promised or contracted to do this say that we are not under an obligation to obey a tyrannous government since, in failing to protect us, it is not keeping its side of the bargain (549-50); the conclusion that we are not obliged to obey a tyrannous government is true, though the reasons given for it are erroneous (550); the correct explanation is that, since our natural obligation to obey the government arises directly from the fact that government is to man's interest, this obligation ceases when it is not (550-1); though general rules are often morally obligatory in cases unlike those which first gave rise to them, this does not mean that our obligation to obey the government does not cease when government is not of any advantage to us, for the likelihood of our governors abusing their power causes us to allow exceptions to the rule demanding obedience (551-2); again, the consensus of opinion shows that men approve of rebellion against a tyrant, and, although they cannot make explicit the reason for this, they have an implicit notion of it (552-3); only interest could produce obedience, and imitation and custom will only reinforce a conformity originally produced for other reasons (553).

COMMENTS

(1) Hume sometimes speaks as if obedience to the government were an all-or-nothing affair. If the government is useful, and protects its subjects and gives them security, my duty to obey it is absolute; if, on the other hand, it does none of these things, there is no reason why I should not take every possible step to overthrow it. There are, however, intermediate stages between absolute obedience and armed insurrection. If I have moral scruples about paying my tithes, vaccinating my children, or fighting for my country, I may disobey the government to a certain limited extent, without thinking that government is entirely useless, and without wishing to overthrow the government. I do not think this point affects Hume's argument, however.

(2) Our natural obligation to obey the government arises when it is in our interest to obey it. We have already seen that by 'natural'

obligation, Hume means that sense of 'obligation' in which we are obliged to do something in order to secure an end which we want. A sea captain, for example, may be obliged in this sense to jettison his cargo in order to save his ship, and men may be obliged—naturally obliged—to obey the government, in this sense, in order to secure their interest.

Hume is therefore wrong in speaking as if no man had a natural obligation to obey a government which does not give security and protection to its subjects. It will be in the interest of some men, the government's paid servants, for example, to obey even a government which does not give its subjects security and protection. Since men's interests differ, some men may have a 'natural' obligation to obey a government, although other men do not.

For this reason, our moral obligation cannot arise from a natural obligation; since men's moral obligation to obey the government arises from the fact that it is useful to its citizens, even men whose interest it would be to disobey it may have a duty to obey it. Conversely, men whose interest it is to obey it might have no duty to obey it, and might have a duty to disobey it. (Hume does not draw a distinction between saying that men sometimes do not have a duty to obey the government, and saying that men sometimes have a duty to disobey the government. He says, 'whenever the civil magistrate carries his oppression so far as to render his authority perfectly intolerable, we are *no longer bound to submit to it* [my italics]' (551); and '*no nation*, that cou'd find any remedy . . . *were blam'd* for their resistance [my italics]' (552); 'the moral obligation . . . must cease' (552-3). However, he says that 'those who took up arms against *Dionysius* or *Nero*, or *Philip the second, have the favour* [my italics] of every reader in the perusal of their history . . .' (552), and I think Hume must often have positively approved, as opposed to failing to disapprove, of rebellion against a tyrannous government.)

One must not suppose that Hume's utilitarian account of our duty of allegiance would justify armed rebellion merely against a bad government, or a violent attempt to replace a bad government with one believed to be better. We are justified in rebelling only if the government is so bad as to make it even worse than the alternative of civil war, which means that it would have to be very bad indeed. In the first paragraph of the next section (Section X, 'Of the objects of allegiance') Hume says, 'We ought always to weigh the advantages, which we reap from authority, against the disadvantages; and by this means we shall become more scrupulous of putting in practice the doctrine of resistance. The common rule requires submission; and 'tis only in cases of *grievous* [my italics] tyranny and oppression, that the exception can take place' (554). Hence though Hume sometimes speaks as if we were under no obligation to obey a tyrannous government, his more mature and more consistently utilitarian view is that we are under such an obligation unless the consequences of obedience are worse than the consequences of civil war.

(3) With Hume's view that the reason why we have an obligation to obey the government is that it is a useful institution, and the reason why we have an obligation to keep our promises is that promise-keeping is necessary to society, I am in entire agreement. Hence I agree with Hume that it is an unnecessary circumlocution to attempt to derive an obligation to obey the government from a contract, even were his other objections to the social contract theory (547-9) not conclusive. It follows from this that the social contract theory's explanation of how it comes about that we sometimes do not have a duty to obey the government is incorrect, as Hume says it is. I believe that his own explanation of this, which is that our obligation to obey the government ceases when it is no longer advantageous that people obey it, is the right one; this means that, if anarchists were right, and governments were unnecessary, undesirable, and evil, we would have no obligation to obey them. Personally, however, I do not think anarchists *are* right. If men were endowed with unlimited benevolence it might be that governments would then be unnecessary. They would not be needed to protect their countries from foreign enemies by war, for their countries would have no enemies. They would not be needed to defend their citizens from the assaults of criminals, for in a state where everyone was benevolent no one would make such assaults. Governments would not be needed to protect people's possessions, for no one would wish to take them, or to enforce promise-keeping or contracts, for no one would wish to break them. The only reason why governments might be necessary would be to organize certain large-scale enterprises, such as building nuclear power stations or harnessing the tides, but such an attenuated organization would not deserve the name of government, especially as people as benevolent as men would then be could probably manage it all by mutual agreement. Men, however, do not have unlimited benevolence, and I dare say never will have.

(4) Hume is too extreme in suggesting (551) that there are no exceptions to rules of justice where these concern property and promise-keeping.[1] Just as he has argued that it is possible to make exceptions to

---

[1] But this is not his usual view. 'What governor of a town makes any scruple of burning the suburbs, when they facilitate the approaches of the enemy? Or what

the rule demanding obedience to the government, so long as the cases where applying this rule is harmful may be excepted as a class, so there is no reason to suppose that certain rules about promising may not give rise to exceptions in the same way. For example, if promises made to insane persons are ones which it is harmful to keep, then there is no reason why these promises should not be excepted as a class, and hence no reason why the rule demanding promise-keeping should not be modified so that it becomes 'One must keep one's promises, except when these are made to people who are insane.'

There is a distinction to be made here, however, which Hume ignores. Hume might be thinking of whether the social rule practised and enforced by a given country demands all promise-keeping, or whether it demands the keeping of promises except when these are made to insane persons. On the other hand, he might be thinking of a situation where, given that the social rule certainly demands all promise-keeping, we are wondering whether we are under an obligation to obey this rule when it in fact demands the keeping of promises to insane persons. Keeping such promises, we are supposing, *is* harmful, but the social rule in question makes no exception in favour of breaking them. Hence Hume might be saying that, when the keeping of certain kinds of promises is harmful, the social rule demanding promise-keeping may be *modified* to exclude the keeping of such promises, or he might be saying that a social rule demanding the keeping of all promises may be *disobeyed* when it demands the keeping of a kind of promise which it is harmful to keep.

What I think he *ought* to be saying is that keeping harmful promises is not obligatory if this class of promises is one which it is harmful to keep, but that one factor bearing upon our decision whether it is harmful to keep this class of promises is whether or not a social rule in the community in which we live demands it. For there is a *tendency* for it to be harmful to break social rules, even when these demand actions which would be harmful ones to perform, were they not demanded by a social rule, and this tendency may override the tendency for keeping such promises to be harmful otherwise.

(5) Some philosophers have thought that an individual would have a

general abstains from plundering a neutral country, when the necessities of war require it, and he cannot otherwise subsist his army? The case is the same with the duty of allegiance; and common sense teaches us, that, as government binds us to obedience only on account of its tendency to public utility, that duty must always, in extraordinary cases, when public ruin would evidently attend obedience, yield to the primary and original obligation. *Salus populi suprema Lex*, the safety of the people is the supreme law' ('Of Passive Obedience', Ess.261).

duty to resist the government for reasons other than its having become
so bad as to make the consequences of obedience worse than the consequences of disobedience. For example, some philosophers have
thought that a government might or ought to be resisted if it infringed
people's right to freedom. Since the citizens of a government which
encroached upon the freedom of its subjects would not have a *legal*
right to freedom—the government would have taken it away from them
—it must be supposed that people's right to resist arises from the
government's infringing their moral right to freedom. It does not seem
to me, however, that people's moral right to freedom is entirely unaffected by what laws a government may make restricting it. To the
extent that government is necessary men have a duty not to undermine
it by disobeying its laws, even sometimes laws restricting individual
freedom.

However, though many, if not most, limitations of individual freedom
may have to be tolerated because of the great desirability of having a
government, it cannot be that some limitations ought to be resisted for
other than utilitarian reasons, or for considerations which have nothing
to do with balancing the advantages of obedience against its disadvantages. For the reasons why people have a moral right to freedom are
themselves utilitarian, and have to do with the benefits gained from
respecting the freedom of others. Men's freedom ought to be respected
for the following utilitarian reasons. It is something most of them enjoy
possessing. Most people are more likely correctly to decide for themselves what they want than other people are to decide this for them. If
a very stereotyped existence is imposed on everybody, the life so
imposed is unlikely to be well adapted to the needs of everybody and
people will not be permitted to experiment with new, and perhaps
more satisfactory, ways of life, and will not be able to profit from such
experiments when these are made by others. Lack of freedom will be
the result of some people imposing ways of life and opinions upon
people who do not approve of the way of life or agree with the opinions.
Hence unless we suppose preternatural wisdom on the part of those in
power, many wrong ways of living and wrong opinions will be imposed.
Less bigotry would mean that wrong views were more exposed to the
test of criticism, and the claims of actual ways of life to be the best
ways of life more exposed to the test of allowing people to try to find
better alternatives. Restrictions on freedom are usually the offspring of
a strong interest in one's own beliefs being true or one's own ways of
life being satisfactory, coupled with a deep-seated fear that they might
be discovered not to be.

There are two kinds of academic subjects. There are those like mathematics or physics, where knowledge is possible, and imposing opinion therefore unnecessary and ridiculous, and there are those like religion, politics, or philosophy, where knowledge is virtually impossible, and so where imposing one's views on other people involves a very high chance of error. It is an interesting psychological fact that the greater the room for error in a view, the more likely it is that it will be imposed upon others by force.

That governments restrict people's freedom, therefore, is not an extra reason for resisting them, over and above the utilitarian advantages of resisting. Freedom is one good thing among others, and governments which do not preserve it are to that extent not worth preserving; if a government does not preserve it, it will be just so much more likely that the consequences of disobeying it will be better than the consequences of obeying it.

It must not be supposed, however—and I am sure that Hume himself would not have supposed this—that freedom has an 'absolute' value, and must be preserved in all conceivable circumstances. Some men do not want it, other men do not know what to do with it, yet others manage their lives so badly that they would be positively better off without it. The chances that many experiments in living will add much to the stock of human wisdom is small, and it is not likely that many people will have original and heterodox ideas which the authorities need take the trouble to repress. Nor is freedom necessarily restricted by frightened people, desperate to preserve from attack their own authority and their own beliefs. It may be restricted by benevolent people, convinced, and perhaps with some justice convinced, of the need of their subjects for firm guidance, and of the rectitude of their own opinions about the way in which their subjects may best go. The existence even of democratic communities involves some people restricting other people's freedom, which supposes that the former must be convinced of the superiority of their wisdom over the latter.

What may offend some people in this is the appearance of inequality and injustice in some people being rulers and other people being ruled. How can it be just, it may be asked, unless the people ruled have voluntarily surrendered their rights, that some people should rule and other people be ruled over? And by what right should some people command, and other people obey? What difference is there between one man and another that one should govern and the other be a subject? This suggests that there is some prima-facie appearance of inequality of treatment in the fact that some men have power, and other men are merely compelled to obey them.

This appearance, however, is only superficial. Given that government is necessary, some men *must* rule and others obey. Hence, even if all men were similar, *some* men would have to have the duty of commanding, and others that of obeying. Even if rulers were selected by lot, there would be no case for saying that this arrangement involved the injustice of making some people rulers, and other exactly similar people subject to their authority; the fact that the lot had fallen on them would *create* a difference between them and the people over whom they ruled. And, of course, people are not all similar, but enormously different. Some people are by nature much more fitted to be rulers than others, and it could be argued that even if power goes to the strongest, those most successful in the battle for it are most likely to be those who have the qualities which will enable them to rule successfully. Since power is something all men want, those who succeed in getting it are likely to be more intelligent, more single-minded, and more disciplined than others, and to have those attributes which other men respect. There is some reason, *pace* Plato, for thinking that those who achieve power are likely to be more fitted for it than those who do not. Even if this were not so, the very fact that some people are in fact rulers constitutes a difference between them and other men, a difference which is made a relevant one by the fact that, because of the necessity of government, already sufficiently emphasized, we have some duty, arising from the advantages of doing so, to obey whatever government we may happen to find ourselves subject to. Hence rulers do not have to be by *nature* different from other people in order to have a right to rule. Since the nature of ruling involves some restriction in the liberties of those who are subjects, it is simply a mistake to suppose that there must be a natural difference between rulers and ruled for some people (the rulers) to have a right to restrict the liberties of other people (the ruled), and for the ruled to have a duty to obey. Nor is there any unjust inequality involved in this arrangement, for considerations of advantage mean that the artificial differences constituted by such things as being in fact a ruler, or the heir of a ruler, give rise to a difference in their rights and duties as compared with the rights and duties of those over whom they rule. Since government is a necessary, albeit artificial, institution, the differences which it entails demand that some people have the right to restrict the liberties of other, possibly similar, people for utilitarian reasons. One hopes, however, that they do not carry this too far.

(6) Hume's argument from the consensus of opinion (552) needs a little comment. It is not, properly speaking, an argument from consensus of *opinion*, for it is an argument based upon what people feel, not upon people's opinions about what people feel, and, on the view of

Hume's which is predominant in Part II of Book III of the *Treatise*, it is the latter in which an opinion about what is right or wrong consists. (To have a moral opinion, on this view, is to have an opinion *about* what most people approve of, not to have a feeling of approval oneself.) His argument then should be that because most men, although they may not explicitly realize it, feel approval of obedience when it is useful, and feel disapproval of it when it is not, this shows that our duty of allegiance arises from the usefulness of having and obeying a government. If Hume were right in thinking that morals is an empirical science, which discovers what is right by finding out what people approve of (provided they are not mistaken on matters of fact about what they approve of, are adequately informed about it, and are not biased, but have an approval which is disinterested) and discovers why it is right by discovering which are the features of things which determine this approval, then his argument would be cogent.

SECTION X

Of the Objects of Allegiance

THE advantages of government are so enormous, however, that rebellion is justified only in very exceptional circumstances[1] (553-4); since government first arises from the voluntary agreement of men, men must know who their *first* rulers are (554); but after government has been in existence for some time, it acquires an authority independent of this agreement, and our rulers are then not chosen by us (554-5); though the advantage of government is the reason for our duty of allegiance, it would be harmful to select our rulers because of their usefulness, rather than by general principles (555-6); the authority of the magistrates will not be diminished if the reasons which determine us to favour one ruler rather than another are less compelling than the reasons for having rulers at all (556); *long possession*, our approval of which is the effect of custom, is the first of these principles, though the length of time necessary to produce a sentiment of allegiance is greater than that which is necessary to make us treat something as someone's property (556-8); *present possession* is the second of these principles; the imagination disposes us to join constant possession to it, and the maintenance of peace militates against taking the government away from its present possessor (the same not being true of property) (557); most governments are founded upon usurpation in any case (557-8); *conquest* the third principle, and has superior force to present possession on account of the glory and honour we ascribe to conquerors (558-9); *succession* the fourth principle, and depends, like the others, on its appeal to the imagination, as is particularly shown by the succession in Poland and the dispute between Artaxerxes and Cyrus (559-61); fifthly, governments derive their authority from the *public laws*,

---

[1] 'And here I must confess, that I shall always incline to their side, who draw the bond of allegiance very close, and consider the infringement of it, as the last refuge in desperate cases, when the public is in the highest danger, from violence and tyranny. For besides the mischiefs of a civil war, which commonly attends insurrection; it is certain, that, where a disposition to rebellion appears among any people, it is one chief cause of tyranny in the rulers, and forces them into many violent measures which they never would have embraced, had every one been inclined to submission and obedience' ('Of Passive Obedience', Ess. 461-2).

which derive their authority from a legislature which owes its authority to the aforementioned principles; this, Hume thinks, explains why the legislature cannot always change the law (561-2); most disputes concerning the legitimacy of government are incapable of a rational solution, as is instanced by the dispute between Germanicus and Drusus, and should be treated as subordinate to the interest of peace and liberty (562-3); though resistance (as in the revolution of 1688) in some cases is lawful, the laws cannot say when resistance is lawful, or even publish the fact that sometimes it is[2] (563); the people, however, cannot be deprived of the right of resistance, which right is greater in a constitutional government than in a despotic one, as every part of the constitution must be supposed to have a right to protect its share of authority (563-4); if a ruler is deposed, it is a natural effect of the imagination that we should also wish his heirs to be deposed (565-6); not only does time make a government lawful, it also (retrospectively) makes its first origins lawful (566-7).

COMMENTS

(1) Some of the ground covered by Hume in this section has been discussed in the *Comments* on Section III, 'Of the rules, which determine property' (501-13).

It is tempting to say that according to Hume, the principles which determine the objects of allegiance, i.e. the people to whom we owe allegiance, have an irrational appeal. For we feel that we owe allegiance to the son of the preceding monarch, for example, not because the principle that sons should succeed their fathers is seen to have advantages, but simply because it appeals to our imaginations. Hume thinks that there *are* some advantages in having the king's son succeed the king to the throne—'the interest, which the state has in chusing the person, who is most powerful, and has the most numerous followers' (559)— but the principle that sons should succeed to their father's thrones is adopted only partly from a perception of its advantages. It is adopted also partly because of a 'basic instinct', if this is the right expression. Our imaginations give us a tendency to *cause* to be related by one relation (in this case, to be related by the relation 'successor of') things which are *already* related by another. Hume could also have said that

---

[2] 'Besides, we must consider, that as obedience is our duty in the common course of things, it ought chiefly to be inculcated; nor can any thing be more preposterous than an anxious care and solicitude in stating all the cases, in which resistance may be allowed' ('Of Passive Obedience', Ess.462).

'the same love of order and uniformity, which arranges the books in a library, and the chairs in a parlour' (504 n.) determines the fate of nations and princes.

These principles, which determine who shall govern, though they sometimes have direct advantages, and are sometimes partly adopted because they are seen to have these advantages, always have indirect advantages to the extent that they determine who shall possess the government, and do not leave power to be fought for, with all the bloodshed and turmoil which results from this. That is to say, though they may or may not have advantages over other principles, which might determine to whom we owed allegiance, they always have the advantage of causing us to come to a decision about who shall rule us; it is better that who governs should be determined by some principle or other, however trivial, than that it should not be determined by any principle at all.

One hesitates to say, however, that it is Hume's view that this appeal to the imagination is an irrational appeal, as opposed to the appeal made by the fact that a principle is perceived to have *advantages*. For it is just a brute fact that certain things appeal to the imagination, and it is just a brute fact that we desire what is of advantage, and Hume has himself said that wanting one thing is neither more nor less rational than wanting another. ''Tis not contrary to reason for me to chuse my total ruin, to prevent the least uneasiness to an *Indian* or person wholly unknown to me' (416). One feels, however, that there is something irrational about selecting the principles which determine who our governors shall be for any other reason than the advantages and disadvantages of these principles, though this is not to say that it might— as Hume thinks it does—so happen that we irrationally hit upon principles which are of advantage to society. I suspect that the reason for this is that what is of advantage to society is logically determined by what society's ends are—which means that it is determined by the ends of individual members of society—and hence, if society does not choose its rulers by principles which have advantages, it is behaving irrationally in the sense that it is not choosing means to the ends that it in fact has.[3]

(2) Hume holds the view that the identity of the person to whom we owe allegiance is determined by people's sentiments. A person or group of persons has the right to rule if people in fact feel that they owe him allegiance, approve of obedience to his edicts, and disapprove of disobedience. In order, therefore, to establish what principles give rise to a right in certain individuals to govern, one has to enquire what factors

---

[3] See my *Hume's Moral Epistemology*, pp. 80–2.

work on men's sentiments in such a way to cause them to feel that they owe allegiance to these individuals rather than to any other individuals. This enquiry is, of course, an empirical one, which accords well with Hume's most mature and considered contention that morality is an empirical science, and that moral questions must be settled by observing what things people approve of and why.

But how, then, does Hume's view that factors, such as that being the son of a deceased monarch gives one the right to govern (other things being equal), square with Hume's prevailing utilitarianism? For though Hume never enunciates any general utilitarian formula, as did Bentham and Mill, he was certainly a utilitarian in that he constantly and consciously attempts to justify the practices of mankind by appealing to their advantages. One would, therefore, expect him to hold the view that what caused men to feel that they ought to obey one rule, in preference to any other, was always their *belief* that this rule was more useful than any other, and that they were justified in thinking that this rule ought to be obeyed, if this rule was *in fact* more useful than any other. Yet Hume continually emphasizes that we do *not* feel that we ought to obey George, rather than Charles, because we perceive that obedience to George would have advantages over obedience to Charles, or because we perceive that the rule that prescribes that George should have the government has advantages over the rule that prescribes that George should have it. The factors that Hume thinks determine our sentiments to approve of obedience to one person rather than another are to a large extent, though not completely, independent of any awareness we may have of their advantages.

One might try to deal with this problem in a way similar to that in which some philosophers attempt to deal with an analogous problem in Book I of the *Treatise*. For in Book I of the *Treatise* Hume constantly says that the only thing which confers force and vivacity upon an idea (i.e. gives rise to belief) is the fact that we are aware of a present impression of a kind which has always in the past been constantly conjoined with other impressions which this idea resembles (constant conjunction), but at other times he mentions a number of other factors, such as resemblance, contiguity, education, ferment of the blood and spirits, and eloquence, which also confer force and vivacity upon an idea. Some philosophers have held that Hume thought that though all these factors gave rise to *belief*, only constant conjunction with a present impression gave rise to *rational belief*. Similarly, it might be maintained that though long possession, present possession, conquest, succession, and positive laws produce sentiments favourable to allegiance, only being demanded by a useful rule produces a rational belief that a government instituted in accordance with this rule ought to be obeyed. For example, being the successor to the successor to the successor of someone who once governed, he thinks, produces sentiments of allegiance, but no rational belief that such a government ought to be obeyed; being moved by such considerations, Hume thinks, savours of bigotry, and trying to depose the present government, which has present possession in its favour, has the enormously disadvantageous consequence of civil war. Conversely, a government which it *is* useful to obey, for example, one in present possession of authority, might not produce any actual sentiments in its subjects favourable to allegiance to it, or, at any rate, not until some time has elapsed. But though, when Hume is himself recommending a rule (for example, the rule that governments which have been in existence for a long period of time ought to be obeyed) as opposed to making statements about the attitude of other people to it, he usually does this on the grounds that keeping it has advantages and departing from it has disadvantages, he never actually makes the generalization that governments which owe their office to the application of a useful rule ought to be obeyed. In any case, it is doubtful whether Hume can draw a distinction between rational and irrational belief that a rule ought to be applied, when you consider the views expressed about moral epistemology in Part I of Book III of the *Treatise*. For if morals depend on the brute fact that we have certain sentiments, then, if our sentiments are favourable to doing something, it must be right to do that thing (provided that our sentiments are not based on a mistake about a matter of fact, or affected by various factors for which Hume says allowances should be made). Hence, if succession does produce in us sentiments favourable to allegiance, then it must (other things being equal) be right to obey a successor; there is no court of appeal, outside our sentiments, to which the pronouncements of our sentiments may be taken, and by which they can be set aside. Hume, however, is himself quite prepared to criticize, usually if not invariably from utilitarian principles, the morality of actions and rules and practices that he knows evince favourable sentiments in people. His practice, therefore, is inconsistent with his theory.

Hume holds that virtues are qualities which are useful or agreeable to their possessors or to other people. To say that a *quality* of character is a *virtue* if it is useful or agreeable, is not the same thing as to say that a *rule ought* to be obeyed if it is a useful rule. There must, however, be some connection between the fact that certain characteristics of men are virtues and the fact that certain rules ought to be obeyed. It would not be reasonable, for example, to maintain both that a *disposition* to obey governments is a vice, and at the same time to maintain that the *rule* demanding obedience to the government ought to be obeyed. A utilitarian theory of the virtues carries utilitarianism along with it, in a rough and ready way, at any rate. Hence there is some incompatibility between Hume's contention that characteristics of men are virtues if they are useful, and his contention that we are caused to feel we owe allegiance to governments by factors other than utility. For if we feel we owe allegiance and loyalty to a prince for no better reason than that once upon a time his ancestors ruled over us, our disposition to support and obey him may sometimes not be a useful characteristic; hence our approval of it cannot be determined by our belief that it is useful, even if, by a merciful dispensation of providence, giving allegiance to such a person does have good results. (As Hume points out, it will at least have the good result of avoiding strife over who is to rule.)

(3) Hume attempts to reconcile the fact that people feel they owe allegiance to one person or group of persons rather than another for reasons which have nothing to do with the advantages of giving him or them allegiance, with his quite proper tendency to think that what justifies human practices is the advantage of having them, in three ways. Sometimes he says it would in fact be harmful to be guided 'directly' by considerations of advantage; it would, for example, be harmful, because it would cause dissension and dispute, to attempt to select those rulers that it would be most advantageous to have. Secondly, he sometimes suggests that though we select our rulers by principles which have nothing to do with utility, these principles in fact lead us to select rulers that it is advantageous to have. For example, though we choose to be governed by the son of a deceased monarch for reasons which have little to do with our perception of the advantages of being so governed, there are *in fact* advantages in choosing him rather than any of his rivals. Thirdly, he sometimes holds that our tendency to be moved by factors which have nothing to do with utility in giving allegiance to a ruler has utilitarian advantages, in that anything, however eccentric, that causes us to settle unequivocally on one would-be ruler rather than another is useful; by doing so, it prevents bloodshed, and internal strife.

Though Hume's attempts to show that man's being guided by these non-utilitarian features is justified by their utility are quite compatible with *Hume*'s being a utilitarian, they are not compatible with the view that *men in general* are utilitarians. For if men in general were utilitarians, they would not be moved by factors such as succession in selecting their rulers unless they thought that it was useful to be so moved; whereas it is clear that Hume thinks that succession has an immediate appeal, which is not capable of being derived from its utility. Hence, though Hume could hold what he does and be a utilitarian himself, he ought not to hold what he does and be a utilitarian, when he also holds that any moral theory (including utilitarianism) has to be justified by appeal to the sentiments which men in fact have. For, whether utilitarianism is right or not, and whether Hume held it or not, he quite explicitly says that the sentiments of other men are in fact determined by things other than the utility of the principles and practices they approve of. According to his *own* account of the derivation of moral distinctions, then, utilitarianism should be false.

(Presumably, it would be possible for a utilitarian philosopher to generalize these remarks, and to hold that though other men are often moved to approve of actions for reasons other than their utility, and approve of debt-paying, promise-keeping, truth-telling, and so on, for reasons other than that they produce good consequences, there are in fact utilitarian advantages in their attitudes to actions being determined in this way; harm would result, for example, if everybody broke a promise when it seemed that he could do more good than harm by breaking it. Hence man's irrational, non-utilitarian tendency to disapprove of breaking promises, even when more good than harm could be done by breaking them, is a useful tendency, though men do not have it because they see that it is useful. The utilitarian philosopher himself, however, would not have this tendency to approve of actions on non-utilitarian grounds—otherwise he would not be a utilitarian philosopher. He himself, presumably, would then have to justify his own abstention from, say, promise-breaking, when promise-breaking did more good than harm, on the grounds that if everybody broke his promises, when breaking them did more good than harm, this would do more harm than good.)

Is it possible to hold that to do something because of the advantages of doing it will in fact produce harm (as Hume holds that to select rulers because of the advantages of having them will in fact do the harm of causing civil strife)? The paradox involved in this contention is the same as that involved in what is known as the paradox of hedonism, according to which, if you aim at your own happiness, you will not find it. You will achieve happiness only if you aim at something other than happiness, say, devoting yourself to a socially useful and generally approved occupation for which you have some native aptitude. There is an inconsistency in holding that doing what has advantages, or will bring happiness, in fact does not have advantages, or does not bring happiness. There is no inconsistency, however, in holding that what has advantages if done by one or a few people on one or a few occasions—

aiming at utility, for example—will have disadvantages if done by all people on all occasions, and there is no inconsistency in holding that what seems to have advantages will in fact have disadvantages (or in holding that what it seems will make one happy will in fact not make one happy). But there does seem to be an inconsistency in holding that someone who deliberately is not being guided by the advantages of what he does, because of the advantages of not being guided by the advantages of what he does, or who deliberately does not aim at his own happiness because he thinks that by aiming at something else he will in fact bring about his own happiness, is not being guided by advantage, or not aiming at his own happiness. It is contradictory to hold that some-one both is and is not aiming at advantage or happiness. In the case of the paradox of hedonism, the solution is probably that the person who thinks he can best achieve his own happiness by not aiming at it, *is* in fact aiming at it, and is in no way *not* aiming at it; what he is perhaps doing is aiming at it, but not aiming at it directly (as someone who attempts to hit a target by causing his bullet to ricochet off something else *is* aiming at the target, although his gun is not pointed in the direction of the target) or is aiming at his happiness, though not at his short-term happiness, or is aiming at happiness, but not at sensual pleasure, or is *aiming* at his happiness, but thinks he will best achieve it by *devoting himself* to something other than his happiness, or is aiming at his happiness, but thinks he can secure his happiness only by not continually dwelling on whether or not he is being successful in getting it. Alice was aiming at reaching the house, although she eventually realized that she would have to get there by walking away from it.

The solution to the problem raised by Hume's contention that it is advantageous not to be guided in choosing a ruler by the advantages of having one person rule rather than another is, I think, that if you aim at the advantage of having the best ruler, you will quite likely not secure this advantage, which is problematic and admits of dispute, whereas you will certainly produce the disadvantage of causing dissension and strife; and partly that the advantage you hope to achieve by *not* aiming at the advantage of having the best ruler is a *different* advantage from the advantage of having the best ruler. You give up what chance there is of obtaining the advantage of having the best ruler in order to secure the advantage of *avoiding civil strife*. Hence, by not aiming at one advantage, you secure another advantage; since you do not both forgo and aim at the very same advantage, there is no contra-diction involved in Hume's remark.

There is no contradiction in Hume's second contention, that non-utilitarian factors—succession or long possession, for example—by appealing to our imaginations, cause us to adopt principles for selecting rulers which in fact have utilitarian advantages, although we do not necessarily see that they have, or, even if we do see that they have, we do not adopt them for this reason. Nevertheless, if non-utilitarian reasons frequently cause us to act in a utilitarian way, this rather surprising fact does need some explanation, which Hume does not attempt to give. One possible reason for it is that we have been 'educated' —in Hume's sense of the word, which savours more of indoctrination than of education—by men wiser and more powerful than ourselves, who did see the advantages of these principles, into accepting them, though *we* accept them only because they have been made to have an immediate appeal. This account suffers from the difficulty that it presupposes that we have been educated by men wiser, cleverer, and more disinterested than experience tells us is likely to be the case. The second explanation is evolutionary. Various non-utilitarian factors might appeal to the imaginations of different people, but the people whose imaginations caused them to settle for principles which were in fact useful would have an advantage over the others, which has caused them and their principles to survive at the others' expense.[4] Similarly, one might argue that though, according to Hume, we accept causal arguments and the existence of bodies not from any rational apprehension of the reasons for accepting them, but solely because our imaginations operate in such a way as to make it psychologically impossible for us not to, our imaginations *must* operate in this way, for, if they did not, we would not survive.

Hume's third contention, that sometimes the non-utilitarian appeal to the imagination of certain non-utilitarian factors in determining us to settle upon our rulers, has the advantage of causing us to decide upon our rulers without contention and strife, needs no particular comment; it is straightforward enough. Unfortunately, it does not always work, for different non-utilitarian factors weigh more with some people than they do with others. Some people, for example, are moved more by long possession than they are by succession, whereas with others it is the other way round. It is partly for this reason that there is sometimes civil strife.

(4) Hume has a predominantly utilitarian theory of why government is necessary, why we ought to obey the government, why we sometimes ought to rebel against the government, and why we ought to obey one government rather than another. We need government because it is useful. It enforces order, in that it compels people to adhere to rules of

---

[4] See my *Our Knowledge of Right and Wrong*, Chapter XI.

justice which their weakness and short-sightedness would cause them to ignore, and organizes large-scale enterprises, including defence in war, which are beyond the capacity of individuals or relatively small groups of individuals. We ought to obey it because government is necessary, and cannot exist unless it is for the most part obeyed. Though we ought to obey even a bad government, because the consequences of rebellion, i.e. civil war, are even worse, a government may become so tyrannous that it is better to attempt to overthrow it than to go on living under it. In this case it may rightly be disobeyed. By and large, it matters much more that we have a government, than what government we have, and matters much more that we are guided by principles which, however irrational, produce agreement and avoid strife, than it matters what government these principles lead us to give our allegiance to. Hume himself does not deduce all the consequences of this view, although in fact they are far-reaching. It would indicate that it would tend to be wrong to rebel against the government established by a *coup d'état*, unless there was a good chance of effectively removing it without civil strife. It would tend to show that it was wrong to rebel against an illiberal government, unless, again, it could be easily removed with little or no bloodshed. It would indicate that it was not right to rebel against a government which was autocratic, and consulted the interests of its subjects but little and their opinions not at all. It would tend to indicate that it was wrong to rebel against the established government in order to restore some previous government, which had a greater hold on one's affections. It would tend to show that it was wrong to overthrow a puppet government, controlled by a nation other than one's own. As a general rule, Hume, like the Vicar of Bray, though for more edifying reasons, is in favour of obedience to whatever government one finds oneself under. It would therefore be wrong to try to replace a democratic government by a communist or fascist one by force, and, I think, equally wrong to use force to replace a communist or fascist government by a democratic one. The really important thing is that there be a government; what this government is, is a matter of subsidiary importance, and a government would have to be very bad indeed before rebellion was justified, for unless it is very bad indeed, civil war, which such rebellion is likely to produce, would be an even worse evil than having the government which a rebellious war aimed at replacing. Hume's defence of the glorious revolution of 1688 seems to me a little inconsistent with the general tenor of Hume's view, but perhaps he was influenced, consciously or otherwise, by the fact that the deposition of James II was accomplished with very little trouble. Had a protracted, bloody, and perhaps unsuccessful, civil war been necessary to overthrow him, perhaps Hume would have been, as he ought then to have been, against it.

That Hume was right in thinking, however inconsistently, that men were moved by other than utilitarian factors in deciding to whom they owed allegiance is shown by how widely the political morality outlined in the preceding paragraph departs from the view of most people. For most people do feel a loyalty to deposed governments, irrespective of their merits, for which loyalty no utilitarian justification is possible. Most people do not feel that they owe allegiance to governments imposed on them by their conquerors—and Hume exaggerates the affection we feel for conquerors (558-9)—even when such governments are administratively more efficient and successful than their own. They feel loyalty to their former laws, and the government these laws legitimized, long after these laws have been rendered inoperative by internal rebellion. It cannot be disguised that the morality that Hume's justification of the duty of allegiance points to would be regarded by most people as somewhat ignoble, and as attaching too high a value to peace and prosperity, and too small a value to loyalty to a government one once had, or loyalty to a government composed of people of the same nation as oneself, or loyalty to a cause one has espoused. I think it follows from utilitarian principles that all such things, to which many people attach such a high value, are manifestations of 'bigotry' rather than good sense, and produce an amount of disruption and strife which can seldom be justified.

(5) The passage in which Hume argues that the legislative power will not always be able to change the positive law is a little confused (561-2). He argues that it will be unable to do this because the positive law will not acquire all the force of the principles (concerning long possession, etc.) from which the authority of the government is derived; some of this force will be lost in the transition. One would have supposed, however, that this was a reason for thinking that the legislative power would quite easily be able to change the positive law, since the legislative power is only one step removed from the principles, whereas the positive law is two steps removed from them. What Hume seems to have in mind is that, when the legislative power is changed, it will not always be able to change the positive laws. The force in the legislative power arising from the aforementioned principles will not necessarily be transferred to any new law it may make, because of the extra step in the passage from original principles, to legislative power, to the authority of the positive law. The premiss he needs to reach this conclusion, however, is not the premiss that the positive law does not *acquire* all the authority of a new government, but that the positive law *retains* some

authority of its own (because it has been in existence longer than the new government). The positive law, in that case, will itself acquire authority *directly* from principles about long possession; consequently, it will *not* acquire all its authority from the legislative powers. The constitution of the USA is a case in point.

The passage I have been discussing (561-2) may possibly be regarded as Hume's psychological explanation for the doctrine of natural law. According to the doctrine of natural law, there are certain laws not made by man, the existence of which is apprehended by reason. In certain circumstances this law may, according to some philosophers, override the positive law. Hume probably thinks that part of the explanation for the view that there is such a thing as natural law is that certain laws are of very great antiquity. It is because they have been in operation for so long that no man can have any recollection or access to any record of their establishment that it has been supposed that they are part of the nature of things, there from all time to be apprehended by anyone with the necessary rational insight. This is not the whole of Hume's explanation of the doctrine of natural law, however. It is also partly explained by the fact that, since men's imaginations work in roughly similar ways, and the same laws have the same appeal to the imaginations of all men, what is in fact the work of the imagination has been wrongly credited to reason. Hume does not explicitly mention natural law in this passage, but the Salic law in France. This is not a natural law, and its origin is not lost in antiquity, so perhaps I am reading too much into what Hume says.

(6) The second of the philosophical morals which Hume draws from the 1688 revolution is interesting. It is that 'Princes often *seem* to acquire a right from their successors' (566). Later in this paragraph (566-7) he drops the word 'seem', and says 'the present *king* of *France* makes *Hugh Capet* a more lawful prince than *Cromwell*' (566) because Hugh Capet successfully founded a dynasty, whereas Cromwell did not. If Hume is contending merely that the success of a man in founding an enduring line of kings or emperors will make him *seem* to have a more legitimate claim to his position, then what Hume says is a true psychological observation. If Hume seriously meant that the claims of a usurper who seized the throne from the lawful monarch are made *legitimate* by the fact that his sons and grandsons became kings after him, and were both regarded by everybody as, and for this reason *were*, legitimate rulers, what Hume says is simply false. The legality of an action is determined by the laws in force at the time at which it was performed, and cannot be altered by anything that happens subsequently to that. It is true that, according to Hume, whether a governor has

authority depends upon whether or not his subjects have feelings of aproval towards obedience to his edicts, but this view is surely only remotely plausible if it is referring to feelings of approval in the minds of his contemporaries, not feelings of approval experienced by men living a century or so after his death. It is natural to think that, since a usurper's successors are legitimate rulers, and because legitimate authority can derive only from authority which is itself legitimate, the alleged usurper's authority, whence the authority of his successors stems, must itself in fact be legitimate. But one of the premisses in this argument—that legitimate authority can derive only from authority which is itself legitimate—is false; what is legitimate *can* be derived from what is illegitimate, for otherwise, as Hume points out (558), since all dynasties were founded upon usurpation, there would be no legitimate rulers at all. It is time, working upon people's sentiments, that causes the change.

I have said that nothing that happens after an action is performed can have any bearing upon whether it was legal at the time at which it was performed. This does not mean that it is not possible to pass retrospective legislation, the object of which is to make illegal some action which has already been performed, perhaps on the grounds that it is something outrageously immoral which escaped any penalty imposed by the law which existed at that time. Such legislation makes it possible to try and punish a man just as if the law had been in existence when he did the things of which he was later accused. Retrospective legislation does not, however, alter the fact that the actions legislated against were perfectly legal at the time they were performed, and so, in the normal sense of that word, legal. It would be possible to use the word 'illegal' in such a way as to describe as illegal an act which is contrary to some law passed after the action was performed. But this is not the usual way, or even a desirable way, of using the word 'illegal'; the contention that actions can be made illegal after they have been performed is, in this sense of the word 'illegal', an uninteresting truism, and not identical with the interesting, but false, assertion made by Hume. For Hume's assertion to be true, it would have to be possible for us to alter the past.

(7) It is presupposed by some of Hume's arguments in this section that there is a connection between legitimacy and force, between legitimacy and people's sentiments, and between legitimacy and what a legislator has or has not the power to do. For a ruler who owes his position to force, not law, may become the legal ruler of his country; that he does so is the result of the operation of time upon people's sentiments; and these same sentiments may make it impossible for the

legislature to change certain 'fundamental' laws. That there is a connection between legitimacy and force, between legitimacy and sentiment, and between what a legislature has the power to do and what it legally *may* do, is paradoxical. For it seems obvious that there is a clear distinction between the legitimate and the illegitimate use of force; between what a man does and what he has a legal right to do; between the laws men approve of and those that actually exist; between what laws a legislator has the right to make and his power to enforce them. If Hume is right, however, what rulers are legitimate (and therefore what laws there are) often depends on force, upon the effects of the imagination upon how people feel, and upon the power of monarchs and legislators to keep themselves in power and to see that their edicts are obeyed.

The resolution of this apparent paradox is as follows. If you consider *individual laws*, there may be some which arouse no sentiments of approval in people, and which it may be impossible to enforce. If you consider a *system of law* as a whole, however, it must be by and large approved of, or, if it is not, it must be predominantly enforced. If there were a body, say some *émigré* government who claimed to have the right to make laws for a given country, but whose promulgations were entirely ignored, whereas the pronouncements of some other body were accepted and enforced, the 'laws' made by the former would not be laws. It may once have had the right to legislate for the country over which it claims authority, but it has this right no longer, simply because it has been deposed by superior force. Of two rival law-making bodies in a given area, the rights of one may simply have decayed by being increasingly ignored, while men paid increasing attention to the dictates of the other. Hence any given law may be a dead letter, but remain a law, because it can be identified as having been promulgated by a body the majority of whose rules are for the most part obeyed, or because it is one of some other system of rules, the majority of which are obeyed by a given community. But, of course, if all the rules promulgated by this body were ignored, the body would not be a law-making body, and its rules, if they could even be called that, would not be laws. The behaviour of no one in the country to which they were intended to apply would be affected by them; no courts would pronounce judgement according to them; no policemen apprehend those who ignored them; no gaolers keep incarcerated those guilty of breaking them.

From this it follows that, though some changes in a system of laws come about through due process of law, other changes come about through force or fraud, accretion or decay. It might be nice to think that all changes in the law come about lawfully, but this cannot be so. For one thing, the very first laws could not come about lawfully, because, prior to their existence, there could be no laws according to which they could either be or fail to be lawful. And subsequently to this, any change, whether lawful or not, which comes to be generally accepted, will become law, whether it came about through due procedure or not. The idea of a sovereign, such that all the laws in existence were promulgated by him, and continue to exist until they have been repealed by him, is therefore a myth. The 'sovereign' must have come to have his position by a process of gradual growth, and he may lose it as the result of a process of gradual decay; even while he has theoretical sovereignty, there are so many laws that he could pass, but does not pass because they would not be generally accepted if he did (and because they would not be generally accepted, would not be laws), that his sovereignty must be regarded as not more than nominal. Law is limited by what subjects will not universally ignore, by what policemen will enforce, by what juries will convict for, by what judges will decide. Practice, rather than due procedure, wears the trousers.

What, then, of Hume's claim that the fact that it has been supposed that there are certain fundamental laws, which the legislature has not the power to change, is due to the effect of custom upon the imagination? Though Hume says 'power' to change, it could be argued that he ought to have said 'right', but I suspect that what he thought was that the legislature did not have the power because it did not have the right, and that it did not have the right because it did not have the power to change people's attitudes to these allegedly fundamental laws. Any attempt it made to change them would be invalidated by the fact that, because of the way people felt about them, these new laws would not be put into operation, would be regarded as being invalid, would not be recognized by the courts, and so would never become laws, except perhaps nominally. (Conversely, there might be a rule prohibiting the legislature from changing certain fundamental laws, or from changing them unless certain more than usually stringent procedures were put into operation, as is demanded by the constitution of the United States. If the legislature attempted to ignore these rules and succeeded, because the laws it passed, though not in accordance with the constitution, were accepted by everyone, including the courts, the legislature would have in fact changed the law by these improper means.)

Hume probably exaggerates the importance of *sentiment* in determining the validity of laws, and what the legislature can or cannot do, or what rulers we owe allegiance to. Practice is more important than sentiment, and sentiment important more because of the fact that, to some extent, it determines practice, than because it directly determines what the law is. It would not matter how much people disapproved of a usurper; so long as he was successful in getting himself accepted, and his edicts obeyed, he would be the lawful ruler, because of the recognition and enforcement of his laws by law enforcement officials such as judges and policemen, and his control over the army and civil service. People might go on calling him a usurper, but the only difference this would make is that the laws would then be made by a usurper. If what is law depends upon what is accepted as being law, or what is treated as being law, then Hume is right in holding that what bounds are set to the legislative power is 'the work more of imagination and passion than of reason' (562); the limits to the laws the legislature can make are determined by what laws it can get accepted, and passion will certainly considerably affect this. That the legitimacy of law depends, in the last resort, upon what people will accept is normally disguised by the fact that lawmakers do not even attempt to pass many laws that they know will not be accepted. If they did, we would be faced with many laws which, though duly promulgated by some allegedly sovereign lawmaking body, were obviously not laws, because they have been universally ignored.

(8) That *passion* will have an effect on what the law is, by causing judges, for example, to make irrational decisions which get sanctified by time and by being treated as precedents, is perhaps a commonplace. Hume's view that the *imagination must* enter into the determination of questions of legality is more interesting and controversial. (Even the statement that passion will affect decisions about the law is not just the commonplace that people will, from passion, irrationally interpret the law wrongly, for Hume thought that there was often *no* rational way of determining legal questions.) The imagination has a bearing upon how people interpret problems of legality, because there is in principle no way in which such questions can be settled by rational means. It is not that the imagination causes us to settle a legal question one way when, logically, it ought to be settled another. There *is* no logical way of settling it. If we were not influenced by the imagination, there would be no way of coming to a decision except, perhaps, by tossing a coin, or by force of arms. That this is so, it must not be forgotten, is not necessarily a bad thing according to Hume. For the question of who is to own property or to be the government of a country cannot be left in abeyance without this leading to civil strife; hence anything that causes us to come to a decision on such questions, whether it is a rational decision or not, and especially if it causes us to come to a decision with a fair degree of unanimity, is to be welcomed.

The imagination might affect decisions about law in two ways, which Hume fails explicitly to distinguish. First, it might affect decisions about what the law *is to be*, as when the imagination causes men to decide to have a law allocating to someone as his property those things which are in his possession. Secondly, it might affect decisions about how the law is to be *interpreted*, and about whether the decisions taken in similar cases in the past are or are not to be taken as precedents. For example, the imagination will affect decisions concerning whether the law is interpreted in such a way that the oldest *natural* son is counted as a son for the purposes of deciding whether he is to inherit his father's throne, or whether the fact that adopted sons had inherited *private estates* is a precedent for determining that an eldest, but adopted, son should inherit his father's *throne*. There is no question of our appealing to logic to enable us to decide such cases. Logic will tell us, syllogistically, that, if an eldest son shall inherit his father's throne, and if an adopted son is a son, then an eldest son, even though adopted, shall inherit his father's throne. It will not, however, tell us whether or not an adopted son is or is not to be counted as a son. In order to settle such questions, we have to decide whether to specify the rules for the use of the word 'son' in such a way that a natural son is a son, or in such a way that a natural son is not a son. This amounts to our having to decide whether certain odd or less familiar cases resemble certain clear, or at any rate, already-settled cases, sufficiently to justify us in applying the principle that was applied to the clear or settled cases to the new cases. The new or odd case will resemble the clear or settled case in some respects, and differ from it in others, or will resemble in some respects cases that have been settled in one way, and resemble in other respects cases that have been settled in the opposite way. On Hume's view, there is no rational way of determining whether to be impressed by the resemblances or the differences, or by the resemblances to one case rather than by the resemblances to another. Certain features appeal to the imagination, while others do not; certain resemblances may irrationally incline us to decide a case as one case was decided; other resemblances may incline us to decide it in the (opposite) way in which a different case was decided.

If Hume is right about this, it will follow that there is a fundamental and irreducible element of irrationality in a large part of legal reasoning. This will manifest itself both in the making and in the interpreting of laws. It will manifest itself in the making of laws, for example, in that sometimes men will make laws laying down that a man's property shall be handed down to his eldest child, and in doing this men are simply yielding to an irrational (or non-rational) tendency to add one relation to another. It will manifest itself in the interpreting of laws, in that sometimes an undecided case will resemble several different clear or decided cases in various different ways, and imagination will be so impressed by certain resemblances as to incline us to decide a case in one way rather than another. The second element of irrationality in legal reasoning is more worrying than the first. Laws always could be made for their usefulness, even though they are not. But, Hume thinks, it is extremely harmful to be guided by utility in interpreting the law; hence it looks as if the second element of irrationality is inescapable.

Hume's view of the effect of the imagination in tempting us to decide cases in some ways rather than others has already been criticized (148-157). We rejected it on the grounds that since every case resembled every other case in some way or other, there was no way in which we could decide a case so as *not* to add a relation which was in our gift, so to speak, to one which was not. Hume, nevertheless, is right in thinking that very often laws are made and cases decided because of some irrational appeal, and he is probably also right in thinking that, in some of these cases, there is no rational way in which they could be decided. He may, of course, be right about this, even if his account of the nature and causes of this irrational appeal is mistaken.

SECTION XI

Of the Laws of Nations

LAWS concerning the stability of possession, its transference by consent, and the performance of promises apply to nations as well as individuals, as also do some other rules not applicable to individuals (567-8); the laws of nations are less stringent than those which govern the behaviour of private persons (568); this is explained by the fact that nations, unlike individuals, can exist without such rules (568-9); the extent to which the laws of nations are less stringent than the rules which apply to individuals is discovered by experience of the world, which fact shows that all men know implicitly that the obligation to obey both kinds of convention depends upon their respective advantages (569).

COMMENTS

(1) Hume is obviously absolutely right in thinking that it is of advantage to nations to observe rules of justice. He is also obviously right in thinking that the observance of these rules is less necessary to human existence than the observance of rules of justice by private individuals. Life could exist if nations were in a state of perpetual war, although it could not exist if individuals were so. He is right, too, in suggesting that the obligations of nations to be just in their dealings with one another is of less force than the obligations of private persons. And I personally agree with Hume that the *reason why* the obligation of nations is less stringent than the obligation of individuals is that justice is less necessary among nations than it is among individuals.

A time may come, however, if it has not done so already, when because of the enormous destructiveness of atomic weapons, peace among nations *is* as necessary as peace among individuals. In that event, injustice among nations should be regarded as being as reprehensible as injustice among individuals. Since moral disapproval attaching to breach of moral codes is not solely the result of a perception of its harmfulness, but is reinforced, as Hume says, by education, custom, and the artifices of politicians, it will probably take time, if it does not come too late, before a breach of the laws of nations is as strongly disapproved of as a breach of the rules of justice among individuals. Obviously, as Hume points out, moral disapproval combined with interest—which interest provides only a weak motive, since it is long-term interest—are not enough in any highly evolved society to secure obedience to rules of justice among individuals; a government is necessary to enforce it. Consequently a world government, with adequate power, is or will be necessary to enforce justice among nations.

(2) Nations are collections of people, and any action performed by a nation is in fact an action, or perhaps a complicated network of actions, performed by individual persons who belong to that nation. Great Britain's declaring war on Germany in 1939, for example, involved individual people, like prime ministers and foreign secretaries, doing certain things, and, if these officials had not done these things, Britain could not have declared war on Germany. (It did not, incidentally, involve individual Britons in *declaring war*, for this is something that only a nation can do, just as only a nation can be a member of the United Nations; but it did involve an individual in doing *something*, e.g. summoning the German ambassador, sending an ultimatum, or broadcasting to the nation.) Hence talking of the obligations of nations is a compendious way of referring to the obligations of the people who are members of those nations; to say that the obligations of nations have less force than the obligations of individuals is to say that the obligations of individuals in their capacity as representatives of nations *vis-à-vis* other nations are of less force than their obligations as private individuals. As Cavour is reputed to have said, if we did for ourselves what we do for our countries, we should all be rogues.

In comparing the degrees of force of the obligations of princes to other princes, and the obligations of private individuals to other private individuals, Hume holds two quite distinct views. First, he thinks that when an action of a prince in failing to observe a law of nations is reprehensible, it is *less* reprehensible than the action of a private individual in breaking a rule of justice. Second, he thinks that it is *permissible* for a prince to transgress a law of nations in circumstances in which it would not be permissible for an individual to break a rule of justice. These two contentions are distinct, and the former is more plausible than the latter. If the laws of nations are less necessary to mankind than the laws which regulate individuals, one would expect breaches of the first to be regarded as being less serious than breaches of the second. It is not so clear, however, that the first may be 'lawfully transgress'd from a more trivial motive'. Breaking a solemn promise may be a more serious offence than breaking a casual one, but this does not mean that it is not wrong to break both. Nevertheless, though it is wrong to break both solemn and casual promises, it does seem to be true that we may be justified in breaking a casual promise for a reason

—one might have a cold, for example—which would not justify us in breaking a solemn one. A utilitarian explanation of this fact—and we must not forget that Hume's views are broadly utilitarian—would be that it is not as serious to break a solemn promise, as it is to break a casual promise, because breaking casual promises is less harmful; just because breaking casual promises is less harmful, circumstances may more easily arise in which one could do more good by breaking them than by keeping them.

This leads us to a difficulty in Hume's view. There is no doubt that he is right in thinking that we do regard breaches of private morality as being more serious than breaches by princes of the laws of nations. A minister may be dismissed for sexual misdemeanour, although he breaks solemn treaties with other states with impunity. But it is in fact the breaches of the laws of nations by princes which usually have much more harmful consequences than the breaches of private morality by individuals. If a 'private gentleman' seizes someone else's land, harm is done, but on nothing like the scale on which it is done when one country seizes the territory belonging to another. The interesting point is that, though it is more necessary to the survival of mankind that private justice be *in general* observed than that the laws of nations be *in general* observed, *particular breaches* of the laws of nations do much more harm than particular breaches of the rules of private justice. Analogously, though diphtheria is a much more serious illness than the common cold, the amount of harm done by the common cold is much greater than the amount of harm done by diphtheria. It is also interesting—and perhaps inconsistent with what Hume says in other places about the observance of general rules—that he should maintain that breaches of the law of nations are less serious than acts of private injustice because *collectively* the former are less harmful, rather than argue that these breaches are more serious because *individually* they are *more* harmful. If the analogy with the common cold is of any value, common views on morality would seem to be against Hume, for, though the common cold does more harm than diphtheria, we would regard a doctor's neglecting to treat a common cold as much less serious than his neglecting to treat diphtheria. (My own view of the matter is that we should *neither* be guided by the consequences of one failure to treat a common cold, or keep the laws of nations, *nor* be guided by the total amount of harm done by failure to treat a common cold, or to keep the laws of nations. We should be guided by the consequences of everybody's failing to treat common colds having consequences as bad or worse than this one, or by the consequences of everybody's failing to keep laws of nations having consequences as serious as or more serious than this failure has. If I am right, Hume is wrong in thinking that breaches of the laws of nations are less serious than breaches of private justice because the latter are collectively more necessary than the former.)

Hume is nevertheless right in thinking that the breaches of the laws of nations by princes are regarded with more indulgence than are acts of private injustice. From this it follows that this greater indulgence must be regarded by a utilitarian, whether a rule utilitarian or an act utilitarian, as irrational. If so, there are perfectly good explanations of *why* we irrationally regard acts of private injustice as more seriously wrong than similar acts performed by the representatives of nations on behalf of their countrymen. One reason, I think, is that there is an enormous amount of bias in these matters. If a statesman of one country takes territory belonging to another, then people belonging to his country are likely positively to approve of the action, because it is in their real or supposed interest, or in the interest of something—their country—with which they identify themselves; but people of the other country are likely to regard his action as worse than a similar act of injustice performed privately by an individual. Nationals of neutral countries are likely to view his action according as to whether it does or does not affect their interests adversely. There is not the same body of impartial opinion where the laws of nations are concerned as that which watches over private justice, and the uncertainty and variability of people's reactions will weaken what moral sanctions against such neglect there are. The absence of any effective means of enforcing justice among nations, too, will weaken the disapprobation felt of omitting it. The existence of written statutes, the police, courts, and prisons constitutes a permanent reminder of the condemnation by society of breaches of private justice, which strengthens the common disapprobation of them, as well as providing sanctions against recurrence; this mark of public disapproval is absent where acts of injustice between one country and another are concerned. For reasons such as these, disapproval of injustice between nations is likely to be weaker than disapproval of injustice between individuals, even when such acts are not less harmful in the former case than they are in the latter.

(3) It is necessary to make a few remarks about Hume's contention that the *moral* obligation to obey the laws of nations is founded upon the *natural* obligation to obey them.

A natural *obligation* should not be confused with a natural *virtue*. Though we have a natural obligation to be just, justice is not a natural virtue at all, but an artificial one. To say that we have a natural obligation to be just is Hume's way of saying that we are obliged to be just in order to promote our interests, as we may be obliged to eat less in

order to lose weight. In the statement that we have a natural obligation
to be just, no mention is made of people's feelings of approval or disapproval, or of what morally ought or ought not to be done. That we
have a natural obligation to obey the laws of nations is simply a natural
or non-moral fact about them.

We come to have a moral obligation, as well as a natural obligation,
to obey the laws of nations because people, from sympathy with the
pleasure of others, feel approval of what is useful or in men's interests.
This is the sense in which the moral obligation is founded upon the
natural obligation. There are, however, some difficulties in this contention, which difficulties Hume obscures. In the first place, Hume never
makes it quite clear whether he is saying that it is in men's interests to
have laws of nations, or whether he is saying that, given that we have
them, it is in our interests to *obey* them. (It could be argued that any
law we have must be mostly obeyed, for a rule which is not obeyed at
all is not a rule.) It is clear that it is in everyone's interests that there
should *be* laws of nations, and that they should, for the most part, be
obeyed, but, given that they exist and are on the whole obeyed, it will
not necessarily be in the interests of every individual nation always to
obey them. What is in the interests of every nation is that other nations
obey them, while it does not. Hence the most plausible line for Hume
to take—though he himself does not make it clear that he is taking it—
is that our moral obligation to obey the laws of nations is founded on
the fact that it is in the interests of every nation that there should be
laws of nations. It is simply not true that it is always in the interests of
any given nation always to obey the laws of nations. The natural
obligation, in this case, is a natural obligation to have such laws, not a
naural obligation to obey them.

The second difficulty arises because of the problem: 'Is it nations, or
individual members of nations acting in a public capacity, who have
natural and moral obligations?' We have seen that, since nations are not
entities over and above individual nationals, talking of the obligations
of nations is really a convenient way of talking of the obligations of
individual people. (It must not be forgotten that though an obligation
of a nation is always an individual's obligation to do *something*, it is
not necessarily an individual's obligation to do what this nation is under
an obligation to do. A nation's obligation to keep a treaty consists in
the obligation of individual men to do something, but not an obligation
to *keep a treaty*, for only nations can do this.) An obligation on the
part of a nation to abstain from seizing territory belonging to another
nation is really an obligation on the part of princes and ministers of the
first nation not to take steps which will result in the nation of which

they are subjects acquiring territory belonging to another nation. (To say that a territory belongs to a nation is not to say that it belongs to any individual member of this nation, but to say something else about them, for example, that officials who are members of the nation have rights over and duties to people living in this territory, which they would not have if it did *not* belong to this nation.)

But then, of course, it is even less clear that it is always in the interests of individuals to perform those acts which would result in the nation of which they are members observing the laws of nations. It may not be in the interests of the relevant officer of a country to do what is in the interests of his country. The two things, the interests of the individual minister, and the interests of the country to which he belongs, may even cancel one another out, so that it is in the interests of the minister that his country should observe a law of nations which it is in the interests of his country to break. This should make it even clearer that it is impossible to found a moral obligation to obey the laws of nations on the natural obligation of any country or individual minister to keep the laws of nations; the only thing this moral obligation can be founded upon is the fact that it is in the interests of nations that there should be laws of nations, and that it is in the interests of nations and individuals collectively that all nations should keep these laws, even when it is not in their individual interests to keep them. This explains why there is a uniform moral obligation to keep the laws of nations, even though the interests of individual nations, their princes, and ministers, are different.

(4) In this section, Hume again (569) uses an argument from what most people's attitudes are (in this case, their attitude to keeping and breaking the laws of nations) to what man's duties or obligations are. This argument is that because in fact men disapprove of breaches of the laws of nations less strongly than breaches of private justice, and because the former are less necessary to mankind than the latter, this shows that men are in fact determined by the advantages or disadvantages of a practice in approving of disapproving of it. This is not an argument from the consensus of opinion. An opinion about what is obligatory would be on Hume's most usual view an opinion about what most men approve of. Hume, however, is not arguing from men's *opinions* about what most people approve of to what is right, but from what in fact most men approve of to what is right.

His argument is that since men feel approval of both the laws of nations and of private justice, but feel stronger approval of the latter than the former, and since both the laws of nations and private justice are useful, but the latter more useful than the former, these facts show that our approval of both the laws of nations and of private justice must be determined by this usefulness. This is perfectly in accord with the epistemological view which is most prominent in Part II of Book III of the *Treatise*, which is that right and wrong are determined by what most people feel approval of (provided the approval is well informed and unbiased), and that those characteristics which make a thing right are those characteristics which cause men to approve of it. It introduces a new consideration, however, which Hume has not alluded to before, namely that there are degrees of obligation, which are determined by the degrees of strength with which approval is felt, which in its turn is determined by the degree to which what is approved of is useful.

No moral philosopher, to my knowledge, has talked much about degrees of morality. This is an important omission. Morality is too frequently spoken of as if it were an all-or-nothing matter, which usually it is not. Common sense, however, certainly regards duties and obligations as capable of being more or less stringent, and I am sure it is just a crude error to suppose that all duties are absolutely stringent, and allow of no exceptions in favour of interest or inclination, but only, perhaps, exceptions in favour of other conflicting duties.

Some men are clearly better than others. There is no particular problem presented by the fact (which philosophers have commonly recognized) that there are degrees of moral goodness, for men can possess the different virtues in varying degrees, and possess a larger or smaller number of those virtues. Nor is there any especial problem presented by the fact that virtues can vary in the degrees of their goodness. On Hume's view, which has always struck me as being extremely sensible, that virtues are those characteristics which are useful or agreeable to their possessor or to others, there can be no difficulty in explaining why some virtues are better than others, for some traits of character can clearly be more useful or more agreeable than others. Even on a Kantian view, according to which there is only one virtue, consisting in the disposition to do one's duty for the sake of duty, there is no difficulty in explaining why virtue can vary in degree, for people may possess this desire to do their duty in varying strengths, may be able to overcome temptations of different degrees of seductiveness, and may actually do their duties with varying degrees of frequency.

Again, when we consider those goods which are the *objects* of desire and action, such as possessing knowledge and enjoying pleasure, there is no reason why some of these should not be described as being better than others, though it might be a little stupid to make statements such as that *knowledge* is better than *pleasure*, when it seems fairly obvious that whether it is better to choose knowledge or pleasure would depend very much on the circumstances. A very knowledgeable man who got little enjoyment from life might be wise to choose some pleasure rather than the possession of even more knowledge, whereas an ignorant man given to short-lived pleasures might be wise to choose the latter. This is at least partly explained by the fact that additional increments of knowledge or of pleasure have progressively diminishing value. Hence it might behove a wise man so to organize his life as to choose an additional increment of pleasure or an increment of knowledge according as to which increment has the most value.

The fact that there is no difficulty with explaining how there can be degrees of the goodness of men, the goodness of nations, and the goodness of good things is marked by the fact that we have the words 'good', 'better', and 'best'. That it is difficult to explain how the expressions 'duty' and 'obligation' admit of degrees is marked by the fact that we do not have the analogous expressions 'more right', 'more obligatory', and 'more of a duty'. However, though no action can be more right than another, some *wrong* actions can be worse than others, and we do have the expression 'very wrong', although we do not have the expression 'very right'. 'Worse' is ambiguous. Sometimes it is the comparative of 'bad', as in 'Smith is a bad man, but Jones is worse'. At other times it is compared with 'wrong', as in 'it would be wrong to do so-and-so, but worse to do such-and-such'. Although 'duty' does not have a comparative, duties do admit of degrees of stringency, and some duties are more stringent than others.

Let us now discuss the question of degrees as it applies to the right/wrong, duty/not a duty, obligatory/not obligatory distinctions, starting with the first. I suspect that all wrong actions are bad in some degree, which may be very small, from which it follows that some wrong actions are worse than others. I do not think that what makes an action bad is, as has commonly been held, the motive for which it is performed, although, of course, some bad motives are worse than others. It is worse to be unkind to children than to break one's dinner engagements irrespective of the motives from which either is performed. I suspect that what makes the former worse than the latter is that it is more harmful than the latter. Performing more harmful actions is normally a sign of having a worse character than performing less harmful actions because, in normal circumstances, it indicates a greater degree of ruthlessness or egotism or callousness in overriding the interests of others in order to get what one wants. It may also be that some good actions are better than others, irrespective of the motive from which they are performed, and that what makes them better is the amount of good that they do. As performing a very bad action is usually a sign of having a worse disposition than is performing a less bad action, omitting a very good action is evidence of having a worse disposition than is omitting a less good one, provided that either could have been done with the same amount of inconvenience to oneself. However, since both very good actions and very bad actions are usually fairly difficult to perform—it takes more trouble to rob a bank than to steal from a supermarket, and it demands a greater sacrifice to give large amounts to charity than it does to give small ones—performing a very bad action is usually evidence of a worse disposition than omitting a very good one.

Though all wrong actions are in some degree bad, it is not the case that all right actions are in some degree good. For 'right' very often simply means 'not wrong' or 'permissible', and all sorts of indifferent actions can be right. (Performing an indifferent action can be a sign of great virtue on the part of the agent if all its alternatives are very wrong, and he is greatly tempted to perform one of them. The goodness of an action and the goodness of the man who performs it are, however, as we have seen, two very different things, though Hume was wrong when (477) he said that actions were only virtues in so far as they were signs of virtuous motives.)

What makes one thing more obligatory than another, and what makes a duty more stringent than another? Hume's view appears to be that what makes 'the morality of princes' have less force than that of private persons is that it may 'lawfully be transgressed' from a more trivial motive (568). If you generalize this view, what it comes to is that one obligation or duty is more stringent than another if a motive which will permit you to ignore the second will not permit you to ignore the first. This view, I suspect, looks lax because it seems to suggest that duty does not have to be done, but this is a mistake. The proposition that duty must always be done must not be confused with the proposition that one of the circumstances which causes something not to *be* duty is that doing it is, say, greatly contrary to the interest of the man who would have to perform it. For example, one must not confuse the statement that one may not have a duty to keep a promise, if it causes one a very great deal of inconvenience to keep it, with the (contradictory) statement that it may be permissible not to do one's duty of keeping a promise, if it would cause one a very great deal of inconvenience to keep it. And it seems just obviously true that one would not have a duty to keep casual promises if it would cause one much inconvenience to keep them, whereas one would have a duty to keep solemn promises, even when keeping them would cause one very much inconvenience. Nevertheless, if one *has* a duty to keep any sort of promise, it is not permissible not to do this duty, for it is logically contradictory to assert that one has a duty which it is permissible not to do.

One might try to evolve an at least apparently less lenient view of what makes some duties and obligations more stringent than others. One might say that though all duties and obligations are equally stringent, in that none ceases to be a duty on account of any conflicting motive, however weighty; omitting them, however, though not *permissible*, is nevertheless *excusable*, and very little *blame* would attach to the agent were he wrongly to omit them. Or one might say that some duties and obligations are more stringent than others in that, in the event of a less stringent duty conflicting with a more stringent one, the agent ought to perform the latter, rather than the former.

Both the above propositions are, I think, true. When we do omit a duty which is not very stringent, less blame *does* attach to us than when we omit one which is very stringent. (Though it is not necessarily excusable to omit a duty which is not very stringent, what would count as a good excuse for omitting such a duty would not necessarily count as a good excuse for omitting a duty which was very stringent.) And when a less stringent duty conflicts with a more stringent one, it is likely that one ought to perform the latter rather than the former. But these two propositions, though true, are not identical with the proposition that some duties are more stringent than others. For one thing, it is both the case that if a promise is rather a casual one, breaking it when it ought to be kept is more excusable than breaking a more solemn promise, and also the case that, because of the inconvenience involved in keeping it, circumstances more easily arise in which one is under no obligation to keep it at all. For another, though if one were faced with the choice between keeping a casual promise and a solemn one, one ought to keep the solemn one, this is not the same thing as to say that one might lawfully break the casual one on account of the amount of inconvenience which would not justify one in breaking the solemn one. I suspect that, when one duty or obligation is less stringent than another duty or obligation, it is true that the first may be transgressed from more trivial motives, that it is more excusable to transgress it even when it is not right to transgress it, and that it is more likely to be overridden by conflicting duties or obligations.

It is an interesting point that we seem to be able to raise the question which of two duties ought to be done, or which of two obligations ought to be performed in the event of a conflict, for our being able to raise this question seems to suggest that perhaps one of those conflicting duties or obligations ought not to be performed. But is it not odd to speak of one's having a duty to perform an action, or of an action's being obligatory, when we ought *not* to perform it?

Again, the appearance that the fact that some duties or obligations are less stringent than others implies that some duties or obligations ought not to be performed is illusory. To say that, of two conflicting duties or obligations, one ought not to be performed, does not imply that a duty or obligation ought not to be performed, but that one of the actions which *would* be a duty or an obligation, if it did not conflict with some other duty or obligation, ought not to be performed. There is not necessarily anything wrong with duties or obligations which ought not to be performed. We can certainly have legal or social duties or obligations which ought not to be performed. But in the present context we are talking about moral duties and moral obligations, and these logically ought always to be performed.

When we come to apply these remarks to what Hume says about the comparative force of the morality of princes and the morality of private persons, though it is clear that there is nothing in principle wrong with Hume's view that the former has less force than the latter—for duties and obligations do differ in stringency—it is doubtful whether he is right in saying that the former do in fact have less force than the latter. For, as I have said, the consequences of breaches of the laws of nations may be much more harmful than the consequences of breaches of private morality, and to argue, as Hume does, that, because the laws of nations are less necessary than private morality, individual breaches of the laws of nations are less serious than individual breaches of private morality might be analogous to arguing that, because refuse collectors are more useful than professors of philosophy, individual refuse collectors ought to be paid more than individual professors of philosophy. My own feeling, as I have already hinted, is that though Hume is right in thinking that the morality of princes is commonly regarded as being of less force than private morality, he is wrong in the explanation he gives of this fact and wrong in thinking that this means that they *are* of less force. For when we consider the enormous amount of harm done by individual breaches of the laws of nations, one might suspect that the leniency with which we regard them is partly due to bias (for which Hume himself thinks allowances ought to be made) and partly due to their remoteness, (for which Hume also thinks allowances ought to be made). It is because breaches of the laws of nations are often performed by our compatriots, and because their harmful consequences are often remote in space and time, and also because they harm people of a different nation from ourselves, that we do not condemn them as strongly as we ought. It is also the case that since we have not been *educated* to disapprove of breaches of the laws of nations as strongly as breaches of the laws of individuals, we will disapprove of the former less strongly than we will disapprove of the latter.

(5) In the final paragraph of this section occurs a passage that I find very difficult to understand, and which I shall quote in full. 'One may safely affirm, that this proportion [the proportion between the strength of our obligation to obey the laws of nations and that of our obligation to observe private justice] finds itself, without any art or study of men; as we may observe on many other occasions. The practice of the world goes farther in teaching us the degrees of our duty, than the most subtile philosophy, which was ever yet invented' (569).

I can make sense of the first sentence in this passage only if, by 'finds itself, without any art or study of men', Hume means 'can be determined, without *academic* study, but instead [as the second sentence in this passage indicates] by knowledge of the practice of the world'. One could, of course, say that the practice of the world can be made a matter of academic study, though most people obtain it, as Hume assumed they would, by mixing with the world.

But why does Hume think that knowledge of our duty can be obtained by knowledge of the practice of the world? It is rather as if he assumed that morality was a matter of conforming to the actual practices of the world, i.e. that man's duties are determined by a practice or rule which assigns them to him, whereas, of course, Hume thought that man's duties are determined by their sentiments. The resolution of this apparent inconsistency, however, may simply be that our sentiments confer morality upon what is advantageous to mankind, and that, given that the practices of the world are advantageous, knowledge of these practices is obtained by experience of them. The remark that knowledge of the practice of the world teaches us the degrees of our duty suggests that the rules actually adopted and applied by mankind are much more complicated, multifarious, and discriminating than anything that could be worked out *a priori* by a philosopher in his study, which may well be true. This does not alter the fact, however, that these multifarious rules may all stem from the unifying principle that what is useful is approved. Alternatively, Hume may simply mean that we know the degrees of duty empirically from observations, which living in the world gives us the opportunity to make, of how severely men condemn breaches of different duties.

The view of one part of morality which this paragraph suggests is that it is a complicated system of social practices, sanctioned by the disapproval which breaches of those practices arouses. Discovering our duties and obligations would consist in discovering what these practices in fact are, which can only be done by experience and by acquiring knowledge of the world. That these practices are useful ones causes men to approve of our conforming to them and, since that men approve of conforming to them is what makes it true to say that conforming to them is a virtue, conforming to them both is a virtue, and is a virtue because it is useful.

SECTION XII

Of Chastity and Modesty

OBSERVANCE of another set of rules, concerning chastity and modesty, will, Hume thinks, confirm his account of the laws of nature and of nations (570); men will not be induced to care for their offspring through a long infancy unless they can be assured that their wives' children are also their own, which assurance is much more difficult to obtain in the case of men than women (570-1); an *a priori* philosopher would suppose that it could be obtained by punishing women for having bad reputations, by punishing infidelity more than natural justice demands and on inadequate evidence, and by punishing immodesty (or the approaches to infidelity) (571); though such an *a priori* philosopher would not expect to find these devices to secure fidelity in women actually adopted, on account of the strength and the biological necessity of the temptation to transgress them (572); he would, however, be mistaken, as education makes women subservient to those who have an interest in their fidelity (572); men, because they do not themselves bear children, are in a large measure excepted from the rule demanding chastity and modesty, but women who are barren, or too old or too young to have children, are not exempted (572-3); the proportion between the strength of the obligations of men and women in respect of chastity and modesty is the same as the proportion between the strength of the obligations of nations and of individuals to obey rules of justice (573).

COMMENTS

(1) In the section on the laws of nations, Hume asserts that our obligation to obey the laws of nations has less force than our obligation to obey the laws of private justice, because the former are less necessary than the latter. In this section, he asserts that men's duties in respect of fidelity and modesty not only have less force than women's: the laws they are obliged to obey are also different. He does not say, however, in what way they are different. And, in the section on the laws of nations, he does say that there are laws—those concerning the sacredness of ambassadors and abstention from poisoned arms, for example—which apply to nations, but not to individuals. I think it is his

view that there are more rules concerning the general behaviour of women than there are those concerning men, and that those rules which apply to both sexes apply more stringently to women than they do to men.

(2) In the fifth paragraph of this section (571), Hume speaks as if his speculative philosopher, having evolved an *a priori* solution to the problem of ensuring fidelity in women, would, when confronted with the empirical facts, discover it to be insufficient. He is not supposed, however, to know the facts until the two succeeding paragraphs, when he finds to his surprise that the solution that he invented in his study has actually been adopted by human beings (572-3). This inconsistency can be resolved if, when Hume says 'our philosopher wou'd quickly discover, that it wou'd not alone be sufficient' (571), he means 'discover by more *a priori* reasoning'. Whether he does mean this or not, I cannot say.

(3) Why does Hume introduce an attempt by a speculative philosopher to produce *a priori* a way of securing fidelity in women? I think it is a rhetorical device to underline the ingenuity of nature. A philosopher might work out *a priori* that it would be very advantageous to living organisms to have eyes, but not expect to find them, because he had not realized that they would evolve by a process of natural selection, rather than be deliberately invented. Similarly, Hume's idea seems to be, a disapprobation of infidelity and immodesty arises 'naturally', rather than is deliberately invented to secure a necessary end, and nature, in this case, does more for man than could be expected from his own ingenuity.

Hume's explanation of how disapprobation of infidelity and immodesty grows up, however, is lame. He says, 'Those, who have an *interest* [my italics] in the fidelity of women, *naturally* [my italics] disapprove of their infidelity, and all the approaches to it' (572), but this seems inconsistent with his usual view that it is not *interest*, but *sympathy* with those to whom something is harmful which causes disapprobation; it is further inconsistent with his view, expressed in the very same section, that disapproval of infidelity and immodesty *must* be caused by a perception of the usefulness of these characteristics, since only in this way can we explain why we disapprove of infidelity and immodesty less strongly in men than in women. Hume says, 'Those, who have no interest, are carried along with the stream' (572), but, if men's moral sentiments are determined by the usefulness of a characteristic to people *other than themselves*, there is no reason why disapprobation of infidelity and immodesty, even in those without an interest in it, should not be caused directly by a perception of this fact. Hume says that 'Education takes possession of the ductile minds of the fair sex in their infancy' (572), but what exactly are the fair sex being educated in? It would be inconsistent to say that they were being educated in the *harmfulness* of infidelity and immodesty, for their approval of these qualities, like others' approval of the same qualities, is supposed to be formed 'naturally, and without reflection' (572). It would also be inconsistent for Hume to suppose that an unreflecting abhorrence of inchastity and infidelity is produced in young women by those who *do* perceive the usefulness of these qualities. Hume cannot have it both ways: he cannot both hold that our approval of chastity and fidelity is unreflecting, and *not* caused by our perception of the fact that demanding it is necessary to give men security that their wives' children are theirs, and also hold that it is caused by our perception of the fact that these qualities are desirable in men and women, but less necessary in men than in women.

Hume's speculative philosopher, incidentally, cannot be supposed to reason wholly *a priori*, for he must know those facts about human beings which cause inchastity and infidelity to be harmful. He must know enough facts about human nature to know what the problem is, but not enough about human nature to know that it has hit upon a solution, or what that solution is.

(4) One of the expedients which Hume's speculative philosopher devises to ensure fidelity in women, which expedient, Hume thinks, is actually found to have been adopted, is to impose penalties not only on infidelity itself, but also upon the *reputation of* having been unfaithful. This solution is not without formidable difficulties. For one thing, Hume does not make it entirely clear whether it is having a bad reputation, or having behaved in such a way as to have acquired a bad reputation, to which penalties must be and are attached. If it is the latter, then a woman is punished for having actually committed an offence, say the offence of being in a bachelor's rooms without a chaperone, but then she is punished for something she has actually done, and is known or reasonably believed to have done. In this case, however, it is arguable that the offence she has committed is one of immodesty, in a wide sense, and falls under the head of Hume's speculative philosopher's *second* expedient, that of attaching penalties to all the approaches to infidelity. If, on the other hand, it is the former ('the punishment of bad fame or reputation'), then a woman can be guilty of an offence, to which severe penalties are or were attached, without having done anything to deserve it, for her bad reputation may arise not even from her own carelessness of it, but simply from malicious gossip.

It is no use replying that in *all* cases, not just this one, someone may

incur penalties for being supposed, because of such gossip, to have committed an offence he or she has not committed; for in the other cases
punishment is inflicted because an offence is, through scandal, wrongly
supposed to have been committed, whereas in this case, according to
Hume, an offence has been committed, namely, the offence of having
been (wrongly) supposed to have committed another offence. Hume,
furthermore, says that punishment for having a bad reputation may be
inflicted 'upon surmizes, and conjectures, and proofs, that wou'd never
be receiv'd in any court of judicature' (571). But here he is confused, for a
woman, if she is punished for having a bad reputation, is not punished
on the *surmise* of having a *bad reputation*. It could, and usually would,
be *known* that she had one. She is punished on the *surmise* of having
been unfaithful. Might it not have been better if Hume had said, not
that a woman may, and indeed must, be punished for having a bad
reputation, but that though what she is punished for is infidelity, this
punishment may be inflicted not only upon its being established that she
has been unfaithful, but upon evidence which may give this a probability
which may not amount even to making it more likely that she has than
that she has not?

This might be more logical, but it would not be true to the empirical
facts. If a woman is not invited to dinner, it is not usually because she
has been unfaithful to her husband, a fact about which her host may
care little, but because she has a bad reputation, and he may not invite
her for this reason even though he privately thinks her bad reputation
unjustified.

There is, however, no difference in this respect between infidelity
and any other crime. A man may not be invited to dinner because he
has a reputation of being a thief, not because his host supposes he is a
thief. It is a fact about human beings that they often do not wish to
associate publicly with those who have bad reputations in any respect.
This fact does impose an added sanction to prevent people from doing
the things which would justify their bad reputations, and also upon
their doing other things which would give them bad reputations without
justifying it, but it is not a fact about sexual morality only. Nor does it
mean that having a bad reputation is ever by itself an offence, though,
naturally, harm comes to those who have one. For to say that it is an
offence implies that those who have a bad reputation are justly punished
simply for having it, even though they have done nothing to deserve
their reputation, and even by people who know that their reputation
is justified neither by their having done what they are suspected of
doing, nor by their having carelessly acted in such a way as to give rise
to such suspicion. Such a way of securing marital fidelity in women

would give an intolerable power to the purveyors of gossip, in that they would be able to create an actual offence, as well as what they cannot be prevented from doing, create the reputation of having committed an offence.

(5) Hume's speculative philosopher also reasons that 'In order, therefore, to impose a due restraint on the female sex, we must attach a peculiar degree of shame to their infidelity, *above what arises merely from its injustice* [my italics] , and must bestow proportionable praises on their chastity' (571). This, though Hume does not seem to realize it, is a different device from attaching a punishment to having a bad reputation, for penalizing people for the suspicion of being unfaithful, and attaching severer penalties than justice demands to actually being unfaithful, are clearly distinct. It is difficult to see what Hume can mean by attaching a degree of shame to infidelity above what arises from its injustice. For justice, according to Hume, is a conventional virtue, which means that if, because of the demands of utility, something be made a severe offence, to which severe penalties are attached, it is a severe offence. Perhaps help may be found from a passage on the following page (572), where Hume's speculative philosopher argues that men will *not* in fact attach severer penalties to infidelity than to other crimes, because ''tis evident they are more excusable, upon account of the greatness of the temptation'. In this case, I shall discuss it later. It may be, however, that he is expressing himself badly; what he means, though it is not what he says, is that the shame attaching to having incurred the reputation of having been unfaithful is 'above' the shame (which justice demands) of actually having been unfaithful. This would explain the occurrence of the word 'therefore' in this sentence, but it does not explain the word 'above'—for one might have incurred the suspicion of having been unfaithful, without actually having been so— and one might have expected him to say 'contrary to [rather than above] what arises merely from its injustice'.

One possible explanation of Hume's remark that the penalties of infidelity in women are (and must be, if domestic life is to be preserved and children properly brought up) above what justice demands is that what he means is that the penalties must be more severe than those attached to other offences which are equally socially harmful, on account of the fact that they are more difficult to detect. The clear implication of this is that some offences must and ought to be punished more severely than they *deserve* to be punished, in order that men and women be adequately deterred from committing them. Marital infidelity, then, because it is difficult to detect, ought to be punished more severely than 'justice' demands. But, if that is what Hume meant, it is difficult to say why he thought he had to make a special case for severe penalties for immodesty and infidelity in women.

(6) In my preceding comments, I have assumed that by 'There seems to be no restraint possible, but in the punishment of bad fame or reputation' (571), Hume meant 'punishing women for *having* a bad reputation'. Perhaps, however, he meant 'punishment consisting in bad fame or reputation'. This interpretation would mean that Hume was not confused when he speaks of this punishment being 'inflicted by the world upon surmizes, and conjectures, and proofs, that would never be received in any court of judicature', for, on this interpretation, he would quite properly be talking about the evidence for a woman's having been unfaithful, and not the evidence for her having the reputation of having been unfaithful. Interpreting the word 'of' in this sentence in this way, however, does not adequately explain the word 'therefore' in the following sentence. From the fact that an offence is punished because those who commit it acquire a bad reputation, it does not *follow* that this punishment is more severe than justice demands. And it is difficult to see how the reputation of having been supposed to have committed an offence can be, as Hume says it must be, greater than what justice demands, for it seems obvious that the dislike which people have of being supposed to have committed an offence must depend almost entirely upon the seriousness of the offence committed. It would be inconsistent for Hume to say that, though marital infidelity (in women) is not more serious than certain other offences, it is worse to be supposed to have been unfaithful than to be supposed to have committed one or other of these other offences. And these interpretations of Hume's would not explain why society deliberately decides to impose the punishment of bad fame or reputation, for there is nothing society can do to stop people from supposing that women are sometimes unfaithful. Nor will it explain why marital infidelity in women has extraordinary sanctions attached to it, for, where any offence is concerned, people will dislike having been supposed to have committed it.

(7) Hume's speculative philosopher, when he despairs of mankind having adopted his *a priori* remedy against the infidelity of women, argues, 'For what means, wou'd he say, of persuading mankind, that the transgressions of conjugal duty [presumably only in women] are more infamous than any other kind of injustice, when 'tis evident they are more excusable, upon account of the greatness of the temptation?' (572). As these remedies have in fact been adopted, does Hume think that their adoption manifests a delusion on the part of mankind, the delusion of supposing that marital infidelity (in women) is a more serious crime than it is, which delusion it is necessary mankind should

labour under in order that fidelity in women should be secured? It is difficult to see how Hume could consistently maintain this, for he thinks that justice is a conventional virtue, and that what kind of behaviour is unjust is determined by the rules society actually adopts; from this it follows that, if mankind have adopted certain rules to secure marital fidelity, behaviour in accordance with these rules is just. Hume cannot, as we have seen, even plead that the behaviour is not just, because the rules attach severer penalties than is socially desirable to the offence they create, for he thinks the penalties are not too severe but, on the contrary, are necessary.

In any case, Hume's reasons for thinking that, in attaching severe penalties to infidelity, we are penalizing more heavily than other crimes something which is more excusable, are not good ones. The fact that there is a strong temptation in mankind to a certain offence is normally a good reason for penalizing it *more* severely. There is a greater temptation to steal a million pounds than ten, and for that very reason, more severe penalties have to be imposed to prevent the former crime than the latter. One does not, of course, legislate against something simply because there is, in mankind, a strong motive for performing it; but given that something ought to be legislated against, the penalties used to enforce the law must be strong enough to deter people from acting on whatever motive he thinks would normally cause them to break the law in question. (That there is in man a strong motive for performing a kind of action which is harmful, but not very hamful, is one reason for *not* legislating against it at all.) Hume is right, of course, in thinking that strong temptation does mitigate the serious-ness of a breach of a rule, but I suspect that what we take into con-sideration here is not the normal motive for breaking the rule, but an exceptionally strong motive in a given individual. Hence if, through extreme poverty, someone has an unusually strong temptation to steal a small amount of money, this is a reason for treating him with more than usual leniency; everyone's having a strong temptation to steal small amounts, however, would not be a reason for leniency. But Hume, of course, is thinking of the *usual* strength of the motive to marital infidelity, and this is a reason for imposing a greater penalty, not a less, on those who are unfaithful.

It may be that what Hume has at the back of his mind, though he does not explicitly say so, is the idea that marital infidelity is less serious than is indicated by the penalties that it is necessary to attach to it, because there is nothing wrong with the motive which normally prompts men and women to be unfaithful; it is, as Hume says, the very same motive to which it is necessary to yield in order to propagate the species (571). But then, the motive which normally prompts men to steal money is not a different motive from the one which normally prompts them to make money; but this is no reason for thinking that taking money is really less serious than the penalties attached to it would suggest.

In general, it seems that the penalties attached to an offence are determined by how harmful are the effects of committing it, the strength of the motive which normally prompts people to commit it, and the difficulty of detecting it. The more harmful its effects, the stronger the motive, and the more difficult it is to detect, the more severe its penalties have to be. Since marital infidelity, especially in women, is, according to Hume, very harmful, one to which we are prompted by a strong motive, and very difficult to detect, these are all reasons for attaching a severe penalty to it. In this it is in no way exceptional.

Hume's speculative philosopher, of course, would not have had the benefit of reading the works of Freud. Had he done so, he might have been less surprised than he was to find that the solution to the problem of securing fidelity in women, which he had devised *a priori*, had in fact been unreflectingly adopted by mankind. For, according to Freud, there is in the mind of man a device which makes him disapprove most strongly in others of those crimes to which he is himself most prone, and the strength of the tendency to marital infidelity in most people would then explain why they condemn it so severely in others. The strength of their condemnation would not be determined rationally, but it would produce the same attitude to infidelity in women that a rational man would have if he were clever enough to see its harmfulness.

(Hume sometimes puts an argument into the mouth of someone other than himself as a device for expressing an opinion which might be unpopular. The most notorious example of the use of this device is the *Dialogues Concerning Natural Religion*, but it is also used in Section XI of the *An Enquiry Concerning Human Understanding*. If he puts an argument into the mouth of a speculative philosopher partly for this reason, it is presumably to disguise the fact that the opinion that infidelity and immodesty are more excusable than other vices, on account of the greatness of the temptation and the fact that yielding to sexual appetite is necessary for the propagation of the species, was his, if it was his. I cannot, however, think that Hume regarded this opinion as so heterodox as to make it necessary to disguise the fact that he held it.)

(8) Hume says, 'And when a general rule of this kind [enjoining fidelity and modesty upon married women] is once establish'd, men

are apt to extend it [to women not capable of bearing children] beyond
those principles, from which it first arose' (572). He is guilty of a
logical mistake in thinking that the rule is extended to bachelors,
and he says nothing about unmarried women *capable of having children*,
though he presumably thinks it is extended to them also. Hume speaks
as if the tendency to extend the rules enjoining fidelity and modesty to
women incapable of childbirth is an irrational one, but, whether or not
he is right about this, there may be a rational justification for it, even
though men have not extended the principle because they have seen
that there is a justification. It may be that it would be impracticable
to impose fidelity and chastity upon married women if they could look
back to a time when this was not expected of them, and forward to a
time when it will be expected of them no longer. It is not, however,
impracticable to expect men to work, although they can look back
upon a time when this was not expected of them, and forward to a
time when it will be expected of them no longer. It could be argued
that the reason for this difference is that men have a rational appreciation of the need to work, whereas they do not have a rational appreciation of the need for fidelity and modesty in women. Hence if fidelity
and modesty were not expected of women, even in those cases when
nothing is gained by it, they would not be faithful and modest at all.
Though a rational rule for rational people would not expect fidelity
and modesty of women outside the age of childbirth, a rational rule
for irrational people, who would not be capable of making permissible
exceptions to it without also making impermissible ones, does expect
these things. On Hume's own principles, one has to allow that it is
irrational of people to demand chastity and modesty of women beyond
the age of childbirth, for he has himself asserted (551-2) that, where a
number of cases, which are not themselves harmful, may be excepted
as a class, the rule may be modified to exclude them. The fact that
women's duties of chastity and modesty arise from the need to assure
their husbands that they are really the biological fathers of their children
does not explain why women past the age of childbirth have such a
duty, except that it sets a bad example to other women not intelligent
enough to perceive the difference between infidelity in women capable
of having children and that in women not capable of having children.

(9) Hume speaks as if there were a natural instinct to care for and
lavish affection on children who are in fact one's own. In this he must
be mistaken. What instinct there is is directed to caring for and giving
affection to children *believed* to be one's own. In this the parental
instinct does not differ from any other kind of instinct. Birds have an
instinct to migrate north when they 'believe' it is spring, and can be

deceived into migrating too early if the weather is especially clement for the time of year. Why then do men care when they care for and lavish affection upon children who are not their own? The answer is that they do not care while they believe they are their own, and only come to care when they believe they are not their own. If there were an instinct in men to give affection only to children who were their own, there would be no problem, for then they would always know which children were their own, and would not have to worry about lavishing affection on children who were not.

It is doubtful whether there is in men even an instinct to care for children whom they believe to be their own, as opposed to other children. The paternal instinct is more likely to be an instinct to care for children in general, rather than one's own children—it would be difficult to explain the satisfaction some parents get from adopted children otherwise—and sometimes even to care for helpless objects like animals and invalids. But in that case, why do we not *welcome* other men's giving us children by our wives, because it provides us with more objects by which the paternal instinct can satisfy itself? One *possible* reason is that the paternal instinct is not strong enough to give enough satisfaction to compensate us for the labours of bringing up children. Society has allocated to fathers the onerous task of providing for their children. (Might not Hume have said society does this because men are impressed by the biological relation between parent and child, which causes them to wish to link those already linked by the relation 'father of' with the further relation of 'being responsible for'?) If men indulge in sexual pleasure, they may have to pay for it by rearing the children which result. Hence if one man has the pleasure, and another man the burden of rearing the child, the latter is likely to be annoyed about the fact, and perhaps refuse to carry the burden.

This is doubtless part of the explanation why men do not want their wives to have children which are not also theirs, but it is obviously not the whole of it. It assumes that having children is wholly onerous, or, at any rate, that the satisfaction does not compensate men for the burden. But this cannot always, or even usually, be true (though Hume, who lived before the days of effective contraception, might have supposed that it was), for otherwise people would not have the children that they can quite easily prevent. What is still needed is an explanation more satisfactory than Hume's of the fact that men generally do not like bringing up their wives' children if these are not also biologically theirs. It will not do to say that the child is a perpetual reminder of one's wife's infidelity, for this, though doubtless often true, presupposes that there is some explanation, which Hume has not given, of the fact that the husband objects to his wife's infidelity, *other* than that it results in her having children which are not also his. One might say that the paternal instinct, strong though it is, is not strong enough to compensate a man for the burden of bringing up children unless it is stimulated by what the late Professor Broad[1] called an 'egoistic motive stimulant', but this does not explain why it is being one's own biological child, and not one's wife's child, that provides this stimulant.

I suspect that the explanation why men are reluctant to bring up their wives' children by other men is the fact that the paternal instinct, in order to compensate them for the burdens it entails, must usually be reinforced by the presence of another motive, for which I know no name. One of the reasons why men want children is that they believe that their own characteristics, which they may be expected to value too highly, are handed on to their own children, whereas they are not handed on to their wives' children by other men. By having children a man may hope to make an indelible mark on the course of future history, survive his own death, and bask in the reflected glory of their achievements, which he naturally exaggerates, and which he flatters himself are the results of endowments that they would not have had, had they not received them from him. His wife's having children by other men, however much it may satisfy his paternal instinct, does not give him this satisfaction. Without it he feels cheated, for he is labouring to perpetuate the virtues of another man, and the situation in which this happens might be described as unfair.

(10) It is often objected to the view, which was Hume's, that infidelity is a more serious offence in women than it is in men, *on the grounds that*, since this offence involves a man and a woman in co-operating in the same act, it must be equally serious for both of them. This statement is presumably made on logical grounds, but there is no contradiction involved in denying it. The man and the woman perform numerically different acts, which have different descriptions. A bachelor, for example, performs the act of copulating with a married woman, and the married woman the act of copulating with a bachelor, and there is no logical reason why different assessments should not be made of these different acts. Similarly, there is no reason why severer moral condemnation should not be attached to the acts of buying than of selling stolen goods, or alcohol, or nicotine, or heroin. It is just conceivable, however, that it was because Hume supposed that the shame arising from the injustice of infidelity must be equal in men and in

---

[1] In 'Egoism as a Theory of Human Motivation', in *Ethics and the History of Philosophy*, Routledge and Kegan Paul, 1952.

women that he thought that a shame more than was demanded by its injustice had to be attached to infidelity in women, though not in men (571).

But though there is no logical reason why the blame annexed to the act of the man and the woman who illegitimately copulate with one another should not be different, this does not mean that it has to be different. In general, if two people co-operate in an illegal or wrong act, their blame varies with the following factors. The instigator or ring-leader is held to be more to blame. The more responsible of the two is held to be the more to blame. The one with the greater temptation to transgress is often held to be the less to blame. If, in addition to the immorality of the act, one of them is neglecting a duty arising from his situation or office, as when a guard steals the money that is in his custody, then he is the more to blame. Motive, too, is relevant. We regard someone selling opium as doing something worse than someone who merely buys it, partly because the former ruins in a calculated way the lives of many from desire for financial gain, whereas the latter simply risks his own health from weakness, curiosity, love of pleasure and excitement, and, in the later stages, because he has no alternative.

If we apply these generalizations—they are too prone to exception to be called principles—to the case of marital infidelity, it would be impossible to say whether the man or the woman was usually the instigator, the ringleader, or the more responsible. The man might usually be the less to blame, in that men are commonly supposed to be tempted more. The parallel with buying and selling opium, to the extent that there is one, might suggest that the woman is the less to blame, in that she is more likely to be harming herself than the man. On the other hand, it might be argued that one has a greater duty to preserve one's own family than to preserve the families of others, which would mean that the woman was the more to blame, for she is running the risk of intro-ducing unwanted children into her household, whereas the man is running the risk only of introducing them into the household of some-one else. One might also suggest that society has appointed women rather than men to the role of guardians of public morality, to which they are by nature more fitted than are men, and that, in consequence, the woman's act of infidelity, unlike that of the man who copulates with her, is aggravated by dereliction of this duty. But I suspect that the main reason why the act of a married woman is worse than that of a man who copulates with her (and why her 'immodesty' is more seriously wrong than his) is that there is an offence, which a married woman can commit, but which a man, without an amount of ingenuity only likely to be found in science fiction, cannot commit, namely, the offence of causing one's spouse to have doubts about the parentage of his children. This would be wrong, both on the grounds that it was unkind to him, and on the grounds that the woman who behaved like this would be risking the happiness of her children. Its motive would normally be concupiscence, but could be deliberate malice (as it is in Strindberg's play, *The Father*).

This gives a perfectly good explanation of Hume's problem, why infidelity and immodesty are worse in married women than in men, which explanation is not in the least irrational, as Hume supposed the more stringent demands imposed by society on women to some extent were. Hume almost hit on it, but that he did not quite hit on it is shown by the fact that, with his love of paradox (or, sometimes, simply of impishly putting things in an unnecessarily paradoxical way), he tends to suggest that the public interest demands that more severe penalties be attached to the *same* thing when performed by women than when performed by men. But it is not the same thing; it is a quite different thing, which for the biological reasons Hume mentions, a man cannot do. This explains why infidelity is more serious in married women than in men, without the need of having to attach penalties to possessing a bad reputation. Possessing a bad reputation is not an offence; behaving in such a way as to cause one's husband to doubt whether his children are really his is an offence. Hence, too, immodesty in women is not an offence because, or only because, she is heading for a situation where she may be tempted to be unfaithful to her husband. It is also an offence because she may be causing her husband to doubt whether he is the father of the children, which will probably give him pain, may cause the disruption of their married life, and harm their children in consequence. What a woman would have to do to be guilty of this offence would obviously vary very much from one age to another.

Unfortunately, however, this does not quite solve the problem. For though there is no offence that a man can commit of causing his wife to doubt the parentage of her children, there is an offence that he could commit of causing other men to doubt the parentage of their children, or of aiding and abetting a man's wife in causing her husband to doubt the parentage of her children. The man's offence, however, may be supposed to be less serious than the offence the woman commits. For each married person is allocated by society a special responsibility to look after his or her own family, and to the extent that the joint act is condemned because the doubts the woman's behaviour arouse in her husband's mind undermine the happiness of her family, she is not discharging this responsibility, while the man may be discharging his responsibility to his family. The man's act of aiding and abetting is generally considered a less serious offence than the woman's act he aids and abets. And perhaps it can be argued that applying moral pressure to women is a more effective way of stopping marital infidelity than applying it to men (in Hume's day, at any rate, men were more mobile than women), more or less as it is simpler to lock one's doors than it is to catch burglars. It should not be forgotten that the preceding remarks are intended to explain only why women's duties in respect of chastity and modesty are more stringent than men's, given that we have roughly the marriage rules we do at present. They might not be more stringent in a community having drastically different marriage rules from ours, for example, one in which women copulated with whichever man they pleased, and were exclusively assigned the task of bringing up any children who might result.

(11) On Hume's view, the rule enjoining fidelity is the corollary of another rule, which demands that one man associate with one woman for a long period of time in order that they may rear children. That these children have to be their joint children is explained by the fact that they will object to carrying this burden if they are not, and the fact that different and stricter rules are applied to women than to men is explained by the fact that it is much easier for men than it is for women to be deceived about which children are theirs. (Hume does not mention that it is also partly explained by the fact that women introduce children into their own homes, but men introduce them into other people's homes.) In other words, the rule restricting a woman's sexual liberty to one man, and, to a (considerably) less extent, restricting a man's sexual liberty to one woman, is entirely due to the fact that Hume considers it a necessary means to the bringing up of children. Is Hume right about this?

If Hume supposed that the only reason why a man objects to his wife's being unfaithful to him was that she thereby risked his having to bring up children who were not his own, he was mistaken. If he did suppose this, or speak as if he supposed it, it was presumably because he was over-emphasizing that reason for objecting to infidelity which explains why women's duty to be faithful is more stringent than men's. In Hume's defence one might argue that some of the other reasons why men object to their wives' infidelity presuppose the existence of the rule which demands it, and so cannot explain why there is such a rule. A man may partly object to his wife's being unfaithful to him, for example, for the same reason that he objects to her shoplifting; by doing so, she makes herself liable to social penalties, which incon- venience him, and she thereby perhaps shows herself to be, in the wide sense of the word, a dishonest person, who cannot be trusted to keep society's other rules as well as this one. This, however, only explains why, given that there is a rule proscribing infidelity, he should object to his wife's breaking it. If there were not such a rule, she would not incur the social penalties he objects to, and would not show herself to be dishonest by breaking it. If I am right, incidentally, in suggesting that one reason why a man objects to his wife's being unfaithful to him is that, if a child results, he will be carrying a burden which ought to be carried by someone else, this is a reason for objecting to infidelity which is *also* the product of the convention demanding it, for it is just a convention that a man is expected to bring up children of whom he is the biological father. Even the statement that men object to their *wives'* being unfaithful to them presupposes a rule, for one's wife is a woman in relation to whom conventional rules give one both certain privileges and certain duties; in the absence of such rules there could be no such thing as a wife.

Are there, then, any facts about men and women which would make it necessary or desirable to have rules or conventions limiting those with whom they may legitimately copulate, apart from the need of a stable union in order to rear children? These facts, it must be remembered, must exist independently of the conventions they are intended to explain; it is no use using facts such as that men object to other men copulating with the women over whom a rule ascribes them exclusive rights for, in the absence of such a rule, there would be no such women, and, consequently, no such objection.

Hume discusses the problem of sexual morality in his essay 'Of Polygamy and Divorces' (Ess.231). The problems he discusses there are all ones which arise, given that you have the institution of marriage, which he says 'has as its end the propagation of the species'. He mentions group marriage, in which he finds some advantages, and condemns polygamy, on the grounds that it destroys love and friendship between men and women, causes jealousy between one man and another, and makes it impossible for a man to educate his children. He opposes divorce, on the grounds that men and women will be happier in the bonds of marriage if they know there is no escape from them (life imprisonment could be preferred to a term in prison for the same reason); on the grounds that the children of divorced parents will have to be brought up by their stepmother, because it nurtures diversity of interest between a man and his wife; and because it dangerously increases the power of men. (Presumably Hume is thinking only of a man divorcing his wife, and had not contemplated the converse possibility.)

His only hint at there being a reason for marriage, apart from its being necessary for rearing children, is contained in the story from

The History of the Sevarambians,[2] 'where a great many men and a few women are supposed to be shipwrecked on a desert coast; the captain of the troop, in order to obviate those endless quarrels which arose, regulates their marriages after the following manner: He takes a handsome female to himself alone; assigns one to every couple of inferior officers, and to five of the lowest rank he gives one wife in common' (Ess.232).

The suggestion here is that marriage is necessary in order to prevent quarrels (in this case, if not in all, presumably, among men over women). But one does not know whether Hume thought that marriage would still be necessary in order to prevent quarrels (not only quarrels among men over women, but among women over men) in normal situations, where the numbers of men and women are more nearly equal. And it is an important question whether the quarrels which arose were due to the fact that the men took it for granted that the women would have to be allocated to one man each, so that there would not be enough women to go round, in which case the reasons which necessitated the distribution actually adopted would presuppose a convention—one man to one woman—similar to the one it was introduced to explain. More generally, it is no good trying to explain marriage rules by saying that they are to govern the distribution of, and prevent quarrelling over, a scarce resource, if the scarcity is itself produced by the marriage rules they are intended to justify. For if any man was allowed to copulate with any woman, then perhaps there would be no scarcity of either.

Whether there would be quarrels among men and women of such a kind and to such an extent as to make necessary rules allocating certain women, or groups of women, to certain men, or groups of men, and restricting their right to copulate with anyone else, should be settled by observation. This, however, is difficult, for everywhere there are marriage rules, and what limited communities there are without them exist against a background of such rules. (Experiments would be virtually impossible to organize.) Hence the best one can do is to apply one's knowledge of human nature to this imaginary situation.

Let us imagine a world where men and women have all the desires and emotions they have now, but are reproduced fully grown and independent from incubators; let us suppose that they are in most respects like ourselves, but with no marriage rules or any idea of the marriage rules possessed by other people. *Sexual desire* would cause no dissension. The inhabitants of such a world would, *ex hypothesi*, have sexual desires, but, since these could be satisfied by more than one

[2] By Denis Vaivasse d'Allais, Amsterdam, 1702.

woman or by more than one man, to a very large extent interchange-
ably, there should not be a shortage of sexual objects to produce strife.
Love might cause more quarrelling, for it is usually confined to one or a
few members of (usually) the opposite sex, which means that an
alternative object is more difficult to secure; it is perhaps less ephemeral
than lust, and may be naturally (i.e. independently of being moulded
by conventions) more prone to produce possessiveness. On the other
hand, since not all men love the same women, though the objects
which satisfy love are fewer, the competition is less keen.

I suspect that, in such a world, sexual rules akin to those we have in
this world regulating marriage might develop. For men and women are
inherently conservative, tend to become dependent upon one another,
and love security. Hence permanent or relatively permanent relationships
of various kinds between the sexes would grow up, and interfering with
them would tend to be disapproved of. This would be especially so if
economic circumstances were such that men and women were of
financial advantage to one another. To the extent that marriage rules
regulate the allocation of scarce resources they would be analogous to
rules governing the distribution of property, though they would not be
quite analogous to them unless men and women could buy and sell
their wives or husbands. First possession or occupation and prescription
would, I think, certainly have some force. Accession could not. Succession might or might not.

(12) That a man must know that his wife's children are his will
explain only why married women have a duty not to be unfaithful to
their husbands, and why men (whether married or not) have a (less
stringent) duty not to copulate with married women. It is fairly easy
to explain why married men have a duty to be faithful to their wives,
if their being unfaithful will harm them and their families, and why
even unmarried women, therefore, are under some obligation not to
help cause such harm by copulating with married men. But this has
no tendency to show that, or explain why, unmarried men and unmarried women have a duty not to copulate with people to whom
they are not married (which means, of course, not with anybody).
Hume gives a psychological explanation of why it is *supposed* that
unmarried women (and married women past the age when they can
bear children) have such a duty but no justification of their having
it. His explanation (572) is that we extend the principle to cases other
than those which gave rise to it. Though he does not mention the
imagination in this section, it is the kind of extension that he usually
puts down to the imagination. Unfortunately, he has himself undermined his own account (552-3). In explaining why we do not have a

duty of allegiance to the government in all circumstances, he states that where there is a large class of cases, all having something in common, in which it is not useful to apply a rule, we should make an exception of these cases, and not apply the rule to them. It seems from this, then, that if it is not useful to apply the rule restricting sexual liberty to unmarried men and women, their liberties should not be restricted and, as we have seen, Hume has given no reasons why it *is* useful to apply this rule to such people. In Hume's day, of course, there was such a reason, though he himself does not mention it; if an unmarried woman were to have a baby, this was likely to be embarrassing and inconvenient for herself and her family. (The embarrassment would be a consequence of the rule, and so not an explanation of it, but the inconvenience would not be.) Nowadays, when there is effective contraception, and a woman is more easily able to support herself and, if necessary, a child, the utilitarian reasons for a prohibition on the sexual liberty of un- married men and women are by no means obvious.

Though sexual liberty in unmarried people should not, on utilitarian grounds, be restricted *per se*, other moral rules, for which there are utilitarian reasons, will necessarily impose some restriction upon it. The rules prohibiting causing unnecessary pain, and those demanding promise-keeping, telling the truth, and loyalty to people with whom one has formed relationships, and who may have become dependent on one, still apply. It is my personal opinion that such rules will impose a very considerable restriction upon the liberty of unmarried people.

(13) A presupposition of the above argument is that the sexual act outside marriage is not necessarily wrong. (There are, of course, religious reasons for thinking that it is, but one may suspect these on the grounds that the usual reason for thinking that something is condemned by the deity are that one is inclined to think it wrong anyway.) It is a corollary of Hume's view of the nature of promises and contracts, which view seems to be substantially correct, that the sexual act outside marriage is *naturally* no different from what it is inside marriage. It cannot be that it is sacred inside marriage, but otherwise unclean, any more than a house can be beautiful when it is yours, but become ugly when it is sold to someone else. To suppose that it could be sacred only inside marriage would be, according to Hume, to suppose that the saying of certain words on a ceremonial occasion could have *magical* effects, like changing bread and wine into flesh and blood (524). The effects that the marriage ceremony does have are caused by the fact that there are certain rules demanding that people be treated differently, after they have said certain words in the appropriate circumstances, from before, and assigning to them rights and duties that they did not

have before. The only other effects the ceremony can have, for good or ill, on those who undergo it, apart from minor and temporary ones, such as being deafened by the organ, arise from their knowledge or belief that it has been performed, and their knowledge or belief about the alteration of their position in society that is consequent upon it. (One of Hardy's characters in *Far from the Madding Crowd* could get satisfaction from sleeping with his wife only if he pretended he had never married her.) These may be substantial, but that they are effects not of the ceremony, but of the belief that it has been performed, is shown by the fact that these effects would be the same whether the belief was true or false. It is, I suppose, just possible that, when Hume spoke of the 'peculiar degree of shame' attaching to the infidelity of women, and said that 'transgressions of conjugal duty are more infamous than any other kind of injustice, when 'tis evident they are more excusable' (572), he was thinking of an irrational tendency to regard the sexual act outside marriage as quite different in kind from the sexual act inside marriage. If so, he regarded it as an irrational belief which had socially desirable consequences.

(14) Contraception, of course, must not only affect the duties of unmarried men and women; it must affect the duties of married people as well. What it does is to enable a married woman to have intercourse with a man other than her husband with no risk, or only a very small one, of having children. Hence it makes it possible for her to commit adultery without committing the offence of causing her husband to doubt the parentage of his children, or, since it is impossible in most cases to avoid this risk completely, and the seriousness of her offence may be supposed to depend on the degree of uncertainty her conduct arouses in his mind, to reduce the gravity of this offence to a very considerable degree. Consequently it makes men and women morally more nearly equal in this respect. There never was any suggestion in Hume that men and women were unequal in any objectionable sense, for though equality demands that similar cases be treated similarly, infidelity by men and infidelity by women are not similar, partly for the reasons Hume has given. It is still the case, however, that a married woman who has a child is introducing it into her own home, while a man is introducing it into someone else's home. Also, since women are more independent than they were in Hume's time, a married woman might be able herself to support her own child by another man, which means that she is not trying to force or cheat her husband into providing financially for a child that is not his. Hence the effect of contraception and the increased earning power of women is to reduce the force of a woman's obligation to marital fidelity. For the same reason,

it also reduces the force of men's obligations, for if it is easier for a woman to commit adultery without making her husband insecure about the parentage of his children, it must also be easier for a man to commit adultery with her without aiding and abetting her in this offence. And if women are more independent than they were, this must not only cause their sexual liberty to approximate more closely to men's; it must also mean that the obligations of fidelity of men to them are reduced (though women are reluctant to admit it), for the less a woman is dependent on a man, the less stringent is his obligation to be faithful to her. A point may come, if it has not come already, when the duty of a married man and a married woman to be faithful arises only from the pain infidelity would cause to the other, and the ill effects or lack of it upon the children. But since these can be avoided—provided the partners are not possessive, which is unusual—if the infidelity is mutual, and performed by mutual consent, it is more nearly possible than it has been in the past to have a marriage where fidelity is not demanded of either party. The advantages of such arrangements lie in the greater variety and freedom they give to life. The disadvantages lie in the very severe demands they would make on the tolerance, forbearance, generosity, and sanity of the people involved.

(15) In Section III of *An Enquiry Concerning the Principles of Morals*, entitled 'Of Justice', Hume argues that public utility is the sole reason why justice is a virtue, and attempts to support his case by imagining various circumstances in which justice would not be of any use. He concludes that, in those circumstances it would not exist, because there would be no need for it. One of these circumstances would arise if people were so benevolent that they felt no more concern for their own interest than they did for the interests of others. Hume says, 'it seems evident, that the use of justice would, in this case, be suspended by such an extensive benevolence, nor would the divisions and barriers of property and obligation have ever been thought of. Why should I bind another, by a deed or promise, to do me any good office, when I know that he is already prompted, by the strongest inclination, to seek my happiness, and would, of himself, perform the desired service; except the hurt, he thereby receives, be greater than the benefit accruing to me? in which case, he knows, that, from my innate humanity and friendship, I should be the first to oppose myself to his imprudent generosity. Why raise land-marks between my neighbour's field and mine, when my heart has made no division between our interests; but shares all his joys and sorrows with the same force and vivacity as if originally my own? Every man, upon this supposition, being a second self to another, would trust all his interests to the discretion of every

man; without jealousy, without partition, without distinction. And the whole human race would form only one family; where all would lie in common, and be used freely, without regard to property . . .' (E185). It is a corollary of this, which Hume does not point out, though he must have been aware of it, that in conditions of universal benevolence, there would be no such thing as marriage. It, like the other conventional rules, some of which were what Hume called justice, would not exist because they would not be useful. For what need is there of a rule prohibiting all men other than myself from copulating with a certain woman, when I will not prevent them if doing so gives them pleasure, and they will not do it if they know that they thereby give me pain? And what need is there of rules to preserve the happiness of children, when no man will give a woman a child if this makes her other children unhappy, and the father of her other children— I cannot say 'husband', for in the world I am envisaging there would be no such thing—will love a child she has by another man as much as if it were his own? I do not suppose that, when Christ said that there was no marrying or giving in marriage in heaven, he meant that in heaven everyone would live in sin, but if he had meant it, there are the above reasons for thinking that it would be true.

EPILOGUE

JUSTICE IN THE *ENQUIRY*

IN *An Enquiry Concerning the Principles of Morals* Hume's remarks about justice are contained almost entirely in Section III, entitled 'Of Justice', and in the third appendix, entitled 'Some Farther Considerations with Regard to Justice'. Section IV, 'Of Political Society', contains a simplified and more palatable version of the views Hume expresses in Sections VII to IX, inclusive, of the *Treatise*. These I shall ignore. Since much of what Hume says in the *Enquiry* he has already written about in the *Treatise*, I shall discuss his arguments only when they are new. I shall summarize separately only Part I of Section III.

SECTION III

Of Justice

PART I

THAT justice owes all its merits to its usefulness is shown by the fact that it would not be useful (and perhaps not even thought of) in the following possible situations (E183): (1) it would not be useful if external goods were as unlimited in supply as air (E183–4); or (2) if men loved other men as much as they loved themselves (E184–6); or (3) if goods were too scarce to be usefully partitioned (E186–7); or (4) when a virtuous man falls into the hands of ruffians (E187); or (5) when a man has made himself obnoxious to the public by his crimes (E187); or (6) in war (E187–8); or (7) in regulating the treatment by men of inferior creatures such as women and American Indians (E190–1); or (8) to creatures not needing society (E191–2); justice would be useless where external goods are either very plentiful or very scarce, and where men are either extremely benevolent or extremely rapacious (as was illustrated by the poetic fiction of the golden age and the philosophical fiction of the state of nature), but is useful in our actual state, which is a mean between these extremes (E188–90); justice arises from its usefulness in the family, and is extended first to society, and then to groups of societies (E192).

COMMENTS

(1) Hume is obviously right in thinking that a society which had an unlimited supply of external goods would have no need of *property*. If, however, the people living in this society were sometimes malevolent, the society would need some rules of *justice* to protect each of its members from the others. The question whether they would need any rules governing sexual behaviour has been discussed in my comments on Section XII. They would need some rules to govern behaviour in polite society. Some rules would prohibit behaviour which causes offence (like eating peas with one's knife, or bubbling in one's soup); other rules ought to be obeyed because the mere fact that there was a rule prohibiting certain behaviour would tend to make it offensive to do the thing which was prohibited. If members of such a society ever had to

co-operate together to achieve an end, they would need rules apportioning different tasks to different people in order to prevent chaos. However, if there was an unlimited supply of goods, they would not need to co-operate to produce material commodities. It is a nice question whether they would need rules apportioning 'immaterial' goods. For example, if there were a limited supply of flute teachers, rules would have to be invented governing the apportioning of a teacher's time to his pupils. And perhaps there would have to be some copyright rules unless literature, science, and music count as 'goods', in which case they, too, would be in unlimited supply. I find it difficult to envisage what a society in which immaterial goods were in unlimited supply would be like. If everybody could produce, from his own internal resources, all the art, music, literature, and science he could possibly want, one reason for having society would disappear. Those writers who wanted readers would be disappointed. Such a society might need some rules in order to govern the production of plays or symphonies. Hume is perhaps a little inclined to take for granted that a good limited in supply must be a material object.

Hume says, 'It seems evident that, in such a happy state, every other social virtue would flourish, and receive tenfold increase' (E183). This does not seem evident to me. Nor does it seem evident to those philosophers of religion who regard the existence of evil as a necessary condition of the existence of moral virtue. Would industry flourish, for example, in a society in which everyone could have anything he wanted simply by stretching his hand for it (if it were of the right category to be obtained by stretching his hand)? Hume is being a little optimistic in supposing that, were the supply of external goods unlimited, 'Music, poetry, and contemplation form his [man's] sole business: conversation, mirth, and friendship his sole amusement' (E183). This would suppose not only an alteration in man's circumstances, but an alteration in his nature.

One might wonder how Hume knows that there would be no rules of justice in a society where goods were unlimited. The answer is that he thinks he knows this partly because there are no such rules governing the distribution of commodities which, like air, are in unlimited supply. But I suspect that another part of Hume's reason for thinking that there would be no rules of justice in such a society is that he already thinks that men have rules of justice because they are useful, and because he thinks that in such a society they would not be useful. Hence on the second point his argument begs the question. Nevertheless, with the qualifications I have mentioned, its conclusion is true.

(2) Hume supposes that there would be no need for rules of justice

in a society in which goods were in such limited supply that no good could come of having such rules. It is difficult to agree with him. Even if men were so necessitous as inevitably to perish from starvation and thirst, rules of justice would be necessary in order to ensure that, at the very least, they perished in an orderly way. If there were enough goods to ensure that some people, but not everybody, could survive, they would be necessary to determine which would be the survivors. For example, lots could be cast, or it might be agreed that women and children should be first. Hence even in a starving city such rules would be useful. Hume is probably confusing the true assertion that, in such a city, it would be absurd for men to have any regard for the existing rules of society, with the assertion that it would not be useful to have any rules at all. It might be considered proper to take the superfluous property of some men, but distribute it in an orderly way, for example, as Hume suggests, by 'an equal partition'. But again, the fact that Hume is wrong in supposing that rules of justice would not be necessary in a society in which men were very necessitous would not show that his theory of justice was wrong. This would be shown only by such rules being still obligatory, though *not* necessary.

(3) Hume is wrong in thinking that there would be no need for rules of justice in a society in which 'every man has the utmost tenderness for every man' (E185). There would obviously be no need for rules to prevent violence. But there would have to be rules to prevent disorganization. Different tasks would have to be allocated to different men, or chaos would result. One way of preventing such disorder over producing a limited supply of goods would be to allocate different fields to different men as their property. Hence they would know which fields to work at. There would still have to be means of exchanging commodities, if any use were to be made of the advantages of dividing labour. Hence there would have to be rules about promising. A government would not be necessary to keep the peace, but it would be necessary to organize large-scale productive enterprises. Men would have no temptation to disobey such rules from malevolence or self-interest, but some men might disobey them because they thought the rules mistaken, and did not bring about, as they were meant to, the public interest. Hence there would be some small need to enforce them. It follows that Hume is mistaken when he remarks that, if benevolence were strong enough to be a motive to obey rules of justice, such rules would be unnecessary (495-6).

The fact that Hume is wrong in supposing that there would be no need for rules of justice in a society where there was an abundance of benevolence is no objection to his variety of utilitarianism. It would be an objection only if, in such a society, rules of justice were obligatory but not useful. They would, however, be useful.

(4) Hume thinks that a virtuous man, fallen into the hands of ruffians, would have no obligation to observe rules of justice, and may 'arm himself, to whomever the sword he seizes, or the buckler, may belong' (E187). It is not clear whether Hume is saying that the virtuous man would be under no obligation to obey the ruffians' rules, or the rules of society at large. (Presumably by society's rules, the buckler might belong to Frog, but by their rules to McHeath.) It looks obvious, however, that he would be under no obligation not to take the sword and buckler, even if they belonged, by society's rules, to the former, and by their rules to the latter, and by neither rules to him. Hume thinks that the reason why I am not under this obligation is that, since the society of ruffians is on the edge of dissolution, its rules of justice are doing it no good. It must, *ex hypothesi*, have some rules, or the virtuous man would not be able to break them, and the rules it does have, presumably, are at least delaying its demise. One feels, however, that Hume has given the wrong reason for thinking that the virtuous man would be under no obligation to obey the rules of the society in which he found himself. Even if the society of ruffians had rules which were adequately enforced governing the behaviour of its members, and was in consequence internally flourishing, the virtuous man would not normally be considered to be under any obligation to obey them. I think that the reason for this is that it is not useful to society at large that there be any rules demanding that the 'property' of bands of thieves be respected. It is no objection to Hume's view that rules of justice depend upon their utility for their obligatoriness that this is so, for the reason why the virtuous man is under no obligation to be just to the ruffians is that it is not useful for society to have rules enjoining this. Hume is just wrong in thinking that the reason is that the rules are not useful to the ruffians.

Hume's case is only one of a number of similar cases that he might have considered. A man might voluntarily visit another country, or be involuntarily shipwrecked on the shore of another country, or be captured and taken as a prisoner of war to another country. Similar fates might befall him, but the society be not a 'country', but a rebel group which has some international recognition, or a harmless society of eccentrics living on a remote island, or a group of settlers whose intention it was to sever their bonds with their former home. In which cases would he be obliged, and which not, to obey the rules of the society in which he found himself? If he was obliged to obey some of their rules, but not others, what distinguishes the rules that he is obliged to obey from those he is not? One feels that a man shipwrecked in another country might not be obliged not to steal food, that a prisoner of war would not be obliged not to escape, and perhaps not be obliged not to steal in order to make a safe return to his own nation. One feels that a visitor to another country is obliged to obey most of its rules but not all of them. For example, he might be obliged to show his appreciation of a good meal by belching—unless he could explain that his compatriots showed their appreciation differently—but not necessarily to participate in cruel customs, even though this was by their rules demanded of him.

It is difficult to elicit any general principle distinguishing the cases. Whatever principle it is, it is not the one Hume presupposes, viz. that I ought to obey those rules of justice that are useful to the society in which I find myself, for this would mean that a prisoner of war had an obligation not to escape. Nor can it be that I ought to obey those rules that would be useful to the society from which I originate, for the rules of the society in which I find myself can seldom affect their usefulness one way or another. Even if they did, it would be quite extraordinary to maintain that, when in Rome, I ought to behave in accordance with rules that are such that, if all Romans obeyed them, this would be of advantage to Englishman. Were we to decide to act on all and only those rules of the society in which we found ourselves, which were of benefit to that society, this would be something of an impertinence. It might be regarded as optional whether I obeyed the rules adopted by the aforementioned society of eccentrics, but if they had a rule prohibiting them from succouring strangers shipwrecked on their shores, it would not be considered obligatory for me not to steal from them, though it would be obligatory for me not to kill them; and so on. One might want to suggest that I should act on those, and only those, rules of the society in which I found myself which were of advantage to the human race. But most rules of a society do not affect the human race, except in so far as they affect the society which has them. When they do, since it seems implausible to suggest that Englishmen would be under no obligation to obey a rule of English society, if the rule in question harmed the human race, so *a fortiori* it would be even more absurd to apply this rule to Frenchmen living in England.

The problem may be partly solved by the existence of a kind of second-order rule, dictating how people are to treat rules of societies other than their own. To some extent, these are codified in international law, but obviously such rules are fairly rudimentary, and do not cover all possible cases. And the problem is made somewhat easier when it is not forgotten that the question whether I ought or ought not to obey a given rule is not settled simply by considering whether or not it is a useful rule. It may be harmful to disobey harmful rules, and so sometimes, for this reason, it may be right for me to obey even a harmful rule of that society in which I find myself. The best I can suggest is that I would have a duty to obey such a rule if and only if the consequences of everybody's deciding to obey it in similar circumstances would be better than the consequences of everybody's deciding to disobey it. If I find myself alone in such circumstances, this means that I ought to obey the rule if and only if my obeying it would have better consequences than my disobeying it.

(5) Hume treats punishing a criminal as a case where the laws of justice are suspended, because in this case they are no longer useful (E187). This is a mistake. Someone punishing a criminal is applying the laws of justice, which are not suspended in his case, since they themselves demand that he be punished. On the other hand, of course, Hume is quite right in thinking that it is because of the disutility of not punishing criminals that they are punished. It would, indeed, be entirely pointless having rules of justice if they were not enforced.

(6) The suspension of rules of justice in time of war is a more interesting case than that of punishment. Rules of justice are then suspended in that, for example, there is a rule of justice in all societies prohibiting their members from taking one another's lives, but this rule does not apply to the lives of enemy soldiers. There may, however, be other rules of justice which do apply in time of war, for example, rules preventing the use of poisoned gas, or regulating the treatment of prisoners. Hume thinks that the reason why the rules of peace are suspended and the rules of war grow up is because the former, in time of war, cease to be useful, whereas they are useful in peace time, and the latter become useful, although they are not necessary in peace time (E187-8).

An interesting analogue of the rules of war is the rules of games. Most games (though not all, as Wittgenstein pointed out) involve one person trying to achieve something that his opponent is trying to prevent, for example, to score most goals or win most tricks. The rules of such games are devised in order that the players should get the most enjoyment from the game. For this some rules are necessary to lay down what is to count as winning, for example, mating one's opponent. Rules must lay down what is the starting position, for example, that a member of the team who wins the toss is allowed to kick a ball to another member of the same side from a legally prescribed place in the middle of the field. It will also be necessary to have rules dictating what things players are and are not allowed to do, partly because it will spoil the game if there are no such rules—footballers must not be allowed to kick their opponents, for example—and partly because, as in the case of chess, there could be no game without rules dictating what counts as a permissible move.

The rules of games involving two or more opponents are determined by two overriding considerations. First of all, since there must be competition if there is to be any enjoyment, players are allowed to put their interests before those of their opponents, and hence any moral rule in society there may be which prohibits men from getting the better of other men is, for the purposes of the game, suspended. Since, however, the pleasure men get from playing games and beating their opponents could easily be more than counterbalanced by the harm that would be done to them if opponents were allowed to adopt any means of beating their opponents they choose, there must be rules prohibiting them from doing things which are such that, if they were allowed, their possibility would detract from the pleasure of playing and winning. Hence it is fairly easy to give a utilitarian justification of the rules of games.

The rules of games, however, are not as entirely different from the rules of life as what I have just said might suggest. For in life a certain amount of competition is quite properly allowed. Men are permitted to compete for money and jobs, though the means they may adopt in so competing are fairly closely circumscribed. It is generally considered to be beneficial to allow a certain amount of competition, but it would obviously be harmful to allow men to pursue any means to those ends that they are allowed to compete for. It is certainly not the case that the rules of most societies demand that men should put the interests of others before their own interests in such matters, or even that they should not put their own interests before those of others. Most people consider that it would be harmful if they did, and, quite apart from the harmfulness of the consequences of not allowing such competition, man is a competitive animal, and a life in which competition was not allowed would not be much fun.

Hume treats the rules of war as analogous to the rules of games. War demands that some rules be set aside because in war they are no longer useful, and also demands that there be special rules, which would not be useful in time of peace. There is an apparent disanalogy between fighting wars and playing games, however. Games add to the enjoyment of human beings, but wars are generally considered to be harmful. If they are harmful, how can it be useful to set aside the normal moral rules which, if they were not suspended, would make war impossible, and how can the special rules of war be regarded as useful? The special rules of war could be regarded as useful in that they mitigate the harm that wars do, but, nevertheless, because of the harm wars do, abrogating the normal rules of society in time of war cannot possibly be beneficial.

Hume has himself supplied at least part of the answer to this question. Men do not look so far as the interest of mankind as a whole in deciding upon the utility of the rules they have. Germans sympathize more with the pleasures and pain of Germans than they do with those of Frenchmen, and Frenchmen do the opposite. Hence the rules which normally operate in society are set aside in wartime not for the advantage of mankind as a whole, but because the warring parties suppose, rightly or wrongly, that it is to their own advantage. Obviously at least one of them, and quite likely both, must be mistaken. Hence Hume could, though so far as I know he does not, regard the setting aside of normal rules in wartime as a case of our approving something out of bias and because of a false belief. We approve of war out of bias because we give more weight to the interests of our compatriots than to those of other people, and out of false belief because we have a false belief in the advantages of war, even to our own compatriots. It is likely that the false belief is itself the result of bias; we have it because we irrationally tend to overestimate the chances our own country has of winning, and because we irrationally tend to exaggerate the harm which will be done to it by compromise or surrender. We do the latter from an equally irrational tendency to exaggerate the extent to which it will be worse to be governed by citizens of some other country than to be governed by the citizens of our own country. It is likely that it will be worse, but not as much worse as we suppose. We overestimate the ills we do not know, as compared with the ills we do. There is perhaps another irrational tendency involved in our approval of the setting aside of normal rules in time of war, which Hume does not mention. Each man will tend to regard the welfare of his own country, and consequently its survival as a unit, as something over and above the welfare of its members. Hence men will irrationally suppose that some advantage has been gained, even if all their compatriots are worse off as a result of war, if their country still survives as a country, even though they all might individually have been happier and better off had it not done so. There is no such thing, however, as the happiness of a nation over and above that of its nationals. Nor is it the case that the happiness of one nation, other things being equal, is of any more importance than the happiness of another.

There is, I suppose, some measure of limited agreement in the setting aside of some rules in time of war, and the growth of others. Each of the participants is prepared to pay a certain price for the chance of gaining its objective, but not more than a certain price. It cannot gain its objective at all without war, and war, logically, cannot be undertaken without setting aside some of the rules which normally operate. But both parties can, with the agreement, tacit or otherwise, of their enemy, achieve their objects at a smaller cost, provided that both parties keep certain rules which make war rather less unpleasant than it would otherwise be. It is perhaps for this reason that we are under no obligation to obey the rules of war if the people with whom we are fighting do not observe them. Hume seems to forget that it is an important part of his view here that, though we are under no obligations of justice towards people when we and they do not share any rules governing the activity in which we are jointly engaged, we are still under obligations of humanity towards such people. This is because humanity, unlike justice, is not an artificial virtue.

If, as one ought, one takes the evils of war very seriously, one may, however, be inclined to exaggerate the difference between the rules of war and the rules of games. Many people fight because they enjoy fighting. Hence they must, in order to fight at all, set aside some of the rules which normally regulate civilized society. If, however, they can reduce the risks involved in this reprehensible activity by accepting other rules governing it, without spoiling the enjoyment, then naturally they will adopt them. War, of course, is a selfish form of enjoyment, for, unlike most games, its inconveniences are shared by people other than the participants.

(7) Hume says, 'Were there a species of creatures intermingled with men, which, though rational, were possessed of such inferior strength, both of body and mind, that they were incapable of all resistance, and could never, upon the highest provocation, make us feel the effects of their resentment; the necessary consequence, I think, is that we should be bound by the laws of humanity to give gentle usage to these creatures, but should not, properly speaking, lie under any restraint of justice with regard to them, nor could they possess any right or property, exclusive of such arbitrary lords' (E190). This is meant to be another example, Hume's seventh, of a situation in which justice, because it would not be useful, would not exist. If it did exist it would not be obligatory.

One's first reaction to what Hume says, of course, is to ask, 'To whom would justice not be useful in the circumstances Hume envisages?' It would be of no use to men, but it looks as if it would have been extremely advantageous to the lower creatures intermingled with them, women, perhaps, or American Indians. This point can partly be met by Hume's explicit and repeated statement that one would still be under an obligation to treat such creatures humanely. But what exactly would be the difference? Suppose, for example, that they were allowed some 'property', if one could call it that, as Indians now are in reservations, and that this property was respected, as it well might be, what does it amount to to say that the fact that their property is respected is a matter of humanity rather than of justice, and that they do not have a right to this property? Again, if they were intelligent enough to understand the operation of promising, men might keep promises made to them, though these creatures could not compel men to keep them. What turns such behaviour on the part of mankind from being just to being merely humane?

Hume does not make it clear what his answer to this question is. Perhaps the idea at the back of his mind is this. If a rule of justice is to govern the behaviour of a group of people—or, in this case, a group consisting of some people and some beings of a different kind—there must be penalties for its infringement. A rule which carries no such penalties does not, properly speaking, deserve the epithet 'rule' at all. The inferior creatures would not have the power to enforce any rules that were made in their interest upon those men who broke them. This, however, by itself is not a reason for thinking that there could be no rules compelling men to respect their interests. Men could make such rules, and compel other men to enforce them, as at the moment is done with rules prohibiting cruelty to animals. But the creatures inter-mingled with men would be in no position to do any such thing.

Perhaps, then, Hume refuses to regard such rules as rules of justice because there could be no enforceable agreement between men and these creatures to the effect that these rules should be kept. For there to be such an agreement, it would have to be the case that each party to it would be in a position to offer something to the other in exchange. Each party would have to be in a position to forgo the advantages he would gain from not having any rules—the advantage of not being prevented by these rules from sacrificing the interests of others to his own when it suited him—in order to gain the protection these rules afford against being treated in a similar manner by other people. The inferior creatures, however, would have nothing to offer in exchange for their interests being respected by men, for they would not have the power to cause men any inconvenience, whether there were such rules or not. This account could easily be modified to cover Hume's (correct) contention that the obligation to obey such rules is not a special case of our obligation to keep agreements. There could not even be any mutual understanding, of the kind which takes place when two people co-operate to row a boat, between men and these inferior creatures, to forgo certain advantages in order to obtain others, for men would have no advantage to obtain, and the creatures no advantages to forgo.

Perhaps it is for this reason that Hume refuses to regard any rules there may be regulating intercourse between men and these inferior creatures as rules of justice, for rules there could certainly be. But this is not the only problem to which Hume's interesting idea gives rise. Man (collectively) would have no 'natural' obligation to obey rules of justice with respect to the inferior creatures, for he would have nothing to lose by disobeying them. Would he be under a *moral* obligation to obey them? He would, on Hume's most usual view, be under such an obligation if disobedience aroused disapproval in most men, provided it was not aroused because of ignorance, mistake, or one or another kind of bias. But if this sentiment of approval is aroused only by sympathy with the pleasures and pains of other men, then, *ex hypothesi*, they could feel no sentiments of disapproval when rules were broken which demanded that men respect the interests of these inferior creatures. (Hume could account for any moral disapproval that might be aroused by breaking such rules made in the interests of women and American Indians, but not in the case of animals.)

Hume, however, is just wrong in his contention that we feel sympathy with the pleasure and pain only of other men, though it is probable that he overlooked abovementioned facts. Ought, on Hume's view, the sympathetic pleasure and pain we feel for creatures inferior to men be counted as moral sentiments? Ought the fact that we do not feel sympathetic pain as strongly when non-human animals are hurt as we do when human animals are hurt to be regarded simply as a case of bias? If so, it would be of the same order as the fact that we do not feel sympathetic pain when people not close to us, to whom we are not related, are hurt as strongly as we do when the people hurt are close to us, and are people to whom we are related.

The corollary of this would be that animals were to count for one, i.e. that animal pleasures and pains ought to determine what it is right or wrong for human beings to do, as much as human pleasures and pains do. It would be absurd, however, to suppose that I ought to lose my leg in order to preserve two legs for a flea, supposing that the flea's legs are as useful to it as my legs are to me. It is normally considered not wrong that a flea should pay with his life for causing me some minor annoyance. On the other hand, few people suppose that animal pleasures and pains should count for nothing. This would mean that it would not be wrong for small boys to torture flies, provided it did the boys no harm, or that it was right for humans to eat the brains of live monkeys, or to boil lobsters alive to provide themselves with a delicacy.

But between these two unacceptable extremes it seems impossible to draw a line. Kant would seem to be wrong in suggesting that it is wrong to treat only other rational beings merely as means. It would not normally be considered wrong to treat a 'rational' but non-sentient computer entirely as a means, but it would be considered wrong to treat non-rational but sentient animals entirely as means.

Hume's problem in reverse would be posed if a higher race from another planet were to come to live on earth. Martians, let us suppose, are so much more powerful and more intelligent than men that they can accomplish any end they have without fear of men's thwarting them. Hence they have nothing to gain by regulating their commerce with men by any set of rules, for men, by circumscribing their behaviour by these rules, can prevent themselves from causing Martians no inconvenience which the Martians could not have prevented in any case. Hence, according to Hume, one would have to regard any disposition on the Martians' part to treat men kindly as a manifestation of 'humanity', if one could call it that, rather than of justice. 'Humanity' would only be a virtue in Martians, according to Hume, if it was usual (and in accordance with Martian internal economy and proportion) for Martians to feel 'humanity'; if it was not, then behaving 'inhumanely' would not be a sign of the lack of a motive that it was usual to feel, and so would not be a manifestation of a natural virtue. What was a natural virtue in one species would not necessarily be so in another.

What ought one to say about the duties of human beings to Martians, if, indeed, there are any? If we have a duty, as some utilitarians think we do, to promote the maximum happiness of all sentient creatures, then Martians would have to count for one, just like any other being. But we have seen that it would be absurd to suppose that animals counted for one, so why should Martians? If the reason why animals do not count for as much as one is that they are inferior mentally to men, then perhaps Martians should count for more than one, since we are supposing them to be mentally superior to men. If Hume were right in thinking that virtues were qualities useful or agreeable to ourselves or others, i.e. to me or other men, dispositions that were of benefit to Martians would not be virtues. But the same would have to be true of dispositions that were of benefit to animals. If Hume were right in saying, as he sometimes did, that duties were actions performed in conformity to a man-made rule, then we would have duties to Martians if there were man-made rules dictating that men should treat Martians in certain ways. But why should men want to make such rules? And why should a duty be an action dictated by a man-made rule, and not one that is dictated by a Martian-made rule? Perhaps one ought to say that one's duty is an action dictated by a rule governing the behaviour of one's own kind. In that case, there would be duties to men as such only to the extent that there were rules which applied to all men, and not just to Englishmen or Americans or Russians. And to that extent, perhaps, men would have duties to men, and Martians would have duties to Martians, but neither would have duties to one another, except in the event of there growing up a set of rules governing the behaviour of either to the other. If Hume is right, it is very unlikely that there ever would be such rules, for humans would have nothing to offer Martians in exchange for their consenting to obey such rules.

One feels that, in actual fact, the moral sentiments of men would be dictated partly by necessity and partly by sympathy (a very Humean view). Men would accept that they had duties to Martians if they needed to accept that they had. And they would from sympathy feel that they had duties to Martians, if Martians resembled them physically and in their ways of thought, feeling, and behaviour sufficiently to evoke sympathy, just as men feel under some obligation to respect the feelings of animals whom they resemble, but feel very little regard to the welfare of animals they do not. But this would be an entirely capricous way of settling the question. The fact that it seems quite impossible to draw any reasonable line between the two extremes of allowing Martians and animals to count for one, and allowing them to count for naught, sometimes makes me despair of ever finding a rational basis for ethics. But perhaps I ought not to mind so much, for many philosophers do not think there is one.

It must not be forgotten that there are some human beings (Hume mentions women, but perhaps he had his tongue in his cheek) who, because of their inferior strength or intelligence, would, according to Hume, be incapable of being treated unjustly, though they could be treated inhumanely. The very old and the very young may fall into this category, as perhaps do the physically and mentally sick. One interesting class of cases is foetuses, or unborn infants, if they are old enough to be so called. I think it is another interesting corollary of Hume's view that it is impossible to treat foetuses unjustly, though it is possible to treat them inhumanely. Taken broadly, I have considerable sympathy with this view. For example, much of the controversy over whether abortion is or is not morally permissible seems to turn on the question whether killing the foetus is a case of murder. Various other analogies are drawn, too, for example, one which likens killing a foetus to throwing another man from an overweighted balloon, when he is there only because one invited him in the first place.

Most of these attempts to extend moral rules which govern the behaviour of men to the treatment of foetuses seem to me to be mis-conceived. The main reason why men have a rule prohibiting them from taking the lives of other men is that, were there not such a rule, civilized society, or any society at all, would be impossible. So men forgo the satisfaction of killing other men in order to gain the security of not being killed themselves. Suicide cannot be shown to be morally wrong by appealing to such a rule, for, from the nature of the case, it must always be done with the consent of the person killed; and the same argument applies to aiding and abetting suicide, and voluntary euthanasia. Killing children, or the aged, is not wrong for the reason that it invites retaliation from other children, or other old people, but because it invites retaliation from the parents of the children, or the relatives of the aged. And, of course, killing foetuses cannot be wrong because of the social chaos which would result if other foetuses were to do the same. Hence whether or not it is right to do it can be left to be deter-mined by factors such as the health of the mother and her family, and the needs of society. Incidentally, I suspect that painless killing does not evidence lack of humanity.

There are differences between the moral question whether or not it is right to kill a foetus, and the question whether or not it is illegal to do this. All discussions of medical ethics seem to overlook such dif-ferences. If there is a law proscribing killing people, then it is certainly relevant to consider whether foetuses are people, and at what age they become people. If there is no clear-cut rule of English language laying down that foetuses either are or are not people, such a rule may have to be prescribed. If a judge decides that foetuses should be called people, then he is *ipso facto* making more precise a law which, because of the vagueness of the word 'people', was imprecise. It is difficult to see, however, how the question whether or not it is morally wrong to kill a foetus can be settled by a decision, whether arbitrary or not, to use a *word* in one way rather than another. Hence the question whether it is wrong to kill this particular foetus, in these particular circumstances, cannot be settled by deciding whether foetuses are to be called people. If we decide not to call foetuses people, it can still be wrong to kill this foetus, for actions which cannot be defined as killing people can still be wrong. If we decide that foetuses are to be called people, all that will follow is that, if it is right to kill this foetus, then it is not always wrong to kill people. How we decide to use the word 'people' is entirely irrelevant. To suppose otherwise is to suppose that we can make up our minds upon the validity of a rule, such as that killing people is wrong, without first considering the cases to which it applies. Worse than this, because what is meant by 'people' has not been made clear, it is to suppose that we can make up our minds on whether killing people is wrong without even knowing exactly what anyone who maintains that killing people is wrong is asserting. Of course, if the question is not one of how to use a word, but a question of fact about what characteristics foetuses have, its answer is relevant. It could be, for example, though it is not, that we perfectly well know how to use the word 'people'. What we are in doubt about is the question of fact whether foetuses have those characteristics which qualify them to be called people. But it seems unlikely that any new facts about foetuses will be discovered that will throw a great deal of light on the question. Hence all that is left to be decided is how to use the word 'person', and this can have no bearing upon the question whether or not it is right to kill foetuses.

It can have as little bearing as the question whether a recently discovered, black swan-like bird is to be called a swan can have on the question whether or not all swans are white. If we decide to call it a swan, we must also decide that not all swans are white. If, on the other hand, we decide not to call it a swan, then we are at liberty to go on saying that all swans are white. But, whichever way we decide, no fact about nature is altered by our decision. The bird is just as black as ever it was before, whether we call it a swan or not. The appearance that there is something at issue between the man who, because he has decided not to call these birds swans, goes on saying that all swans are white, and the man who, because he has decided that these birds are to be called swans, says that not all swans are white, is illusory. They have each only decided to use the word 'swan' in a different way. Similarly, it cannot be decided whether or not this white substance resembling chalk dissolves in sulphuric acid by deciding whether or not chalk by definition dissolves in sulphuric acid, and whether or not to call it chalk. If chalk, by definition, does dissolve in sulphuric acid, it does not follow that this substance dissolves in sulphuric acid. All that follows is that if this substance does not dissolve in sulphuric acid, then it is not chalk.

If 'murder' is defined in such a way that murder is necessarily wrong, we cannot properly argue that killing foetuses is murder, and so wrong. The way in which we should argue is that if killing foetuses is not wrong, killing foetuses is not murder. To suppose otherwise is to suppose that a terminological decision upon the question how to use the word 'murder' could have some bearing on what, in a particular situation in which he found himself placed, it would be right for an individual doctor to do. The fact that legal questions can be decided by deciding how to use a word, but moral questions cannot be so decided, is doubtless because the law is a matter of fiat, whereas morals are not.

Hume, I suspect, would have regarded the analogue of the balloon-ist, and many other analogues appealed to in discussions of abortion, as just another of those situations in which the rules of justice were no longer useful—as they would not be, if applying them caused both balloonists to die—and so were no longer obligatory. It is an important fact about men that they tend to believe, perhaps through habit and indoctrination, that useful rules are obligatory in their own right (E203). Hence, because they obey them without any perception of the reasons for doing so in the first place, they go on obeying them, or, at any rate, feeling that they ought to obey them, even when they cease to be useful. The Russian soldiers who stayed at their posts long after the departure of the tsars whom they defended would fall into that category.

Using rules, which govern the relations of one adult human being to another, to decide questions about how a foetus should be treated is, Hume might say, to be guided by resemblances and analogies. The case of killing a foetus is like, but not quite like, the case of killing an adult human being. It is the imagination which determines us to be attracted by some resemblances but not by others, and the question concerning whether foetuses resemble people sufficiently to be brought under some rules governing the behaviour of people is one which, apart from utility, admits of no rational solution. Indeed, it is a matter of fiat rather than of discovery. The question whether it is morally wrong to kill foetuses cannot be settled by the type of reasoning that Hume has in mind, though it may well have a large part in determining any questions about its legality.

(8) Hume's eighth and last case in which rules of justice would not be useful, and so would neither exist nor be obligatory, would obtain if human beings were so made as not to need one another's help, and to be incapable of being harmed by one another. It seems obvious that Hume is right in thinking that such creatures would not need, and would not have, any rules of justice. He has perhaps contradicted his own hypothesis when he suggests that such creatures might 'challenge the preference above every other being' (E191-2). If they could do this they could harm one another, at least to the extent that one could take what another needed, and, if this were so, they might well need rules of justice to distribute the goods for which Hume supposes they are competing. It is perhaps worth mentioning that they would not strictly speaking constitute an exception to ordinary utilitarianism, though I am not suggesting that Hume was an ordinary utilitarian. For the principle that we ought to maximize happiness or good, when more explicitly stated, says that we ought to maximize happiness or good, to

the extent that it is in our power, and it is not within the power of 'humans' like these to affect the happiness of others. Though I have argued that the creatures that Hume imagines would need rules of justice, this is no objection to Hume's fundamental point, which would only be controverted if these creatures had them, but did not need them.

(9) Hume repeats the view, which he has already expressed in the *Treatise* (486), that rules of justice arise from experience of their advantageousness in family life, which is itself the inevitable result of the conjunction of the sexes. These rules are extended from families to societies consisting of groups of families, and then to larger societies of which the smaller societies are members. 'History, experience, reason sufficiently instruct us in this natural progress of human sentiments, and in the gradual enlargement of our regards to justice, in proportion as we become acquainted with the extensive utility of that virtue' (E192). It is a consequence of what Hume says that it would be useful to have rules of justice before men appreciate that it would be useful, and that the existence of such rules lags behind man's realization of their utility. Sometimes it lags a lot behind, which partly explains why men behave as stupidly as they do.

(10) It would do Hume a great wrong to forget that, though he thinks that justice would be suspended in the eight situations he envisages in which it would be useless, he does not think that we would have no obligation to be humane in these situations. For example, talking of the effect of extreme want in causing rules for the allocation of property to cease to be useful, he says, 'and every man may now provide for himself by all the means which prudence can dictate, *or humanity permit* [my italics] ' (E186).

This militates against any interpretation of Hume which says, despite what he himself in some places (e.g. E186-7) remarks, that all words like 'right', 'duty', 'obligation', 'a right to', and so on, are tied in their meaning to the existence of man-made conventions. For the word 'permit' is a word like 'duty', and, Hume unequivocally says, some things (inhumanity, for example) would *not* be permitted even were there no conventional rules of justice to prohibit them.

PART II

Whereas Part I of Section III of the *Enquiry Concerning the Principles of Morals* attempted to show that the mere existence of rules of justice was dependent upon their being useful, Part II attempts to show that the fact that we have certain rules as opposed to others is also due to their utility. This part adds little to what Hume has said about justice in the *Treatise*. Consequently I shall not comment individually on each point as it arises.

Hume expresses the opinion that it would be harmful to have rules which allocated the largest possessions to the most extensive virtue. 'Fanatics may suppose, *that dominion is founded on grace* and *that saints alone inherit the earth*; but the civil magistrate very justly puts these sublime theorists on the same footing with common robbers, and teaches them by the severest discipline, that a rule, which, in speculation, may seem the most advantageous to society, may yet be found, in practice, totally pernicious and destructive' (E193). The view that possessions should be distributed equally is also impracticable. For though 'wherever we depart from this equality, we rob the poor of more satisfaction than we add to the rich, and . . . slight gratification of a frivolous vanity, in one individuals, frequently costs more than bread to many families, and even provinces' (E194), 'men's different degrees of art, care, and industry will immediately break that equality' (E194). '. . . if you check these virtues, you reduce society to the most extreme indigence' (E194). 'The most rigorous inquisition too is requisite to watch every inequality on its first appearance; and the most severe jurisdiction, to punish and redress it' (E194). This, Hume thinks, would cause society to degenerate into tyranny, were it not that, in a situation in which there was equality, there would be no one in a strong enough position to exercise the power that would be necessary to preserve such tyranny.

Hume is perhaps failing to distinguish sufficiently carefully between inequality of wealth and inequality of power, which may not go hand in hand. There might be sufficient inequality of power, in a society in which there was little inequality of income or wealth, to *compel* people to produce, though they themselves did not benefit from producing. Love of power, as opposed to love of wealth, could well be a sufficiently strong incentive to make the governors in such a community govern. Events have shown that Hume was right in thinking that producing greater equality of wealth has produced a more 'rigorous inquisition', and, if it is not as bad as he feared, this may be because it has not yet anywhere produced anything like complete equality. One gains greater equality at the cost of greater government interference, and smaller incentives to produce. Though some greater equality than there would otherwise be may be worth the cost, the cost of complete equality, as Hume himself implies, would probably be too high.

Hume next argues that some (though not much) experience of the world is necessary to determine what is useful and beneficial. (He thinks that no one with such experience would recommend a rule distributing possessions equally.) He lists a number of rules about property, already discussed in the *Treatise*, which he thinks are derived from their utility. He argues that all writers on the laws of nature, whatever principles they *start* from, always *end* by defending their principles by arguing that they are useful. (There is much truth in this remark.) He thinks that there is nothing, apart from the interests of society, which makes one thing mine and another thing someone else's.

Hume thinks that sometimes, when there are several rules of justice which would all be equally useful, we take account of *analogies* in deciding on what rules to have. He thinks that our having a rule allocating property to its possessor or its first possessor are cases in point. In allocating property to its first possessor, we are impressed by the resemblance (analogy) between first possession and something else which *already* determines us to make something someone's property. (In the *Treatise* he thought that the imagination is disposed to add to the already-existing relation of first possession the relation of property. This it could do even were there no analogies, and no other rules about property, in existence.)

He reiterates the view, expressed in the *Treatise*, that 'Many of the reasonings of lawyers are of this analogical nature, and depend on very slight connexions of the imagination.' Hume asserts that 'The safety of the people is the supreme law' (E196), which means that any rule of justice, which is useful in the common course of things, may be set aside when, in extraordinary circumstances, utility demands it, e.g. seizing granaries in time of famine.

When utility fails to predispose us in favour of a law, and there is nothing to appeal to the imagination, the civil law must step in and decide the question in an arbitrary way. Civil laws, for example, must arbitrarily determine just how long it takes for a right to something to lapse. There is no right, antecedently to the making of civil law, by which those who make civil law can be guided. The civil law creates right, e.g. by prescribing how long a person must have possessed something before he has a right to it.

The civil law, indeed, is always the final court of appeal, and can 'extend, restrain, modify, and alter' (E196) any rule of natural justice. It is not easy to see what Hume means by 'the rules of natural justice' (E196). He ought not to have thought that there were any. I take Hume to mean that there is a rule of natural justice tending to make something someone's property if there is a strong tendency in the imagination to cause people to allocate this kind of thing to him. Strictly speaking there is no rule of natural justice to be discovered, for nothing is anyone's property until it has been allocated to him by man. It is not the relations which make something someone's property; men make certain possessions the property of those to whom they are related.

Hume thinks (he is being a bit optimistic) that men make civil laws about property in the public interest. Hence 'the constitution of government, the manners, the climate, the religion, the commerce, the situation of each society' (E196) should all be taken into consideration in deciding what laws are useful. The fact that laws determining property are made in the public interest, he thinks, shows that property is not determined by relations. Hume means that, if property is that which a man is allocated a right to use by civil law (because of the usefulness of so allocating it), something cannot be caused to be someone's property by relations such as first possession; there can be no such fact irrespective of what human beings decide, for human beings to discover. Montesquieu, the author of *L'Esprit des Loix*, is inconsistent in starting off with a theory, according to which property is determined by *relations*, and ending up with a theory according to which it is determined by utility (E197 n.). (In the *Treatise* Hume held that we often allocated property in ways which were useful although in doing so we were guided by the fact that our imaginations were attracted by certain relations, rather than by the perception of the usefulness of having certain rules.)

Hume thinks (E197 n.) that not only may the principles of natural justice be modified by civil law; where the civil law is harmful, we allow ourselves to be guided by 'natural justice' in setting it aside. This is puzzling for the same reason as before. Hume should not have allowed that there was any such thing as natural justice. If there were such a thing, it would be embodied in a set of synthetic *a priori* propositions, recognized by reason, which obviously Hume could not allow. By saying that we appeal to natural law, rather than to civil law, when the civil law is 'so perverse as to cross all the interests of society' (E197), all Hume means is that we set aside the civil law when it is very harmful, and allocate property by means of principles, e.g. that allocating property to its first possessor, which have a strong appeal to the imagination, are useful, and are of great antiquity. (The antiquity of a principle itself appeals to the imagination.) It is simply an empirical fact about human nature that man finds such principles attractive. Thus we alter 'natural justice' by civil law or set aside civil law for natural justice, according to which is more useful.

Hume thinks that another case when justice does not follow civil law is also no objection to his view that justice depends on utility. When an agreement is technically invalid, we would disapprove of a man for not honouring it, although the courts could not enforce it (E197 n.). I think that it is Hume's view that, in expecting a man to honour such an agreement, we are again appealing to natural law, which demands that promises ought to be kept (or contracts fulfilled) and that there is a set of conventions demanding this, although they do not have the force of civil law. Such conventions are regarded as being obligatory because it is useful that they should be acted upon, though, presumably, it is not useful that they should be enforced by law. Hume uses the word 'natural' in opposition to 'civil', not, as he does in the *Treatise*, in opposition to 'artificial'.

Hume says that a man's property is that which the rules give him alone a right to use. In determining the rules, 'we must have recourse to statutes, customs, precedents, analogies, and a hundred other circumstances' (E197). We allow ourselves to be guided by facts such as these only because it is in the public interest that we do. Though in appealing to a precedent or an analogy, we are not appealing to the public interest, it is in the public interest that we appeal to precedent and analogy.

It is the fact that it is in the public interest that we are guided by precedents and analogies, etc., that makes the difference, Hume thinks, between property and superstition. 'This earth or building, yesterday was profane; to-day, by the muttering of certain words, it has become holy and sacred' (E198). No physically detectable change has taken place, however, to the earth or the building. 'Had I worn this apparel an hour ago, I had merited the severest punishment; but a man, by pronouncing a few magical syllables, has now rendered it fit for my use and service.' Again no physically detectable change has taken place to the apparel. One might object that if it is a superstition to suppose that any change has taken place to the building which has been sanctified, it must equally be a superstition to suppose that a change has taken place to the apparel which has been pronounced mine. Hume's answer is that it is in the public interest to have the institution of property, and to allow it to be transferred by consent. Superstitious practices like consecrating buildings, however, are not in the public interest.

He is wrong about the nature of the difference between making promises and consecrating buildings, however. Something impossible is no less impossible because it is in the public interest to suppose it. What makes it superstitious to suppose that sanctifying a building can change it, while not superstitious to suppose that pronouncing certain words can change the ownership of something, is that the latter change is a conventional one, whereas the former change is not. That is to say, the rules of justice prescribe that before certain words are uttered, it is one man's; after these words have been uttered, it is another's. There is nothing perplexing about this, for the change which has taken place to it entirely consists in the way people treat it, and there is nothing at all odd about their treating it in one way before, and in another way after, these words have been uttered. To suppose that uttering words over a building can make any sort of non-conventional change to it, however, is a superstition. The building itself could have no properties that it did not have previously.

Hume thinks that those sentiments demanding that property be sacred and inviolable (he is surely exaggerating) acquire force from the observation that human beings could not exist without 'the *establishment* [my italics] of it [the duty to respect property]' (E201). This remark is true. Hume's choice of words indicates that he does think that certain duties are brought into being by the creation of human rules. He cannot think that the only duty here established is the duty of conforming to the civil law, for he has made it quite clear that I may have a duty to disobey the civil law when it conflicts with 'natural justice' (in his sense) and the latter is more useful.

He argues that the only alternative to his own view, that the sentiment of justice is derived from reflecting on its usefulness, is that it is determined by 'a simple original instinct in the human breast' (E201) which instinct, like 'hunger, thirst, and other appetites' is useful to man. (Thirst impels us to drink water, which is necessary to us.)

Hume seems to think that two things are necessary if the sentiment of justice is to be an instinct. First, there must be some way of telling the difference between one man's property and another's by means simply of inspection, as we can tell the difference between water, which is the object of thirst, and petrol, which is not, by inspection. Secondly, I think Hume means that there is some 'original' sentiment which perception of this physical difference arouses, as thirsting for something is aroused by our perception that it has the physical characteristics of water.

He does not make use of the arguments he has used in the *Treatise* to show that the difference between one man's property and another's is not a physical difference (527). Instead he argues that to tell the difference between one man's property and another's would require a sixth sense, which no man has ever detected. At the top of page 202, he seems to be arguing (wrongly) that, if property were an instinct, we would have to have *a priori* knowledge of such facts as that property could be acquired by 'occupation, by industry, by prescription, by inheritance, by contract &c'. He also argues that a different kind of sense ('ten thousand different instincts' (E201)) would be necessary to discern when we acquire something for each one of the aforementioned different reasons. He also argues from the complexity of ideas such as 'inheritance' and contract to the non-existence of an instinct. He argues that, since justice is closely bound up with civil law, if property is recognized by an instinct, we would have to have innate ideas of 'praetors and chancellors and juries' (E202). Hume is obviously right in thinking that we have no such innate ideas, but it is difficult to see why he supposed that an instinct distinguishing property should imply that we have innate ideas, when he (rightly) did not suppose that the fact that thirst was an instinct implied that we had an innate idea of water. He argues that the fact that all birds of the same species build their nests alike shows that nest building is an instinct in birds; whereas the fact that men build their houses differently shows that house building is not an instinct, but a rational adoption of means to ends in man. Here he seems to be shifting from his original sense of 'instinct' to the (more modern) sense in which an instinct is an unlearned tendency to behave in a certain kind of way. In this sense of 'instinct', an original instinct would not imply a sixth sense, for birds could recognize nests and nest-building material with the same senses that men do. It is obvious that men do not have an unlearned tendency to behave justly.

The uniformity (when the need is the same) in the midst of diversity (when the needs are different) exemplified by house building in men shows, according to Hume, that houses are not built from instinct, but from a perception of their usefulness. The same uniformity in the midst of variety shows that justice is not adopted from instinct, but from a conscious and rational selection of means to an end (the welfare of society). (In the *Treatise* he emphasizes more than in the *Enquiry* the extent to which rules of justice are not useful, and not adopted from an appreciation of their usefulness. In this way, as in many others, the *Treatise* is superior to the *Enquiry*.)

The conclusion which Hume draws, that the difference between one man's property and another's is not discerned by sense (he should have said 'exclusively by sense'), is clearly right. But what about the other half of his contention that justice is not a matter of instinct, viz. that the sentiment involved in property is not *original*? (Obviously there is a sentiment involved in property, for we feel differently about a man's treating in the same way what is and what is not his own.) I have suggested that Hume thinks that there cannot be an original sentiment aroused by property, because there is no physical difference between what is one man's property and what is another's. I suspect that this is a *non sequitur*. By saying that there is not an original sentiment concerning property, I think Hume means that what sentiments we have with respect to property are derivative; that a complete list of all our 'sentiments' would mention hunger and thirst and resentment, but would not mention any feeling we have about property, because to do so would be redundant. Similarly, though we may have sentiments antagonistic to wearing a black tie with tails, there is no 'original' sentiment which is so antagonistic; such a sentiment is a special case of a more general desire not to incur the displeasure of others, and to feel the displeasure of those who do not conform to the rules of polite society. Hume has already argued in the *Treatise* that there can be no original sentiment, for though men determine property by artificial rules, they cannot artificially invent sentiments. They can only redirect sentiments that already exist. There does not seem to be any necessary connection between a sentiment's being original, and its being aroused by our discerning the physical features of things. It could be that some of the sentiments involved in our attitude to property were original even though, because property can be defined only in terms of rules, it could not be recognized by a sense. (The part played by sense in enabling us to recognize property should not, incidentally, be under-estimated. Sense is a necessary, though not a sufficient, condition of our being able to determine what belongs to whom. In order to know that a given car is mine it is not enough that I know rules determining property. It is also necessary that my senses be able to tell the difference between your car and mine. And a man totally devoid of senses would not even know what the rules were.)

Though, Hume thinks, rules of justice are invented because of their usefulness, this fact may be overlooked by his opponents because education and habit cause men to condemn breaches of rules of justice, without their considering their usefulness. It is so obvious that rules of justice are useful that we overlook it, and apply these rules mechanically. (He might have argued, though here he does not, that it is a good thing that we apply the rules mechanically, without appealing to utility in every individual case.) Our tendency to approve of justice because it is useful is reinforced by our tendency to approve of what is merely customary, to approve of what other men approve of, or try to make us approve of. Even in common life, however, men are not so blind to utility as not to ask, 'What must become of the world, if such practices prevail?' (E203.)

Hume ends Part II of Section III by saying that utility 'must, there-fore, be the source of a considerable part of the merit ascribed to humanity, benevolence, friendship, public spirit, and other social virtues of that stamp [the natural virtues] ; as it is the sole source of the moral approbation paid to fidelity, justice, veracity, integrity, and those other estimable and useful qualities and principles [the artificial virtues] '

(E204). He has, of course, inconsistently said that we approve of justice for reasons other than utility, e.g. from education, habit, and the imagination. If Hume could allow himself to make such a distinction, one could say that utility had a rational appeal which was reinforced by the irrational attraction of these other factors. The only reason why Hume thinks that benevolence and the other natural virtues do not derive the whole of their merit from their utility is that he thinks they are approved of because they are agreeable as well as because they are useful. He thinks that his argument is conformable to Newton's chief rule of 'philosophy' (natural science), which is, 'where any principle has been found to have great force and energy in one instance, to ascribe to it a like energy in all similar instances' (E204). (This principle should be applied with some discretion; otherwise it would force us to conclude that because some objects fall to the ground, all do.) Presumably Hume is arguing that, because he has shown that in a large number of cases things which are useful are also obligatory, and vice versa, in the cases which he has not examined usefulness and obligatoriness will also go hand in hand.

A long footnote to page 199 in the *Enquiry* has already been discussed in Section V above.

APPENDIX III

Some farther considerations with regard to justice

I shall not offer individual comments on this appendix as almost everything in it has already been discussed, especially in Sections II and III. It is this appendix which contains Hume's most explicit statement of his view that justice should be applied by universal rules. These rules should be applied even in cases when it is harmful to apply them, if the consequences of applying them in *all* the cases in which it is harmful to apply them will be good. Hume reiterates his view that our obligation to be just cannot be a special case of our duty to keep our promises.

We have not promised to be just. Both our duty to keep our promises and our duty to be just can be explained directly by their utility. There is no need to derive the one duty from the other. In any case, 'The observance of promises is itself one of the most considerable parts of justice, and we are not surely bound to keep our word because we have given our word to keep it' (E306). He argues again that the conventions which determine justice are not promises, but arise from a tendency in men to co-operate when it is in the interest of one man to play his part in a common enterprise, provided the other also plays his. 'Thus, two men pull the oars of a boat by common convention for common interest, without any promise or contract: thus gold and silver are made the measures of exchange; thus speech and words and language are fixed by human convention and agreement' (E306). (The idea of speechless men meeting together to agree upon a language would be as absurd as the idea of faithless men meeting together to promise to keep their promises.)

There follows a discussion, which adds little to those in the *Treatise*, of the sense in which justice is natural. He says, 'In so sagacious an animal, what necessarily arises from the exertion of his intellectual faculties may justly be esteemed natural' (E307). Justice is natural in that it is neither *unusual* nor *miraculous*, but Hume cautiously suggests only that *perhaps* it is not natural in the sense of that word which is opposed to what is artificial. The artificiality of justice is much more strongly emphasized in the *Treatise* than in the *Enquiry*, though there is no reason to suppose that Hume materially altered his view.

Hume seems to think that justice must be governed by general rules, and applied even in cases when it is harmful to apply it, because this is the only way to 'fix the sentence of judges by such general views and considerations as may be *equal* [my italics] to every member of society' (E308). He seems to think that justice must be governed by general rules to prevent partiality on the part of judges. Such partiality would cause men to entertain the strongest ill will against them. The equality he mentions is a safeguard against only a certain kind of injustice; a law prohibiting blacks, but not whites, from owning property could be applied 'equally' or impartially by the judges, but it would itself be an unequal or impartial law. Hence being guided by general considerations is not an adequate safeguard against enmity against the magistrates. He has in the *Treatise* suggested that the law mentions only general considerations which ignore utility because otherwise it will give rise to so much controversy that it cannot be applied; particular utilities may always be disputed. Hume may also have at the back of his mind the idea that it is impracticable for rules to mention anything other than general considerations, since it is impossible adequately to foresee the complexities of any given case.

Hume argues, as he has already done in the *Treatise*, that though it be essential to society to have some rules of justice, *which* rules of justice society has is often not a very important matter. The large part attributed to the imagination in causing men to adopt some rules rather than others is less strongly stressed in the *Enquiry*. However, it is attributed, in a large part, in our adoption of the rule allocating property by succession, and is supposed by Hume entirely to explain the rule allocating property by accession.

Hume thinks that when 'natural reason' cannot determine what laws
are useful, civil laws supply its place. Hume has in mind the contrast
between those cases in which the civil law prescribes something because
it is useful, and those when it must come to some arbitrary decision,
e.g. on the length of time it takes to acquire a prescriptive right. When a
civil law fails to determine a clear decision, a precedent may be used.
A precedent given without good reason may itself be a good reason for
subsequent decisions guided by it. (There is, on Hume's view, nothing
necessarily wrong with a precedent given without good reason, for a
judge must come to some decision or other, and the reasons for any
alternative decision may be equally dependent upon some very slight
turn of thought. Hence a judge has no alternative but to be guided by
some fairly fanciful comparisons.) Since civil laws will not, in many
cases, unequivocally determine what a judge ought to decide, he must
have recourse to 'analogical reasonings and comparisons, and similitudes,
and correspondencies, which are often more fanciful than real' (E308).
Hume has given many examples of these in Section III of the *Treatise*.
His general idea seems to be that when a law does not directly apply to
a case, a judge must consider whether it resembles the cases to which it
does directly apply sufficiently to be brought under it, or whether it
resembles more closely those which fall directly under some other
law. The same thing is true when a new case resembles previous cases
that were decided in different ways. It is often an arbitrary matter
which of two previous cases a new case most resembles, and so 'the
preference given by the judge is often founded more on taste and
imagination than on any solid argument' (E308-9).

Hume makes the interesting remark, 'In general, it may safely be
affirmed that jurisprudence is, in this respect, different from all the
sciences; and that in many of its nicer questions, there cannot properly
be said to be truth or falsehood on either side' (E308). By this I think
Hume means that, to take an example from the *Treatise* (507 n.-
508 n.), it is neither true nor false that the city belongs by law either to
the first or to the second Grecian colony. The business of the judges is
to decide not to whom the city belongs, but to whom it shall belong,
i.e. to bring it about that it belongs to one colony rather than another.
By deciding that it belongs to the first, say, they cause it to belong to
it, as an umpire, by pronouncing a batsman out, causes him to be out.
The similarities and comparisons do not determine to which colony the
city belongs, so much as they determine the judges to award it to the
one colony rather than the other. Many judges appear to be under the
delusion that they are always discovering a fact which is independent of
their decision, but this is a hangover from the theory of natural law.

In clear-cut cases, a judge may decide that a property already belongs to one person rather than to another, but in less clear-cut ('nicer') cases, the judge decides to whom it shall belong. To this extent, I suppose, one function of jurisprudence would not be to lay down rules saying in what circumstances property belongs to one person, rather than to another, but to lay down rules enabling or directing judges in what circumstances to award property to one person, rather than to another.

Hume ends his third appendix by observing that the harm done by any act of injustice can be divided into two parts. It is a breach of a rule useful to society. Some individual or individuals may be harmed, by being deprived of something of which they reckon to have the secure enjoyment. The second kind of harm does not always take place, but, when it does, 'the greatest public wrong is also conjoined with a considerable private one' and 'the highest disapprobation attends so iniquitous a behaviour' (E311). The question whether Hume thinks that actual public harm is done by a single breach of a rule of justice, or whether he thinks that harm would only be done if the breach were regularly repeated, has already been discussed.

In a footnote (E309 n.) Hume reviews a number of particular rules about property, which rules he has already discussed in Section III of Book II, Part II, of the *Treatise*.

APPENDIX:
THREE LATIN TRANSLATIONS

In the pages of the *Treatise* and the *Enquiry* that we have been concerned with there appear three long Latin quotations. I thought the reader might find it helpful to have translations of them.

I. PASSAGE FROM JUSTINIAN, *INSTITUTES*, II.1. § 28 (512 n.)

But if corn belonging to Titius has been mixed with yours, if it is with your consent, it is common property, because the single bodies, that is to say the single grains, which were the private property of each, have now been shared as a result of your agreement. But if it has been mixed by accident, or Titius has mixed it without your consent, it does not appear to be common property, because the grains remain in their original nature. But in these cases the grain would not be common property any more than a herd is understood to be common property if beasts belonging to Titius have been mixed with yours. But if all that corn should be retained by either one of you, it is appropriate to the matter to institute proceedings to recover the proportion of the corn belonging to each, but it lies within the judge's discretion to make his own assessment of the quality of the corn belonging to each.[1]

II. PASSAGE FROM CICERO, *PRO SESTIO*, XLII.91–2 (E189 n.)

Who among you, gentlemen judges, is unaware that nature so ordered things that at a certain time, before either natural or civil law had been properly defined, men wandered about, scattered and dispersed, over the countryside, and possessed only so much as they had been able to carry off or to retain by physical strength through slaughter and wounds? Then those who were the first to be pre-eminent through virtue and outstanding wisdom, after studying the character of human aptitude for learning and of human intelligence, gathered together into one place those who had been scattered, and brought them over from their former condition of savagery to justice and gentleness. Then those things, which we call public, which serve the common good, human associations which were afterwards named states, and concentrations of dwellings which we might call cities: these, after the discovery of the

---

[1] The final sentence as printed in the Selby–Bigge edition is defective. It should read: 'Arbitrio autem judicis continetur, ut ipse. . . .'

law, both the divine and the human, they enclosed with fortifications. Now between this high state of civilization and the former condition of savagery nothing makes so marked a difference as law and violence. Whichever of these we may refuse to employ, we must employ the other. We wish violence to be done away with: then it is essential for law to prevail, that is to say the administration of justice on which all law depends. The administration of justice does not find favour or is not existent: then violence must hold sway. All men see this.

III. PASSAGE FROM GROTIUS, *DE JURE BELLI ET PACIS*, LIB. II CAP. 2, § 2, ARTS. 4 AND 5 (E307 n. 1)

Hence we learn what the reason was why the primeval common ownership of property, at first of chattels and then of real estate, was abandoned. It was of course because, since men were not content to feed themselves on the produce of nature, to live in caves and to go about with their bodies naked or clothed in the barks of trees or the skins of wild animals, and had chosen a more refined way of life, effort was essential which individuals might apply in their individual affairs. But what prevented the proceeds from being contributed to the common good was first of all the distance between the areas to which men had gone their separate ways, and then the lack of justice and love, through which it happened that the appropriate equality was not observed either in the labour or in the consumption of the proceeds. At the same time we learn how things passed into private ownership; not by a solitary mental act, for not only was one group unable to know what another wished to possess in order to keep away from it, but also many men could have the same desire—but through some agreement, either explicit, as in the case of division, or understood, as in the case of seizure.

INDEX